Cisco Field Manual:
Catalyst Switch Configuration

Dave Hucaby, CCIE No. 4594
Steve McQuerry, CCIE No. 6108

Cisco Press

Cisco Press
800 East 96th Street
Indianapolis, IN 46240 USA

Cisco Field Manual: Catalyst Switch Configuration

Dave Hucaby

Steve McQuerry

Copyright © 2003 Cisco Systems, Inc.

Published by:
Cisco Press
800 East 96th Street
Indianapolis, IN 46240 USA

Printed in the United States of America 3 4 5 6 7 8 9 0

Third Printing August 2004

Library of Congress Cataloging-in-Publication Number: 2001090450

ISBN: 1-58705-043-9

Warning and Disclaimer

This book is designed to provide information about configuring the Cisco Catalyst switch series running both the Catalyst operating system and Cisco IOS Software. Every effort has been made to make this book as complete and as accurate as possible, but no warranty or fitness is implied.

The information is provided on an "as is" basis. The authors, Cisco Press, and Cisco Systems, Inc. shall have neither liability nor responsibility to any person or entity with respect to any loss or damages arising from the information contained in this book or from the use of the discs or programs that may accompany it.

The opinions expressed in this book belong to the author and are not necessarily those of Cisco Systems, Inc.

Trademark Acknowledgments

All terms mentioned in this book that are known to be trademarks or service marks have been appropriately capitalized. Cisco Press or Cisco Systems, Inc. cannot attest to the accuracy of this information. Use of a term in this book should not be regarded as affecting the validity of any trademark or service mark.

Feedback Information

At Cisco Press, our goal is to create in-depth technical books of the highest quality and value. Each book is crafted with care and precision, undergoing rigorous development that involves the unique expertise of members from the professional technical community.

Readers' feedback is a natural continuation of this process. If you have any comments regarding how we could improve the quality of this book, or otherwise alter it to better suit your needs, you can contact us through e-mail at feedback@ciscopress.com. Please make sure to include the book title and ISBN in your message.

We greatly appreciate your assistance.

Corporate and Government Sales

Cisco Press offers excellent discounts on this book when ordered in quantity for bulk purchases or special sales.
For more information, please contact:
U.S. Corporate and Government Sales 1-800-382-3419 corpsales@pearsontechgroup.com

For sales outside of the U.S., please contact:
International Sales 1-317-581-3793 international@pearsontechgroup.com

Publisher	John Wait
Editor-In-Chief	John Kane
Cisco Representative	Anthony Wolfenden
Cisco Press Program Manager	Sonia Torres Chavez
Cisco Marketing Communications Manager	Tom Geitner
Cisco Marketing Program Manager	Edie Quiroz
Executive Editor	Brett Bartow
Production Manager	Patrick Kanouse
Development Editor	Christopher Cleveland
Project Editor	Eric T. Schroeder
Copy Editor	Keith Cline
Technical Editors	Steve Daleo Martin Duggan
	Kevin Hamilton Geoff Tagg
Team Coordinator	Tammi Ross
Book Designer	Gina Rexrode
Cover Designer	Louisa Adair
Composition	Mark Shirar
	Octal Publishing, Inc.
Indexer	Tim Wright

CISCO SYSTEMS

Corporate Headquarters
Cisco Systems, Inc.
170 West Tasman Drive
San Jose, CA 95134-1706
USA
www.cisco.com
Tel: 408 526-4000
     800 553-NETS (6387)
Fax: 408 526-4100

European Headquarters
Cisco Systems International BV
Haarlerbergpark
Haarlerbergweg 13-19
1101 CH Amsterdam
The Netherlands
www-europe.cisco.com
Tel: 31 0 20 357 1000
Fax: 31 0 20 357 1100

Americas Headquarters
Cisco Systems, Inc.
170 West Tasman Drive
San Jose, CA 95134-1706
USA
www.cisco.com
Tel: 408 526-7660
Fax: 408 527-0883

Asia Pacific Headquarters
Cisco Systems, Inc.
Capital Tower
168 Robinson Road
#22-01 to #29-01
Singapore 068912
www.cisco.com
Tel: +65 6317 7777
Fax: +65 6317 7799

Cisco Systems has more than 200 offices in the following countries and regions. Addresses, phone numbers, and fax numbers are listed on the
Cisco.com Web site at www.cisco.com/go/offices.

Argentina • Australia • Austria • Belgium • Brazil • Bulgaria • Canada • Chile • China PRC • Colombia • Costa Rica • Croatia • Czech Republic
Denmark • Dubai, UAE • Finland • France • Germany • Greece • Hong Kong SAR • Hungary • India • Indonesia • Ireland • Israel • Italy
Japan • Korea • Luxembourg • Malaysia • Mexico • The Netherlands • New Zealand • Norway • Peru • Philippines • Poland • Portugal
Puerto Rico • Romania • Russia • Saudi Arabia • Scotland • Singapore • Slovakia • Slovenia • South Africa • Spain • Sweden
Switzerland • Taiwan • Thailand • Turkey • Ukraine • United Kingdom • United States • Venezuela • Vietnam • Zimbabwe

About the Authors

David Hucaby, CCIE No. 4594, is a lead network engineer for the University of Kentucky, where he works with health-care networks based on the Cisco Catalyst, IP Telephony, PIX, and VPN product lines. Prior to his current position, David was a senior network consultant, where he provided design and implementation consulting, focusing on Cisco-based VPN and IP Telephony solutions. David has a B.S. and an M.S. in electrical engineering from the University of Kentucky.

Steve McQuerry, CCIE No. 6108, is an instructor and consultant with more than 10 years of networking industry experience. He is a Certified Cisco Systems Instructor (CCSI) teaching routing and switching concepts for Global Knowledge. Steve is also the course developer/director for Global's Advanced Cisco Campus Switching course. Steve holds a B.S. in engineering physics from Eastern Kentucky University.

About the Technical Reviewers

Stephen A. Daleo, president of Golden Networking Consultants, Inc., is a network consultant whose clients include the University of South Florida—St. Petersburg, FL and North Broward Hospital District (Fort Lauderdale, FL). Steve is a frequent contributor to the technical content of Cisco Press books and is an active CCSI (#97025) teaching the BCMSN, BCRAN, CIPT, BSCN and ICND Cisco courses.

Martin J. Duggan, CCIE No. 7942, CCDP, is a technical architect for IBM. He has been in this role for one year and was previously a senior network consultant for NTL. Martin's specialties are large-scale network integration, ATM, and campus LAN design. Martin resides in Hampshire, UK and owes his CCIE qualification to the support given from his wife Adela and children Anna and James.

Kevin Hamilton, CCSI No. 97056, has been in the networking industry for 20 years working with analog and digital communications systems including broadband, Ethernet, FDDI, token ring and ATM networks. He is a coauthor of the Cisco Press title *Cisco LAN Switching* and a contributor to the *Internetworking Technologies Handbook*, Third Edition. Kevin formerly worked for Mentor Technologies as an instructor/consultant teaching ATM, switching, multicast, and security related subjects. Currently, Kevin provides instruction and consultation for service provider networks deploying MPLS, multicast, and switched-based networks. He is a graduate of The Pennsylvania State University in electrical engineering.

Geoff Tagg, runs a networking consultancy in the UK, where he has over 20 years experience of working with companies ranging from small local businesses to large multinationals. Prior to that, he was a systems programmer on a variety of mainframe and minicomputers. Geoff's current specialties include IP, ISDN, Frame Relay, ATM, and Ethernet. Geoff lives in Oxford, England, with his wife Christine and family and is a visiting professor at nearby Oxford Brookes University.

Dedications

Dave Hucaby: This book is dedicated to my wife Marci and my two little daughters Lauren and Kara. For girls who have never seen a Catalyst switch, they sure encouraged me to keep at the writing I enjoy. I'm so grateful to God, who gives endurance and encouragement (Romans 15:5), and who has allowed me to work on projects such as this.

Steve McQuerry: I would like to dedicate this book to the four most important people in my life. Becky, you are the love of my life and my inspiration. Katie, your drive to do your best and your work ethic remind me to keep working hard. Logan, your questions and desire to learn drive me to keep learning. And Cameron, your energy and spirit keep me young. Thank you. I could not be a more content husband, father, or friend.

Acknowledgments

Dave Hucaby: Once again, it is my good pleasure to be involved in writing a Cisco Press book. Technical writing for me is great fun, although it's hard to write a book strictly on lunch hours and after the rest of the family goes to bed. I gratefully acknowledge the good people at Cisco Press for allowing me to work on this project and for their encouragement, patience, and diligence to produce fine work.

In particular, I would like to thank Brett Bartow for making this project a goal we could meet. Writing a book such as this is a long and difficult process. Brett is always able to give us a feel for the big picture, while keeping us on track with the details. I am also very grateful to work with Chris Cleveland again. Chris is probably the hardest working person I know, and is a wonderful editor. Somehow, he is able to take in rough-hewn chapters and turn out smooth text.

I would like to acknowledge the hard work and good perspective of our technical reviewers: Steve Daleo, Martin Duggan, Kevin Hamilton, and Geoff Tagg. This book has been a challenge to put together, because there are a good many ways to configure the same feature on different Catalyst platforms. The reviewers have done a superb job of catching us in inaccuracies and helping us to better organize the technical information. I'm glad I was on the writing end and not the reviewing end!

I would like to express my thanks to my friend and coauthor Steve McQuerry. Next to Chris, Steve is the hardest working guy I know. It's been a pleasure to share the writing load with him again.

Finally, it's time to acknowledge another laptop computer crisis. For this book, I managed to knock my laptop off an equipment rack onto the cold, hard concrete floor. The hard drive survived, although the rest of the laptop didn't. I am very grateful to my good friend Joshua Fried, who went out of his way to provide me with a temporary laptop the same day mine died. Due to his kindness, I was able to keep writing this book.

Steve McQuerry: It seems hard to believe that in three short years I have had an opportunity to be a part of so many fun and challenging projects. Because so many people make these books come together, it doesn't seem fair that we have only a few short lines to thank them. The one thing I've learned to do since I started writing is to read the acknowledgments of any book that I pick up, whether it is a technical, fiction, or nonfiction work. The publishing industry is filled with a great group of people who are as much responsible for the finished product as those who have their names on the front of the book. I would like to take this time to thank the individuals responsible for helping me with my part of this book.

First, I would like to thank my friend and coauthor Dave Hucaby. Dave, I know that you did more than your share of work on this book and I want to thank you for putting in the extra hours when I got myself overcommitted. I can't think of anyone I've worked with in my entire career as dedicated and focused as you are. More important than your focus and dedication to your work, however, is your focus on the importance of God, family, and friendship. I am blessed by having you for a friend and a partner. I hope we can continue to find ways to keep working together in the future.

As always, I want to thank Brett Bartow. I don't think we could finish a book without Brett's consistency and his follow-through. Thanks for the opportunity, and thanks for keeping us motivated. It is truly a pleasure to work with you.

Chris Cleveland, what can I say? You got swept into this project, and you are the biggest part of what makes this book a cohesive and usable product. Your knowledge of what we are trying to do and your expertise as a development editor is unsurpassed. Thank you for making us look good!

To our technical editors—Kevin Hamilton, Steve Daleo, Martin Duggan, and Geoff Tagg—thanks for the sharp eyes and excellent comments. It was a great having you as part of the team.

A special thanks to the fine professionals at Cisco Press: John Kane, Tammi Ross, Amy Lewis, Patrick Kanouse, and Eric Schroeder. You guys are the best in the industry!

Thanks to all my students and fellow instructors at Global Knowledge. Your challenges and questions drive me to have a better understanding.

I want to thank my wife and children for the support they offer for all my projects and for the patience and understanding they have when I work late and act a little grouchy the next day.

Most importantly, I want to thank God, for giving me the skills, talents, and opportunity to work in such a challenging and exciting profession.

Contents at a Glance

Table of Contents

Icons Used in This Book

Throughout this book, you will see a number of icons used to designate Cisco and general networking devices, peripherals, and other items. The icon legend that follows explains what these icons represent.

Switch

Layer 3
Switch

Router

Catalyst
6000

Route/Switch
Processor
(Layer 3 Switch)

PIX Firewall

Access
Server

PC

IP Phone

Cisco
CallManager

File Server

Cisco IP
SoftPhone

Network
Analyzer

Line: Switched Serial

Ethernet Connection

Network Cloud

Command Syntax Conventions

The conventions used to present command syntax in this book are the same conventions used in the IOS Command Reference. The Command Reference describes these conventions as follows:

- Vertical bars (|) separate alternative, mutually exclusive elements.

- Square brackets [ ] indicate optional elements.

- Braces { } indicate a required choice.

- Braces within brackets [{ }] indicate a required choice within an optional element.

- **Boldface** indicates commands and keywords that are entered literally as shown. In actual configuration examples and output (not general command syntax), boldface indicates commands that are manually input by the user (such as a **show** command).

- *Italics* indicate arguments for which you supply actual values.

Introduction

This is the second book in the Cisco Field Manual series, focusing on the Cisco Catalyst switch product lines. Of the many sources of information and documentation about Cisco Catalyst switches, very few provide a quick and portable solution for networking professionals.

Cisco Field Manual: Catalyst Switch Configuration is designed to provide a quick and easy reference guide for all the features that can be configured on Cisco Catalyst switches. In essence, the subject matter from an entire bookshelf of Catalyst software documentation, along with other networking reference material, has been "squashed" into one handy volume that you can take with you. This is also the only book available that presents switch feature configuration with all the different variations of Catalyst operating system commands (COS and IOS).

The idea for this book began as a follow-on to our router configuration book, with the twist that the different Catalyst operating systems be shown together for comparison. In larger switched network environments, it is common to see many different Catalyst platforms in use—each might have a different feature set and different operating system commands. We have found it difficult to remember the configuration steps and commands when moving from one Catalyst platform to another. Perhaps you have too.

As with router configuration, the commands for switch configuration went into a notebook of handwritten notes. This notebook began to travel with me into the field as a network consultant and engineer. When you're on the job and someone requires you to configure a feature that you're not too familiar with, it's nice to have your handy reference notebook in your bag! Hopefully, this book will be that handy reference for you as well.

NOTE   This book is based on the most current Cisco Catalyst software releases at press time. COS-based switches are presented according to Release 7.2, and IOS-based switches according to the 12.2 major release. If you are using an earlier version of either software, you may find that the configuration commands differ slightly.

Features

This book is meant to be used as a tool in your day-to-day tasks as a network administrator, engineer, consultant, or student. As such, we have avoided presenting a large amount of instructional information or theory on the operation of features or commands. That is better handled in other textbooks that are dedicated to a more limited subject matter.

Instead, the book is divided into chapters that present quick facts, configuration steps, and explanations of configuration options for each Cisco Catalyst switch feature. The chapters are as follows:

- **Chapter 1: CLI Usage**—Presents the difference in the COS and IOS operating systems and command-line interface.

- **Chapter 2: Switch Functionality**—Describes LAN switches and how to design a switch campus network.

- **Chapter 3: Supervisor Engine Configuration**—Explains how to configure switch prompts, IP addresses, passwords, switch modules, file management, and administrative protocols.

- **Chapter 4: Layer 2 Interface Configuration**—Describes configuration of Ethernet, Fast Ethernet, Gigabit Ethernet, EtherChannel, Token Ring, and ATM LANE interfaces.

- **Chapter 5: Layer 3 Interface Configuration**—Explains how Layer 3 interfaces are used in a switch.

- **Chapter 6: VLANs and Trunking**—Presents VLAN configuration, private VLANs, trunking, VTP, and dynamic port membership.

- **Chapter 7: Spanning Tree Protocol (STP)**—Discusses STP operation, configuration, and tuning.

- **Chapter 8: Multilayer Switching**—Explains how to configure and use Catalyst switch hardware for Layer 3 switching and redundancy.

- **Chapter 9: Multicast**—Explains how a switch handles multicast traffic and interacts with multicast routers.

- **Chapter 10: Accelerated Server Load Balancing**—Presents Catalyst 6000 features that streamline access to server and firewall farms.

- **Chapter 11: Controlling Traffic and Switch Access**—Discusses broadcast suppression, protocol filtering, user authentication, port security, and VLAN access lists.

- **Chapter 12: Switch Management**—Explains how to configure a switch for logging, SNMP and RMON management, port analysis (SPAN), power management, and connectivity testing.

- **Chapter 13: Quality of Service**—Presents configuration of QoS theory and features in a switched network.

- **Chapter 14: Voice**—Discusses specialized voice gateway modules, inline power, and QoS features needed to transport voice traffic.

- **Appendix A–D**—Present a cabling quick reference, well-known ports and addresses, specialized switch modules, and VLAN extension.

How to Use This Book

All the information in this book has been designed to follow a quick-reference format. If you know what feature or technology you want to use, you can turn right to the section that deals with it. Sections are numbered with a quick-reference index, showing both chapter and section number (5-2, for example, is Chapter 5 section 2). You'll also find shaded index tabs on each page, listing the section number.

Facts About a Feature

Each section in a chapter begins with a bulleted list of quick facts about the feature, technology, or protocol. Refer to these lists to quickly learn or review how the feature works.

Configuration Steps

Each feature that is covered in a section includes the required and optional commands used for common configuration. The difference is that the configuration steps are presented in an outline format. If you follow the outline, you can configure a complex feature or technology. If you find that you don't need a certain feature option, skip over that level in the outline.

You'll also find that each step in a configuration outline presents the commands from both Catalyst COS and IOS operating systems in an adjacent manner. You can stay in the same configuration section, no matter what type or model of Catalyst switch you're dealing with.

Commands labeled "COS" pertain to the Catalyst operating system, as found on switches such as the Catalyst 4000, 5000, and 6000 Supervisor engines. Below that, commands labeled "IOS" pertain to the Cisco IOS Software operating system, as found on the Catalyst 2900XL, 2950, 3500XL, 3550, 4000 Supervisor III, and the Catalyst 6000 running "native IOS" or "Supervisor IOS." In some instances, the "native" or "Supervisor" IOS differs from that of the IOS on the 2900/3500XL switches. We have taken care to separate these commands in the steps and made the appropriate notes where necessary.

Example Configurations

Each section includes an example of how to implement the commands and their options. We have tried to present the examples with the commands listed in the order you would actually enter them to follow the outline. Many times, it is more difficult to study and understand a configuration example from an actual switch, because the commands are displayed in a predefined order—not in the order you entered them. The examples have also been trimmed down to show only the commands presented in the section (where possible).

Displaying Information About a Feature

Where applicable, each section concludes with a brief summary of the commands you can use to show information about the switch feature. You can use these command summaries as a quick reference when you are debugging or troubleshooting switch operation. Again, the **show** commands from both COS and IOS operating systems are presented in an adjacent manner for easy reference.

Further Reading

Each chapter concludes with a recommended reading list to help you find more in-depth sources of information for the topics discussed.

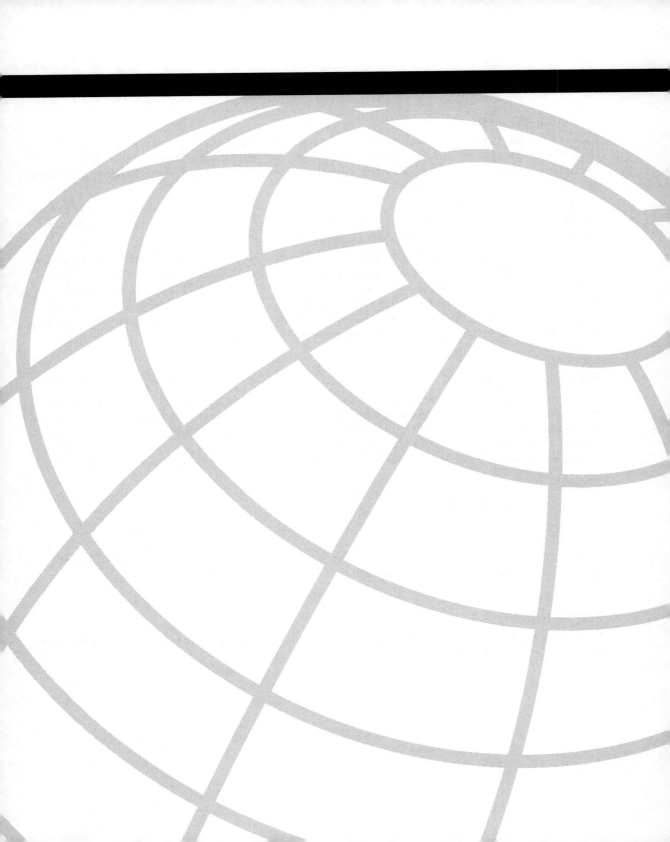

CHAPTER **1**

CLI Usage

Refer to the following sections for information about these topics:

- **1-1: Catalyst Operating System (COS)**—Describes the use of the COS for switching configuration.
- **1-2: Cisco Internetwork Operating System (IOS) Software**—Describes the use of Cisco IOS Software for switching configuration.
- **1-3: ROM Monitor**—Describes the use of the ROM monitor for recovery of a switch and configuration of boot parameters.

1-1: Catalyst Operating System (COS)

- The COS uses a basic command-line interpreter as the user interface for configuration and management.
- The COS runs on the Network Management Processor of Catalyst 4000, 5000, and 6000 series switches.
- The *command-line interface* (CLI) can be accessed through the console port or by Telnet.
- The COS CLI has two basic modes for configuration and management—user mode and privileged mode.
- The COS is not case-sensitive and allows for command abbreviations.
- Help and editing features enhance the COS and make using the operating system easier.
- Syntax and usage prompts help the user deal with syntax errors.
- The COS has default settings for most of the parameters on the switch. These settings allow for the simplification of basic configuration.

Using COS

COS has two basic modes for switch administration, as well as a number of useful commands and options that enable you to interact with the switch for management purposes. The following items describe how to access these modes and use options to configure the switch.

1   User interface modes

a. User mode

```
Cisco Systems Console
Enter password: password
Console>
```

Users can connect to a switch through the console port or a Telnet session. The initial access to a switch places the user in user mode and offers a limited number of commands. When connecting to the switch, a user-level *password* is required. The default user password is *null*—that is no password is set and you just press the Enter key to gain access to user mode. When in user mode, you gain access to the user prompt, which is Console> by default. To close your connection to the console or Telnet facility use the command **logout** or **exit**.

b. Privileged mode

```
Console> enable
Enter password: password

Console> (enable)
```

When a user gains access to the user mode, the **enable** command can be used to enter privileged or enable mode. In this mode, the user has access to all the commands and can set switch parameters. To leave privileged EXEC mode, use the **disable** command. A user can also close the connection using the **logout** or **exit** command.

2   User interface features

a. Entering commands

```
Console> command
Console> (enable) command
```

Commands can be entered from either the user or privileged mode. In user mode, the commands available are limited to switch examination and a few test utilities. To enable a feature or parameter, you must be in privileged mode and use the **set** commands to configure the switch. To establish a parameter, type the command and its options normally, as in *command*.

To disable the commands that you have configured, use the **set** command to reestablish the default parameter or in some instances use the **clear** command. Not all **set** commands have corresponding **clear** commands. To view the configuration changes that have been made in the COS, use the command **show config** in privileged mode. To view all the parameters that are set on the switch, use the command **show**

config all. You can also view the configuration of a particular module using the command **show config** [*mod*] [**all**]; use the **all** option to see both default and nondefault settings.

You can edit a command line by using the left and right arrow keys to move within the line. When editing a line, you are in insert mode. This means that if additional characters are typed, the remainder of the line to the right is spaced over. You can use the Backspace and Delete keys to make corrections.

b. Syntax checking

COS is a command-line interpreter. The operation of the interface is to take user input on the command line and parse it to interpret and perform a function based on the entered commands. If the CLI does not recognize the command entered by a user, a syntax error is generated. A *syntax error* is a message that informs the user of a problem with the typed command. For the COS, syntax errors usually appear in one of the following two forms:

— Help error

A help error occurs when the CLI cannot reconcile the user input with a valid command. If a user were to enter a command such as **set speed port 3/5 100**, for example, a help error would be generated.

```
Console> (enable) set speed port 3/5 100
Unknown command "set speed". Use 'set help' for more info.
```

This error message is telling the user that it does not understand anything beyond the word **set**. If the user were to type **set help** or **set ?**, the user would see a listing of all the valid **set** commands, one of which would be **set port speed**.

— Usage error

A usage error occurs when a valid command has been entered but an error is present in the options selected for that command. The error could be that the options are not there, the options are not in the proper order, or that options have been specified when none are available. If a user were to enter a command such as **set port speed 100 3/5**, for example, a usage error would be generated.

```
Console> (enable) set port speed 100 3/5
Usage: set port speed <mod/port> <10|100|auto>
```

This type of error message is telling the user that it understands the major command (**set port speed**), but that the options (**100** and **3/5**) are not correct. By displaying the usage of the command **set port speed** and all the options, the CLI informs the user of the proper way to format the syntax. Any parameters between the less than (<) and greater than (>) brackets are required, whereas anything in the square brackets ([ ]) are options.

TIP

Sometimes when a user is entering a command, the switch displays console messages while the user is typing. It is common for the user to press the Enter key to move the information out of the way. However, pressing Enter on the CLI causes the interpreter to parse the command or partial command you have typed (which usually was not complete, and which results in a help or usage error). To prevent this and refresh your input, you can press the Ctrl-R or Ctrl-L keys to redisplay the line and continue editing the command.

---

c. Viewing output

```
Console> or Console> (enable) show [parameter]
```

To display information about the switch configuration or operation, use the **show** command followed by the appropriate option. By default the output is formatted to be 24 lines in length. This means that after 24 lines have been displayed, the output pauses and displays the --More-- prompt. To continue the output, press the **Spacebar** key for another page (24 lines) of output or press the Enter key for one line at a time. To stop the output completely, use the key Q or the key sequence Ctrl+C.

d. Terminal screen length

```
Console> (enable) set length lines
```

Use this command to change the length of the output before you receive the --More-- prompt. If you don't want the output displayed by page with a --More-- prompt, use the command **set length 0**. It is important to note that the screen width is not configurable on the COS but can be set on the terminal application used to access the CLI. Output can be long, and output that exceeds the width is typically wrapped by the terminal application. The COS does not count wrapped lines; so if the output contains several wrapped lines you might still have information that scrolls off the top of the page.

TIP

If you are displaying a great deal of information with the **show** command but are only looking for a specific item, you can scroll to the text by entering a slash (/) followed directly by the text you are looking for (/text). If you enter /text and press the Return key at the --More-- prompt, the output searches and the display returns the text starting two lines above the one containing the *text* string. If the *text* string is not found, a "Pattern Not Found" message displays. You can also enter **n** at the --More-- prompt to search for the last entered *text* string. You can use this search method on all **show** commands that use the more buffer to display screen by screen output except the commands **show cam**, **show mls**, and **show tech-support**.

---

e. Context-sensitive help

You can enter a question mark (**?**) or the keyword **help** anywhere in a command line to get additional information from the switch. If the question mark is typed alone on a command line, all available commands for that mode display. Question marks can also be typed at any place after a command—for example for a keyword or an option. If the question mark follows a space, all available keywords or options display. If the question mark follows another word without a space, a list of all available commands beginning with that substring displays.

An abbreviated command can also be typed, followed by the Tab key. The command name is expanded to its full form if no other commands start with the same abbreviation.

f. Command history

— Recalling commands to use again

From any input mode, each press of the Up Arrow ($\uparrow$) key or Ctrl-P recalls the next older command. Each press of the Down Arrow ($\downarrow$) key or Ctrl-N recalls the next most recent command. When commands are recalled from history, they can be edited as if you had just typed them. The **history** command displays the recorded command history. The switch keeps the previous 20 commands for a session. The size of the history is not a configurable parameter for COS.

NOTE   The Up and Down Arrow keys require the use of an ANSI-compatible terminal emulator (that is, VT100).

3 Telnet sessions

a. Start a new session

```
Console> (enable) telnet host
```

This initiates a Telnet connection to *host* (either an IP address or a host name). Then from the switch CLI, you can continue to communicate with the remote host. You can only initiate a Telnet session from privileged mode on a COS device.

b. Closing a Telnet session locally

During an active Telnet session to a host, you can use the key sequence Ctrl-]—that is, hold the Ctrl key while you press the Right Bracket (]) key—to escape back to the Telnet application. This suspends the Telnet session and returns you to the local switch Telnet application prompt telnet>. From here you can type the command **quit** to close the Telnet connection locally instead of logging out remotely. This is useful when your Telnet session has become "locked up" and you get no response form the remote host.

d. Configure session timeout values

```
Console> (enable) set logout time
```

All active sessions on switch—either through the console or the Telnet facility—are logged out if no activity occurs for the number of minutes specified by the *time* parameter. The default setting is 20 minutes. Use this command to change the logout value. If you set the value to 0, sessions will not be timed out.

1-2: Cisco Internetwork Operating System (IOS) Software

- Cisco IOS Software supports user access by CLI or by a web browser.
- The CLI can be accessed through the console port or through Telnet.
- Users can execute Cisco IOS Software commands from a *user level* or from a *privileged level*. User level offers basic system information and remote connectivity commands. Privileged level offers complete access to all switch information, configuration editing, and debugging commands.
- Cisco IOS Software offers many levels of configuration modes, enabling you to change the configuration for a variety of switch resources.
- Cisco IOS Software offers a VLAN database mode to configure and modify VLAN and Virtual Terminal Protocol (VTP) information.
- A context-sensitive help system offers command syntax and command choices at any user prompt.
- A history of Cisco IOS Software commands executed can be kept. As well, command lines can be edited and reused.
- The output from a command can be searched and filtered so that useful information can be found quickly.
- Parameters for the CLI connection to the switch can be set to preferred values.

Using Cisco IOS Software

Cisco IOS Software has two basic user modes for switch administration and a number of other modes that enable you to control the configuration of the switch. In addition to a variety of modes, Cisco IOS Software provides features such as help and command-line editing that enable you to interact with the switch for management purposes. The following items describe how to access these modes and use options to configure the switch.

1 User interface modes

a. User EXEC mode

```
Switch>
```

Users can connect to a switch through the console port or Telnet session. By default, the initial access to a switch places the user in *user EXEC* mode and offers a limited set of commands. When connecting to the switch, a user-level *password* might be required.

b. Privileged EXEC mode

```
Switch> enable
password: [password]
Switch#
```

When a user gains access in user EXEC mode, the **enable** command can be used to enter *privileged EXEC* or *enable* mode. Full access to all commands is available. To leave privileged EXEC mode, use the **disable** or **exit** commands.

c. Configuration mode

```
Switch# configure terminal
```

From privileged EXEC mode, the configuration mode can be entered. Switch commands can be given to configure any switch feature that is available in the IOS software image. When you are in configuration mode you are managing the active memory of the switch. Anytime you enter a valid command in any configuration mode and press Enter, the memory is immediately changed. Configuration mode is organized in a hierarchical fashion. Global configuration mode allows commands that affect the switch as a whole. Interface configuration mode allows commands that configure switch interfaces. You can move in and out of many other configuration modes depending on what is being configured. To move from a lower-level configuration mode to a higher level, type **exit**. To leave the global configuration mode and return to the privileged EXEC mode, type **exit** at the global configuration prompt. To leave any configuration mode and return to privileged EXEC mode, type **end** or Ctrl-Z.

d. VLAN database mode

```
Switch# vlan database
Switch(vlan)#
```

From privileged EXEC mode, you can enter vlan database mode. After you enter this mode, the prompt changes to vlan database mode. Vlan database mode configures and modifies VLAN and VTP parameters using **vlan** and/or **vtp** commands. When making changes to the VLAN database, the changes do not take effect until you use the command **apply** to make the changes active in the database or use the command **exit** to apply the changes and exit the mode. When you make a change and then **apply** or **exit** vlan database mode, the VTP configuration number is incremented. You should first configure a VTP domain or set the VTP mode to transparent to create, change, or edit VLANs. The **abort** command aborts any changes made in the database and leaves the mode. You can also view the current database and the proposed changes to the database using the **show** commands. Context-sensitive help is available in this mode using the question mark (**?**) or **help** command.

2 User interface features

a. Entering commands

```
Switch>, Switch#, Switch(config)# or Switch(vlan)# command
Switch>, Switch#, Switch(config)# or Switch(vlan)# no command
```

Commands can be entered from any mode (EXEC, global config, interface config, subinterface config, vlan database, and so on). To enable a feature or parameter, type the command and its options normally, as in *command*. To disable a command that is in effect, begin the command with **no**, followed by the command. The commands that are in effect can be seen by using the **show running-config** command in privileged mode. Note that some commands and parameters are set by default and are not shown as literal command lines in the configuration listing.

Commands and their options can also be abbreviated with as few letters as possible without becoming ambiguous. To enter the interface configuration mode for Ethernet 0, for example, you can abbreviate the command **interface fastethernet 0** as **int fa 0**.

You can edit a command line using the Left and Right Arrow keys to move within the line. If additional characters are typed, the remainder of the line to the right is spaced over. You can use the Backspace and Delete keys to make corrections.

NOTE   If the switch displays a console informational or error message while you are typing a command line, you can press the Ctrl-L or Ctrl-R key to redisplay the line and continue editing. You can also configure the lines (console, vty, or aux) to use **logging synchronous**. This causes the switch to automatically refresh the lines after the switch output. You might have to wait for the switch in order to see output; if you issue **debug** commands with **logging synchronous** enabled, you might have to wait for the switch to finish the command (such as a ping) before you see the output.

---

b. Context-sensitive help

You can enter a question mark (**?**) anywhere in a command line to get additional information from the switch. If the question mark is typed alone, all available commands for that mode display. Question marks can also be typed at any place after a command, keyword, or an option. If the question mark follows a space, all available keywords or options display. If the question mark follows another word without a space, a list of all available commands beginning with that substring displays. This can be helpful when an abbreviated command is ambiguous and flagged with an error.

An abbreviated command might also be typed, followed by the Tab key. The command name expands to its full form if it is not ambiguous.

If a command line is entered but doesn't have the correct syntax, an error "% Invalid input detected at '^' marker" is returned. A caret (^) appears below the command character where the syntax error was detected.

c. Command history

— *(Optional)* Set the number of commands to save (default 10). To set the history size for the current terminal session, enter the following:

```
Switch# terminal history [size lines]
```

To set the history size for all sessions on a line, enter the following:

```
Switch(config-line)# history [size lines]
```

— Recalling commands to use again

From any input mode, each press of the Up Arrow (↑) key or Ctrl-P recalls the next older command. Each press of the Down Arrow (↓) key or Ctrl-N recalls the next most recent command. When commands are recalled from history, they can be edited as if you had just typed them. The **show history** command displays the recorded command history.

NOTE   The Up and Down Arrow keys require the use of an ANSI-compatible terminal emulator (that is, VT100).

---

d. Searching and filtering command output

— Sift through output from a **show** command

```
Switch# show command ... | {begin | include | exclude} reg-expression
```

A **show** command can generate a long output listing. If the listing contains more lines than the terminal session can display (set using the *length* parameter), it displays a screenful at a time with a --More-- prompt at the bottom. To see the next screen, press the Spacebar. To advance one line, press the Return key. To exit back out to the command line, press Ctrl-C, the Q key, or any key on the keyboard other than Return or the Spacebar.

To search for a specific regular expression and start the output listing there, use the **begin** keyword. This can be useful if your switch has many interfaces in its configuration. Instead of using the Spacebar to eventually find a certain configuration line, you can use **begin** to jump right to the desired line. To display only the lines that include a regular expression, use the **include** keyword. To display all lines that don't include a regular expression, use the **exclude** keyword.

— Sift through output from a **more** command

```
Switch# more file-url | {begin | include | exclude} reg-expression
```

The **more** command displays the contents of a file on the switch. A typical use is to display the startup (**more nvram:startup-config**) or running (**more system:running-config**) configuration file. By default the file is displayed one screen at a time with a --More-- prompt at the bottom.

To search for a specific regular expression and start the output listing there, use the **begin** keyword. To display only the lines that include a regular expression, use the **include** keyword. To display all lines that don't include a regular expression, use the **exclude** keyword.

— Search through output at a --More-- prompt

```
(--More--) {/ | + | -}regular-expression
```

At a --More-- prompt, you can search the output by typing the slash (/) key followed by a regular expression. To display only lines that include the regular expression, press the plus (+) key. To display only lines that don't include the regular expression, press the minus (–) key.

— What is a regular expression?

A regular expression can be used to match against lines of output. Regular expressions are made up of patterns, either simple text strings (that is, *ethernet* or *ospf*) or more complex matching patterns. Typically, regular expressions are regular text words that offer a hint to a location in the output of a **show** command.

A more complex regular expression is made up of patterns and operators. Table 1-1 shows the characters that are used as operators:

Table 1-1 *Operator Characters*

Character	Meaning
.	Matches a single character.
*	Matches 0 or more sequences of the preceding pattern.
+	Matches 1 or more sequences of the preceding pattern.
?	Matches 0 or 1 occurrences of the preceding pattern.
^	Matches at the beginning of the string.
$	Matches at the end of the string.

Table 1-1   *Operator Characters (Continued)*

Character	Meaning
–	Matches a comma, braces, parentheses, beginning or end of a string, or a space.
[ ]	Defines a range of characters as a pattern.
( )	Groups characters as a pattern; if used around a pattern, the pattern can be recalled later in the expression by using the backslash (\) and the pattern occurrence number.

3 Terminal sessions

a. Start a new session

```
Switch# telnet host
```

This initiates a Telnet connection to *host* (either an IP address or a host name). Then from the switch CLI, you can continue to communicate with the remote host.

b. Name a session

```
Switch# name-connection
Switch# Connection number: number
Switch# Enter logical name: name
```

An active session can be assigned a text string name to make the session easier to identify with the **show sessions** or **where** command.

c. Suspend a session to do something else

During an active Telnet session to a host, type the escape sequence **Ctrl-Shift-6** followed by an x (that is press control, shift and 6 together, let up on all the keys then press the letter x) to suspend the session. The suspend sequence is sometimes written as **Ctrl-^ x**. This suspends the Telnet session and returns you to the local switch command-line prompt.

NOTE   You can have nested Telnet sessions open. For example, from the local switch, you can Telnet to another switch A, and then Telnet on to another switch B, and so forth. To suspend one of these sessions, you must also nest your escape sequences. Typing a single **Ctrl-^x** suspends the session to switch A and returns you to the local switch. Typing **Ctrl-^ Ctrl-^x** suspends the session to switch B and returns you to switch A's prompt. (Only type the **x** at the final escape sequence.)

Section 1-2

d. Show all active sessions

```
Switch# show sessions
```

All open sessions from your connection to the local switch are listed, along with connection numbers. You can also use the **where** command to get the same information.

e. Return to a specific session

First, use the **show sessions** command to get the connection number of the desired session. Then, just type the connection number by itself on the command line. The session will be reactivated. You can also just press Return/Enter at the command-line prompt and the last active connection in the list will be reactivated. The last active connection in the list is denoted with the asterisk (*). This makes toggling between the local switch and a single remote session easier.

NOTE   When you resume the connection, you are prompted with the message "[Resuming connection 2 to Switch ...]." After you've resumed your connection, the message shown here does not change and the switch does not display a prompt. Therefore, you must press Enter again to actually resume the connection and get a device prompt.

f. End an active session

```
Switch2#Ctrl-^ x
Switch1# disconnect connection-number
```

When the remote session is suspended, you can use the **disconnect** command to end the session and close the Telnet connection. Otherwise, your session remains open until the remote host times the connection out (if at all).

g. Terminal screen format

— Set the screen size for the current session only

```
Switch#terminal length lines
Switch# terminal width characters
```

— Set the screen size for all sessions

```
Switch(config-line)# length lines
Switch(config-line)# width characters
```

The screen is formatted to *characters* wide by *lines* high. When the number of lines of output from a command exceeds *lines*, the --More-- prompt is used. If you don't want the output displayed by page with --More--, use **length 0**. The default length for sessions is 24 lines and the default width for settings is 80 characters.

h. Configure session timeout values

— Define an absolute timeout for a line

```
Switch(config-line)# absolute-timeout minutes
```

All active sessions on the line are terminated after *minutes* have elapsed. (Default is 0 minutes, or an indefinite session timeout.)

— Define an idle timeout for a line

```
Switch(config-line)# session-timeout minutes [output]
```

All active sessions on the line are terminated only if they have been idle for *minutes*. (Default is 0 minutes, or an indefinite idle timeout.) The **output** keyword causes the idle timer to be reset by outbound traffic on the line, keeping the connection up.

— Define an idle timeout for all EXEC mode sessions

```
Switch(config-line)# exec-timeout minutes [seconds]
```

Active EXEC mode sessions are automatically closed after an idle time period of *minutes* and *seconds* (default 10 minutes). To disable idle EXEC timeouts on the line, use the **no exec-timeout** or **exec-timeout 0 0** command.

— Enable session timeout warnings

```
Switch(config-line)# logout-warning [seconds]
```

Users are warned of an impending logout *seconds* before it occurs. By default, no warning is given. If the *seconds* field is left off, it defaults to 20 seconds.

4 Web browser interface

a. Enable the web interface

```
Switch(config)# ip http server
```

The web interface server is started, enabling users to monitor or configure the switch through a web browser.

NOTE   The switch web interface should not be used for access from a public (Internet) network, because of a major vulnerability with the HTTP server service. This vulnerability is documented as Cisco Bug ID CSCdt93862. To disable the HTTP server, use the **no ip http-server** command. In addition to this bug, the default authentication uses clear-text passwords. If you must use the web interface, make sure to configure a stronger authentication method and limit access in Steps c and d that follow.

---

b. *(Optional)* Set the web browser port number

```
Switch(config)# ip http port number
```

HTTP traffic for the web interface can be set to use TCP port *number* (default 80).

c. *(Optional)* Limit access to the web interface

```
Switch(config)# ip http access-class access-list
```

A standard IP access list (specified by either number or name) can be used to limit the source IP addresses of hosts accessing the web interface. This should be used to narrow the range of potential users accessing the switch's web interface.

d. *(Optional)* Choose a method for user authentication

```
Switch(config)# ip http authentication {aaa | enable | local | tacacs}
```

Users attempting to access the switch's web interface can be challenged and authenticated with several different mechanisms. By default, the **enable** method (the clear-text **enable** password must be entered) is used for authentication. You should use one of the stronger authentication methods: **aaa**, **local** (authentication is performed locally on the switch, using usernames and passwords), and **tacacs** (standard or extended TACACS authentication).

e. View the switch's home page

From a web browser, use the URL **http://**switch/*, where *switch* can be the switch's IP address or host name. The default switch home page is available to users with a privilege level of 15. Only IOS commands available to lesser-privilege levels are available to those users limited to a privilege level less than 15.

1-3: ROM Monitor

- The ROM monitor is a ROM-based program that is executed on power up or reset of the switch.

- The ROM monitor interface can be accessed if the user presses Ctrl+Break during the boot process.

- If the switch fails to load an operating system or if the value of 0 is specified in the BOOT field of the configuration register, the switch enters ROM monitor mode.

- If the switch encounters a fatal exception from which it cannot recover, it enters ROM monitor mode.

- Like the COS and Cisco IOS Software interfaces, ROM monitor is a CLI.

- ROM monitor offers a limited number of commands associated with booting recovery of the switch.

- ROM monitor offers a limited help facility and basic history functions to aid users.

- ROM monitor allows for Xmodem asynchronous transfers to aid in the recovery of OSs.

Using the ROM Monitor Command Set

Many switches have a ROM monitor command set that enables the user to interact with the switch to recover operating systems or alter boot variables during the boot process. The ROM monitor has a basic set of commands and a help facility to aid the user. The following steps outline the use of the ROM monitor facility.

1 User interface modes

```
rommon1>
```

The rommon interface is a simple CLI that allows users to recover from fatal errors or change the boot parameters of the switch. The rommon interface offers a single mode with a limited set of commands typically associated with booting the switch and managing environment parameters.

2 User interface features

a. Entering commands

```
rommon> command
```

The rommon command line interprets input a line at a time like the COS and Cisco IOS Software CLI.

b. Help

You can enter a question mark (**?**) at the beginning of a rommon> prompt to get a list of available commands for rommon.

c. History

The rommon interface keeps a history of the previous 16 commands a user typed. To view the history, use the command **history** or the letter **h** to view the list of commands in history. When the history is listed, users should see a numeric value to the left of each command. The user can recall the commands by using the **repeat** *value* or **r** *value*, where the *value* is the number to the left of the command shown during a history listing.

3 Viewing and changing configuration variables

a. Viewing the configuration variables

```
rommon> set
```

The ROM monitor loads the configuration variables for the switch before giving the user access to the prompt. These variables include the location of the configuration file and the boot image that ROM monitor will look for. Use the command **set** with no options to view these variables.

b. Setting the configuration variables

```
rommon> PARAMETER=value
```

To set a configuration variable, use the parameter value *exactly* as it shows in the **set** command (these are case-sensitive) followed by a value. To nullify a configuration variable, leave the value blank. For example, use the following command to clear the boot image that was specified for the switch.

```
rommon> BOOT=
```

NOTE   When you're in the ROM monitor, it is important to note that any variable or parameter you set should be in all uppercase and any command that is typed should be all lowercase. If you mistype the case, the ROM monitor cannot process the command.

---

c. Saving the configuration variables

```
rommon> sync
```

To save the configuration variables, use the command **sync.** This command saves the new variables to NVRAM to be used the next time the switch is reset.

d. Loading the new configuration variables

```
rommon> reset
```

To load the configuration variables to the ROM monitor, you must power cycle or reset the switch. To reset the switch, use the command **reset**.

4 Booting a switch in rommon mode

a. Viewing the images on Flash devices

```
rommon> dir [device:]
```

ROM monitor is responsible for loading the COS or Cisco IOS Software images for a device. To view an image, use the command **dir** followed by the device name such as **dir bootflash:** or **dir slot0:**.

b. Booting an image from Flash

```
rommon> boot [device:filename]
```

To boot from ROM monitor, use the command **boot**. The command **boot** without any device or filename uses the BOOT field in the configuration variables. If the field is empty or the file is invalid, the user is returned to the rommon> prompt. If you specify the name of the file when using the **boot** command, the variable is ignored and the file is booted.

CAUTION   Boot variables and filenames are case-sensitive. If you specify an invalid name or miss a character or a case setting in the name, the file will not be found and the switch will return you to the rommon mode. It might be useful to view the Flash device and highlight and copy the filename into a buffer using the **edit** commands in the terminal application.

5 Xmodem transfers

```
rommon> xmodem
```

This command initiates an Xmodem receive for the ROM monitor. Using this command, you can boot a switch from a file located on a PC attached to the console port. Use the terminal software on your PC to start an asynchronous transfer using Xmodem and send a file from the PC hard drive to the ROM monitor Flash device. After the switch has booted from the PC, the OS will be active and a valid file can be copied into flash memory. This process can take a very long time and should be considered a last resort to recovering a lost or damaged image.

Section 1-3

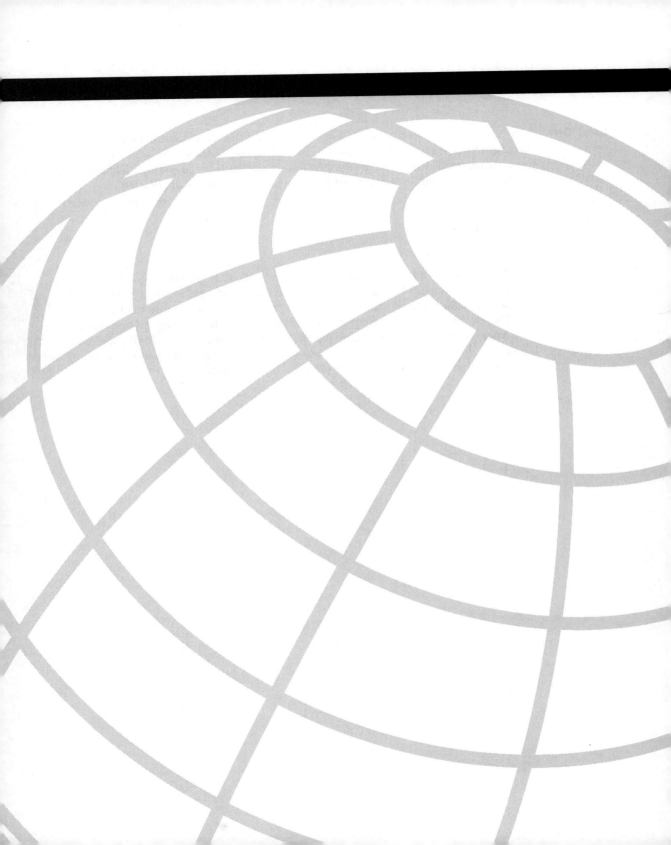

Switch Functionality

Refer to the following sections to configure and use these features:

- **2-1: Catalyst Switch Families**—Gives a brief summary of the Cisco Catalyst switch platforms, their capabilities, and the operating systems that are supported.
- **2-2: Switched Campus Network Designs**—Presents a quick reference checklist of guidelines and ideas you can use when designing your switched enterprise network.

2-1: Catalyst Switch Families

The family of Catalyst switches is an ever-expanding clan. Starting with the acquisition of Grand Junction, Kalpana, and Crescendo in the mid 1990s and with the addition of Granite in 1999, Cisco Systems has put together some of the finest switching engineers in the world. The result it a family of switching products that offer a variety of features for deployment in campus networks.

One of the major challenges in choosing and deploying a switch in your network is understanding what functions that switch performs and how it functions within the network design. The purpose of this section is to give you a brief overview of the current Catalyst switch platforms and their basic functionalities. In addition, a brief section describes the operating systems supported on the various platforms.

Catalyst 3500XL and 2900MXL Series

The Catalyst 3500XL and 2900MXL series switches provide basic connectivity for end-user devices. These switches are referred to as *access switches* and vary in port density from 12 ports to 48 ports. The 3500XL series switches support gigabit interface connectors for gigabit uplinks. The 2900MXL is a modular switch that can support a variety of modular connections including an ATM *LAN emulation client* (LEC) for connectivity to an ATM LANE network. These switches offer a reasonable cost solution for access into a switched network and offer Layer 2 forwarding capabilities with features such as limited *quality of service* (QoS) classification and scheduling, trunking capabilities, and EtherChannel capabilities. In addition, you can cluster many of these switches for management purposes.

Catalyst 2950 Series

The Catalyst 2950 series switch is a switch that typically provides end-user access, but offers advanced features. The 2950 comes in a variety of port densities, with some options for media speeds and connectors. One of the 2950 products offers 10/100/1000 mbps connectivity using copper. This switch allows for deployment of gigabit to the access layer. The 2950 offers Layer 2 forwarding and has many of the same capabilities as the Catalyst XL series switches, such as trunking and EtherChannel capabilities. The 2950 also adds Layer 3 and Layer 4 security using VLAN *access control lists* (ACLs), and enhanced QoS classification and scheduling based on Layer 3 and Layer 4 information. The 2950 is the next generation of access switches for the campus network.

Catalyst 3550 Series

The Catalyst 3550 is a midline switch that can offer Layer 2 services or both Layer 2 and Layer 3 services in the same device, depending on the software. The switch comes in different port densities and offers Fast Ethernet and Gigabit Ethernet support. This switch has ports that can be directly configured as Layer 3 interfaces, or can use virtual (VLAN) interfaces for Layer 3 switching. It also supports Layer 2 functionalities on a port-by-port basis for basic Layer 2 connectivity and enhanced features such as trunking, channeling, QoS classification and marking, in addition to access control for Layer 2 or Layer 3 ports.

Because of its flexibility, the 3550 makes an excellent switch in small to midsize campus environments and can be deployed as an access switch or a distribution switch. The 3550 has replaced the 2948G-L3 switch as a midsized wire-speed Layer 3 switch. The 3550 can run either the *standard multilayer software image* (SMI) for Layer 2 switching or the *enhanced multilayer software image* (EMI) for Layer 2 and 3 switching.

Catalyst 5000 Series

The Catalyst 5000 series switches are some of the staples of Cisco campus switching. This switch is a modular product that offers both a variety of media support and port densities. The 5000 series consists of the 5000 products and 5500 products. The 5500 switches have been used in many networks as distribution and backbone switches, but are now being deployed as access and distribution switches because of the backplane limitations. The switch supports ATM, FDDI, Token Ring, Ethernet, Fast Ethernet, and Gigabit Ethernet modules in addition to routing and WAN modules for connectivity. The 5500 products offer advanced features such as supervisor redundancy and multilayer switching capabilities. These switches also offer some basic QoS classification and scheduling services.

Catalyst 4000 Series

The Catalyst 4000 series switch is a midline switch that can act as a high-port-density access switch and distribution switch as well as a low-density core device. The 4000 series is also a modular switch that offers both Layer 2 and Layer 3 services. This switch offers Ethernet connectivity and a Layer 3 module. The Supervisor III for the 4000 series has an integrated Layer 3 module and can run Cisco IOS Software. These switches also perform Layer 2 trunking functions and provide support for EtherChannels. The 4000 series switch offers some basic QoS classification and scheduling.

Catalyst 6000 Series

The Catalyst 6000 series switch is the flagship of the Catalyst product lines. It is the most robust, has the highest backplane support, and is the most flexible of any of the Catalyst products. This modular switch can act as a high-port-density access switch, as a Layer 2/Layer 3 distribution switch, and as a wire-speed Layer 2 or Layer 3 core switch. In addition to its high-speed Ethernet switching capabilities, it offers a variety of cards to support advanced features such as voice services, content switching, intrusion detection, network analysis, optical services, 10 Gigabit Ethernet, firewall support, and encryption services. All these features function at wire speeds. In addition to these services, the 6500 chassis support connectivity for the fabric module to interconnect the cards rather than the 32 gbps backplane. With this fabric module, a 6509 or 6513 fully populated with fabric-enabled cards has a total of 256 gbps of fabric connectivity. The switch also offers support for redundancy and high-availability features. The Catalyst 6000 series switches continue to evolve as new products provide more flexibility and functionality.

NOTE   Although Cisco officially announced May 15, 2002, as the end of sales for the Catalyst 6006 and 6009 chassis, it is important to note that the only difference in a 6000 chassis and a 6500 chassis is connectors for fabric cards. The chassis themselves offer no enhanced services without the appropriate cards and modules. Therefore, a 6500 without a fabric module and fabric-enabled cards operates the same as a Catalyst 6000 would. To speak of the products in a generic sense, this text refers to the family as the 6000 series.

Switch Operating Systems

Because the variety of Catalyst products that exist are the direct result of acquisitions, mergers, and ongoing developments, it is not hard to believe that there is also a variety of operating systems (OSs) that configure and manage these devices. A major challenge when working with Cisco switches is understanding the difference between the OSs and how to go about configuring the same functionality on the different platforms. A main purpose of this book is to identify the necessary steps to configure a feature and to distinguish how those steps vary among the different operating systems. Before you can configure these OSs, it is import to be able to differentiate between how the systems work on the different platforms.

The Cisco switch product lines consist of two major OSs. The first is the *Cisco Internetwork Operating System* (Cisco IOS). This OS is based on the same Kernel and shell used for routers. In the switch world, this OS has three derivatives:

- **Layer 2 IOS**—This is Cisco IOS that runs on a device that forwards packets based on Layer 2 information only. Some example devices that run Layer 2 IOS include the 3500XL and the 2950.

- **Layer 3 IOS**—Layer 3 IOS runs on a switch device that performs Layer 3 packet forwarding for its interfaces. This OS is the same that runs on a router; in the switch environment, however, it is found on the 2948G-L3 products, the Route Switch Module (RSM) and Multilayer Switch Module (MSM), and the Route Switch Feature Card (RSFC) and Mutilayer Switch Feature Card (MSFC).

- **Layer 2/Layer 3 IOS**—This is an IOS that runs on a device that can have a port that acts like a router port (Layer 3) or like a switch port (Layer 2) depending on the device's configuration. The Layer 2/Layer 3 IOS is sometimes referred to as *integrated IOS* because it integrates the functions of both *Open System Integration* (OSI) layers. The 3550 runs this OS. This OS can also be run on a 4000 series switch with a Supervisor III card or a 6000 series switch with a MSFC. When the code runs on one of these platforms, it is also referred to as *native* or *Supervisor* IOS.

The IOS flavors are similar in command structure, configuration steps, and system management; but they do differ slightly in support and some configuration parameters. Where this is the case, this book points out the differences between the OSs.

The other major OS for the Catalyst family of switches is the *Catalyst Operating System* (COS), sometimes referred to as *CatOS*. This OS offers only Layer 2 support and runs on the 4000, 5000, and 6000 series switches. COS is very popular for Layer 2 switching because of the ease of use in its command structure. Table 2-1 shows the different OSs and the platforms that support them.

Table 2-1   *OS Platform Matrix*

OS	Cisco IOS			Catalyst OS
OSI Layer Support	Layer 2 only	Layer 3 only	Layer 2 and Layer 3	Layer 2 only
Platform	2900MXL 3500XL 2950	2948G-L3 4980G-L3 RSM/MSM RSFC/MSFC All routers Layer 3 services module	3550 4000 series[1] 6000 series[2]	5000 series 4000 series 6000 series

[1] The Catalyst 4000 series switch requires a Supervisor III to run the integrated (Supervisor) IOS.

[2] The Catalyst 6000 series switch requires a supervisor with a MSFC to run the integrated (Supervisor) IOS.

A variety of Cisco switches and OSs will be used for the design and configuration of a campus network based on Cisco products. While using this book, keep in mind which OS and which platform you are using.

2-2: Switched Campus Network Designs

When you design a switched network, you must consider many things. Adding to or redesigning a large enterprise or campus network can seem complex or overwhelming. There is an accepted, organized approach to switched network design that can simplify the design process, as well as make the network more efficient and scalable.

This section is organized as a quick reference "checklist" of guidelines, rules of thumb, and ideas to help you think through the overall network architecture and configuration. Many of the checklist items include a reference to the appropriate sections of this book that deal with the switch features.

1 Segment LANs into the smallest collision domains possible by using LAN switches.

2 Organize your enterprise network into a hierarchical structure.

A network designed around a layered structure gives the foundation for predictable behavior, consistent latency (number of switch hops) from anywhere in the network, and scalability. If the network needs to be expanded, you can add more switch blocks into the existing structure.

Figure 2-1 shows the basic network hierarchy divided into three distinct layers:

- **Access layer**—Consists of switches that connect to the end users
- **Distribution layer**—Consists of switches that aggregate traffic from the access layer
- **Core layer**—Consists of switches that aggregate traffic from the distribution layers

Figure 2-1   *Layers of a Hierarchical Network Design*

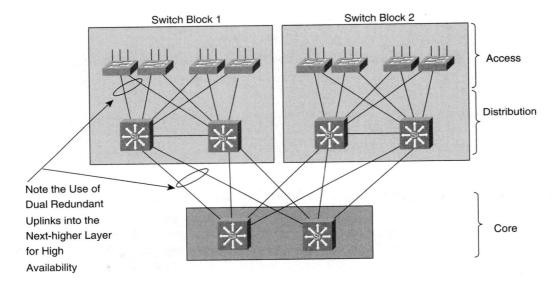

TIP   In small to medium sized enterprise networks, the distribution layer can be omitted. The access layer switches uplink directly into the core layer. This is referred to as a *collapsed core* design.

To provide high availability, each switch in a network layer should have dual or redundant uplinks to two switches in the next higher layer. In the event of a link failure or the failure of an entire switch, the extra uplink can be quickly used. The uplink failover is handled by the *Spanning Tree Protocol* (STP) at Layer 2, or by routing protocols at Layer 3.

3 Place switching functionality at each layer of the hierarchy.

     — **Access**—Switches at this layer generally have a high port density, lower cost, features that address user access or security, and several high-speed uplink ports. Usually, Layer 2 switching is sufficient, although Layer 3 switching can provide higher availability for applications such as IP telephony.

     — **Distribution**—Distribution switches have a port density made up of high-speed ports, and offer higher switching performance, ideally at Layer 3.

     — **Core**—The core layer should be built from the highest performance switches in the network, aggregating traffic from the distribution switches. Layer 2 switches can be used effectively, although switching at Layer 3 adds higher availability and enhanced QoS. Usually, a dual-switch core layer is sufficient to support an entire enterprise.

4 Identify resources in your network that serve common functions. These will become the modules or building blocks of your network design. Figure 2-2 shows some examples of these blocks and how they fit within the network hierarchy.

TIP
     The network in Figure 2-2 is shown with single uplinks to higher layers for simplicity. In a real network, you should always add dual redundant uplinks to two switches in the next higher network layer for the highest network availability.

In this case, each access layer switch would have two uplinks to the two nearest distribution switches. In addition, each distribution switch in each block of the diagram would have two uplinks to the two core layer switches. In other words, the basic principles of Figure 2-1 should be applied to the enterprise layout of Figure 2-2.

     — **Server farms and mainframes**—These are called *server blocks* and *mainframe blocks*, respectively.

     — **Internet access, e-commerce or extranet server farms, and firewall farms**—These are called an *Internet block*.

     — **Remote access**—This is called a *WAN block*.

     — **Telephony servers and gateways**—This is called a *PSTN block*.

     — **Legacy networks (Token Ring, FDDI, and so on)**—This is very similar to the WAN block, using a router to provide connectivity to various network media types.

— **Common workgroups of users**—End users located in the same
building, on the same floor, or in the same area of a floor are called
switch blocks. A switch block typically groups access layer
switches and the distribution switches to which they connect.

Figure 2-2   *Modular Approach to a Campus Network Design*

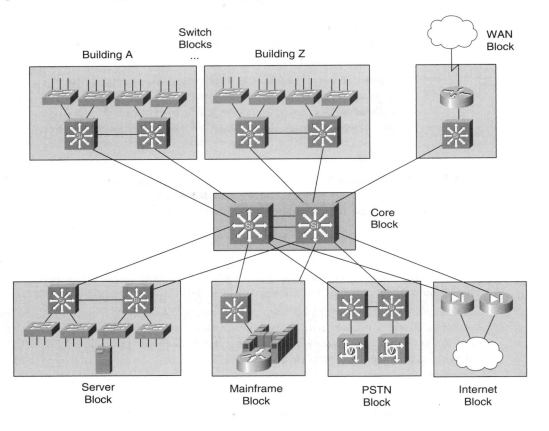

5 Consider high availability or redundancy features that can be used in each network
building block:

a. Core

— If Layer 2 switches are used, don't create a spanning-tree loop by
connecting the two core switches.

— Be sure to identify and configure both primary and secondary root
bridge switches for each VLAN. Typically, the root bridge should
be placed close to the core layer. See section "7-2: STP
Configuration."

— If Layer 3 switches are used, connect the core switches with multiple links. See section "4-4: EtherChannel."

— In a Layer 3 core, make use of Hot Standby Router Protocol (HSRP) to provide redundant gateway addresses. See section "8-6: Router Redundancy with HSRP."

— Each core switch should connect to each distribution switch for full redundancy. If Layer 3 is not used in the core or distribution layers, use STP BackboneFast to reduce STP convergence time. See section "7-2: STP Configuration."

b. Server block

— Use redundant uplinks into the distribution or core layer. Utilize STP UplinkFast (section "7-2: STP Configuration") or HSRP (section "8-6: Router Redundancy with HSRP") for fast failover.

— Consider using dual *network interface cards* (NICs) in servers for redundancy. Connect the NICs into different switch cards or modules.

c. Internet block

— Use Server Load Balancing to distribute traffic across multiple servers in a server farm. See section "10-1: SLB."

— Use Firewall Load Balancing to distribute traffic across multiple firewalls in a firewall farm. See section "10-2: SLB Firewall Load Balancing."

d. Switch blocks

— Each access layer switch has dual uplinks to two separate distribution switches.

— Use STP UplinkFast on access layer switches to reduce uplink failover time.

— Use STP PortFast on access layer ports to reduce startup time for end users.

— To load balance across the access layer uplinks, adjust the STP parameters so that one access VLAN travels over one uplink while another VLAN travels over the other uplink (Layer 2 distribution layer). Otherwise, adjust the HSRP priorities in a Layer 3 distribution so that one distribution switch supports one access VLAN and the other distribution switch supports another VLAN.

— If Layer 3 is used in the distribution layer, use passive interfaces toward the access layer where no other routers reside.

6 Other considerations

a. For each VLAN, configure an STP root bridge and a secondary root bridge as close to the core layer as possible. See section "7-2: STP Configuration."

b. Broadcast domains

— Limit the size of broadcast domains by controlling the size of VLANs. It is permissible to extend VLANs anywhere in the network, but broadcast traffic will follow it.

— Consider using broadcast suppression on switch ports. See section "11-1: Broadcast Suppression."

c. *VLAN Trunking Protocol* (VTP)

— Configure VTP servers nearest the core layer.

— Use VTP pruning or manually configure specific VLANs to be transported on trunks. This reduces the unnecessary broadcast traffic on the trunks.

d. Scaling trunks

— Bundle multiple trunk links together into an EtherChannel. For fault tolerance, divide the EtherChannel across switch modules. See section "4-4: EtherChannel."

— Do not configure trunk negotiation; use the "on" mode. See section "6-3: Trunking."

e. QoS

— Configure QoS on every switch in your network. QoS must be properly supported end-to-end. See section "13-2: QoS Configuration."

— Extend the QoS trust boundary to edge devices (IP phones, for example) that can provide trust.

— Use policers to control non-mission-critical traffic flows.

f. Redundant switch modules

— Consider using redundant supervisors in server farm switches where hosts are single-attached (one NIC).

— If redundant uplinks are provided at each network layer, two physically separate switches will always provide redundancy. Use redundant supervisors in distribution or core layer switches where only single uplinks are available.

— Use high-availability redundancy between supervisors in a chassis. Enable versioning so that the OS can be upgraded without a switch downtime. See section "3-5: Redundant Supervisors."

h. Port security, authentication

— You can control the end-user MAC address or the number of users connected to an access layer switch port with port security. See section "11-4: Port Security."

— Authenticate users at the access layer switch ports using 802.1x authentication. See section "11-2: AAA."

— Control access to VLANs with VLAN ACLs. See section "11-5: VLAN ACLs."

Further Reading

Refer to the following recommended sources for further information about the topics covered in this chapter.

Catalyst Switch Families

Cisco Product Quick Reference Guide (CPQRG) at: www.cisco.com/warp/customer/752/qrg/. For Catalyst LAN switches, go to: www.cisco.com/warp/customer/752/qrg/cpqrg2.htm

Software Advisor—A tool to compare and match Catalyst COS and IOS features, releases, and hardware platforms. Go to: www.cisco.com/cgi-bin/Support/CompNav/Index.pl (CCO login required).

Integrated (Native) IOS White Paper

www.cisco.com/warp/public/cc/pd/si/casi/ca6000/tech/cat65_wp.htm

Switched Campus Network Designs

Gigabit Campus Network Design—Principles and Architecture at: www.cisco.com/warp/public/cc/so/neso/lnso/cpso/gcnd_wp.htm

Gigabit Campus Design—Configuration and Recovery Analysis at: www.cisco.com/warp/public/cc/so/neso/lnso/cpso/camp_wp.htm

Designing High-Performance Campus Intranets with Multilayer Switching at: www.cisco.com/warp/public/cc/so/cuso/epso/entdes/highd_wp.htm

Section 2-3

Cisco Internetwork Design by Matthew Birkner, Cisco Press, ISBN 1-57870-171-6

Building Cisco Multilayer Switched Networks by Karen Webb, Cisco Press, ISBN 1-57870-093-0

CCNP Switching Exam Certification Guide by Tim Boyles and David Hucaby, Cisco Press, ISBN 1-58720-000-7

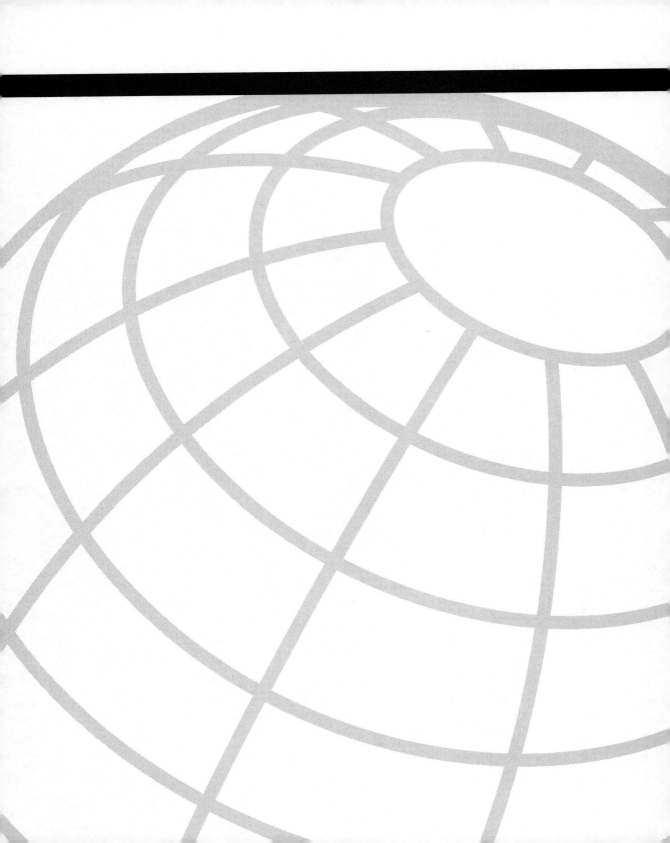

CHAPTER **3**

Supervisor Engine Configuration

See to the following sections for configuration information about these topics:

- **3-1: Prompts and Banners**—Describes the method for configuring prompts and banners for switch identification.

- **3-2: IP Addressing and Services**—Explains how to configure an IP addressing and services for switch management using the TCP/IP protocol.

- **3-3: Passwords and Password Recovery**—Covers the processes used to set passwords for switches and the methods used to recover lost and unknown passwords.

- **3-4: Managing Modules**—Describes how to control power to a module, reset a module, and manage the configuration of individual modules for modular switches.

- **3-5: File Management and Booting**—Explains the process for management of configuration and system files and how to control the boot process.

- **3-6: Redundant Supervisors**—Explains the feature by which redundant Supervisor modules synchronize their configurations and how to manage this feature.

- **3-7: Cisco Discovery Protocol**—Describes the interaction of the *Cisco Discovery Protocol* (CDP) with other Cisco devices and how to control CDP functions for switch ports.

- **3-8: Time and Calendar**—Presents the basic steps needed to configure date and time information on the switch using both manual configuration techniques and *Network Time Protocol* (NTP).

3-1: Prompts and Banners

- Switch prompts help users identify the device they are managing by providing a useful name at each command-line entry point.

- In most switch operating systems, the prompt will follow the system or host name, but can be altered.

- System banners both identify switches and provide information about security policies and monitoring procedures.

- The configuration of prompts and banners is optional.

Configuration of Prompt

1 *(Optional)* Configuring the prompt.

a. Configure a prompt by setting a device name:

COS	`set system name` *string*
IOS	`(global)` `hostname` *string*

By default the host name for an IOS device is Switch or Router, depending on the function (Layer 2 or Layer 3) of the switch. COS switches have no name, so the default prompt is console.

NOTE   In early Catalyst operating systems (COS 3.2 and below), setting the system name had no effect on the prompt. To configure the prompt on a COS device running these versions of software, refer to Step 1b.

---

b. Specifically configure a prompt:

COS	`set system prompt` *string*
IOS	`(global)` `prompt` *string*

By default, the host name for an IOS device is Switch or Router, depending on the function (Layer 2 or Layer 3) of the switch. COS switches have no name, so the default prompt is console.

Configuration of Banner

1 *(Optional)* Configure a *Message of the Day* (MOTD) banner.

MOTD banners are not required to make any system operational; however, they are extremely useful for identifying any security policies pertaining to accessing network devices. For COS devices, this is a way to identify the switch without logging in to the device.

a. Configure an MOTD banner:

COS	`set banner motd &` *string* `&`
IOS	`(global)` `banner motd &` *string* `&`

The banner text is typed in between delimiting characters (in the table, the ampersand [**&**]). The delimiting character is typed at the beginning and end of the banner, which can include multiple lines, line breaks, and words. The delimiting character can be any character that is not part of the banner text.

NOTE   Banners are limited in size by device and operating system. There is no consistent number or limitation. The old 1900 and 2800 series switches have a limitation of 400 characters or 20 lines. The latest version of the COS has a limitation of 3070 characters.

Feature Example

This example shows a typical configuration for setting the system name, prompt, and banner.

An example of the Catalyst OS configuration follows:

```
Console (enable)>set system name Core_Switch1
Core_Switch1 (enable)>set banner motd *
This is Core_Switch1 for the XYZ corporation.
You have accessed a restricted device, unauthorized logins are prohibited.
*
Core_Switch1 (enable)>
```

An example of the Supervisor IOS configuration follows:

```
Switch(config)#hostname Core_Switch1
Core_Switch1(config)#banner motd *
This is Core_Switch1 for the XYZ corporation.
You have accessed a restricted device, unauthorized logins are prohibited.
*
Core_Switch1(config)#end
Core_Switch1#copy running-config startup-config
```

3-2: IP Addressing & Services

- Switches use IP addresses and services for management purposes.
- IP addresses can be set or obtained using *Dynamic Host Configuration Protocol* (DHCP), *BOOTstrap Protocol* (BOOTP), or *Reverse Address Resolution Protocol* (RARP).
- Gateways, routes to networks, and default routes are established to allow communications with devices that are not local to the management network.
- Static entries or DNS servers can be used to resolve computer names.
- *Hypertext Transfer Protocol* (HTTP) services are available for some switches to provide a configuration interface.
- *Simple Network Management Protocol* (SNMP) service allows for switch configuration and management.

Section 3-2

Configuring an IP Management Address

IP addresses are used in Layer 2 switches for management purposes only. This step is not required to make the switch operational. If you do not configure an IP address, however, the only way to manage the switch is by using the console connection.

1 *(Optional; recommended)* Configure the IP address.

a. Configure the IP address manually:

COS	`set interface sc0` [*vlannumber*] *address mask*
IOS	(global) `interface vlan` *vlannumber*
	(interface or subinterface) `ip address` *address mask*
	(interface or subinterface) `management`

Catalyst switches can have an active management address in only one VLAN. The management command on the Layer 2 IOS switches specifies which VLAN is active. VLAN 1 is the default management VLAN for both IOS and COS switches. On a Layer 2 IOS switch, if VLAN 1 is not the management VLAN, the prompt reads "subinterface."

On COS switches running COS 5.x or above, you can also configure the mask using bitwise or *classless interdomain routing* (CIDR) notation (for example, **set interface sc0 10.1.1.1/24**).

To view the IP configuration, use the command **show interface** for COS devices or **show interfaces vlan** *n* (where *n* is your VLAN number) for IOS devices.

NOTE   This addressing section deals exclusively with Layer 2 management addresses and interfaces only. Layer 3 interfaces are discussed in Chapter 5, "Layer 3 Interface Configuration."

---

b. (*Not recommended*) Automatically obtain an IP address.

You can have the switch request an address from a service, such as RARP, BOOTP, or DHCP. This is not recommended because it is conceivable that the address could change for DHCP unless the lease is permanent or static (meaning that the lease never expires or a specific IP address is reserved for the switch MAC). This also means that a change of hardware could create a problem with BOOTP and static DHCP address. Not all switches support all of these services. A COS device requests a RARP and BOOTP/DHCP address upon boot if there is no address configured (which is the default setting). If you want to remove an address and configure the COS switch for automatic IP address resolution, you must set the address to 0.0.0.0 and then reset the switch, assuming that there is a valid RARP or DHCP/BOOTP server available. If you are using a static DCHP entry, BOOTP, or a RARP server, you must know the MAC address used by the switch during the request. You can use the command **show module** to locate the last address for module 1 (the Supervisor engine).

For Layer 2 IOS switches, you can obtain an address via DHCP/BOOTP if you have configured the device for autoconfig. The command **service config** enables autoconfig. If automatic configuration is enabled, the switch ignores any manual IP configuration parameters:

COS	```show module```
	```set interface SC0 0.0.0.0```
	```reset```

IOS	(global) ```service config``` (privileged exec)```reload```

For the COS devices, you can renew or release the DHCP address with the command **set interface sc0 dhcp release** or **set interface sc0 dhcp renew**.

NOTE Service configuration loads a complete configuration for the switch automatically. It is referred to as *autoinstall* in the router community. Autoconfig also requires that a configuration file be available on a TFTP server for a full configuration. For more details on autoconfig, consult the Cisco web site at www.cisco.com/univercd/cc/td/doc/product /lan/c2900xl/29_35wc/sc/swgsyst.htm#xtocid100303.

Configuring a Default Gateway

Because you might be accessing your switch from various networks throughout your environment, it is important to configure the gateway address or default route to access a Layer 3 device to access other networks.

 1 *(Optional; recommended)* Configure the default gateway:

COS	```set ip route default``` *gatewayaddress*
IOS	(global) ```ip default-gateway``` *gatewayaddress*

The gateway address is the IP address of the Layer 3 interface that is acting as a router for traffic generated by the switch. To view your default gateways, use the command **show ip route** for COS devices or **show ip route default** for IOS devices.

NOTE The option **default** in the COS configuration is an IP alias and cannot be abbreviated. You can also use 0.0.0.0 instead of the word *default*.

Setting Up DNS Services or Host Tables

Each Catalyst switch can resolve common names, such as URLs or fully qualified domain names, into IP addresses if the proper IP service is configured. This service is a *Domain Name System* (DNS) server or a local host table. By default DNS services are enabled on IOS switches, but the server is not specified. On COS switches, you must enable the service and specify the server. To configure the switch for DNS operation, use the following guidelines.

1 *(Optional)* Enable the DNS service on the switch:

COS	`set ip dns enable`
IOS	`(global) ip domain-lookup`

This command enables the switch to use DNS for name lookups. The IOS default is for **ip domain-lookup** to be on.

TIP If you are not going to use DNS, it is recommended that you disable DNS lookups on IOS switches with the global configuration command **no ip domain-lookup**. This command prevents the switch from trying to resolve mistyped commands.

2 *(Optional)* Define the address of the DNS server:

COS	`set ip dns server serveraddress [primary]`
IOS	`(global) ip name-server serveraddress1 [serveraddress2. . . serveraddress6]`

Use this command to specify the addresses of one or more DNS servers. For COS switches, you can enter up to three different addresses using separate command-line entries. The COS keyword **primary** specifies the first server that will be queried. If there is no answer, the other two will be checked. For IOS switches, you can specify up to six addresses on a single command-line entry. For IOS switches, the first address is the primary.

-or-

(Optional) Specify host entries for name resolution:

COS	`set ip alias` *name address*
IOS	`(global)` `ip host` *name address*

By specifying the name and address of the device on the switch, the name is resolved in the local table. DNS can be enabled or disabled when using local host names.

Configuring HTTP Services

For IOS switches, an HTTP server can be enabled so that the switch can be managed using a web browser. The web-based *graphical user interface* (GUI) is a straightforward management option that gives users another configuration option. HTTP server services are not supported across all platforms.

1 *(Optional)* Configure HTTP service for switch configuration:

COS	N/A
IOS	`(global)` `[no] ip http server`

The IOS command **ip http server** is on by default. You can choose to disable it with the **no** command.

CAUTION Starting with Cisco IOS Release 11.3, the HTTP server was enabled by default. Some switches can be vulnerable to a bug (CSCdt93862) that enables users to access the HTTP services at privileged level without being prompted for the password. The initial workaround to this bug was to disable the HTTP services. See www.cisco.com/warp/ public/707/IOS-httplevel-pub.html for more information.

Feature Example

This example shows a typical configuration for setting the IP address, gateway, and DNS servers for a switch in an administrative VLAN 986. For the IOS switch, this example disabled the HTTP server service.

An example of the Catalyst OS configuration follows:

```
Console (enable)> set interface sc0 986 10.1.1.5/24
Console (enable)> set ip route default 10.1.1.1
Console (enable)> set ip dns enable
Console (enable)> set ip dns server 10.1.1.254
```

An example of the Supervisor IOS configuration follows:

```
Switch(config)#interface vlan 986
Switch(config-subif)#ip address 10.1.1.5 255.255.255.0
Switch(config-subif)#management
Switch(config-subif)#ip default-gateway 10.1.1.1
Switch(config)#ip name-server 10.1.1.254
Switch(config)#no ip http server

Switch(config)#end
Switch(config)#copy running-config startup-config
```

3-3: Passwords and Password Recovery

- Passwords provide a layer of protection for the switch to prevent unauthorized use.
- Catalyst switches have basically two levels of password protection (user level and privileged level).
- Privileged passwords are encrypted for tighter security.
- If a password is lost, each OS offers a password recovery process to gain access to the device.

Configuration of Passwords

1 *(Optional; highly recommended)* Configure a user-level password:

COS	`set password`
IOS	`(line) login`
	`(line) password` *password*

The user-level password prevents anyone who is not authorized from accessing the *command-line interface* (CLI) from Telnet or console sessions. For COS machines, the command **set password** enables an applet that queries the user for the current and new password. On IOS machines, the command **login** and a **password** must be configured on each line (**con0** or **vty 0 4**). The command **login** is a default setting on the Telnet lines for an IOS switch, which prevents a user from logging in via Telnet until after a password has been configured.

NOTE	On an IOS switch, you can configure a different user-level password for any line, such as Telnet or console connections. For a COS switch, the user password is always the same regardless of how the switch is accessed (Telnet or console).

2 *(Optional; highly recommended)* Configure a privileged-level password:

COS	`set enablepass`
IOS	`(global)` `enable secret` *password*

The privileged password prevents anyone who is not authorized from gaining access to privileged level, where configuration changes can be made to the switch and other features. For COS machines, the command **set enablepass** enables an applet that queries the user for the current and new password. On IOS machines, the command **enable secret** followed by the password is used to configure the password.

NOTE	On a COS device, both passwords are encrypted. For the IOS machine, only the secret, privileged password is encrypted by default.

Feature Example

This example shows a typical configuration for setting the user and privileged passwords for COS and IOS switches.

An example of the Catalyst OS configuration follows:

```
Console (enable)>
Console (enable)>set enablepass
Enter old password: oldenablepass
Enter new password: san-fran
Retype new password: san-fran
Password changed
Console (enable)> set password
Enter old password: oldpass
Enter new password: cisco
Retype new password: cisco
Password changed
Console (enable)>
```

An example of the Supervisor IOS configuration follows:

```
Switch(config)#enable secret san-fran
Switch(config)#line vty 0 4
Switch(config-line)#password cisco
Switch(config-line)#line con 0
Switch(config-line)#login
Switch(config-line)#password cisco
Switch(config-line)#end
Switch1#copy running-config startup-config
```

Section 3-3

Password Recovery on a COS Device

If you have lost or forgotten your passwords, you can use the COS password-recovery process to gain access to the device. The COS procedure is among the easiest of all the recovery procedures.

For the initial 30 or so seconds after the switch CLI becomes available, all passwords are null, so users only need to press Enter when prompted for a password (including prompts during password management). The following steps outline the procedure:

1 Attach a device to the console of the switch and power cycle the device.

2 As the switch comes up, press Enter to gain access to the user prompt.

NOTE You should see a message about the device being available, but it might scroll by quickly. Because it is important to complete the next few steps in a timely fashion, you might want to press Enter every few seconds until you get the user prompt.

3 After accessing the user prompt, access privileged mode by typing the command **enable** and pressing Enter when prompted for a password.

4 In privileged mode, changed the user password with the command **set password**. Press Enter for each of the prompts.

5 In privileged mode, change the user password with the command **set enablepass**. Press Enter for each of the prompts.

At this point, you have set all the passwords back to the default (which is null). Because timing is critical for Steps 2 through 5, it is best to set the passwords to null and then go back and change the passwords to the desired setting using the **set password** and **set enablepass** commands again after Step 5.

TIP Because you have a limited time to complete this process, it is helpful to create a text file with the commands and carriage returns needed to complete the process. Then when you get the prompt to log in, you can paste in the text file to complete the password-recovery process.

Feature Example

This example shows a typical password-recovery process for a COS switch:

```
System Bootstrap, Version 5.3(1)
Copyright (c) 1994-1999 by Cisco Systems, Inc.
c6k_sup1 processor with 65536 Kbytes of main memory
```

```
Autoboot executing command: "boot bootflash:cat6000-sup9k.6-1-1c.bin"

Uncompressing file: ################################################
######################################################################
######################################################################
System Power On Diagnostics
DRAM Size ...................64 MB
Testing DRAM.................Passed
Verifying Text segment ......Passed
NVRAM Size ..................512 KB
Saving NVRAM ................Done
Testing NVRAM ...............Passed
Restoring NVRAM .............Done
Level2 Cache ................Present
Testing Level2 Cache ........Passed

System Power On Diagnostics Complete

Boot image: bootflash:cat6000-sup9k.6.1.1(c).bin

Running System Diagnostics from this Supervisor (Module 1)
This may take up to 2 minutes....please wait


Cisco Systems Console

Enter password: (press Enter)

2000 Jan 09 23:09:27 %SYS-1-SYS_NORMPWRMGMT:System in normal power management
operation
2000 Jan 09 23:09:27 %SYS-5-MOD_PWRON:Module 3 powered up
2000 Jan 09 23:09:34 %SYS-5-MOD_OK:Module 1 is online

Console> enable
Enter password: (press Enter)
Console> (enable) set password
Enter old password: (press Enter)
Enter new password: (press Enter)
Retype new password: (press Enter)
Password changed.

Console> (enable) set enablepass

Enter old password: (press Enter)
Enter new password: (press Enter)
Retype new password: (press Enter)
Password changed.

Console> (enable)

Console> (enable) set password
Enter old password: (press Enter)
Enter new password: (type your new password)
Retype new password: (type your new password)
Password changed.

Console> (enable) set enablepass
Enter old password: (press Enter)
Enter new password: (type your new password)
Retype new password: (type your new password)
Password changed.
```

Section 3-3

Password Recovery on IOS Devices: Procedure 1

Password-recovery procedure 1 covers the 2900/3500XL, 2950, and 3550. If you have lost or forgotten your passwords, or if you want to bypass the configuration file, you can use this recovery process to gain access to the device.

To recover from a lost IOS password, you have to stop the boot process and then direct the IOS switch to not use the configuration file. When the switch loads without a file, you have no passwords and can enter into privileged mode. From there, you can copy the configuration file into active memory and then change and save the passwords. To complete the recovery process, follow these steps:

1 Attach a device to the console of the switch. Make sure you have connectivity, and then unplug the power cord from the switch.

2 Press and hold the mode button and plug the switch back in. Release the mode button after the LED above port 1x has been on for at least 2 seconds.

3 You will receive some information indicating that the Flash initialization has been interrupted. After you receive this information, at the prompt type the command **flash_init**.

4 Next type the command **load_helper**.

5 You need to get a listing of the Flash with the command **dir flash:** (the colon [:] is required).

6 Rename the file to config.text with the command **rename flash:config.text flash:config.old**.

7 Continue the boot process with the command **boot**.

8 Answer **n** to the question about entering setup mode.

9 Press Enter to access the user mode and enter into privileged mode with the command **enable**.

10 Rename the configuration file back to config.text with the command **rename flash:config.old flash:config.text**.

11 Copy the configuration file into active memory with the command **copy flash:config.text system:running-config**.

12 Enter configuration mode with the command **configure terminal**.

13 Change the line and secret passwords as covered earlier in this section.

14 Save the configuration.

Feature Example

This example shows a typical password-recovery procedure 1 for IOS switches.

The system has been interrupted prior to initializing the Flash file system. The following commands initialize the Flash file system and finish loading the operating system software:

```
flash_init
load_helper
boot

flash_init
load_helper
dir flash:
 Directory of flash:
2 -rwx 843947 Mar 01 1993 00:02:18 C2900XL-ms-12.2.8.bin
4 drwx    3776 Mar 01 1993 01:23:24 html
66 -rwx     130 Jan 01 1970 00:01:19 env_vars
68 -rwx 1296   Mar 01 1993 06:55:51 config.text
1728000 bytes total (456704 bytes free)
rename flash:config.text flash:config.old
boot
Continue with the configuration dialog? [yes/no] : N
Switch>enable
Switch#rename flash:config.old flash:config.text
Switch# copy flash:config.text system:running-config
Switch#configure terminal
Switch(config)#enable secret newpassword
Switch(config)#line vty 0 4
Switch(config-line)#password newpassword
Switch(config)#line con 0
Switch(config-line)#password newpassword
Switch#(config-line)#end
Switch#copy running-config startup-config
```

Password Recovery on IOS Devices: Procedure 2

Password-recovery procedure 2 covers the 6000 series switch running IOS. If you have lost or forgotten your passwords, or if you want to bypass the configuration file, you can use this recovery process.

To recover from a lost IOS password, you must stop the boot process of the route processor and then direct the IOS switch to not use the configuration file. When the switch loads without a file, you have no passwords and can enter into privileged mode. From there you can copy the configuration file into active memory and then change and save the passwords. To complete the recovery process, follow these steps:

1   Attach a device to the console of the switch and power cycle the device.

2   Watch the console output. When you see the message "%OIR-6-CONSOLE: Changing console ownership to route processor," initiate the break sequence from your terminal emulator (typically Ctrl-Break).

3   You should see a rommon1> prompt. At this prompt, type **confreg 0x2142** to tell the switch to ignore the current configuration.

Section 3-3

4 Now type **reset** at the rommon2> prompt to reset the switch and restart to boot process.

5 Answer **no** to the question about entering setup.

6 Press Enter to gain access to the Router> prompt and enter the command **enable** to access privileged mode.

7 At the Router# prompt, copy the startup configuration into the running configuration with the command **copy startup-config running-config**.

8 Enter global configuration mode with the command **configure terminal**.

9 Change the line and secret passwords as covered earlier in this section.

10 Reset the configuration register with the command **config-register 0x2102**.

11 Exit setup mode with the command **end**.

12 Save the configuration with the command **copy running-config startup-config**.

Feature Example

This example shows a typical password-recovery procedure 2 for IOS switches:

```
%OIR-6-CONSOLE: Changing console ownership to route processor
issue break
rommon1>confreg 0x2142
rommon2>reset
<switch output omitted>
Continue with the configuration dialog? [yes/no] : N
Router>enable
Router# copy startup-config running-config
Router#configure terminal
Router(config)#enable secret newpassword
Router(config)#line vty 0 4
Router(config-line)#password newpassword
Router(config)#line con 0
Router(config-line)#password newpassword
Router#config-register 0x2102
Router#(config-line)#end
Router#copy running-config startup-config
```

3-4: Managing Modules

- Many devices have multiple blades or modules used for switching services.
- Some of these modules have their own operating systems and can be accessed directly for configuration.
- Most modules can be power cycled or reset individually.
- For some switches, it is possible to power down a module.
- For COS switches, you can view the configuration of each module individually.
- For COS switches, you can clear the configuration of a single module.

Viewing Modules

In both IOS and COS, you can use modular switches to effect a more flexible switch configuration. To view the modules installed on a switch, use one of the following commands:

COS	`show modules`
Supervisor IOS	(privileged) `show module all`
L2 IOS	(privileged) `show hardware` or `show version`

These commands show the hardware or module information for the switches.

Accessing Modules

Most modules and ports are configured through the main CLI for the switch. However, a handful of modules, such as the *Multilayer Switch Feature Card* (MSFC) or the ATM interface on a 2900MXL, must be accessed individually and configured separately. To access these interfaces, use the **session** command:

COS	`session` *mod#*
IOS	(privileged) `session` *slot#*

The *slot#* or *mod#* indicates in which slot or module in the switch the card is. For a 2900MXL, this is slot 1 or 2. For a Layer 3 module—an RSM or MSM in a Catalyst 4000, 5000, or 6000 switch—this corresponds to the module number into which the card is plugged. For a *Route Switch Feature Card* (RSFC) or MSFC, this is 15 for the MSFC or RSFC in slot 1 and 16 for the MSFC or RSFC in slot 2.

NOTE   You can also access many of these modules with a console port directly on the blade. For console access to the MSFC on the Catalyst 6000, use the command **switch console**.

Resetting Modules

You can reset modules on an individual basis. Therefore, you can jumpstart a group of ports without having to reset the entire switch:

COS	`reset` *mod#*
IOS	(privileged) `power cycle module` *slot*

Section 3-4

The **reset** command causes an entire module to be powered down and then back up, and forces the module to go through *Power-On Self-Test* (POST) as it reloads. Some IOS switches do not offer this option. For those switches, you can reset a port with the **shutdown** and **no shutdown** commands.

Powering Modules Up and Down

For the IOS and COS modular switches, you can power down a module. Powering down disables the module and all its ports. If the switch is reset or power cycled, the module remains in a powered-down state. This state can be useful for troubleshooting a boot problem or if the power supply cannot handle the complete switch power load:

COS	`set module power down` *mod*
IOS	(global) `no power enable module` *slot*

These commands disable the modules. For an IOS switch, none of the module's configuration are saved; and if the switch is reset, all the configuration entries for that module are lost. To re-enable the modules, use the following commands:

COS	`set module power up` *mod*
IOS	(global)`power enable module` *slot*

Viewing Module Configurations

For COS devices, you can view the configuration of a specific module as follows:

COS	`show configuration` *mod#* [`all`]
IOS	N/A

Use the module number to specify which module's parameters you want to view. If you do not specify the **all** option, only the nondefault configuration parameters display.

Clearing Module Configurations

For COS devices, you can clear the configuration of a specific module as follows:

COS	`clear config` *mod#* `all`
IOS	N/A

Use *mod#* to specify which module you want to clear. This command is particularly useful if you remove a card and replace it with a different one. If you remove an 8-port Gigabit Ethernet module and replace it with a 16-port module, for example, you must clear the configuration of the slot before the new module will be active.

3-5: File Management and Boot Parameters

- Cisco operating systems have many files and file systems that require management.
- File management consists of managing configuration files and operating system files.
- COS switches do not require you to save configuration changes.
- File system commands replace many older file management commands.
- File system commands enable you to view and classify all files, including files on remote servers.
- File system commands enable you to copy files with complete path information to eliminate the need for system prompting.
- Cisco platforms support various Flash file system types.
- When copying various files into Flash memory, it is important to configure the switch to boot the proper file with boot parameters.

Section 3-5

NOTE   Both COS and IOS switches have a new set of file system commands that facilitate file management. Cisco refers to the file system as the   *IFS* or *IOS file system*. This file system provides an extremely powerful way to manage files within the switch devices and on remote systems. Because it is new, many people are unfamiliar with the commands. To provide backward compatibility, many aliases map to older commands for file management. See Table 3-3 at the end of this section for a listing of the older commands and the IFS equivalent.

Navigating File Systems

1 View the available file system devices:

COS	**show flash devices**
IOS	(privileged) **show file systems**

This command gives a listing of the file systems available on the device. The COS command lists the writeable file devices. This IOS command lists the total size and the amount of free space on the file system in bytes, the type of file system, the flags for the file system, and the alias name used to access the file system. For IOS devices, file system types include Flash, *nonvolatile random-access memory* (NVRAM), and network (and some others, such as ROM file systems, that contain microcode). Table 3-1 lists some of the available file systems. Note that not all file systems are available on all platforms.

Table 3-1   *Cisco File Systems*

Prefix	File System
system:	Contains the system memory, including the running configuration.
nvram:	Nonvolatile random-access memory. This contains the startup configuration.
flash:	Flash memory. Typically the location of the IOS. This is the default or starting file system for file system navigation. The prefix *flash:* is available on all platforms. For platforms that do not have a device named *flash:*, the prefix *flash:* is aliased to slot0:. Therefore, you can use the prefix *flash:* to refer to the main Flash memory storage area on all platforms.
bootflash:	Boot flash memory. Typical location for Rxboot IOS image.
supbootflash:	The boot flash for the Supervisor *network management processor* (NMP). This is from where the Catalyst OS is run.
slot0:	First PCMCIA Flash memory card.
tftp:	Trivial File Transfer Protocol network server.
ftp:	File Transfer Protocol network server.
slave-nvram:	NVRAM on a redundant Supervisor module running native IOS.
slave-supbootflash:	The boot flash for the Supervisor NMP on a redundant Supervisor module.
slave-bootflash:	Internal Flash memory on a redundant MSFC running native IOS.
slave-slot0:	First PCMCIA card on a redundant Supervisor module.
null:	Null destination for copies. You can copy a remote file to null to determine its size.
rcp:	*Remote Copy Protocol* (RCP) network server.

2 Change the default file system directory:

COS	**cd** [*filesystem:*]
IOS	(privileged) **cd** [*filesystem:*]

Use this command to move to a specific file system or directory within that file system. By moving to a specific file location, you can use file system commands without having to specify the *file system:* option. If you do a **dir** command without specifying the *file system:*, for example, it uses the directory that has been specified by the default directory or the **cd** command. The default file system directory is Flash.

3 List the current directory:

COS	**pwd**
IOS	(privileged) **pwd**

This command prints or displays the name of the working directory to the screen. This command enables you to determine the default file system directory. Use this command to verify that you have moved into the appropriate directory when using **cd** command.

4 Display information about the files:

COS	**dir** [[*m/*]*device:*][*filename*] [**all**	**deleted**	**long**]
IOS	(privileged) **dir** [**/all**] [*filesystem:*][*path/filename*]

This command displays a directory of the default directory structure as specified by the **cd** command. The option **/all** for IOS or **all** for COS switches enables you to see all files, including those that have been deleted but not permanently removed from a file system. For COS the option **deleted** shows you only the files that have been deleted but not permanently removed. The option **long** shows filenames in long-name format. For COS machines, you can use the **m** before the device name to specify a module number. You can also specify a file system by using the *filesystem:* or *device:* option. If you want to view a single file, provide the path and filename also. You can use an asterisk (*) as a wildcard to display a group of files with common starting characters. You can use this command to get a list of files off of any available local file system:

COS	**show** *filesystem:*
IOS	(privileged) **show** *filesystem:*

This command displays the contents of a file system. It is similar to the **dir** command, but the output is formatted differently. This command does not enable you to display individual files or remote file systems.

5 View the information about a local or remote file:

COS	N/A
IOS	(privileged) **show file information** *filesystem:path*

This command enables you to view information about a file on a remote or local file system. The output displays the image type and size.

6 View the contents of a local or remote file:

COS	**show file** [*device:*] *filename* [**dump**]
IOS	(privileged) **more** [**/ascii**	**/binary**	**/ebcdic**] *filesystem:path*

Use this command to view the contents of a remote or local file. The options **ascii**, **binary**, and **ebcdic** enable you to specify the type of format in which you want to have the file presented. For COS the default is ASCII format. If you specify **dump**, it shows the file in binary format. The *filesystem:path* options enable you to specify a particular file on a valid file system—for example, **more /ascii flash:myconfig.txt** displays the file myconfig.txt in ASCII format located in the current Flash device.

Deleting Files from Flash

Cisco switch platforms have three different classifications of file systems. Each of these file systems deals differently with deleting and permanently removing files from the Flash file system. Table 3-2 shows the three types of file systems and the platforms that use these file systems.

Table 3-2 *Switch File System Types*

File System Type	Platforms
Class A	Catalyst 5000, 6000, 4000, 2948G, 4908G
Class B	Catalyst 2948G-L3, 4908G-L3
Class C	Catalyst 2900/3500XL, 3550, 2950

1 Delete a file from Flash memory:

COS	**delete** [*filesystem:*]*filename*
IOS	(privileged) **delete** [*filesystem:*]*filename*

This command deletes a file from Flash on any of the three classifications of file systems. For Class A and B file systems, the file is marked as deleted and shows up only if the command **dir /all** is used. You can restore files that are marked as deleted by using the **undelete** command. For Class C file systems, the **delete** command permanently removes the file from the system. The file system must be a Flash file system.

2 Restore a deleted file:

COS	**undelete** *index* [*filesystem:*]
IOS	(privileged) **undelete** *index* [*filesystem:*]

For a Class A file system, if a file has been deleted, you can restore the file by using the **undelete** command. You must provide the *index* number of the file listed by using the **dir /all** command. If the file is not located in your working directory, determined by the **pwd** command, you can specify the *filesystem:* option.

3   Permanently remove a file from Class A Flash memory:

COS	`squeeze` *filesystem:*
IOS	(privileged) `squeeze` *filesystem*

If you want to permanently remove a file that has been deleted from a Class A file system, you must **squeeze** the file system. This command permanently removes any file on the file system that has been marked as deleted.

4   Remove a file from Class B Flash memory or NVRAM:

COS	N/A
IOS	(privileged) `delete` [`flash:`/*filename* | `bootflash:`/*filename* | `nvram:`/*filename*]

To remove a file on a Class B Flash device, use the **delete** command. When you delete a file from a Class B Flash device, it remains in Flash memory and retains the memory space used. To permanently remove a file from a Class B file system, you must reformat the file system. Because this removes all files, you should save OS files and copy them back to memory after you reformat the device:

COS	`format` *filesystem:*
IOS	(privileged) `format` *filesystem:*

For Class A and Class C devices, you can also remove all the files and reformat the device by using the **format** command.

Moving System Files

Like on most computer systems, it is important to move the files from one location to another. To move system files, you can use the **copy** command. This command, along with path parameters, moves the system files. The results of some file system moves are unique—when a file is copied into the system:running-configuration file, for example, the result is a file merge. This section discusses some common **copy** commands and the results. On the whole, however, you can move files into file systems that enable you to write to the system. The command structure for **copy** commands is **copy** [**/erase**] *source-location destination-location*. The source location and destination location can be any writeable file system and path. By using the **/erase** option, you can always erase the destination of a writeable file system before source the file is copied. The source location can be any file system that contains files that need to be moved. With all of these commands, you can specify the address and filename or you can leave them out and the system will prompt you for information.

1 Save the active configuration file to be used for startup:

COS	Not required (this is automatic)
IOS	(privileged) **copy system:running-config nvram:startup-config**

This command copies the system's current active configuration into the startup configuration file. When anything is copied into the location nvram:startup-configuration, it is a complete overwrite—that is, any information that was in that file is completely lost and overwritten with the source file. The startup configuration file is loaded at startup. For COS, this is automatic and not required.

2 Copy a file into active configuration:

COS	**copy** [[*m/*]*device:*][*filename*] **config**
IOS	(privileged) **copy** *source* **system:running-config**

This command copies a file into the current running configuration. The source/device can be any location that contains a text file that has configuration parameters framed in the appropriate syntax. When files are copied into running configuration, they are merged with the current configuration. That is, if a configuration parameter (such as an address) exists in both places—running configuration and the source configuration—the running configuration will be changed by the parameter that is being copied from the source location. If the configuration parameter exists only in the source location, it is added to the running configuration. In the case that a parameter exists in running configuration, but is not modified in the source configuration, there is no change to the running configuration. The source location can be a file in any location, including a file on a TFTP server, FTP server, or a text file that has been written to Flash memory.

3 Save a file to a TFTP server:

COS	**copy** [[*m/*]*device:*][*filename*] **tftp**
IOS	(privileged) **copy** *source* **tftp://**address/filename

This command enables you to save any readable file from an IFS source location to a TFTP server specified in the address of the destination parameter. If you do not supply a filename and address, the system prompts for this information.

4 Save a file to Flash memory:

COS	**copy** [[*m/*]*device:*][*filename*] *flash-filesystem:*//*path*/*filename*
IOS	(privileged) **copy** *source* ***flash-filesystem:***//*path*/*filename*

You can copy a file into any Flash file system of a router with the **copy** commands. Some writeable file systems, such as a Class A file system, enable you to create and write to directories and files. This **copy** command enables you to move files into a Flash file system. Files that are moved into Flash are usually IOS files; however, you can use Flash to store any file as long as you have room to place the file. If fact, after a file has been placed into Flash memory, the router can be configured as a TFTP server and can then serve that file to other devices. Refer to the related commands portion of section "1-2: Cisco Internetwork Operating System (IOS) Software" for more information about configuring your router to act as a TFTP server.

File System Boot Parameters

1 Specify an OS image to boot from in a Flash file system:

COS	**set boot system flash** *device:*[*filename*] [**prepend**] [**mod**]
IOS	(global) **boot system flash** *flash-filesystem:*/*directory*/*filename*

By default, switches boot the first valid image in the default Flash location. If you have more than one file in Flash memory and you do not want to boot the first file, you must specify which file is to be used as the IOS image. For COS devices, you can manipulate the order with the **prepend** option in the command. The **boot system flash** command specifies which file to use.

2 Change the configuration file environmental parameter for Class A file systems:

COS	**set boot auto-config** *device:directory/filename*
IOS	(global) **boot config** *device:directory/filename*

For a Class A file system, you can copy configuration files to the Flash file system. You can also specify that some switches are to load a configuration from Flash instead of the startup configuration file located in NVRAM. To do this, you must first copy the active configuration into the Flash file system, and then in global configuration use the **boot config** parameter followed by the file system name and file location and name. After you save this configuration, the router attempts to load the configuration from the specified location.

Section 3-5

Alias Commands

Because the new file system functionality is the third generation of file management system for Cisco IOS and COS, alias commands have been established to provide backward compatibility for commands that existed in previous operating systems. This backward compatibility enables you to use file management commands that you might have learned in previous releases without having to relearn the new command structure. Table 3-3 show the alias commands and the IFS equivalent command and COS command.

Table 3-3   *File Management Alias Commands*

Cisco IOS Software Release 10.2 and Earlier Command	Cisco IOS Software Release 10.3 to 11.3 Command	Cisco IOS Software Release 12.0 and Later (IFS) Command	COS Commands
write terminal	show running-config	show system:running-config or more system:running-config	show config -or- write terminal
show config	show startup-config	show system:startup-config or more system:startup-config	show config or write terminal
write memory	copy running-config startup-config	copy system:running-config nvram:startup-config	No equivalent. Automatically saves all configuration changes.
write erase	erase startup-config	erase nvram:	clear config all
write network	copy running-config tftp:	copy system:running-config tftp://*address/filename*	Write network or copy config tftp
config memory	copy startup-config running-config	copy nvram:startup-config system:running-config	No equivalent. There is no difference between startup and running.
config network	copy tftp running-config	copy tftp://*address/filename* system:running-config	config network or copy tftp config
config overwrite	copy tftp startup-config	Copy tftp://*address/filename* nvram:startup-config	No equivalent.

Cisco's official stance on older commands is that they might not be supported in future releases, so it is conceivable that commands that existed before Release 12.0 might not be supported in future releases of Cisco IOS.

3-6: Redundant Supervisors

- When identical Supervisor hardware is placed in slots 1 and 2 of Catalyst 5500 and 6000 series switches, one Supervisor is active and the other is in standby mode.

- In the event of a failure, the redundant Supervisor takes over switch functionality.

- Configuration files and operating system files are synchronized between switches.

- Layer 2 tables are synchronized between the supervisors for quick transitions between modules.

- Parameters such as the Layer 2 synchronization and operating system synchronization can be managed for the modules.

- Layer 3 MSFC cards operate independently of the COS and must be managed manually or configured for redundancy in the MSFC IOS. See section "8-4: MSFC Redundancy with Single Router Mode" and "8-5: MSFC Redundancy with Configuration Synchronization" for more information.

- Catalyst 6000 series switches provide both Layer 2 and Layer 3 synchronization within the same operating system and configuration.

By placing identical Supervisor hardware and software in slots 1 and 2 of a Catalyst 5500 or Catalyst 6000 series switch, you have activated system redundancy. No parameters enable you to activate this feature. The first Supervisor to come online is active, and the second one is in standby mode. The standby Supervisor has an orange system light, and the console port is not active. However, the interfaces on the module are active.

You can remove or insert Supervisor cards while the switch is powered on. If a second Supervisor is added or a standby Supervisor is replaced, the card being inserted into the switch goes through the power-on diagnostics, but does not test the backplane (because this would interrupt traffic flow) and then goes into standby mode. The standby Supervisor becomes active if there is a failure in the primary Supervisor or if you force a change by resetting the primary Supervisor.

Section 3-6

Forcing a Change to the Standby Supervisor

1 Reset the active Supervisor engine:

COS	`reset` *mod#*
	-OR-
	`switch supervisor`
IOS	(privileged)`reload`

For the COS device, you can reset the module that is active and thereby force the standby to take over. In the **reset** *mod#* command, the *mod#* would be that of the active module. Use the command **show module** to determine which Supervisor is active. The command **switch supervisor** automatically chooses to reset the active Supervisor and forces a switch to the secondary.

As configuration changes are made to the Supervisor in the active Supervisor module, these changes are also propagated to NVRAM of the standby Supervisor. If there is a change or a difference in the Supervisor images, the active Supervisor also forces a synchronization of images to ensure compatibility of features. Several items influence the synchronization of COS images between the switches, including the following:

- Changing the boot parameters for the switch
- Overwriting the runtime COS image
- Deleting the runtime COS image
- Different time stamps on the runtime COS images stored in *bootflash: or slot0:*

Catalyst 6000 native IOS switches do not automatically synchronize images. Therefore, to have redundancy operational, you must have the same images on both the active and redundant Supervisor modules. To manually synchronize the images, make sure you have IOS on both Supervisor modules and then copy the image from the active Supervisor to the "slave" Supervisor.

Synchronizing IOS Images

1 *(Required)* Manually synchronize the images for IOS Supervisor modules:

COS	Automatic; not required
IOS	(privileged) # **copy** *source_device:source_filename destination_device:target_filename*

The destination device can be one of the following:

- **slaveslot0:** — The PCMCIA card on the redundant Supervisor
- **slave-supbootflash:** — The Supervisor boot flash on the redundant Supervisor
- **slave-bootflash**: — The MSFC boot flash on the redundant Supervisor.

As each Supervisor boots, it checks the configuration register to determine how the device is to boot and where to look for the image. Typically the image is specified in a Flash location using boot variable parameters. In the Catalyst operating systems, the configuration registers are not synchronized automatically to enable you to control booting each individually, but the boot variables are synchronized. For Cisco IOS devices, the configuration registers are synchronized by default, but the boot variables are not automatically synchronized. The boot variables specify the operating system location, the bootloader file, and configuration files to be used on boot.

It is important that both modules have configuration parameters that allow them to automatically boot the same image before redundancy actually takes place. By default the configuration registers of both operating systems use boot system commands to load the OS. Therefore, they are correctly configured. When you specify a boot location of a COS image, this initiates an OS synchronization. If the configuration register is altered, you must manually configure the register on each module (1 and 2) of a COS device so that it automatically loads the image. The IOS devices synchronize the configuration register by default. If you change the boot parameters, however, saving the configuration on the active Supervisor will not change to boot variables on the standby Supervisor.

Synchronizing Boot Parameters

1 *(Required)* Synchronize the configuration register:

COS	(privileged) **set boot config-register boot {rommon	bootflash	system}** [*module*]
IOS	Automatic; not required

When setting the configuration register on the COS device, specify which Supervisor you're setting with the *module* option. During startup, the Supervisor boots from one of: **rommon** (ROM-monitor; no system image is run), **bootflash** (the first image file stored in the onboard Flash memory), or **system** (the system image given by the BOOT environment variable). Try to avoid using the **bootflash** keyword, as the first image stored in flash will not always be the desired image.

2 *(Required)* Synchronize the location of the boot image:

COS	Automatic; not required
IOS	(global) **redundancy** (redundancy) **main-cpu** (redundancy-maincpu) **auto-sync bootvar** (redundancy-maincpu) **end** (privileged) **copy running-config startup-config**

After you have redundant Supervisors operational, you can check the status with the command **show module** for COS switches or **show module all** for IOS switches to verify that one Supervisor is active and the other in standby mode.

When you have two Supervisors installed in the switch, your switch is in redundancy mode for COS switches and enhanced systems high availability mode for IOS switches. This means that the configurations are synchronized between the switches and that if one module fails, the standby will take over. When the redundant module takes over for a COS switch, however, it must initialize the ports and run the *Spanning Tree Protocol* (STP) to determine the port states. This failover takes about 30 to 40 seconds. To provide a quicker failover for the Supervisors, you need to enable high availability on your COS switch. In this mode, the switches are also synchronizing forwarding information between the modules. Including STP, some features are incompatible with high parameters so that the failover will be more efficient. In the case of the IOS switch, the Layer 2 and Layer 3 processors are running the same software, and the forwarding tables and configurations are automatically synchronized.

With the COS devices, however, you must consider a few things before enabling high availability. Remember that some features are incompatible with high availability, including the following:

- Dynamic VLANs
- *GARP VLAN Registration Protocol* (GVRP)
- Port security
- Protocol filtering

If you want to run any of these features, you cannot enable high availability. If you do enable high availability, you will not be able to configure these features. Keeping high availability disabled does not stop the secondary Supervisor from becoming active; it only prevents the synchronization of forwarding tables and therefore causes the secondary Supervisor to have to learn all the forwarding information in order after it becomes active.

Enabling High Availability

1 *(Optional)* Enable high availability:

COS	(privileged) `set system highavailability {enable	disable}`
IOS	N/A

The default configuration is that high availability is disabled. To enable high availability, use the keyword **enable**. If you want to disable the feature, use the keyword **disable**.

Enabling High-Availability Versioning

It is sometimes desirable to upgrade the active Supervisor image, but not that of the standby image in the event that you need to back out of an upgrade. Another feature of high availability on COS machines is something called *versioning*. Versioning enables you to have separate runtime images between Supervisor images within supported tolerances. For example, versions 6.1(3) and 6.1(4) are fully compatible images. See the Release Notes on your image to find out more about versioning. The active Supervisor engine exchanges image version information with the standby Supervisor engine and determines whether the images are compatible for enabling high availability. To enable high-availability versioning, perform the configuration that follows.

1 *(Required)* Enable high availability:

COS	(privileged) **set system highavailability enable**
IOS	N/A

This is a default and has to be enabled only if high availability was previously disabled.

2 *(Required)* Enable high-availability versioning:

COS	(privileged) **set system highavailability versioning enable**
IOS	N/A

3-7: Cisco Discovery Protocol

- CDP is used to identify directly connected Cisco devices.
- CDP is enabled on all Cisco devices.
- CDP identifies neighbor address, operating system, VLAN, *VLAN Trunking Protocol* (VTP) domain, and duplex information between Cisco switches.
- CDP can be disabled globally or on a per-port (interface) basis.

Configuration of CDP

1 *(Default)* Enable CDP globally:

COS	**set cdp enable**
IOS	(global) **cdp run**

CDP is enabled by default. The default commands are shown in Step 1. To disable CDP for the entire device, use the command **set cdp disable** for COS devices or **no cdp run** for IOS devices.

2 *(Optional)* Set the update time for CDP advertisements:

COS	**set cdp interval** *interval*
IOS	(global) **cdp timer** *interval*

Section 3-7

CDP sends advertisements ever 60 seconds by default. Use these commands to change the update interval in seconds. Keep in mind that the update interval must be less than the holdtime.

3 *(Optional)* Specify the holdtime of CDP information:

COS	set cdp holdtime *interval*
IOS	(global) cdp holdtime *interval*

If CDP does not hear an update for the specified amount of time in the holdtime interval in seconds, that information is purged from the CDP table. Use these commands to change the holdtime. The holdtime should be greater than the advertisement (usually three times the value of the update timer).

4 *(Default)* Set the CDP version send parameters for the switch:

COS	set cdp version {v1 | v2}
IOS	(global) cdp {advertise-v2 | advertise-v1}

CDP has two versions (v1 and v2). These versions are compatible, but version 2 has enhanced *type-length-values* (TLVs) that support VTP domain name, native VLAN, and duplex information. This information is very important in the operation of switch ports. If you receive CDP mismatch messages, the errors are not fatal, but they can indicate a problem.

5 *(Optional)* Disable CDP on an interface or port:

COS	set cdp disable *mod/port*
IOS	(interface)no cdp enable

CDP is enabled by default on every port. For ports that are not connected to Cisco devices, it makes no sense to have CDP running. Use the commands in Step 2 to disable CDP on a port-by-port basis. To reenable CDP, use the command **set cdp enable** *mod/port* for COS devices and **cdp enable** for IOS switches.

The command **show cdp** displays global information about CDP configuration on both operating systems. Use the commands **show cdp neighbors** for both operating systems to view neighbor information. The command **show cdp interface** *type mod/port* or **show cdp port** *mod/port* displays port-specific information about CDP.

Feature Example

This example shows a switch with the CDP timers altered so that the holdtime is 480 seconds and the update time is 120 seconds. It also shows CDP disabled for port 3/1 through 3/48 on the COS switch and Fast Ethernet ports 1 to 12 on an IOS switch.

An example of the COS configuration follows:

```
Console (enable)> set cdp interval 120
Console (enable)> set cdp holdtime 480
Console (enable)> set cdp disable 3/1-48
```

An example of the Supervisor IOS configuration follows:

```
Switch(config)# cdp timer 120
Switch(config)# cdp holdtime 480
Switch(config)# interface fastethernet 0/1
Switch(config)# no cdp enable
Switch(config)# interface fastethernet 0/2
Switch(config)# no cdp enable
Switch(config)# interface fastethernet 0/3
Switch(config)# no cdp enable
Switch(config)# interface fastethernet 0/4
Switch(config)# no cdp enable
Switch(config)# interface fastethernet 0/5
Switch(config)# no cdp enable
Switch(config)# interface fastethernet 0/6
Switch(config)# no cdp enable
Switch(config)#end
Switch#copy running-config startup-config
```

3-8: Time and Calendar

- System time is maintained by the software. When a switch is initialized, the system time is set from a hardware time clock (system calendar) in the switch.

- An accurate system clock is important to maintain, especially when you need to compare the output of logging and debugging features. A switch timestamps these messages, giving you a frame of reference.

- System time is maintained as *coordinated universal time* (UTC, also known as *Greenwich mean time*,GMT). The format of time as it is displayed can be configured with operating system commands.

- System time can be set manually or by *Network Time Protocol* (NTP). In addition, the hardware time clock in a switch can be updated by NTP if desired.

- NTP uses a concept of *stratum* to determine how close an NTP speaker is to an authoritative time source (an atomic or radio clock). Stratum 1 means that an NTP server is directly connected to an authoritative time source. NTP also compares the times reported from all configured NTP peers and will not listen to a peer that has a significantly different time.

- NTP associations with other NTP peers can be protected through an encrypted authentication.

NTP version 3 is based on RFC 1305 and uses UDP port 123. You can find information about public NTP servers and other NTP subjects at www.eecis.udel.edu/~ntp/.

NOTE	Catalyst 4000 and 6000 series switches running native IOS and 2948G-L3 and 4908G-L3 switches can also be configured as NTP authoritative time sources. For configuration information on these devices, visit the Cisco web site at www.cisco.com/univercd/ cc/td/doc/product/software/ios122/122cgcr/ffun_c/fcfprt3/fcf012.htm#41044 or refer to *Cisco Field Manual: Router Configuration* by David Hucaby and Steve McQuerry, Cisco Press, ISBN 1-58705-024-2.

Configuration

You can set the system time using in two different ways:

- Manually
- Using the NTP

For manual configuration, you will be setting the time and date on the router along with the time zone and whether to observe summer hours. With manual configuration, the router has no way to preserve the time settings and cannot ensure that time remains accurate. NTP is defined by RFC 1305 and provides a mechanism for the devices in the network to get their time from an NTP server. With NTP, all the devices would be synchronized and will keep accurate time.

Setting the System Time Manually

1 Set the time zone:

COS	**set timezone** [*zone_name*] [*hours* [*minutes*]]
IOS	(global) **clock timezone** zone *hrs-offset min-offset*

The time zone is set to the abbreviated name *zone* (that is, EST, PST, CET). This name is only used for display purposes and can be any common zone name. The actual displayed time is defined by an offset in hours (*hrs-offset*) and minutes (*min-offset*) from UTC.

2 *(Optional)* Configure *daylight savings time* (DST):

COS	**set summertime** {**enable** | **disable**} [*zone*]
	set summertime recurring [*week day month hh:mm week day month hh:mm*} [*offset*]]
	set summertime date *month date year hh:mm month date year hh:mm* [*offset*]
IOS	(global) **clock summer-time** *zone* **recurring** [*week day month hh:mm week day month hh:mm* [*offset*]]
	(global) **clock summer-time** *zone* **date** [*date month* | *month date*] *year hh:mm* [*date month* | *month date*] *year hh:mm* [*offset*]

For COS, you can enable and disable summertime manually with the command **set summertime** {**enable** I **disable**}. This causes the switch to set the time ahead 60 minutes (the U.S. standard for DST).

If DST begins and ends on a certain day and week of a month, use the command with the **recurring** keyword. To start and stop DST, you can give the *week* number (including the words "first" and "last"), the name of the *day*, the name of the *month*, and time *hh:mm* in 24-hour format. If no arguments are given, the U.S. standard of beginning at 2:00 a.m. on the first Sunday in April, and ending at 2:00 a.m. on the last Sunday in October is used. The *offset* value can be given to set the number of minutes that are added during DST (default 60 minutes).

Otherwise, you can use the **date** keyword to specify the exact date and time that DST begins and ends in a given year.

3 *(Optional)* Set the system clock (IOS clock):

COS	**set time** [*day*] [*mm/dd/yy*] [*hh:mm:ss*]
IOS	(exec) **clock set** *hh:mm:ss* [*day month* | *month day*] *year*

The clock is set when this command is executed. The time is given in 24-hour format; *day* is the day number, *month* is the name of the month, and *year* is the full four-digit year for IOS switches; and the date is in the international format for COS switches.

4 *(Optional)* Set the system calendar (hardware clock):

COS	N/A
IOS	(exec) **calendar set** *hh:mm:ss* [*day month* | *month day*] *year*

The hardware clock is set to the given time (24-hour format) and date. The *month* is the name of the month, *day* is the day number, and *year* is the full four-digit year. As an alternative, you can set the system calendar from the system clock using the (EXEC) **clock update-calendar** command.

Section 3-8

Setting the System Time Through NTP

1 Define one or more NTP peer associations:

COS	`set ntp server` *ip-addr* [`key` *public-keynum*] `set ntp client enable`
IOS	(global) `ntp peer` *ip-address* [`version` *number*] [`key` *keyid*] [`source` *interface*] [`prefer`]

The NTP peer is identified at *ip-address*. The NTP version can be given with the
version keyword (1 to 3, default is version 3). If NTP authentication is used, the **key**
keyword identifies the authentication key to use (see Step 3b in this section). If
desired, you can take the source address used in NTP packets from an interface by
using the **source** keyword. Otherwise, the router uses the source address from the
outbound interface. The **preferred** keyword forces the local router to provide time
synchronization, if contention exists between peers.

2 *(Optional)* Configure NTP broadcast service:

COS	`set ntp broadcastclient enable` `set ntp broadcastdelay` *microseconds*
IOS	(global) `ntp broadcast client` (global) `ntp broadcastdelay` *microseconds*

By default, NTP sends and receives unicast packets with peers. Broadcasts can be
used instead, if several NTP peers are located on a common network. The **ntp
broadcast** command enables sending broadcast packets. The **ntp broadcast client**
command enables the reception of broadcast packets. The **ntp broadcastdelay**
command sets the round-trip delay for receiving client broadcasts (1 to 999,999
microseconds, default is 3000 microseconds).

3 *(Optional)* Restrict access to NTP using authentication.

a. Enable NTP authentication:

COS	`set ntp client enable`
IOS	(global) `ntp authenticate`

b. Define an authentication key:

COS	`set ntp key` *public-key* [`trusted`	`untrusted`] `md5` *secret-key*
IOS	(global) `ntp authentication-key` *key-number* `md5` *value*

An MD5 authentication key numbered *key-number* is created. The key is given a text-string *value* of up to eight clear-text characters. After the configuration has been written to NVRAM, the key value displays in its encrypted form.

c. Apply one or more key numbers to NTP:

COS	**set ntp server** *ip-addr* [**key** *public-key*]
IOS	(global) **ntp trusted-key** *key-number*

Remote NTP peers must authenticate themselves using the authentication key numbered *key-number*. You can use this command multiple times to apply all desired keys to NTP.

Example

This example shows a switch that is configured for the U.S. eastern time zone and daylight savings time. The time is manually set.

An example of the COS configuration follows:

```
Console (enable)> set timezone EST -5
Console (enable)> set summertime recurring 1 Sunday april 2:00 last Sunday
  October 2:00
Console (enable)> set time Saturday 08/11/90 15:30:00
```

An example of the Supervisor IOS configuration follows:

```
Switch(config)# clock timezone EST -5
Switch(config)# clock summer-time EST recurring 1 sunday april 2:00
  last sunday october 2:00
Switch(config)#end
Switch# clock set 15:30:00 August 11 1990
Switch#copy running-config startup-config
```

In this configuration, NTP is enabled and NTP is configured for authentication. One key, source1key, authenticates a peer at 172.17.76.247, while another key, source2key, authenticates a peer at 172.31.31.1.

An example of the COS configuration follows:

```
Console (enable)> set ntp client enable
Console (enable)> set ntp key 1 trusted md5 sourcekey1
Console (enable)> set ntp key 2 trusted md5 sourcekey2
Console (enable)> set ntp server 172.17.76.247 key 1
Console (enable)> set ntp server 172.31.31.1 key 2
```

An example of the Supervisor IOS configuration follows:

```
Switch(config)# ntp authenticate
Switch(config)# ntp authentication-key 1 md5 sourceA
Switch(config)# ntp authentication-key 2 md5 sourceB
Switch(config)# ntp trusted-key 1
Switch(config)# ntp trusted-key 2
Switch(config)# ntp peer 172.17.76.247 key 1
Switch(config)# ntp peer 172.31.31.1 key 2
```

Section 3-8

Further Reading

Refer to the following recommended sources for further information about the topics covered in this chapter.

CCNP Switching Exam Certification Guide by Tim Boyles and David Hucaby, Cisco Press, ISBN 1-58720-000-7

Cisco Field Manual: Router Configuration by David Hucaby and Steve McQuerry, Cisco Press, ISBN 1-58705-024-2

Cisco Enterprise Management Solutions, Volume 1, by Michael Wynston, Cisco Press, ISBN 1-58705-006-4

CHAPTER **4**

Layer 2 Interface Configuration

See the following sections to configure and use these features:

- **4-1: Switching Table**—Explains how to view and add entries to the switching table of *Media Access Control* (MAC) addresses.
- **4-2: Port Selection**—Discusses the various ways you can select switch ports to be configured.
- **4-3: Ethernet**—Presents the steps needed to configure Ethernet, Fast Ethernet, Gigabit Ethernet, and 10 Gigabit Ethernet switch ports.
- **4-4: EtherChannel**—Covers the configuration steps necessary to bundle several switch ports into a single logical link.
- **4-5: Token Ring**—Discusses Token Ring switch ports and how to configure them.
- **4-6: ATM LANE**—Covers *LAN emulation* (LANE) configuration and how switches bridge Ethernet segments over an ATM network.

4-1: Switching Table

- The switching table contains MAC addresses and the switch ports on which they were learned or statically configured.
- Packets or frames are forwarded by looking up the destination MAC address in the switching table. The frame is sent out the corresponding switch port.
- The switching table entries are normally dynamically learned as packets flow. Entries can also be statically defined.

Configuration

1 *(Optional)* Assign a static switching table entry:

COS	**set cam** {**dynamic** | **static** | **permanent**} {*mac-addr* | *route-descr*} *mod/port* [*vlan-id*]
IOS	(global) **mac-address-table** {**dynamic** | **static** | **secure**} *mac-addr* {**vlan** *vlan-id*} {**interface** *int1* [*int2 ... int15*] [**protocol** {**ip** | **ipx** | **assigned**}]

An entry for the destination MAC address *mac-addr* (use dashed format on COS, dotted-triplet format on IOS switches) is made to point to one or more switch ports (*mod/port* on COS, a list of interfaces for IOS). If the destination port is a trunk, you must also specify the destination VLAN number *vlan-id*.

Switching table entries can be **static** (not subject to aging), **dynamic** (entries are aged; not available on Catalyst 6000 IOS), **permanent** (entries are stored in NVRAM and preserved across switch reboots; not available on Catalyst 6000 IOS), or **secure** (MAC address entry can exist on only one port; not available on Catalyst 6000 IOS).

A Catalyst 6000 IOS switch also associates the MAC address with a protocol: **ip** (TCP/IP), **ipx**, or **assigned** (other protocols, such as DECnet or AppleTalk). If the **protocol** keyword is not used, an entry is made for each of the three protocol types.

2 *(Optional)* Set the switching table aging time:

COS	`set cam agingtime` *vlan-id seconds*
IOS	(global) `mac-address-table aging-time` *seconds* [`vlan` *vlan-id*]

For VLAN number *vlan-id* (COS: 1-1005 and 1025-4094; IOS: 2-1001), entries are aged out of the switching table after *seconds* (0, 10 to 1,000,000 seconds; default 300 seconds). A value of 0 disables the aging process. On an IOS switch, the VLAN number is optional. If not specified, the aging time is modified for all VLANs.

3 *(Optional)* Remove a switching table entry:

COS	`clear cam` *mac-addr* [*vlan-id*] -OR- `clear cam {dynamic	static	permanent}` [*vlan-id*]
IOS	(global) `no mac-address-table static` *mac-addr* {`vlan` *vlan-id*} [`interface` *int1* [*int2 ... int15*] [`protocol {ip	ipx	assigned}`]

You can remove an entry by referencing its MAC address *mac-addr* (use dashed format on COS, dotted-triplet format on IOS switches). If it is defined on more than one VLAN, the *vlan-id* must also be given. IOS switches allow the specific destination interfaces to be given, along with a specific protocol.

On a COS switch, you can clear all entries of a particular type: **dynamic**, **static**, or **permanent**.

4 *(Optional; Catalyst 2900/3500XL only)* Define a default destination port:

COS	N/A
IOS	(interface) `port network`

Switches that have a limited switching table size can't learn all the destination addresses in a large network. Therefore, you can identify one interface that serves as the "default" or "network" destination for a VLAN.

If a destination MAC address is not known in the switching table, the switch automatically forwards the packet on the network port instead of flooding it to all ports on the VLAN.

Displaying Information About the Switching Table

Table 4-1 lists some switch commands that you can use to display helpful information about the Layer 2 switching table contents.

Table 4-1   *Switch Commands to Display Layer 2 Switching Table Content Information*

Display Function	Switch OS	Command
Show dynamically learned addresses based on a port or VLAN number	COS	`show cam dynamic [{mod/port}	vlan]`
	IOS	`(exec) show mac-address-table dynamic [{address mac-addr}	detail	{interface interface interface-number}	{protocol protocol}	{Vlan vlan-id}]`
Show statically defined addresses based on a port or VLAN number	COS	`show cam {static	permanent	system} [{mod/port}	vlan]`
	IOS	`(exec) show mac-address-table static [address mac-addr	detail	interface interface interface-number	protocol protocol	Vlan vlan-id]`
Show the port or VLAN associated with a MAC address	COS	`show cam mac_addr [vlan]`
	IOS	`(exec) show mac-address-table address mac-addr [detail	{interface interface interface-number}	{protocol protocol}	{Vlan vlan-id}	all]`
Show the switching table aging time	COS	`show cam agingtime [vlan]`
	IOS	`(exec) show mac-address-table aging-time [Vlan vlan-id]`
Show the switching table address count and size	COS	`show cam count {dynamic	static	permanent	system} [vlan]`
	IOS	`(exec) show mac-address-table count [Vlan vlan-id] [slot slot-num]`

Switching Table Example

Suppose you need to locate the switch port where a specific PC is connected. The PC's MAC address is 00-b0-d0-f5-45-0e:

COS	`show cam 00-b0-d0-f5-45-0e`
IOS	`(exec) show mac-address-table address 00b0.d0f5.450e`

On a COS switch, the command output looks like this:

```
switch-cos (enable) show cam 00-b0-d0-f5-45-0e
* = Static Entry. + = Permanent Entry. # = System Entry. R = Router Entry.
X = Port Security Entry $ = Dot1x Security Entry

VLAN  Dest MAC/Route Des     [CoS]  Destination Ports or VCs / [Protocol Type]
----  ------------------     -----  -------------------------------------------
534    00-b0-d0-f5-45-0e            1/2 [ALL]
Total Matching CAM Entries Displayed  =1
```

An IOS switch can have this output:

```
switch-ios#show mac-address-table address 00d0.b7e5.4dc3
Non-static Address Table:
Destination Address  Address Type  VLAN  Destination Port
-------------------  ------------  ----  --------------------
00d0.b7e5.4dc3       Dynamic       534   FastEthernet0/2
```

Suppose you need to find a list of all the MAC addresses that have been learned on a specific switch port:

COS	**show cam dynamic 3/1**
IOS	(exec) **show mac-address-table dynamic interface gigabit 0/1**

The COS switch produces the following output:

```
cos-switch (enable) show cam dynamic 3/1
* = Static Entry. + = Permanent Entry. # = System Entry. R = Router Entry.
X = Port Security Entry $ = Dot1x Security Entry

VLAN  Dest MAC/Route Des     [CoS]  Destination Ports or VCs / [Protocol Type]
----  ------------------     -----  -------------------------------------------
999    00-00-0c-45-21-00            3/1 [ALL]
64     00-00-1b-04-2f-76            3/1 [ALL]
57     00-00-48-9a-3b-0b            3/1 [ALL]
Total Matching CAM Entries Displayed  =1
```

The IOS switch produces output like this:

```
switch-ios#show mac-address-table dynamic interface gig 0/1
Non-static Address Table:
Destination Address  Address Type  VLAN  Destination Port
-------------------  ------------  ----  --------------------
0000.0c45.2100       Dynamic       999   GigabitEthernet0/1
0000.1b04.2f76       Dynamic       64    GigabitEthernet0/1
0000.489a.3b0b       Dynamic       57    GigabitEthernet0/1
```

TIP

If you need to locate a specific MAC address within a large network and you have no idea where to start, begin looking on a core layer switch near the center of the network. Look for the MAC address in the switching table there. After finding it, move to the neighboring switch that is connected to the destination port.

Keep looking for the address in the switching tables, and then moving to the next neighboring switch. Repeat this process until you reach the edge of the network, where the device is physically connected.

4-2: Port Selection

- When configuring a Layer 2 port or interface, the port must first be selected or identified.
- COS switches allow a single port, a list of ports, a range of ports, or a combination of these in a single command.
- IOS switches allow only a single interface to be specified at a time.
- Catalyst 6000 IOS switches allow a range of interfaces to be defined. Any subsequent interface configuration commands are applied to the range of interfaces.

Section 4-2

Configuration

1 Select a port:

COS	`set ... mod/port ...`
IOS	`(global)` **`interface`** `type mod/num`

A COS switch port is identified by its module number *mod* and port number *port*. This nomenclature applies to any COS port command. An IOS switch port is called an interface, and is identified by its type (**fastethernet**, **gigabitethernet**, and so on), module number *mod*, and port number *num*.

TIP

Often, you will make the same configuration changes to several ports on a switch. On a COS switch, you can easily reference multiple ports in a single command (see the next step). However, IOS switches only allow interfaces to be configured one at a time. This makes changing the access VLAN or port speed on all 48 ports of a Catalyst 3548XL switch very tedious.

Instead of typing in 48 individual port configurations, consider using a text editor on a PC to create a configuration template. You can copy and paste commands and use global change or replace functions to change large numbers of parameters. Then you can copy and paste the file into a terminal emulator or upload the file into the switch through TFTP.

Another alternative is to use the web interface into a cluster of switches. Individual port configuration changes can be quickly made using the graphical tools.

2 Select a range of ports:

COS	`set ... mod/port ...`
IOS	`(global)` **`interface range`** `port-range`
	-OR-
	`(global)` **`define interface-range`** `macro-name port-range`
	`(global)` **`interface range macro`** `macro-name`

COS switches allow multiple ports to be specified by separating them with commas (no spaces). A range of port numbers on the same module can be given by separating them with a dash. For example, module 4 port 1 and module 5 port 1 would be listed as **4/1,5/1**; whereas ports 1 through 4 on modules 4 and 5, along with module 6, port 3 would be specified as **4/1-4,5/1-4,6/3**. You can use a list or range of ports wherever a module and port number are needed in any COS command.

The Catalyst 6000 IOS switches allow lists or ranges of interfaces to be given once, so that subsequent commands are applied to each of the interfaces. A *port-range* is defined as the interface type (**ethernet**, **fastethernet**, **gigabitethernet**, **tengigabitethernet**, or **vlan**) followed by the module number, a slash (/), and the starting port number. The end of the range is given by a space, a hyphen, another space, and the ending port number. If additional ranges are given, the ranges must be separated by a comma.

The basic range format is *type slot/first-port - last-port* [*,type slot/first-port - last-port* ...], where up to five different ranges can be listed. Following the **interface range** command, you are placed into interface configuration mode.

If you need to make several configuration changes to a range of interfaces, you can define a macro that contains a list of interface ranges. Use the **define interface-range** command, with a *macro-name* (arbitrary text name) and a *port-range* (list of interface ranges as defined earlier). This macro can be saved in the switch configuration so that it can be referenced in the future. To invoke the interface range macro, use the **interface range macro** command, along with the *macro-name*.

Port Selection Example

Module 1 ports 1 and 2, along with module 6 ports 1 through 4, are to have their port speed set to autonegotiate mode. (Any port configuration function could be used; port speed is shown here only as a demonstration of port selection.) The COS switch allows all the ports to be configured in a single command. The IOS switch (Catalyst 2900/3500XL) must have each interface configured individually. Finally, the Catalyst 6000 IOS switch allows the ports to be identified as two ranges and their speeds to be set with a single interface configuration command:

COS	`set port speed 1/1-2,6/1-4 auto`
IOS	`(global) `**`interface gig 1/1`**
	`(interface) `**`speed auto`**
	`(global) `**`interface gig 1/2`**
	`(interface) `**`speed auto`**
	`(global) `**`interface gig 6/1`**
	`(interface) `**`speed auto`**

IOS (*Cont.*)	(global) `interface gig 6/2`
	(interface) `speed auto`
	(global) `interface gig 6/3`
	(interface) `speed auto`
	(global) `interface gig 6/4`
	(interface) `speed auto`
Catalyst 6000 IOS	(global) `interface range gigabitethernet 1/1 - 2, gigabitethernet 6/1 - 4`
	(interface) `speed auto`
	-OR-
	(global) `define interface-range AnnexPorts gigabitethernet 1/1 - 2, gigabitethernet 6/1 - 4`
	(global) `interface range macro AnnexPorts`
	(interface) `speed auto`

4-3: Ethernet

- Autonegotiation of link speed and duplex mode for 10/100/1000BASE-T is possible through the functions standardized in IEEE 802.3u and 802.3ab. The two endpoints of a connection exchange capability information and choose the highest common speed and duplex supported by both.

- Ethernet ports are referenced by module and port numbers (*mod/port*) on COS switches and by interface type and number (**interface** and one of **ethernet**, **fastethernet**, **gigabitethernet**, or **tengigabitethernet**) on IOS switches.

- If certain problems are detected on a port, the switch automatically moves that port into the *errDisable* or "error disabled" state. This minimizes the effect that the problem port could have on the rest of the network.

- Ports in errDisable can be automatically reenabled or recovered after a timeout period, or they can be manually recovered. In either case, determine and correct the problem condition before attempting to recover errDisable ports.

Configuration

1 *(Optional)* Assign a descriptive name to the port:

COS	`set port name` *mod/port* [*port-name*]
IOS	(interface) `description` *port-name*

The description *port-name* (text string) is assigned to the port for human use. Usually the description includes a reference to the location, function, or user of the port.

Section 4-3

2 *(Optional)* Set the port speed:

COS	`set port speed mod/port {10	100	1000	auto}`
IOS	`(interface) speed {10	100	1000	auto	nonegotiate}`

You can set the port speed to one of: **10** (10 mbps for 10, 10/100, and 10/100/1000BASE-T ports), **100** (100 mbps for 10/100 and 10/100/1000BASE-T ports), **1000** (1000 mbps for 10/100/1000BASE-T ports), **auto** (autonegotiate the speed for 10/100 and 10/100/1000BASE-T ports; the default), or **nonegotiate** (don't autonegotiate the speed; IOS only). The speeds of 10BASE-T, 100FX, and *Gigabit Interface Converter* (GBIC) ports are fixed and cannot be set with this command.

TIP   Choosing the **auto** speed for a port (the default) enables the port to *participate in a negotiation* with the far end of the link. The two endpoints exchange information about their capabilities and choose the best speed and duplex mode supported by both. If one endpoint of a link has autonegotiation disabled, however, the other endpoint can only sense the link speed from the electrical signals. The duplex mode can't be determined and is left to the current default mode.

If you need to set the speed and duplex mode of the switch port to something other than **auto**, be sure to set the device at the far end of the link to the same values.

Generally, if a 10/100/1000BASE-T switch port is connected to another similar switch port or to a mission-critical device such as a server, router, or firewall, it is best to set the speed and duplex to a fixed value. By so doing, you eliminate any possibility of autonegotiation forcing the port to a lower speed in the future.

---

3 *(Optional)* Set the port duplex mode:

COS	`set port duplex mod/port {full	half	auto}`
IOS	`(interface) duplex {full	half	auto}`

You can set the duplex mode to one of **full**, **half** (IOS default), or **auto** (autonegotiate the duplex mode; COS default). The **auto** option is not available on the Catalyst 6000 IOS; if the speed is set to **auto**, the duplex follows suit.

TIP   The duplex mode can be autonegotiated only if the port speed is also set to **auto** (or autonegotiate). Gigabit and 10 Gigabit Ethernet ports can be set to either full- or half-duplex. Beware of a port that has a duplex mismatch, in which one end is full- and the other is half-duplex. This condition can cause poor response and a high error rate. Make sure that both ends of a link are set to autonegotiate or the same duplex setting.

4 *(Optional)* Set the port traffic flow control:

COS	`set port flowcontrol` *mod/port* `{receive	send} {off	on	desired}`
IOS	`(interface) flowcontrol {send	receive} {desired	off	on}`

A switch port can receive *pause* frames, causing transmission to stop for a short time while buffers at the far end are full. By default, **receive** processing is **off** for all switch port types (except 10 Gigabit Ethernet). A port can also send pause frames if its buffers get full. By default, **send** is **on** for Fast Ethernet, **desired** for Gigabit, and **off** for all other port types. The **desired** keyword is available for Gigabit ports only, where autonegotiation is inherent.

5 *(Optional)* Control port negotiation:

COS	`set port negotiation` *mod/port* `{enable	disable}`
IOS	`(interface) [no] negotiation auto`

By default, link negotiation (flow control, duplex, fault information) is enabled on Gigabit Ethernet ports. To disable negotiation, use the **disable** or **no** keyword.

6 *(Optional; Catalyst 6000 only)* Enable the port debounce timer:

COS	`set port debounce` *mod/port* `{enable	disable}`
IOS	N/A

By default, the linecards wait 300 milliseconds (10 milliseconds for fiber Gigabit ports) before announcing to the main processor that a port has changed state. This "debounces" the up/down state change so that quick changes do not trigger *Spanning Tree Protocol* (STP), *Port Aggregation Protocol* (PAgP), *Simple Network Management Protocol* (SNMP) traps, and so on. This debounce gives a port the chance to settle down to a stable state. If you find that this period is too short, you can **enable** an extended port debounce for specific ports. When enabled, the debounce period becomes 3.1 seconds (100 milliseconds for fiber Gigabit ports).

Section 4-3

NOTE   When this is enabled, port up/down detection is delayed. The normal STP state progression, along with PAgP negotiation, can make a very long delay before a port can become usable. Use this with caution.

7 *(Optional)* Optimize the port as a connection to a single host:

COS	`set port host` *mod/port*
IOS	`(interface)` **`spanning-tree portfast`**
	`(interface)` **`switchport mode access`**
	`(interface)` **`no channel-group`**

Several options are set for the port: STP PortFast is enabled, trunk mode is disabled, EtherChannel is disabled, and no dot1q tunneling is allowed. This optimizes the link startup time when the port is attached to only one host. Notice that COS switches can accomplish this in one command, whereas IOS switches require several.

8 *(Optional)* Use inline power where an IP phone is connected:

COS	`set port inlinepower` *mod/port* `{`**`off`** `|` **`auto`**`}`
IOS	`(interface)` **`power inline`** `{`**`auto`** `|` **`never`**`}`

On ports or linecards that can support inline power to IP phones, power is supplied if an IP phone is detected on the port by default (**auto**). If power should never be supplied to a connected device, choose the **off** or **never** keyword. See Chapter 14, "Voice," for more configuration information.

9 *(Optional)* Allow large or *jumbo* frames:

COS	`set port jumbo` *mod/port* `{`**`enable`** `|` **`disable`**`}`
IOS	`(interface)` **`mtu`** *bytes*

By default, the maximum frame size or *maximum transmission unit* (MTU) that can be switched is 1548 bytes (COS; default **disable**) and 1500 bytes (IOS; **mtu 1500**). Sometimes you might need to switch larger packets to improve performance from server to server. To allow switching of packets up to 9216 bytes, use the **enable** keyword (COS) or set an MTU size of *bytes* (IOS; 1500 to 9216 bytes).

Section 4-3

TIP	Enabling jumbo frame support allows large frames to be *switched*. If they also need to be routed, make sure that the MTU on the respective router interfaces is set to the same size. Jumbo frame support is available on an MSFC2 with the **mtu** interface command, but is not available on the *Multilayer Switch Feature Card* (MSFC).

10 *(Optional)* Automatically reenable ports from the errDisable state.

a. Set the timeout period before ports are automatically reenabled:

COS	`set errdisable-timeout interval {interval}`
IOS	`(global) errdisable recovery {interval interval}`

If ports in errDisable are automatically reenabled, the ports remain in the errDisable state for *interval* (30 to 86400 seconds, default 300 seconds). This command is not available in the Catalyst 2900XL and 3500XL IOS families.

b. Choose the causes that will automatically reenable ports:

COS	`set errdisable-timeout {enable	disable} reason`
IOS	`(global) [no] errdisable recovery cause reason`

By default, ports in the errDisable state are not automatically recovered or reenabled. If automatic recovery is desired for an errDisable condition, use the **enable** keyword (COS) or the **errdisable recovery cause** command (IOS). The ports will be recovered after the errDisable timeout period has expired. Choose one of the following reasons:

— **BPDU Port Guard**—A *bridge protocol data unit* (BPDU) is received on a port in the STP PortFast state; use *reason* **bpduguard** (COS) or **bpduguard** (IOS).

— **UDLD**—A unidirectional link is detected; use *reason* **udld** (COS and IOS).

— **STP Root Guard**—Use *reason* **rootguard** (IOS only).

— **EtherChannel misconfiguration**—The EtherChannel ports no longer have consistent configurations; use *reason* **channelmisconfig** (COS) or **pagp-flap** (IOS).

— **Trunk negotiation flapping**—*Dynamic Trunking Protocol* (DTP) is detecting changes from one trunk encapsulation to another; use *reason* **dtp-flap** (IOS only).

— **Duplex mismatch**—A high amount of excessive and late collisions are being detected; use *reason* **duplex-mismatch** (COS only).

— **Port is going up and down**—Use *reason* **link-flap** (IOS only).

— **Some other port problem**—Problems detected by a switch process not in this list; use *reason* **other** (COS only).

— **All known errDisable causes**—Ports are put into errDisable if any problem from this list is detected; use *reason* **all** (COS and IOS).

The **errdisable recovery cause** command is not available in the Catalyst 2900XL and 3500XL IOS families.

11 Enable or disable the port:

COS	`set port enable mod/port`
	-OR-
	`set port disable mod/port`

IOS	`(interface) shutdown`
	-OR-
	`(interface) no shutdown`

By default, a port is enabled (**enable** or **no shutdown**). To disable the port, use the **disable** or **shutdown** keywords.

Ethernet Example

A 10/100/1000 switch port connects a mail server. The port is set to 100 mbps, full duplex. The port is also tuned for a single host so that there are no port startup delays because of PAgP, STP, or trunk negotiations:

COS	`set port name 3/1 Mail server`
	`set port speed 3/1 100`
	`set port duplex 3/1 full`
	`set port host 3/1`
	`set port enable 3/1`

IOS	`(interface) description Mail server`
	`(interface) speed 100`
	`(interface) duplex full`
	`(interface) spanning-tree portfast`
	`(interface) switchport mode access`
	`(interface) no channel-group`
	`(interface) no shutdown`

Displaying Information About Layer 2 Interfaces

Table 4-2 lists some switch commands that you can use to display helpful information about Layer 2 interfaces.

Table 4-2   *Switch Commands to Display Layer 2 Interface Information*

Display Function	Switch OS	Command
Port status	COS	`show port [`*mod* `|` *mod/port*`]`
	IOS	`(exec) show interfaces [`*type num*`]`
Port error counters	COS	`show port mac [`*mod* `|` *mod/port*`]`
	IOS	`show interfaces counters [broadcast	errors	{module` *mod-num*`}	{trunk [module` *mod-num*`]}]`
Port MAC address used by the switch	COS	`show port mac-address [`*mod*`[`*/port*`]]` -OR- `show module` *mod*

	IOS	`(exec) show interfaces [`*type num*`]`
		-OR-
		`show catalyst6000 chassis-mac-address`

Port flow control	COS	`show port flowcontrol [`*mod*`[`*/port*`]]`
	IOS	`show interfaces [`*interface* `[`*mod*`]] flowcontrol`
Port negotiation	COS	`show port negotiation [`*mod*`[`*/port*`]]`
	IOS	N/A
Port debounce	COS	`show port debounce [`*mod* `|` *mod/port*`]`
	IOS	N/A
Port inline power	COS	`show port inlinepower [`*mod*`[`*/port*`]`
	IOS	`show power inline [`*interface-id*`] [actual	configured]`
Jumbo frame support	COS	`show port jumbo`
	IOS	`(exec) show interfaces [`*type num*`]`
errDisable recovery and port status	COS	`show errdisable-timeout`
	IOS	`(exec) show errdisable recovery`

On COS switches, you can generate and view reports of utilization, traffic volume, and errors on each port in the switch. These *TopN* reports can prove useful if you don't have network management applications that can generate statistical reports about the switch ports.

1 Run a TopN report:

COS	`show top [N] [metric] [interval interval] [port-type] background`
IOS	N/A

The report should include the top *N* (1 to the maximum number of switch ports; default 20 ports) entries using the *metric* as a sorting key. *Metric* can be one of **util** (utilization; the default), **bytes** (bytes in/out), **pkts** (packets in/out), **bcst** (broadcast packets in/out), **mcst** (multicast packets in/out), **errors** (input errors), or **overflow** (buffer overflows).

The TopN report can sample the port data over an *interval* (0 or 10 to 999 seconds; default 30 seconds). If *interval* is 0, the report uses the absolute port counters (as seen with **show port** or **show port mac**). In addition, reports can be run for specific types of ports as *port-type*: **all** (all port types; the default), **eth** (all types of Ethernet ports), **10e** (10 mbps Ethernet), **fe** (Fast Ethernet), **ge** (Gigabit Ethernet), or **10ge** (10 Gigabit Ethernet).

The switch prompts when the report has started and ended. Be sure to note the report number that is being generated. With the **background** keyword, you can issue other switch commands while the report is in progress.

2 View a stored TopN report:

COS	`show top report [report-num]`
IOS	N/A

A specific TopN report numbered *report-num* can be viewed. To see a list of all the stored TopN reports, omit the report number. Reports are stored in switch memory and remain there until the switch is rebooted or loses power. To clear TopN reports from memory, use the **clear top** [**all** | *report-num*] command.

4-4: EtherChannel

- You can aggregate several individual switch ports into a single logical port or EtherChannel.

- Fast Ethernet ports, when bundled together, form a *Fast EtherChannel* (FEC). Gigabit ports form a *Gigabit EtherChannel* (GEC).

- You can manually configure EtherChannels or aggregate them through the use of dynamic protocols. PAgP is a Cisco proprietary protocol, whereas *Link Aggregation Control Protocol* (LACP) is a standards-based protocol defined in IEEE 802.3ad (also known as IEEE 802.3 Clause 43, "Link Aggregation").

- Frames are distributed onto the individual ports that make up an EtherChannel by using a hashing algorithm. The algorithm can use source, destination, or a combination of source and destination IP addresses, source and destination MAC addresses, or TCP/UDP port numbers, depending on the hardware platform and configuration.

- Frame distribution is deterministic; that is, the same combination of addresses or port numbers always points to the same port within the EtherChannel.

- The frame distribution hashing algorithm performs an *exclusive-OR* (XOR) operation on one or more low-order bits of the addresses or TCP/UDP port numbers to select on which link a frame will be forwarded. For a two-port bundle, the last bit is used; a four-port bundle uses the last two bits; an eight-port bundle uses the last three bits. (With XOR, if two bits are identical, a 0 bit results; if two bits are different, a 1 bit results.)

- If a link within an EtherChannel fails, the traffic that normally crosses the failed link is moved to the remaining links.

- EtherChannel links can be static access ports or trunk ports. However, all links to be bundled must have consistent configurations before an EtherChannel can form.

NOTE   PAgP sends frames to destination address 01:00:0C:CC:CC:CC, as an 802.2 *Subnetwork Access Protocol* (SNAP) protocol 0x000C0104. LACP sends frames to destination address 01-80-c2-00-00-02 using protocol 0x8809.

Section 4-4

Configuration

1 *(Optional; Catalyst 6000 COS only)* Select an EtherChannel protocol for a module:

COS	`set channelprotocol {pagp	lacp}` *mod*
IOS	N/A

By default, each module uses the PAgP protocol (**pagp**) for dynamic EtherChannel control. You can use the **lacp** keyword to select LACP for the module number *mod* instead, if desired.

TIP   PAgP and LACP are not interoperable. Therefore, use the same protocol on the modules and ports at both ends of a potential EtherChannel.

2 *(Optional)* Adjust the STP costs for an EtherChannel.

a. Set the STP port cost:

COS	`set spantree channelcost {`*channel-id* `|` **all**`}` *cost*
IOS	N/A

By default, the STP port cost for an EtherChannel is based on the port cost of the aggregate bandwidth. For example, a single 100 mbps port has a port cost of 19. When two 100 mbps ports are bundled as an FEC, the port cost for 200 mbps is 12. A bundle of four 100 mbps ports gives a port cost of 8 for the 400 mbps bandwidth. Refer to Table 7-1 in Chapter 7, "Spanning Tree Protocol (STP)," for STP port cost values.

You can change the port cost for all EtherChannels by using the **all** keyword, or a single EtherChannel by giving its *channel-id* number. To find this index, use the **show channel group** (PAgP) or **show lacp-channel group** (LACP) command. The *channel-id* is a unique number that is automatically assigned to the EtherChannel.

The STP port cost is given as *cost* (1-65535 in 16-bit "short mode" or 1-4294967296 in 32-bit "long mode"). Refer to section "7-1: STP Operation" for more cost information.

b. Set the STP port cost per VLAN:

COS	`set spantree channelvlancost` *channel_id cost*
	`set spantree portvlancost` *mod/port* [**cost** *cost*] [*vlan-list*]
IOS	N/A

Use the **set spantree channelvlancost** command to allow the port cost per VLAN to be configured for the EtherChannel with *channel-id*. The STP port cost is set to *cost* for all VLANs that will be carried over the EtherChannel. Then you should adjust the port cost for specific VLANs by using the **set spantree portvlancost** command. Refer to section "7-1: STP Operation" for more cost information.

3 *(Optional)* Use PAgP on an EtherChannel:

TIP   When you make configuration changes to add or remove ports from an EtherChannel, be aware of the effects this has on the STP. This is especially important in a live production network where you might cause an interruption of service.

STP operates on an EtherChannel as if it were a normal switch port. After ports have been assigned to an EtherChannel, STP moves through its various states to guarantee a loop-free topology. Switch ports within the EtherChannel administrative group can be enabled and disabled without triggering an STP topology change. As a result, the other links in the EtherChannel remain in the STP "forwarding" state.

If you attempt to add a new port into an active EtherChannel administrative group, however, an STP topology change is triggered. The same result occurs if you change the administrative group number on an active EtherChannel. You have now reconfigured the logical link, so STP moves the EtherChannel (and all of its ports) back through the "listening" and "learning" states. This interrupts traffic on the EtherChannel for up to 50 seconds.

a. Assign ports to the EtherChannel:

COS	`set port channel` *mod/port* [*admin-group*]
IOS	N/A

One or more ports, given by *mod/port*, are assigned as an EtherChannel. A specific administrative group number *admin-group* can be given if desired. If this is omitted, the switch automatically assigns these ports a new unique group number. If you do specify a group number and that number is already in use, the new EtherChannel receives the group number and the ports that were previously assigned are moved to a different unique group number.

On an IOS switch, ports are assigned to an EtherChannel group at the same time as the PAgP mode is set. This is done in Step 3b.

TIP

You must list all the ports that will belong to the EtherChannel in this one command. To add or delete individual ports from the bundle, reissue this command with an updated list of all the desired ports.

b. Set the PAgP mode:

COS	`set port channel` *mod/port* `mode {on	off	desirable	auto} [silent	non-silent]`
IOS	(interface) `channel-group` *number* `mode {on	auto [non-silent]	desirable [non-silent]}`

The channel is referenced by one of its ports as *mod/port* (COS) or by selecting the interface and the group *number* (IOS). You can configure PAgP in one of these modes: **on** (EtherChannel is used, but no PAgP packets are sent), **off** (EtherChannel is disabled), **desirable** (switch is actively willing to form an EtherChannel; PAgP packets are sent), or **auto** (switch is passively willing to form an EtherChannel; no PAgP packets are sent; the default).

Section 4-4

When in **auto** or **desirable** mode, PAgP packets are required before an EtherChannel can be negotiated and brought up. However, there might be times when one end of the EtherChannel (a server or network analyzer) doesn't generate PAgP packets or is "silent." You can use the **silent** keyword (the default) to allow a port to become an EtherChannel with a silent partner after a 15-second delay. Use the **non-silent** keyword to require PAgP negotiation before bringing the EtherChannel active.

TIP PAgP is not available on the Catalyst 2900 or 3500XL platforms. An EtherChannel on these switches is either "on" or "off" with no negotiation. If you connect an EtherChannel from another switch platform to one of these, make sure that PAgP is not used for negotiation. In other words, use the **on** mode to force the use of an EtherChannel.

---

c. *(Optional)* Choose a load-balancing algorithm:

COS	`set port channel all distribution {ip	mac	session} [source	destination	both]`
IOS	`(global) port-channel load-balance` *method*

Choose a load-balancing *method*:

— Source IP address— **ip source** (COS) or **src-ip** (IOS)

— Destination IP address— **ip destination** (COS) or **dst-ip** (IOS)

— Source and destination IP— **ip both** (COS) or **src-dst-ip** (IOS)

— Source MAC address— **mac source** (COS) or **src-mac** (IOS)

— Destination MAC address— **mac destination** (COS) or **dst-mac** (IOS)

— Source and destination MAC— **mac both** (COS) or **src-dst-mac** (IOS)

— Source port number— **session source** (COS) or **src-port** (IOS)

— Destination port number— **session destination** (COS) or **dst-port** (IOS)

— Source and destination port— **session both** (COS) or **src-dst-port** (IOS)

| TIP | Load balancing based on **session** or **port** is available only on the Catalyst 6000 Supervisor Engine 2 with a *Policy Feature Card 2* (PFC2) (both COS and IOS). |

4 *(Optional; COS only)* Use LACP on an EtherChannel.

a. Set the system priority:

COS	`set lacp-channel system-priority` *value*
IOS	N/A

The system ID is an 8-byte quantity formed from a 2-byte priority of *value* (1 to 65535; default 32768) followed by the switch MAC address. A lower *value* means a higher priority. The switch with the lowest overall system ID value can modify which ports are actively participating in an EtherChannel at any given time.

b. Set the port priority for individual ports:

COS	`set port lacp-channel` *mod/ports* `port-priority` *value*
IOS	N/A

The switch with the lowest system ID value selects ports with the lowest port ID value for use in an EtherChannel. The port ID is made up of a 2-byte priority *value* (1 to 255, default 128) followed by a 2-byte port number. Ports that cannot be used are placed in a "standby" state; they are held inactive until another link in the EtherChannel fails.

c. Group ports by setting their administrative keys:

COS	`set port lacp-channel` *mod/ports* [*admin-key*]
IOS	N/A

Ports that have the potential to become an EtherChannel should have their administrative key, *admin-key* (1 to 65535), set to the same value. Up to eight ports can be assigned the same administrative key value. Ports that have a unique value are considered to be individual ports and do not become part of an EtherChannel.

By default, each group of four consecutive ports in a module has the same unique key value. Key values are only locally significant. However, ports with the same key value on one switch can potentially form an EtherChannel with ports sharing another common key value on another switch.

Section 4-4

If the *admin-key* value is not specified, the switch selects an unused, unique value for the ports listed. If you do specify a key value and that value is already in use, the ports already assigned are moved to another unique key value.

d. Set the EtherChannel mode:

COS	`set port lacp-channel` *mod/ports* `mode {on | off | active | passive}`
IOS	N/A

LACP can be configured in one of these modes: **on** (EtherChannel is used, but no LACP packets are sent), **off** (EtherChannel is disabled), **active** (switch is actively willing to form an EtherChannel; LACP packets are sent), or **passive** (switch is passively willing to form an EtherChannel; no LACP packets are sent; the default).

TIP   Although PAgP and LACP are not compatible or interoperable, you can form an EtherChannel between one switch that uses PAgP on a module and another switch that uses LACP on its module. In this case, set the PAgP switch to the **on** mode and the LACP switch to the **on** mode. Neither protocol will be used to negotiate an EtherChannel, but the EtherChannel will be formed.

EtherChannel Example

Figure 4-1 shows a network diagram for this example. A switch has three linecards with Ethernet ports. Modules 4 and 5 use PAgP to aggregate ports, whereas module 6 uses LACP. One EtherChannel is made up of ports 4/1, 4/2, 5/1, and 5/2, demonstrating that an EtherChannel can be split across multiple linecards. This EtherChannel uses PAgP in the desirable mode to dynamically bundle the ports together. The nonsilent mode requires a PAgP speaker on the far end before the EtherChannel will be built. Both source and destination IP addresses distribute traffic across the bundled ports.

Figure 4-1   *Network Diagram for the EtherChannel Example*

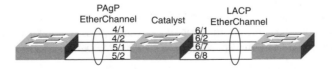

A second EtherChannel is configured to use LACP. The LACP system priority is set to 8192 so that this switch will become the higher-priority decision maker. Ports 6/1, 6/2, 6/7, and 6/8 all belong to LACP administrative key 101, forming a common aggregate link. Ports

6/1 and 6/2 are given a port priority of 100, which is less than the default 128. These ports are used in the LACP bundle first. If for some reason ports 6/7 or 6/8 are not able to be used in the EtherChannel, they are placed in a "standby" state and used if another port fails. Each of the bundled ports is put into the active LACP mode and is willing to initiate an EtherChannel with the far-end switch:

COS	```set channelprotocol pagp 4```
	```set channelprotocol pagp 5```
	```set channelprotocol lacp 6```
	
	```set port channel 4/1-2,5/1-2```
	```set port channel 4/1 mode desirable non-silent```
	```set port channel all distribution ip both```
	
	```set lacp-channel system-priority 8192```
	```set port lacp-channel 6/1-2 port-priority 100```
	```set port lacp-channel 6/1-2,6/7-8 101```
	```set port lacp-channel 6/1-2,6/7-8 mode active```

IOS	```(global) interface fastethernet 4/1```
	```(interface) channel-group 100 mode desirable non-silent```
	```(global) interface fastethernet 4/2```
	```(interface) channel-group 100 mode desirable non-silent```
	```(global) interface fastethernet 5/1```
	```(interface) channel-group 100 mode desirable non-silent```
	```(global) interface fastethernet 5/2```
	```(interface) channel-group 100 mode desirable non-silent```
	```(global) port-channel load-balance src-dst-ip```

Displaying Information About EtherChannels

Table 4-3 lists some switch commands that you can use to display helpful information about EtherChannel links.

Table 4-3   *Switch Commands to Display EtherChannel Link Information*

Display Function	Switch OS	Command
EtherChannel protocol used on each module	COS	```show channelprotocol```
	IOS	N/A
EtherChannel capabilities on a module	COS	```show port capabilities [mod[/port]]```
	IOS	N/A

continues

Table 4-3 *Switch Commands to Display EtherChannel Link Information (Continued)*

Display Function	Switch OS	Command
EtherChannel ID numbers	COS	`show channel group` *admin-group* -OR- `show lacp-channel group` *admin-key*
	IOS	N/A
EtherChannel load balancing	COS	`show channel` [*channel-id*] `info`
	IOS	`(exec)` `show etherchannel` [*channel-group*] `load-balance`
EtherChannel traffic utilization	COS	`show channel traffic` [*channel-id*] -OR- `show lacp-channel traffic` [*channel-id*]
	IOS	`(exec)` `show pagp` [*group-number*] `counters`
Outgoing port for an address or port number	COS	`show channel hash` *channel-id* {*src* | *dest* | *src dest*} -OR- `show lacp-channel hash` *channel-id* {*src* | *dest* | *src dest*}
	IOS	N/A

TIP If you are debugging an EtherChannel that will not form, remember that all ports with the bundle must have the same attributes. For example, all the ports should have the same speed, duplex, VLAN (or native VLAN for a trunk), trunk mode, trunk encapsulation, allowed VLAN range, and so on.

The commands listed in Table 4-3 provide a great deal of information about EtherChannels that are already formed. To be sure that the ports are all configured consistently, use other **show** commands that display the port attributes . Beyond that, you sometimes have to resort to looking through the switch configuration to spot port configurations that are not identical.

4-5: Token Ring

- Token Ring ports are capable of running at 4 or 16 mbps, and either half- or full-duplex.
- Token Ring ports can operate as Token Ring concentrators or as end stations.
- The following bridging modes are supported:
  - *Source-route bridging* **(SRB)**—*Routing Information Fields* (RIFs) forward packets from rings to bridges, instead of learning MAC addresses. Both the IBM and IEEE STPs are supported.

— *Source-route transparent* (**SRT**)—SRB is combined with transparent bridging. Packets with a RIF are forwarded through SRB, whereas packets without a RIF are forwarded through transparent bridging. Only the IEEE STP is supported.

— *Source-route switching* (**SRS**)—Packets can be forwarded based on MAC addresses or RIFs.

Configuration

1 *(Optional)* Assign a descriptive name to the port:

COS	`set port name` *mod/port* [*port-name*]
IOS	N/A

The description *port-name* (text string) is assigned to the port for human use. Usually, the description includes a reference to the location, function, or user of the port.

2 Set the port speed:

COS	`set port speed` *mod/port* {**4** | **16** | **auto**}
IOS	N/A

The port speed can be set to **4** or **16** mbps. If the **auto** (the default) keyword is used instead, the port automatically senses the speed of the connected ring. If the speed is changed on a port, the port leaves and reenters the ring at the new speed.

CAUTION   If the default autosensing speed is not used, be careful to choose the correct speed for the attached ring. If the port's transmission speed is different from the ring, the port sends beacon frames—effectively making the entire ring inoperable.

3 Set the port mode:

COS	`set tokenring portmode` *mod/port* {**auto** | **fdxcport** | **hdxcport** | **fdxstation** | **hdxstation** | **riro**}
IOS	N/A

Depending on how the port is used, its mode can be set to one of **auto** (automatically detect the connection mode; the default), **fdxcport** (act as a full-duplex concentrator when connected to a single station), **hdxcport** (act as a half-duplex concentrator when

Section 4-5

connected to a single station), **fdxstation** (act as a full-duplex station when connected to another Token Ring switch), **hdxstation** (act as a half-duplex station when connected to a MSAU), or **riro** (act as a ring-in/ring-out when using a fiber connection).

4 *(Optional)* Use *early token release* (ETR):

COS	set tokenring etr *mod/port* {enable | disable}
IOS	N/A

With ETR, the port is allowed to release its token onto the ring immediately after transmitting (**enable**; the default). Ordinarily, the port must wait to release the token until after the transmitted frame has returned around the ring (**disable**). ETR is only possible on ports participating in 16 mbps rings.

5 *(Optional)* Control the use of explorer frames.

a. *(Optional)* Use *All-Routes Explorer* (ARE) reduction:

COS	set tokenring reduction {enable | disable}
IOS	N/A

When a Token Ring network has parallel paths, ARE frames are flooded onto all possible paths. The amount of ARE frames can be reduced (**enable**; the default) by discarding the identical explorers that have already been seen on the ring where the port is attached.

b. *(Optional)* Throttle the amount of incoming ARE frames:

COS	set tokenring explorer-throttle *mod/port maximum-explorers*
IOS	N/A

The number of ARE frames is limited to *maximum-explorers* (frames per second; default 0, or no throttling). After the throttle threshold has been reached during a 1-second interval, the additional ARE frames received on the port are dropped.

6 *(Optional)* React to error conditions on a port.

a. *(Optional)* Use soft error monitoring:

COS	set station softerror *mod[/port]* {disable | enable}
IOS	N/A

By default, soft error monitoring is disabled. When enabled, soft error statistics are collected on the module or port. Soft errors normally occur on a ring, indicating noncritical errors.

b. *(Optional)* Set a soft error threshold:

COS	`set station softerror` *mod*[*/port*] `threshold` *thres-num* `interval` *int-num*
IOS	N/A

A threshold for the number of soft errors from a single station can be set to *thres-num* (1 to 255; default 100) errors per time interval *int-num* (0 to 65534 seconds; default 60 seconds). When the threshold is reached, the switch sends a "soft error exceeded" trap, unless the interval is set to 0 seconds.

c. *(Optional)* Remove an error-producing station from the ring:

COS	`clear station` *mod/port mac-addr*
IOS	N/A

If a station is seen to produce a large number of soft errors and is degrading the ring performance, it might be a candidate to be removed from the ring. Give the station's *mac-addr* in noncanonical format (00:11:22:33:44:55). Be aware that the switch will send a "Remove Station" MAC frame to the station, which will force it to remove itself from the ring.

d. *(Optional)* Automatically disable a port with configuration losses:

COS	`set tokenring configloss` *mod/port* [`threshold` *thresh-num*] [`interval` *int-num*]
IOS	N/A

A configuration loss occurs when a port enters the ring, passes data, and then closes or is removed from the ring for some reason. A threshold for the number of configuration losses can be set to *thres-num* (1 to 100; default 8) losses per time interval *int-num* (0 to 99 minutes; default 10 minutes). When the threshold is reached, the switch disables the port. To regain use of the port, you must reenable it with the **set port enable** command.

7 *(Optional)* Use a filter to control MAC addresses or protocols entering a port:

COS	`set port filter` *mod/port* {*mac-addr*	*protocol-type*} {**permit**	**deny**}
IOS	N/A

Section 4-5

You can **permit** or **deny** frames containing the MAC address *mac-addr* (either source or destination, entered in canonical format, 00-11-33-44-55, or noncanonical format, 00:11:22:33:44:55) or the protocol type given as *protocol-type* on a switch port.

The *protocol-type* can be a four-digit hex value (0x1234, for example) for the Ethernet type, as given in "Appendix B-5: Ethernet Type Codes", a four-digit hex value for a SNAP (0x1234, for example), or a two-digit hex value for a *destination service access point* (DSAP) (0x12ff, for example, always ending in ff).

Up to 16 MAC address filters and 16 protocol filters (8 SAP and 8 DSAP) can be defined per Token Ring port.

Token Ring Example

Token Ring switch port 2/5 is connected to a 3745 FEP in a data center, using a 16 mbps speed. The port is set to autodetect its role on the ring. Early token release is enabled. Port 2/5 is also set to be disabled if 5 or more configuration losses occur during a 15-minute interval.

Switch port 2/6 is connected to a *multistation access unit* (MSAU), which also connects to several other hosts. This port is set for hdxstation mode, to properly connect with the MSAU. Early token release is used on the 16 mbps ring. ARE reduction is enabled for the entire switch:

COS	
	`set port name 2/5 3745 FEP`
	`set port speed 2/5 16`
	`set tokenring portmode 2/5 auto`
	`set tokenring etr 2/5 enable`
	`set tokenring configloss 2/5 threshold 5 interval 15`
	`set port name 2/6 1st floor MSAU`
	`set port speed 2/6 16`
	`set tokenring portmode 2/6 hdxstation`
	`set tokenring etr 2/5 enable`
	`set tokenring reduction enable`
IOS	N/A

Displaying Information About Token Ring

Table 4-4 lists some switch commands that you can use to display helpful information about Token Ring links.

Table 4-4   *Switch Commands to Display Token Ring Link Information*

Display Function	Switch OS	Command
Token Ring port status	COS	`show tokenring`
	IOS	N/A
Status of stations on a ring	COS	`show station controltable` [*mod*[*/port*]]
	IOS	N/A
Connection order of stations on a ring	COS	`show station ordertable` [*mod*[*/port*]]
	IOS	N/A
Soft error configuration	COS	`show station softerror config` [*mod*[*/port*]]
	IOS	N/A
Soft error statistics	COS	`show station softerror counters` *mod*/*port* [*mac-addr*]
	IOS	N/A
Token Ring filters	COS	`show port filter` [*mod*[*/port*]] [`canonical`]
	IOS	N/A

4-6: ATM LANE

- LANE provides an emulated IEEE 802.3 Ethernet or IEEE 802.5 Token Ring network over an ATM network. You can use LANE to transport traditional LANs over an ATM backbone or an ATM WAN cloud.

- LANE uses the concept of *emulated LANs*, or ELANs, to segment traffic into logical networks within the ATM domain.

- LANE consists of several logical components, each configured on a router, switch, or an ATM switch:

  - *LAN Emulation Configuration Server* (**LECS**)—The central administrative control point for all ELANs in a domain. The LECS keeps a database of ELANs and the ATM addresses of the LANE servers that control each ELAN. (Each administrative domain has only one LECS.)

  - *LAN Emulation Server* (**LES**)—The central control point for all LANE Clients in an ELAN. The LES provides MAC to ATM *Network Service Access Point* (NSAP) address translation for each LANE Client. (Each ELAN has only one LES.)

  - *Broadcast and Unknown Server* (**BUS**)—The BUS handles all broadcasts sent from a LANE host. The LANE Client must forward any broadcast or multicast from an end user to the BUS. The BUS is then able to replicate the broadcast to all other LANE Clients in the domain.

Section 4-6

— *LAN Emulation Client* (**LEC**)—Provides the basic ELAN function at the edge of the ATM network. The LEC emulates an interface to a tradition LAN and provides data forwarding, address resolution, and MAC address registration with the other LANE components. A LEC is needed at any location where network layer addresses are used.

- You can configure multiple LANE components in the network for redundancy. *Simple Server Redundancy Protocol* (SSRP) handles the communication between the active and standby components so that no single point of failure can exist within the components.

NOTE   ATM addresses use the NSAP format, a 20-byte value. Typically, NSAP addresses are written out as groups of four hex digits separated by dots. The leftmost and rightmost two hex digits are usually grouped by themselves. The address is composed of the following parts:

- **Prefix**—A 13-byte field that uniquely identifies every ATM switch in the network. Cisco ATM switches use a predefined 7-byte value of 47.0091.8100.0000 followed by the 6-byte MAC address of the switch.

- *End-System Identifier* (**ESI**)—A 6-byte field that uniquely identifies every device attached to an ATM switch. Typically, this is the 6-byte MAC address of the device (an ATM router interface or LANE module, for example).

- **Selector**—A 1-byte field that identifies a process running on an ATM device. Cisco devices usually use the ATM subinterface number as the selector value. Be sure to convert the ATM subinterface number from decimal to hex before configuring the selector byte on a Cisco switch.

The prefix value always comes from the ATM switch. The ESI value is determined from the ATM interface MAC address as follows: LEC (MAC address), LES (MAC address + 1), BUS (MAC address + 2), and LECS (MAC address + 3). The selector is the ATM subinterface number except for the LECS, which must always be configured on a major ATM interface (selector 00).

Configuration

1 Access the ATM LANE module session:

COS	`session module`
IOS	N/A

A Telnet session is started with the LANE module in slot number *module*. To find
the slot number, use the **show module** command. After the session has been opened,
you communicate with the LANE module's IOS CLI. When you are finished and need
to return to the COS switch, type **exit**.

2 Define the control *permanent virtual circuits* (PVCs).

a. Select the major ATM interface:

COS	N/A
IOS	(global) **interface atm 0**

b. *(Optional)* Select the preferred PHY to use:

COS	N/A
IOS	(interface) **atm preferred phy {A | B}**

On a dual PHY ATM module, you can select either the **A** or **B** physical interface to be
the preferred PHY.

c. Define the ATM signaling PVC:

COS	N/A
IOS	(interface) **atm pvc** *vcd* **0 5 qsaal**

The signaling PVC uses QSAAL and usually operates over VPI/VCI 0/5. The *vcd* is
the virtual circuit descriptor, an arbitrary number (1 to 2047) used to uniquely identify
the PVC.

d. Define the ILMI PVC:

COS	N/A
IOS	(interface) **atm pvc** *vcd* **0 16 ilmi**

Interim Local Management Interface (ILMI) is a protocol used between the LANE
module and the ATM switch to communicate and set various ATM parameters. Specifically, ILMI can be used to pass the LECS address to any switch in the LANE
cloud. ILMI is usually configured over VPI/VCI 0/16. The *vcd* field can be arbitrarily
set to identify the PVC.

3 Display the default LANE addresses on the ATM PHY interface:

COS	N/A
IOS	(exec) **show lane default-atm-addresses**

Section 4-6

The default NSAP addresses for the LANE components are shown. If the LANE module has received the prefix portion of the address from an ATM switch, the entire NSAP address is shown. Otherwise, only the ESI or MAC address portion displays. These NSAP addresses are used in further LANE configuration steps. An example of the output from a LANE module follows:

```
(lane-module) show lane default-atm-addresses
interface ATM0:
LANE Client:        47.00918100000000E01E35A801.00503ED30C10.**
LANE Server:        47.00918100000000E01E35A801.00503ED30C11.**
LANE Bus:           47.00918100000000E01E35A801.00503ED30C12.**
LANE Config Server: 47.00918100000000E01E35A801.00503ED30C13.00
  note: ** is the subinterface number byte in hex
```

4 *(Optional)* Define the LECS.

a. Name the LECS database:

COS	N/A
IOS	(global) **lane database** *database-name*

The LECS database is named *database-name* (1- to 32-character string).

b. Define an ELAN and its LES:

COS	N/A
IOS	(lane-database) **name** *elan-name* **server-atm-address** *atm-address* [**restricted**] [**index** *index*]

The ELAN named *elan-name* (1- to 32-character string) is bound to the LES at *atm-address* (20-byte NSAP address). The NSAP address can be obtained from the **show lane default-atm-addresses** command on the router or LANE module that will have the LES component. You can use the **restricted** keyword to restrict ELAN membership to only those clients explicitly listed in the database as shown in the bulleted steps that follow.

NOTE   To use SSRP for redundancy, multiple LES components can be defined for a given ELAN. You must use the **index** keyword to assign a priority to each LES (0 is the highest priority).

— *(Unrestricted ELAN membership)* Define a default ELAN name:

COS	N/A
IOS	(lane-database) **default-name** *elan-name*

For an unrestricted membership ELAN, any client attempting to register itself with the LECS will be joined to the ELAN named *elan-name* (1- to 32-character string).

— (Restricted ELAN membership) Define specific LECs and their ELAN:

COS	N/A
IOS	`(lane-database)` **`client-atm-address`** `atm-address` **`name`** `elan-name`

For a restricted membership ELAN, any client attempting to register itself with the LECS must be specifically identified by its *atm-address* (20-byte value, 40 hex digits; * can match any digit, ... can match any number of digits). The matching client is joined to the ELAN named *elan-name* (1- to 32-character string).

c. Enable the LECS.

— Select an ATM major interface:

COS	N/A
IOS	`(global)` **`interface atm 0`**

— Use a specific LECS database

COS	N/A
IOS	`(interface)` **`lane config database`** `database-name`

— Determine the LECS ATM address.

NOTE To use redundant LECS components, you must configure each LECS ATM address in the ATM switch. As each LEC initializes, it contacts the ATM switch through ILMI and is provided a list of all the LECS addresses. If multiple ATM switches are used within the ELAN domain, all ATM switches must have an identical list of LECS addresses in the same order. In addition, each redundant LECS must have an identical database.

You can choose from three different ATM addresses for the LECS.

Section 4-6

To use the automatic or predetermined address, use the following command:

COS	N/A
IOS	(interface) `lane config auto-config-atm-address`

The LECS address is created from the value shown by the **show lane default-atm-addresses** command.

To use the well-known LECS address, use the following command:

COS	N/A
IOS	(interface) `lane config fixed-config-atm-address`

The LECS address is the well-known NSAP 47.0079000000000000000000000.00A03E000001.00.

To use a specific ATM address, use the following command:

COS	N/A
IOS	(interface) `lane config config-atm-address` *nsap-address*

The LECS receives the *nsap-address* (20-byte value, or 40 hex digits). The address can be given as a template, using * to match any single hex digit, or ... to match any number of leading, middle, or trailing hex digits.

5 *(Optional)* Define a LES/BUS pair.

a. Select an ATM subinterface:

COS	N/A
IOS	(global) `interface atm 0.`*subinterface*

You can use an arbitrary *subinterface* number for the LES/BUS components. However, you can configure only one LES/BUS on a subinterface, serving only a single ELAN. In addition, only one LES/BUS pair is needed to support an ELAN.

b. Enable the LES/BUS:

COS	N/A
IOS	(interface) `lane server-bus ethernet` *elan-name*

A LES and BUS are created for the ELAN named *elan-name* (1- to 32-character string). The emulated LAN acts as an *Ethernet* network.

6 *(Optional)* Define a LEC.

a. Select an ATM subinterface:

COS	N/A
IOS	(global) **interface atm 0.***subinterface*

You can use an arbitrary *subinterface* number for the LEC component. You can configure a LEC on the same subinterface as the LES/BUS pair, although this is not required. However, you can create only one LEC on a single subinterface, serving a single ELAN.

b. Enable the LEC:

COS	N/A
IOS	(interface) **lane client ethernet** *vlan-id* [*elan-name*]

The LEC is configured to emulate an Ethernet network. When the LEC joins the ELAN, the LECS will already have the ELAN name for the client in its database. The ELAN name, *elan-name*, can be given so that the LEC will present the ELAN name to the LECS for additional matching. The VLAN number *vlan-id* will be bridged to the ELAN.

ATM LANE Example

A Catalyst LANE module is configured to participate in LANE in a hospital environment. After the signaling and ILMI PVCs have been configured, the LANE module is able to complete all of the parts for the default ATM addresses. The default addresses on the local LANE module are shown in the example, although the default addresses of other devices are also collected. A LECS database for the hospital is configured as *hospital-db*. An ELAN named *radiology* is configured with restricted membership. Two LES addresses are listed for redundancy: The local LANE module's LES as priority zero, and another device's LES as priority one. For simplicity, only one LEC is listed and able to join the radiology ELAN—the LEC on the local LANE module.

A second ELAN named *surgery* is also configured with unrestricted membership. By default, a LEC is joined to the surgery ELAN.

The LECS is configured on interface atm 0, a LES/BUS for radiology on interface atm 0.1, and a LES/BUS for surgery on interface atm 0.2. Finally, a LEC in the radiology ELAN is configured on interface atm 0.3 to bridge to VLAN 10. Notice that the ATM addresses listed in the database have the correct LANE component value in the last ESI digit (0 = LEC, 1 = LES, 2 = BUS, 3 = LECS). The selector value also has the appropriate subinterface number used in the interface configuration:

COS	N/A
IOS	(see below)

```
(global) interface atm 0
(interface) atm pvc 1 0 5 qsaal
(interface) atm pvc 2 0 16 ilmi
(interface) no shutdown
(interface) exit
(global) exit

(exec) show lane default-atm-addresses
LANE Client:       47.00918100000000E01E35A901.00E0FE1400C0.**
LANE Server:       47.00918100000000E01E35A901.00E0FE1400C1.**
LANE Bus:          47.00918100000000E01E35A901.00E0FE1400C2.**
LANE Config Server: 47.00918100000000E01E35A901.00E0FE1400C3.00
(This command is also run on other LES and LEC routers and
switches, so that the LANE component addresses can be added into
the configuration.)
(exec) config terminal
(global) lane database hospital-db
(lane-db) name radiology server-atm-address
47.00918100000000E01E35A901.00E0FE1400C1.01 restricted index 0
(lane-db) name radiology server-atm-address
47.00918100000000E01E35A901.00E0FE121042.01 restricted index 1
(lane-db) client-atm-address
47.00918100000000E01E35A901.00E0FE1400C0.03 name radiology
(lane-db) name surgery server-atm-address
47.00918100000000E01E35A901.00E0FE1400C1.02 index 0
 (lane-db) name surgery server-atm-address
47.00918100000000E01E35A901.00E0FE121041.02 index 0
(lane-db) default-name surgery
(lane-db) exit

(global) interface atm 0
(interface) description LECS for hospital ATM network
(interface) lane config database hospital-db
(interface) lane config auto-config-atm-address

(global) interface atm 0.1
(interface) description LES/BUS for radiology ELAN
(interface) lane server-bus ethernet radiology

(global) interface atm 0.2
(interface) description LES/BUS for surgery ELAN
(interface) lane server-bus ethernet surgery

(global) interface atm 0.3
(interface) description LEC for radiology ELAN
(interface) lane client ethernet 10 radiology
```

Displaying Information About ATM LANE

Table 4-5 lists some switch commands that you can use to display helpful information about ATM LANE.

Table 4-5   *Switch Commands to Display ATM LANE Information*

Display Function	Switch OS	Command
LECS status	COS	N/A
	IOS	(exec) **show lane config**
LECS database	COS	N/A
	IOS	(exec) **show lane database**
LES status	COS	N/A
	IOS	(exec) **show lane server**
BUS status	COS	N/A
	IOS	(exec) **show lane bus**
LEC status	COS	N/A
	IOS	(exec) **show lane client**
Default NSAP ATM addresses	COS	N/A
	IOS	(exec) **show lane default-atm-addresses**

TIP

If you are having trouble passing traffic over a LEC, use the **show lane client** command to see whether the LEC has been able to join the ELAN. The output for a successfully joined LEC is as follows:

```
lane-module# show lane client
LE Client ATM0.1  ELAN name: elan48  Admin: up  State: operational
Client ID: 1                        LEC up for 7 days 18 hours 6 minutes 40 seconds
Join Attempt: 3
HW Address: 00e0.1499.6410   Type: ethernet          Max Frame Size: 1516
        VLANID: 62
ATM Address: 47.00918100000000E01E35A901.00E014996410.01

  VCD  rxFrames  txFrames  Type      ATM Address
    0         0         0  configure  47.00918100000000E01E35A901.00E0FE1400C3.00
   16         1    211337  direct     47.00918100000000E01E35A901.00E014996411.01
   87    761437         0  distribute 47.00918100000000E01E35A901.00E014996411.01
   90         0    916712  send       47.00918100000000E01E35A901.00E014996412.01
   91  34484839         0  forward    47.00918100000000E01E35A901.00E014996412.01
  198  13033702  11492132  data       47.00918100000000E01E35A901.00E0FE1400C0.01
```

Section 4-6

Further Reading

Refer to the following recommended sources for further information about the topics covered in this chapter.

Ethernet

Charles Spurgeon's Ethernet Web Site at: wwwhost.ots.utexas.edu/ethernet/

Ethernet: The Definitive Guide by Charles Spurgeon, O'Reilly and Associates, ISBN 1-56592-660-9

Fast Ethernet

Cisco Fast Ethernet 100-Mbps Solutions at: www.cisco.com/warp/public/cc/so/neso/lnso/lnmnso/feth_tc.htm

Gigabit Ethernet

The Gigabit Ethernet Alliance at: www.gigabit-ethernet.org

The 10 Gigabit Ethernet Alliance at: www.10gea.org/index.htm

IEEE 802.3ae Standard at: http://grouper.ieee.org/groups/802/3/ae/index.html

EtherChannel

Understanding and Configuring FastEtherChannel on Cisco Switching and Routing Devices at: www.cisco.com/warp/public/473/4.html

Understanding and Designing Networks with FastEtherChannel at: www.cisco.com/warp/public/cc/techno/media/lan/ether/channel/prodlit/faste_an.htm

LACP—Link Aggregation Task Force at: http://grouper.ieee.org/groups/802/3/ad/

Token Ring

Token Ring / IEEE802.5 at: www.cisco.com/univercd/cc/td/doc/cisintwk/ito_doc/tokenrng.htm

ATM LANE

Cisco ATM Solutions by Galina Diker Pildush, Cisco Press, ISBN 1-57870-213-5

The ATM Forum at: www.atmforum.com

CHAPTER 5

Layer 3 Interface Configuration

See the following sections for configuration information about these topics:

- **5-1: Layer 3 Switching**—Describes the process involved with Layer 3 switching and the switching elements needed to perform Layer 3 switching.

- **5-2: Layer 3 Ethernet Interfaces**—Explains the steps needed to configure Ethernet interfaces for Layer 3 processing.

- **5-3: Layer 3 EtherChannels**—Covers the method for configuring multiple interfaces into a single logical channel that can be configured for Layer 3 processing.

- **5-4: WAN Interfaces**—Describes how to configure Layer 3 WAN interfaces installed in Catalyst 5500 or Catalyst 6500 switches.

- **5-5: Layer 3 Virtual Interfaces**—Explains how to configure a logical VLAN or BVI to perform Layer 3 processing for members of a VLAN or bridge group.

- **5-6: Routing Tables**—Explains the basic process for populating and viewing the Layer 3 routing tables.

5-1: Layer 3 Switching

- Layer 3 switching is the movement of data between devices using tables or pathways containing Layer 3 network addressing.

- To perform Layer 3 switching, the device must have a Layer 3 switching processor that can be a separate module or card.

- A Layer 3 switching processor will use Layer 3 IOS to configure the Layer 3 switching components.

- To allow Layer 3 switching, the switch must have the routing function enabled for a given protocol.

- To provide connectivity between the different networks, the switch must have knowledge of available pathways for these networks.

Configuration

To perform Layer 3 switching on a device, you must have a switching processor that makes decisions based on Layer 3 protocol addressing. This engine will run Cisco IOS and the configuration task will be performed in configuration mode of IOS only. This switching processor can be in the form of a *route switch module* (RSM), *route switch feature card* (RSFC), *multilayer switch module* (MSM), *multilayer switch feature card* (MSFC), Layer 3 services module, or integrated into the hardware in the switch like that of the 3550 or 2948G-L3.

1   Access the Layer 3 switching processor.

If the switching processor is a card that runs as a subsystem in a COS device, you need to access this device to perform any configuration. To access the device, use the **session** command. This command is not required for a switch running Supervisor IOS, because you are communicating directly with the Layer 3 switch processor. If you are using a COS switch, you access the switch processor as follows:

COS	(privileged)**session** *mod*

The *mod* number specifies the module number of the switch processor. Use the command **show modules** to locate this processor if you do not know where it is located in the switch.

NOTE	For an MSFC or RSFC on a Supervisor in slot 1, the module number is always 15. For an MSFC or RSFC on a Supervisor in slot 2, the module number is always 16.

2   Enable the routing process.

In addition to having the processor, it must be configured to perform the switching process. This is accomplished by going to global configuration mode and enabling the routing process for the protocol in question:

IOS	(global) *protocol* **routing**

This command enables the routing process. The *protocol* option specifies the protocol you want to enable. Some examples are **appletalk**, **ip**, and **ipx**. The default for all protocols except IP is that routing is disabled, so this command would not be required for IP packets to be switched by the Layer 3 engine.

If you have configured your switch to perform *integrated routing and bridging* (IRB), you will also have to enable the routing process for any bridge group that needs access outside of their broadcast domain. Use the following command to enable Layer 3 switching for the bridge groups:

IOS	(global) **bridge** *groupnumber* **route** *protocol*

This command allows all the members of the bridge group, specified by the *groupnumber* option, to use a virtual interface to communicate through Layer 3 switching. The *protocol* option specifies which protocols will be Layer 3 switched.

NOTE   If you specify this command for a specific protocol on a bridge group, but do not assign the virtual interface a protocol address, the bridging function will be disabled for that protocol.

5-2: Layer 3 Ethernet Interfaces

- Layer 3 switching requires an interface on the switch that can forward packets based on Layer 3 addressing.

- Each Layer 3 interface defines a separate broadcast domain and therefore a separate network.

- After a Layer 3 interface has been configured with a protocol, it can act as a gateway for other devices in the same broadcast domain.

- On some switches, you can configure an Ethernet port (interface) as a Layer 3 interface.

Configuration

A Layer 3 interface is a direct routed interface that is designed to provide Layer 3 processing of packets entering and exiting the interface. Not every physical interface on every switch is designed to be a Layer 3 interface; however, on some switches, each port is, or can be, configured to be a direct routed port. To configure these interfaces for Layer 3 processing, use the following steps.

1 Select the physical Layer 3 interface:

IOS	(global) **interface** *type mod/port*

Section 5-2

Access global configuration mode and use this command to specify the interface and move to interface configuration mode in the device. You must specify the type of interfaces: **ethernet**, **fastethernet**, **gigabitethernet**, or **tengigabitethernet**. The *mod/port* specifies the module and port number of the interface. Fixed-configuration switches, such as the 2948G-L3, have no module option; and for the 3550 switches, the module (or slot) is always **0**.

2 Configure the interface for Layer 3 operation:

IOS	(interface)`no switchport`

For multilayer IOS switches, such as the 4000 or 6000 running Supervisor IOS or such as the 3550, ports can be configured to act as Layer 2 (switchport) ports or Layer 3 (routed) ports. To configure a port to act as a Layer 3 port, use the **no switchport** command to disable Layer 2 operation and enable Layer 3 operation.

NOTE　When the **switchport** or **no switchport** command is issued, the port will be disabled then reenabled.

NOTE　The default port operation for the 4000 and 6000 series switches running Supervisor IOS is routed mode; the 3550 defaults to switchport mode.

3 Configure protocol information.

a. Assign an IP address:

IOS	(interface) `ip address` *address netmask*

When an interface begins acting as a Layer 3 interface, you must configure it with information about the network connected to the broadcast domain. For IP networks, this means the interface must be given an IP address. This address becomes the gateway address used by clients in the broadcast domain to which the interface is connected.

NOTE
Although all Layer 3 switch-routed interfaces support IP, not all of them support other protocols. For example, the 3550 and 4000 running Supervisor IOS support only the configuration of IP on a physical interface. Check your device notes for more details.

b. Assign the IPX network number:

IOS	(interface) **ipx network** *networknumber*

To enable the IPX process on an interface, you must specify the network number with the *networknumber* option. Contact the NetWare administrator for the proper network number and encapsulation type.

c. Assign an AppleTalk cable range and zone:

IOS	(interface) **appletalk cable-range** *beginrange-endrange*
	(interface) **appletalk zone** *zonename*

To enable AppleTalk, you must specify the cable range using the *beginrange-endrange* option to specify the range numbers and configure at least one zone using the command **appletalk zone**.

NOTE
The information presented here for configuring protocol information on a Layer 3 interface is the minimal requirements. You can find more detailed information concerning protocol configuration in *Cisco Field Manual: Router Configuration*, published by Cisco Press.

4 Enable the interface:

IOS	(interface) **no shutdown**

The default status of many Layer 3 interfaces is **shutdown**, which is a disabled state. To ensure that the interface is operational, enable the interface with the command **no shutdown**.

Verifying the Configuration

After you have configured a protocol on an interface, use the following command to verify the configuration:

IOS	(privileged) **show** *protocol* **interface** *type mod/port*

The protocol option is **ip**, **ipx**, **appletalk**, or other configured interface.

Feature Example

The following example shows the configuration of interface Gigabit Ethernet 1/1 on Distribution_Switch_A for Layer 3 processing. This interface acts as the gateway for all the clients connected to Access_Switch_A. Figure 5-1 shows the network topology for this example.

Figure 5-1 *Network Topology for Layer 3 Interface Configuration*

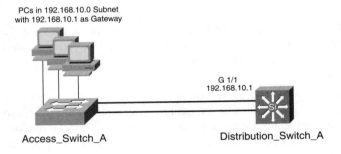

PCs in 192.168.10.0 Subnet
with 192.168.10.1 as Gateway

G 1/1
192.168.10.1

Access_Switch_A

Distribution_Switch_A

An example of the configuration for Distribution_Switch_A follows:

```
Distribution_Switch_A(config)#interface gigabitethernet 1/1
Distribution_Switch_A (config-if)#no switchport
Distribution_Switch_A (config-if)#ip address 192.168.10.1 255.255.255.0
Distribution_Switch_A (config-if)#no shut
Distribution_Switch_A (config-if)#end
Distribution_Switch_A #copy running-config startup-config
```

5-3: Layer 3 EtherChannels

- An *EtherChannel* is the aggregation of multiple physical channels into a single logical connection.

- The single logical connection is referred to as a *port channel*.

- You can configure the port channel to operate as a Layer 3 interface on some switches.

- When assigned with an IP address, the port channel becomes the logical Layer 3 interface.

- If any single link of the channel fails, the port channel interface is still accessible through the other links.

- Layer 3 EtherChannel operation is the same as Layer 2 EtherChannels for traffic distribution and channel establishment.

Configuration

An EtherChannel offers the capability to bond multiple physical connections for greater throughput for links that carry traffic for multiple hosts. Because EtherChannel operates at an almost physical layer, multiple Layer 3 interfaces can be bonded into a single channel. After the channel has been formed, a virtual interface known as a *port channel* interface will act as the Layer 3 conduit for all the members of the channel. To configure a Layer 3 EtherChannel, use the following steps.

1 Access the Layer 3 switching processor (see Note).

   If the switching processor is a card that runs as a subsystem in a COS device, you need to access this device to perform any configuration. To access the device, use the **session** command. This command is not required for a switch running Supervisor IOS because you are communicating directly with the Layer 3 switch processor if you are running this software:

COS	(privileged)**session** *mod*

   The *mod* number specifies the module number of the switch processor. Use the command **show modules** to locate this processor if you do not know where it is located in the switch.

NOTE   You have to access the Layer 3 switching processor only when creating a channel to the backplane on the Layer 3 services module. All the other Layer 3 interfaces would be configured directly using the IOS Software.

---

2 Create a logical port channel:

IOS	(global) **interface port-channel** *number*

In global configuration mode, use this command to create the logical port channel interface. This acts as the Layer 3 interface for all the members of the channel. The *number* option specifies the channel group number with which each channel member will be configured.

3 Configure protocol information on the port channel:

IOS	(interface) **ip address** *address netmask*

Use the appropriate command to configure the Layer 3 interface with network addressing. The example here shows configuration of an IP address. Refer to Step 3 the of section "5-2: Layer 3 Ethernet Interfaces" for other protocol options.

CAUTION   If you are creating a channel that will use an address that is currently configured on the interface, you must first remove that address before assigning it to the port channel interface. Step 4b describes how to remove a protocol address.

---

4 Assign physical Layer 3 interfaces to the channel group.

a. Select an interface:

IOS	(global) **interface** *type mod/port*

Select a Layer 3 interface to assign to the channel group. Because you are creating a Layer 3 channel, the interface must be a Layer 3 interface. For switches that allow an interface to act as a Layer 2 or Layer 3 interface, issue the command **no switchport** to ensure the interface operates at Layer 3.

b. Remove any protocol addressing:

IOS	(interface) **no ip address**

If the interface has been configured with any protocol addressing, such as IP, you must remove the protocol address with the **no** form of the command that established the addressing—for example, the **no ip address** command would remove an IP address from the interface.

c. Assign the interface to the channel group:

IOS	(interface) **channel-group** *number* **mode {auto | desirable | on}**

For a physical Layer 3 interface that you want to be part of the channel, you will specify the **channel-group** command. The *number* option specifies with which port channel interface the physical interface is associated. The modes specify how the channel
communicates to the other side of the link. (Refer to the section "4-4: EtherChannel"
for more details on the channel modes.)

d. Verify that the interface is enabled:

IOS	(interface) **no shutdown**

The default status of many Layer 3 interfaces is **shutdown**, which is a disabled state.
To ensure that the interface is operational, you should enable the interface with the
command **no shutdown**.

e. Repeat Steps 4a through 4d for each same-speed interface that will be a member of
the channel.

Verifying the Channel

After you have configured a channel, you can verify the operation with the following
command(s):

IOS	(privileged) **show etherchannel** *number* **port-channel**
	(privileged) **show interfaces** *type number* **etherchannel**

When using the **show etherchannel** command, the *number* option specifies the port
channel or channel group number of the channel you want to view. The **show interfaces**
command enables you to specify individual members of the channel and view the
EtherChannel parameters for those interfaces.

Feature Example

The following example shows the configuration of interfaces Gigabit Ethernet 1/1 and
Gigabit Ethernet 2/1 on Distribution_Switch_A as a Layer 3 channel. This interface acts
as the gateway for all the clients connected to Access_Switch_A. Figure 5-2 shows the
network topology for this configuration example.

Figure 5-2   *Network Topology for Layer 3 Channel Configuration Example*

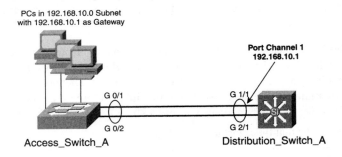

An example of the configuration for Distribution_Switch_A follows:

```
Distribution_Switch_A(config)#interface port-channel 1
Distribution_Switch_A (config-if)#ip address 192.168.10.1 255.255.255.0
Distribution_Switch_A (config-if)#interface gigabitethernet 1/1
Distribution_Switch_A (config-if)#no switchport
Distribution_Switch_A (config-if)#no ip address
Distribution_Switch_A (config-if)#channel-group 1 mode on
Distribution_Switch_A (config-if)#no shut
Distribution_Switch_A(config-if)#interface gigabitethernet 2/1
Distribution_Switch_A (config-if)#no switchport
Distribution_Switch_A (config-if)#no ip address
Distribution_Switch_A (config-if)#channel-group 1 mode on
Distribution_Switch_A (config-if)#no shut
Distribution_Switch_A (config-if)#end
Distribution_Switch_A #copy running-config startup-config
```

An example of the configuration for Access_Switch_A (a 3500XL) follows:

```
Access_Switch_A (config)#interface gigabitethernet 0/1
Access_Switch_A (config-if)#port group 1
Access_Switch_A (config)#interface gigabitethernet 0/2
Access_Switch_A (config-if)#port group 1
Access_Switch_A (config-if)#end
Access_Switch_A #copy running-config startup-config
```

5-4: WAN Interfaces

- The Catalyst 5000 and 6000 series switches offer support for WAN interfaces to be added to the switch chassis.

- WAN interfaces are only known to the Layer 3 switching processor and must be configured from an IOS interface.

- The 5000 series switch allows for the addition of a RSM/VIP2 card, which can provide support for a variety of *port adapter modules* (PAMs) for WAN connectivity.

- The 6000 series switch supports a FlexWAN card, which provides support for a variety of WAN PAMs for WAN connectivity.
- In addition to the FlexWAN card, the 6000 series switch offers a variety of optical services modules, which can be connected to high-speed optical networks.

Configuration

WAN interfaces enable users to connect to remote services from the Catalyst switch chassis. These interfaces typically operate as Layer 3 interfaces and require some type of Layer 3 switching processor, such as an RSM or MSCF, to provide access and connectivity to the cards. The interfaces are accessible only in Cisco IOS Software, so they can only be configured from the Layer 3 switch processor or the switch must be running the Supervisor IOS.

NOTE   This section offers an abbreviated look at configuring some basic parameters for Layer 3 switching using these interfaces. For a more detailed look at these interfaces and WAN connectivity, see the "Further Reading" section at the end of this chapter.

Each of the following sections details the steps to configure the different WAN interfaces for basic network connectivity.

Configuring VIP2 WAN Interfaces

A VIP2 interface is a component that allows for PAMs to be installed into a subsystem of the route switch module. The VIP2 is a component of the RSM/VIP2 combination card. This card takes up two slots in the chassis of the Catalyst 5000 series switch. As a part of the RSM, it allows for the installation of a variety of Layer 3 interfaces into the switch, including WAN interfaces. The following steps show how to configure the WAN interfaces for a VIP2 PAM.

1 Access the RSM.

To access the RSM, use the **session** command. You will configure the WAN interfaces from the RSM:

COS   (privileged)**session** *mod*

The *mod* number specifies the module number of the switch processor. Use the command **show modules** to locate the RSM if you do not know where it is located in the switch.

2 Configure the WAN interface:

IOS	(global) **interface** *type bay/number*

In global configuration mode, use this command to create and access a WAN interface. The option *type* specifies the type of WAN interface. The *bay* indicates in which location in the VIP the WAN PAM is placed. The bays are numbered 0 and 1 from left to right. The *number* specifies the port number in a given bay.

NOTE   The VIP2 processor supports several different PAMs. Go to www.cisco.com/univercd /cc/td/doc/product/lan/cat5000/cnfg_nts/rsm/rsm_pa/index.htm for a complete listing of Layer 3 modules supported by this component.

3 Assign a protocol address to the interface:

IOS	(interface) **ip address** *address netmask*

Use the appropriate command to configure the Layer 3 interface with network addressing. The example here shows configuration of an IP address. See Step 3 of the section "5-2: Layer 3 Ethernet Interfaces" for other protocol options.

4 Enable the interface:

IOS	(interface) **no shutdown**

The default status of many Layer 3 interfaces is **shutdown**, which is a disabled state. To ensure that the interface is operational, you should enable the interface with the command **no shutdown**.

Configuring a FlexWAN Interface

The FlexWAN card for the 6000 series is similar to the VIP2 card for the 5000 series. This module allows for the installation of a limited number of WAN PAMs to be used by the Layer 3 switching processor for WAN connectivity. The major difference is that the Flex-WAN card is not coupled with any other card (such as an RSM) and attaches directly to the backplane of the switch. However, the FlexWAN does require that an MSFC be installed into the switch before it will operate. The following steps describe the process for configuring the FlexWAN ports.

1 Access the Layer 3 switching processor (for hybrid mode).

If the switching processor is a card that runs as a subsystem in a COS device, you need to access this device to perform any configuration. To access the device, use the **session** command. This command is not required for a switch running Supervisor IOS because you are communicating directly with the Layer 3 switch processor if you are running this software:

COS	(privileged)**session** *mod*

The *mod* number specifies the module number of the switch processor. Use the command **show modules** to locate this processor if you do not know where it is located in the switch.

NOTE If the switch chassis contains two active MSFCs, the FlexWAN ports are available only to the MSFC in slot 15, or the active router if you are using configuration synchronization. If the active router or MSFC 15 fails, you must manually configure the ports on the remaining router before they will become operational again.

---

2 Configure the WAN interface:

IOS	(global) **interface** *type slot/bay/number*

In global configuration mode, use this command to access the WAN interface. The *type* option specifies the type of WAN interface (for example, **serial**, **hssi**, or **atm**). The *slot* indicates the slot in the switch chassis, the *bay* is the bay number on the FlexWAN card (bays are numbered 0 to 1 from left to right), and interface *number* on the PAM (interface numbers start at 0).

NOTE You can use only a select number of PAMs with a FlexWAN module. See www.cisco.com/univercd/cc/td/doc/product/lan/cat6000/cfgnotes/flexwan/flex_pa/index.htm for a complete list of support adapters.

---

3 Assign a protocol address to the interface:

IOS	(interface) **ip address** *address netmask*

Section 5-4

Use the appropriate command to configure the Layer 3 interface with network addressing. The example here shows configuration of an IP address. See Step 3 of the section "5-2: Layer 3 Ethernet Interfaces" for other protocol options.

4 Enable the interface:

IOS	(interface) **no shutdown**

The default status of many Layer 3 interfaces is **shutdown**, which is a disabled state. To ensure that the interface is operational, enable the interface with the command **no shutdown**.

Configuring a Gigabit Ethernet WAN Interface

The Gigabit Ethernet WAN OSM is a four-port gigabit module that you can use to connect to *metropolitan area networks* (MANs) for Gigabit WAN services. The card requires a 6500 series switch with a Supervisor 2 and MSFC2. Each port on this blade acts as a Layer 3 port and can be configured with an IP address only, along with a variety of traffic-control features. To provide basic configuration for these interfaces, use the following steps:

1 Access the Layer 3 switching processor (for hybrid mode).

If the switching processor is a card that runs as a subsystem in a COS device, you need to access this device to perform any configuration. To access the device, use the **session** command. This command is not required for a switch running Supervisor IOS, because you are communicating directly with the Layer 3 switch processor:

COS	(privileged)**session** *mod*

The *mod* number specifies the module number of the switch processor. Use the command **show modules** to locate this processor if you do not know where it is located in the switch.

2 Access the interface:

IOS	(global) **interface ge-wan** *slot/number*

In global configuration mode, use this command to access the interface. The *type* will be a **ge-wan**, the *slot* will be the chassis slot, and the *number* will be the port number.

3 Assign an IP address:

IOS	(interface) **ip address** *address netmask*

Use this command to enable IP processing for the port. The Gigabit Ethernet WAN ports support only IP processing.

4 Enable the interface:

IOS	(interface) **no shutdown**

The default status of many Layer 3 interfaces is **shutdown**, which is a disabled state. To ensure that the interface is operational, you should enable the interface with the command **no shutdown**.

Configuring a Packet-over-SONET Interface

The *packet-over-SONET* (POS) interfaces offer another method for connecting the 6500 series switches to high-speed metropolitan area networks. In addition to a 1-, 4-, or 16-port POS interface, these cards also offer 4 Gigabit Ethernet cards for connectivity to the core network. This card requires a 6500 series switch with a Supervisor 2 and MSFC2. Use the following steps to provide basic configuration for POS interfaces.

1 Access the Layer 3 switching processor (for hybrid mode).

If the switching processor is a card that runs as a subsystem in a COS device, you need to access this device to perform any configuration. To access the device, use the **session** command. This command is not required for a switch running Supervisor IOS, because you are communicating directly with the Layer 3 switch processor:

COS	(privileged)**session** *mod*

The *mod* number specifies the module number of the switch processor. Use the command **show modules** to locate this processor if you do not know where it is located in the switch.

2 Access the POS interface:

IOS	(global) **interface pos** *slot/port*

In global configuration mode, use this command to access the POS interface. The *slot* option designates the slot in the switch chassis, and the *port* option indicates which POS port you are configuring.

3 Specify an encapsulation:

IOS	(interface) **encapsulation {hdlc	ppp}**

You need to ensure that the Layer 2 encapsulation between the devices is compatible. *high-level data link control* (HDLC) is typically used if attaching to another Cisco device; if not, use PPP.

4 *(Optional)* Specify an clocking:

IOS	(interface) **clock source {line	internal}**

If you are connecting two switches back-to-back using dark fiber, you need to configure one of the switches with the option **clock source internal**; otherwise, the default is **line**.

5 Assign an IP address to the interface:

IOS	(interface) **ip address** *address netmask*

Use this command to enable IP processing for the port.

6 Enable the interface:

IOS	(interface) **no shutdown**

The default status of many Layer 3 interfaces is **shutdown**, which is a disabled state. To ensure that the interface is operational, enable the interface with the command **no shutdown**.

Verifying Configurations

After you have configured your WAN interfaces, use the following command to verify configuration:

IOS	(privileged) **show interface** *type number*

Feature Example

This configuration shows an example of a 5500 (Core_switch_1) using a VIP2 with a serial interface connecting to a 6500 (Core_switch_2) using a FlexWAN interface across a Frame Relay network. The *data-link connection identifier* (DLCI) number for the 5500 is 110, and the DLCI for the 6500 is 120. In this example, the 6500 is running Supervisor IOS. Figure 5-3 shows the network topology associated with this configuration example.

Figure 5-3   *Network Topology for WAN Interface Configuration Example*

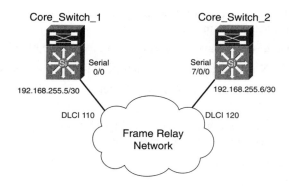

An example of the Core_switch_1 configuration follows:

```
Core_switch_1> (enable)session 4
Core_switch_RSM>enable
Core_switch_RSM#config t
Core_switch_RSM(config)#interface serial 0/0
Core_switch_RSM(config-if)#encapsulation frame-relay
Core_switch_RSM(config)#interface serial 0/0.110
Core_switch_RSM(config-if)#frame-relay interface-dlci 110
Core_switch_RSM(config-if)#ip address 192.168.255.5 255.255.255.252
Core_switch_RSM(config-if)#no shutdown
Core_switch_RSM(config-if)#end
Core_switch_RSM#copy running-config startup-config
Core_switch_RSM#quit
Core_switch_1> (enable)
```

An example of the Core_switch_2 configuration running Supervisor IOS follows:

```
Core_switch_2>enable
Core_switch_2#config t
Core_switch_2(config)#interface serial 7/0/0
Core_switch_2(config-if)#encapsulation frame-relay
Core_switch_2(config)#interface serial 7/0/0.120
Core_switch_2(config-if)#frame-relay interface-dlci 120
Core_switch_2(config-if)#ip address 192.168.255.6 255.255.255.252
Core_switch_2(config-if)#no shutdown
Core_switch_2(config-if)#end
Core_switch_2#copy running-config startup-config
```

NOTE   Although this configuration shows a 6500 using IOS to configure the FlexWAN, FlexWAN can be configured using the MSFC IOS in hybrid mode.

5-5: Virtual Interfaces

- Virtual interfaces exist for configuration where there is no single physical attachment to a broadcast domain.

- For switches with Layer 2 interfaces, VLANs define broadcast domains.

- The VLAN interface is a Layer 3 interface for any member of the given VLAN.

- For switches or routers with Layer 3 interfaces, broadcast domains are defined as bridge groups.

- To route between bridge groups and other broadcast domains, a *bridged virtual interface* (BVI) is used as a Layer 3 interface.

- In some instances, a physical Layer 3 interface can support traffic from multiple VLANs.

- To provide Layer 3 interfaces for each VLAN on the physical connection, a subinterface is configured as the Layer 3 interface for the members of the VLAN.

Configuring a VLAN Interface

1 Access the Layer 3 switching processor (for hybrid mode).

If the switching processor is a card that runs as a subsystem in a COS device, you need to access this device to perform any configuration. To access the device, use the **session** command. This command is not required for a switch running Supervisor IOS because you are communicating directly with the Layer 3 switch processor:

COS	(privileged)**session** *mod*

The *mod* number specifies the module number of the switch processor. Use the command **show modules** to locate this processor if you do not know where it is located in the switch.

2 Configure a VLAN interface:

IOS	(global) **interface vlan** *number*

In global configuration mode, use this command to create and access a VLAN interface. This interface will be in the same broadcast domain as the members of the VLAN number. For this interface to be active, it must first exist in the VLAN database of the switch (see the section "6-1: VLAN Configuration").

NOTE The VLAN interface on a Layer 2 switch, such as a 2900/3500XL or a 2950, does not do Layer 3 switching and will not function as described in this section. The Layer 2 IOS VLAN interface is an administrative interface only.

3 Assign a protocol address to the interface:

IOS	(interface) **ip address** *address netmask*

Use the appropriate command to configure the Layer 3 interface with network addressing. The example here shows configuration of an IP address. See Step 3 of the section "5-2: Layer 3 Ethernet Interfaces" for other protocol options.

4 Enable the interface:

IOS	(interface) **no shutdown**

The default status of many Layer 3 interfaces is **shutdown**, which is a disabled state. To ensure that the interface is operational, you should enable the interface with the command **no shutdown**.

Configuring a Bridged Virtual Interface

1 Access the Layer 3 switching processor (for hybrid mode).

If the switching processor is a card that runs as a subsystem in a COS device, you need to access this device to perform any configuration. To access the device, use the **session** command. This command is not required for a switch running Supervisor IOS because you are communicating directly with the Layer 3 switch processor:

COS	(privileged)**session** *mod*

The *mod* number specifies the module number of the switch processor. Use the command **show modules** to locate this processor if you do not know where it is located in the switch.

NOTE Although you can configure a BVI using bridge groups for virtual interfaces on an RSM or RSFC, this is usually only configured when you have a need to provide Layer 2 communications between devices in separate VLANs.

Section 5-5

NOTE   Bridge groups and BVIs are not supported on interfaces that can be either Layer 2 or Layer 3 using the **switchport** command.

   2 Configure a bridge group:

IOS	(global) **bridge** *number* **protocol ieee**

To configure a BVI, you must first establish the bridge group for which you will be using the BVI to route. This command configures a bridge group running the IEEE protocol. The *number* here is used to associate ports with the group.

   3 Enable *integrated routing and bridging* (IRB):

IOS	(global) **bridge irb**

Because the ports in the bridge group will be both routed and bridged, you must enable the IRB process.

   4 Enable routing for the bridge group:

IOS	(global) **bridge** *number* **route** [**ip** | **ipx** | **appletalk**]

By default, when you enable IRB, ports that are members of a bridge group will not attempt to route the packets because they are now considered bridged ports. If you are going to configure a Layer 3 interface to be used by these bridge ports, you must specify that the bridge group can now route. The *number* parameter specifies which bridged ports you are routing for, and the *protocol* specifies which Layer 3 protocol(s) you will be routing.

   5 Assign interfaces to the bridge group:

IOS	(interface) **bridge-group** *number*

You must assign each interface that will be in the same broadcast domain to the bridge group. The clients off of this interface will be in the same IP subnet and will use the BVI as the Layer 3 interface or gateway out of the subnet. The *number* option will correspond to the bridge number in Steps 2 and 4.

   6 Configure the BVI interface:

IOS	(global) **interface BVI** *number*

In global configuration mode, use this command to create and access a BVI interface. This interface will be in the same broadcast domain as the members of the bridge group number. The *number* option specifies to which bridge group the interface belongs.

7 Assign a protocol address to the interface:

IOS	(interface) **ip address** *address netmask*

Use the appropriate command to configure the Layer 3 interface with network addressing. The example here shows configuration of an IP address. See Step 3 of the section "5-2: Layer 3 Ethernet Interfaces" for other protocol options.

8 Enable the interface:

IOS	(interface) **no shutdown**

The default status of many Layer 3 interfaces is **shutdown**, which is a disabled state. To ensure that the interface is operational, enable the interface with the command **no shutdown**.

Configuring Subinterfaces

1 Create and access the subinterfaces:

IOS	(global) **interface** *type number.subnumber*

In global configuration mode, use this command to create and access a subinterface. The *type* will be the controller type of the interface (for example, **fastethernet** or **gigabitethernet**). The *type* could also be **port-channel** for a channeled connection. The *number* specifies the location or logical number of the interface, and the *.subnumber* creates a logical Layer 3 subinterface off the main connection.

2 Specify an encapsulation and VLAN:

IOS	(sub-interface) **encapsulation** {**dot1q**	**isl**} *vlannumber* [**native**]

In subinterface mode, you will specify which VLAN is associated with a given subinterface using the encapsulation command. The type (**dot1q** or **isl**) depends on the type of trunk connected to the router interface. The *vlannumber* option specifies which VLAN is associated with the subinterface—that is, in which broadcast domain this subinterface will act as a Layer 3 interface.

Section 5-5

For dot1q trunks only, the option **native** specifies which one of the VLANs will be the native VLAN. This is important because native VLAN packets are not tagged as per the 802.1Q specification.

NOTE	Subinterfaces are used in configurations for routers or interfaces connected to a trunk link. Layer 3 interfaces do not run the *Dynamic Trunking Protocol* (DTP), and any switch connected to these interfaces must be configured in trunk on mode.

NOTE	Layer 3 interfaces on the Catalyst 4000 series and 6000 series running Supervisor IOS and 3550 switches do not support subinterfaces. Instead, use a trunk port and VLAN interfaces described in this section.

3 Assign a protocol address to the subinterface:

IOS	`(sub-interface) `**`ip address`**` address netmask`

Use the appropriate command to configure the Layer 3 subinterface with network addressing. The example here shows configuration of an IP address. See Step 3 of the section "5-2: Layer 3 Ethernet Interfaces" for other protocol options.

4 Enable the interface:

IOS	`(interface) `**`no shutdown`**

The default status of many Layer 3 interfaces is **shutdown**, which is a disabled state. To ensure that the interface is operational, enable the interface with the command **no shutdown**.

TIP	The Catalyst 4000 Layer 3 switch engine connects to the Layer 2 switch through 2 internal gigabit interfaces. These interfaces (Gigabit Ethernet 3 and Gigabit Ethernet 4) are each Layer 3 interfaces that can be configured individually (if you are only routing for one or two VLANs) or they can be configured with subinterfaces as described in this section. Another option is to channel these interfaces together and trunk across the channel, creating subinterfaces for the port channel.

Verifying Configurations

After configuring your subinterfaces, use the following commands to verify configuration:

IOS	(privileged) **show interface** *type number.subnumber*
	(privileged) **show vlan** [*number*]

Feature Example

This example shows the configuration of a 2948G-L3 connected to a 3550 through an 802.1Q trunk link between ports G49 on the 2948G-L3 and G0/1 on the 3550. A virtual interface for VLAN 10 has been configured on both switches. Figure 5-4 shows the network topology for this example.

Figure 5-4   *Network Topology for Virtual Interface Configuration Example*

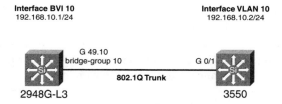

An example of the 2948G-L3 configuration follows:

```
2948G-L3 (config)#bridge 10 protocol ieee
2948G-L3 (config)#bridge irb
2948G-L3 (config)#bridge 10 route ip
2948G-L3 (config)#interface gigabitethernet 49.10
2948G-L3 (config-subif)#encapsulation dot1q 10
2948G-L3 (config-subif)#bridge-group 10
2948G-L3 (config-subif)#no shutdown
2948G-L3 (config-subif)#interface BVI 10
2948G-L3 (config-if)#ip address 192.168.10.1 255.255.255.0
2948G-L3 (config-if)#no shutdown
2948G-L3 (config-if)#end
2948G-L3 #copy running-config startup-config
```

```
3550 #vlan database
3550 (vlan)#vlan 10
3550 (vlan)#exit
3550 #config t
3550 (config)#interface gigabitethernet 0/1
3550 (config-if)#switchport mode trunk
3550 (config-if)#switchport mode on
3550 (config-if)#switchport trunk encapsulation dot1q
3550 (config-if)#interface vlan 10
3550 (config-if)#ip address 192.168.10.2 255.255.255.0
3550 (config-if)#no shutdown
3550 (config-if)#end
3550 #copy running-config startup-config
```

Section 5-5

5-6: Routing Tables

- To move packets between separate networks, the switching processor must have knowledge of the destination network.
- Networks that are connected to a physical or virtual interface are connected routes and are automatically known by the switching processor.
- You can configure the Layer 3 switching processor with statically defined routes by entering the routes into the configuration file.
- One of the most common ways to learn and maintain routes is to use a dynamic routing protocol, such as *Open Shortest Path First* (OSPF) *Protocol* or *Enhanced Interior Gateway Routing Protocol* (EIGRP).

Configuration

1 Access the Layer 3 switching processor.

If the switching processor is a card that runs as a subsystem in a COS device, you need to access this device to perform any configuration. To access the device, use the **session** command. This command is not required for a switch running Supervisor IOS because you are communicating directly with the Layer 3 switch processor:

COS	(privileged)**session** *mod*

The *mod* number specifies the module number of the switch processor. Use the command **show modules** to locate this processor if you do not know where it is located in the switch.

2 Establish connected routes:

IOS	(interface) **ip address** *address mask*

By specifying a network address on an interface, you have also established an entry for that network in the routing table. This step shows the configuration for an IP address, but the same would hold true for other protocols (as shown in the section "5-2: Layer 3 Ethernet Interfaces").

3 Establish static routes:

IOS	(global) **ip route** *network netmask {nexthop	interface} [admin-distance]*

This command specifies a static route for the network using the mask specified. The *nexthop* address or *interface* shows how to get to the network configured.

4 Enable dynamic routes:

IOS	(global) **router** *protocol*
	(router)**network** *network*

The **router** command along with a protocol such as *Routing Information Protocol* (RIP), OSPF, or EIGRP places you in router configuration mode. In this mode, you specify the networks for which you want to run the protocol.

NOTE   This section is an abbreviated look at establishing and maintaining routes. It is intended as a reminder and not as a comprehensive configuration of routing protocols. A Layer 3 switch works exactly like a router for maintaining routes. Refer to *Cisco Field Manual: Router Configuration* by Cisco Press for more detailed configuration information. For more general information on routing and routing technologies, see the "Further Reading" section at the end of the chapter.

Verifying Routes

After you have configured a port for trunking, use one of the following commands to verify the VLAN port assignments:

IOS	(privileged) **show** *protocol* **route**

The *protocol* option enables you to look at the routing table for a given protocol, such as IP, IPX, or AppleTalk.

Further Reading

Refer to the following recommended sources for further information about the topics covered in this chapter.

Layer 3 Switching (Routing) and Routing Updates

Interconnections: Bridges, Routers, Switches, and Internetworking Protocols, Second Edition, by Radia Perlman, Addison-Wesley, ISBN 0-20163-448-1

Interconnecting Cisco Network Devices, edited by Steve McQuerry, Cisco Press, ISBN 1-57870-111-2

Routing TCP/IP, Volume I, by Jeff Doyle, Cisco Press, ISBN 1-57870-041-8

Section 5-6

Routing TCP/IP, Volume II, by Jeff Doyle and Jennifer DeHaven Carroll, Cisco Press, ISBN 1-57870-089-2

Cisco Field Manual: Router Configuration by David Hucaby and Steve McQuerry, Cisco Press, ISBN 1-58705-024-2

WAN Interfaces

Route Switch Module Catalyst VIP2-15 and VIP2-40 Installation and Configuration Note at:
www.cisco.com/univercd/cc/td/doc/product/lan/cat5000/cnfg_nts/rsm/4780vip2.htm

Catalyst 6000 Family FlexWAN Module and Port Adapter Documentation at:
www.cisco.com/univercd/cc/td/doc/product/lan/cat6000/cfgnotes/flexwan/index.htm

Optical Services Modules Installation and Configuration Note at: www.cisco.com/univercd/cc/td/doc/product/core/cis7600/cfgnotes/osm_inst/index.htm

CHAPTER 6

VLANs and Trunking

See the following sections for configuration information about these topics:

- **6-1: VLAN Configuration**—Describes the method for configuring, creating, and configuring VLANs on a switch.

- **6-2: VLAN Port Membership**—Explains how to assign a port to a VLAN using static or dynamic methods.

- **6-3: Trunking**—Covers the method for extending a VLAN beyond the boundaries of a single switch through tagging mechanisms.

- **6-4: VLAN Trunking Protocol**—Describes the Cisco proprietary protocol for maintaining a forwarding path between switches that are trunking and how to prune for unused VLANs.

- **6-5: GVRP**—Explains the industry standard process management of traffic across trunk links and how to maintain VLANs on switches for forwarding purposes.

- **6-6: Private VLANs**—Explains the feature that allows for more granular traffic control within the VLAN using the private VLAN structure.

6-1: VLAN Configuration

- *VLANs* are broadcast domains defined within switches to allow control of broadcast, multicast, unicast, and unknown unicast within a Layer 2 device.

- VLANs are defined on a switch in an internal database known as the *VLAN Trunking Protocol* (VTP) *database*. After a VLAN has been created, ports are assigned to the VLAN.

- VLANs are assigned numbers for identification within and between switches. Cisco switches have two ranges of VLANs, the *normal range* and *extended range*.

- VLANs have a variety of configurable parameters, including name, type, and state.

- Several VLANs are reserved, and some can be used for internal purposes within the switch.

Creation of an Ethernet VLAN

VLANs are created on Layer 2 switches to control broadcasts and enforce the use of a Layer 3 device for communications. Each VLAN is created in the local switch's database for use. If a VLAN is not known to a switch, that switch cannot transfer traffic across any of its ports for that VLAN. VLANs are created by number, and there are two ranges of usable VLAN numbers (normal range 1–1000 and extended range 1025–4096). When a VLAN is created, you can also give it certain attributes such as a VLAN name, VLAN type, and its operational state. To create a VLAN, use the following steps.

1 Configure VTP.

VTP is a protocol used by Cisco switches to maintain a consistent database between switches for trunking purposes. VTP is not required to create VLANs; however, Cisco has set it up to act as a conduit for VLAN configuration between switches as a default to make administration of VLANs easier. Because of this, you must first either configure VTP with a domain name or disable VTP on the switch. VTP is explained in detail in section "6-4: VLAN Trunking Protocol."

NOTE	For Catalyst 4000 and 6000 switches running IOS Supervisor 12.1(8a) or above (native IOS), you can configure the VTP parameters in global configuration mode as well.

— Specify a VTP name:

COS	`set vtp domain` *domain-name*
IOS	`(vlan) vtp domain` *domain-name* -OR- `(global) vtp domain` *domain-name*

By default, the VTP is in server mode and must be configured with a domain name before any VLANs can be created. These commands specify the VTP domain name. For IOS switches, you enter vlan database mode, **(vlan)**, by entering the command **vlan database**, at the privileged-level prompt.

NOTE	The global configuration command **vtp domain** is not available on all switches that run IOS.

-OR-

— Disable VTP synchronization:

COS	`set vtp mode transparent`
IOS	(vlan) `vtp transparent` -OR- (global) `vtp mode transparent`

Another option is to disable VTP synchronization of the databases. Disabling it enables you to manage your local VTP database without configuring and relying on VTP. For Catalyst 4000 and 6000 switches running IOS Supervisor 12.1(8a) or above (native IOS), you can configure the VTP parameters in global configuration mode as well.

NOTE The global configuration command **vtp mode transparent** is not available on all switches that run IOS.

-OR-

— Disable VTP:

COS	`set vtp mode off`
IOS	N/A

With the introduction of COS version 7.1.1, an option now exists to disable VTP completely. Use the command **set vtp mode off** to turn off VTP. After doing so, you can administer the local VTP database.

2 Create the VLAN.

VLANs are created by number. The two ranges of VLANs are as follows:

— The standard range consists of VLANs 1 to 1000.

— The extended range consists of VLANs 1025 to 4096.

Extended VLANs are currently supported only on switches running COS software version 6.1 or greater. When you create a VLAN, you have many options to consider. Many options are valid only for FDDI and Token Ring VLANs. Some of the items configured deal with options, such as private VLANs, which are discussed in other sections in this book. VLANs are created using the **set vlan** command for COS devices or with the **vlan** command in vlan database mode for IOS switches. For Ethernet VLANs, you can also configure the standard parameters in Table 6-1.

Table 6-1   *Configurable VLAN Parameters*

Parameter	Description
name	A description of the VLAN up to 32 characters. If none is given, it defaults to VLAN00XXX, where xxx is the VLAN number.
mtu	The maximum transmission unit (packet size, in bytes) that the VLAN can use; valid values are from **576** to **18190**. The MTU can extend up to 1500 for Ethernet, but beyond for Token Ring or FDDI. The default is **1500**.
state	Used to specify whether the state of the VLAN is active or suspended. All ports in a suspended VLAN will be suspended and not allowed to forward traffic. The default state is **active**.

NOTE   Many other options are available during the VLAN configuration command; however, most of these deal with the configuration of FDDI and Token Ring VLANs. Because these are not widely used topologies, the options and descriptions of Token Ring and FDDI VLAN configuration and parameters have not been included in this book. For information on Token Ring or FDDI VLANs, refer to www.cisco.com/univercd/cc/td/doc/product/lan/cat5000/rel_6_3/config/vlans.htm.

a. Create a VLAN in the standard range:

COS	`set vlan` *vlan-id* [`name` *name*] [`state` *state*] [`mtu` *mtu*]
IOS	`(vlan) vlan` *vlan-id* [`name` *vlan-name*] [`state {suspend	active}`] [`mtu` *mtu-size*]
	`(global) vlan` *vlan-id*
	`(vlan-config) vlan` *vlan-id* [`mtu` *mtu-size*] [`name` *vlan-name*] [`state {suspend	active}`]

The **vlan-id** specifies the VLAN by number. For COS you can specify a range of VLANs in the *vlan-id* section; you cannot configure the name for a range of VLANs, however, because each VLAN is to have a unique name. For IOS switches, VLANs are created in vlan database mode. For Catalyst 6000 and 4000 switches running Supervisor IOS 12.1(8a) and above, you can create VLANs in global configuration mode if the switch is in VTP transparent mode. To do this, enter the **vlan** *vlan-id* command to move to vlan-config mode. From vlan-config mode, you can manage the parameters of the VLANs.

NOTE	You cannot modify any of the parameters for VLAN 1.

b. Create a VLAN in the extended range.

Extended VLANs support VLANs up to 4096 in accordance with the 802.1Q standard. Currently only switches running COS 6.1 or greater can support creation and assignment of VLANs in the extended range. You cannot currently use VTP to manage VLANs in the extended range, and these VLANs cannot be passed over an *Inter-Switch Link* (ISL) trunk link.

1 Enable spanning-tree MAC reduction:

COS	`set spantree macreduction enable`
IOS	N/A

To allow these switches to use the extended range, you must first enable **spanningtree macreduction** to allow the switch to support a large number of spanning-tree instances with a very limited number of MAC addresses and still maintain the IEEE 802.1D bridge ID requirement for each STP instance.

NOTE	After you have created a VLAN in the extended range, you cannot disable this feature unless you first delete the VLAN.

2 Create a VLAN in the extended range:

COS	`set vlan` *vlan-id* [**name** *name*] [**state** *state*] [**mtu** *mtu*]
IOS	N/A

Here the *vlan-id* would be a number from 1025 to 4096. Numbers 1001 to 1024 are reserved by Cisco and cannot be configured.

CAUTION	For Catalyst 6000 series switches with FlexWAN cards, the system identifies these ports internally with VLAN numbers starting with 1025. If you have any FlexWAN modules, be sure to reserve enough VLAN numbers (starting with VLAN 1025) for all the Flex-WAN ports you want to install. You cannot use these extended VLANs if you install FlexWAN ports.

Feature Example

In this example, the switches Access_1 and Distribution_1 are going to be configured with VLANs 5, 8, and 10 with the names Cameron, Logan, and Katie, respectively. Also the distribution switch will be configured with VLAN 2112 with the name Rush.

An example of the Catalyst OS configuration for Distribution 1 follows:

```
Distribution_1 (enable)>set vtp mode transparent
Distribution_1 (enable)>set vlan 5 name Cameron
Distribution_1 (enable)>set vlan 8 name Logan
Distribution_1 (enable)>set vlan 10 name Katie
Distribution_1 (enable)>set spantree macreduction enable
Distribution_1 (enable)>set vlan 2112 name Rush
Distribution_1 (enable)>
```

An example of the Supervisor IOS configuration for Distribution 1 follows:

```
Distribution_1#vlan database
Distribution_1(vlan)#vtp transparent
Distribution_1(vlan)#exit
Distribution_1#conf t
Distribution_1(config)#vlan 5
Distribution_1(config-vlan)# name Cameron
Distribution_1(config-vlan)#vlan 8
Distribution_1(config-vlan)# name Logan
Distribution_1(config-vlan)# vlan 10
Distribution_1(config-vlan)# name Katie
Distribution_1(config-vlan)# end
Distribution_1 #copy running-config startup-config
```

NOTE   For the Supervisor IOS, extended VLANs such as 2112 are not supported.

An example of the Layer 2 IOS configuration for Access 1 follows:

```
Access_1#vlan database
Access_1 (vlan)#vtp transparent
Access_1 (vlan)#vlan 5 name Cameron
Access_1 (vlan)#vlan 8 name Logan
Access_1 (vlan)#vlan 10 name Katie
Access_1 (vlan)#exit
Access_1#copy running-config startup-config
```

6-2: VLAN Port Assignments

- VLANs are assigned to individual switch ports.
- Ports can be statically assigned to a single VLAN or dynamically assigned to a single VLAN.
- All ports are assigned to VLAN 1 by default.

- Ports are active only if they are assigned to VLANs that exist on the switch.
- Static port assignments are performed by the administrator and do not change unless modified by the administrator, whether the VLAN exists on the switch or not.
- Dynamic VLANs are assigned to a port based on the MAC address of the device plugged into a port.
- Dynamic VLAN configuration requires a *VLAN Membership Policy Server* (VMPS) client, server, and database to operate properly.

Configuring Static VLANs

On a Cisco switch, ports are assigned to a single VLAN. These ports are referred to as *access ports* and provide a connection for end users or node devices, such as a router or server. By default all devices are assigned to VLAN 1, known as the *default VLAN*. After creating a VLAN, you can manually assign a port to that VLAN and it will be able to communicate only with or through other devices in the VLAN. Configure the switch port for membership in a given VLAN as follows:

1 Statically assign a VLAN:

COS	**set vlan** *number mod/port*
IOS	(global) **interface** *type mod/port*
	(interface) **switchport access vlan** *number*

To change the VLAN for a COS device, use the **set vlan** command, followed by the VLAN *number*, and then the port or ports that should be added to that VLAN. VLAN assignments such as this are considered static because they do not change unless the administrator changes the VLAN configuration.

For the IOS device, you must first select the port (or port range for integrated IOS) and then use the **switchport access vlan** command followed by the VLAN *number*.

CAUTION	If the VLAN that the port is assigned to does not exist in the database, the port is disabled until the VLAN is created.

Configuring Dynamic VLANs

Although static VLANs are the most common form of port VLAN assignments, it is possible to have the switch dynamically choose a VLAN based on the MAC address of the device connected to a port. To achieve this, you must have a VTP database file, a VTP server, a

VTP client switch, and a dynamic port. After you have properly configured these components, a dynamic port can choose the VLAN based on whichever device is connected to that port. Use the following steps to configure dynamic VLANs:

1 Create a VTP database file.

Using a text editor, such as WordPad or vi, create a VTP database file and place it on a VMPS or *Remote Copy Protocol* (RCP) server. The VTP database file contains the following elements:

— A header that includes a VMPS domain name

— The VMPS operational mode

— The fallback VLAN name

— A list of MAC address mapped to VLAN names

The basic outline of a VMPS database file is as follows:

```
vmps domain Switchblock1
vmps mode open
vmps fallback default
vmps no-domain-req deny
!
vmps-mac-addrs
!
!
address 0001.0387.0943 vlan-name GroupA
address 0050.0491.F950 vlan-name GroupB
address 0050.DA8F.1134 vlan-name GroupC
```

The very first thing that should be in the VTP database file are the letters **vmps** followed by the word **domain** and a domain name. The domain name matches that of the VTP domain name of the switch(es) sending the VMPS request. (VTP is discussed further in section "6-4: VLAN Trunking Protocol.") This name is used in the request for VMPS mapping information. The next three lines in the file are information about how VMPS should operate. The **mode open** indicates whether a request comes in that is not in the MAC address list. The switch should place that device in a default VLAN. The next line specifies that VLAN by name. The name **default** is that of VLAN 1. You can also configure the mode as **closed**; if this is the case, the port will be suspended if the device is not in the MAC address table. The **no-domain-req deny** option states that any device that sends a request with no domain name should not be given any port VLAN mapping information. Each **!** (exclamation point) is a comment and is ignored by the VMPS server.

The **vmps-mac-addrs** entry indicates the start of the MAC address to VLAN mapping. The entries are entered with the format **address** *address* **vlan-name** *vlan_name*, where the address is in dotted-hexadecimal format and the VLAN name is the exact name (including case) as found in the VLAN database of the requesting switch. When a request is sent, this mapping is returned to the requesting switch. The VLAN assignment is based on the name returned. If the name is not found on the local switch, the assignment is not made.

2 Configure the VMPS server.

a. *(Optional)* Set the VMPS download method:

COS	`set vmps downloadmethod {rcp	tftp}`
IOS	N/A

Specify how to download the VMPS database file using **rcp** or **tftp**. If you do not choose a method, the default is **tftp**.

b. Set the VMPS download server and filename:

COS	`set vmps downloadserver `*ipaddress*` [`*filename*`]`
IOS	N/A

Configure the IP address of the RCP or TFTP server and specify the *filename* of the VMPS database.

c. Enable the VMPS server service:

COS	`set vmps state enable`
IOS	N/A

When you enable the VMPS server service, it will read the file from the server into the memory of the switch and will then be able to respond to request from the VMPS client switches. Use the commands **show vmps**, **show vmps mac**, **show vmps vlan**, and **show vmps statistics** to verify the operation of the VMPS server.

NOTE   After the VMPS server service has been enabled and the VMPS information loaded into the memory of the server, the VMPS database file is no longer referenced. If you make changes to the VMPS database file, you must either disable and reenable the server service or reload the file with the command **download vmps**.

---

3 Configure the VMPS client:

COS	`set vmps server `*ipaddress*` [`**primary**`]`
IOS	`(global) vmps server `*ipaddress*` `**primary**

Any switch that will have dynamic ports is considered a VMPS client. For this switch to request the dynamic VLAN information from the server, you must configure the client with the server address. Use the primary option to specify the IP address of the main VMPS server. You can also specify up to three other IP addresses for VMPS servers. Use the command **show vmps server** for COS and **show vmps** on IOS devices to confirm the server configuration.

NOTE	If the a switch is configured as a VMPS server and it will also have dynamic ports, it must also be configured as a client using Step 3 and pointing to its own IP address as server.

4 Configure the port for dynamic VLAN assignments:

COS	`set port membership` *mod/port* `dynamic`
IOS	`(interface)` `switchport access dynamic`

This places the port in dynamic VLAN mode. The switch must first be configured as a client (Step 3) before you configure a port as dynamic. After this has been configured, the port is assigned to the local switch's VLAN that has a name that matches the one mapped to the MAC address of the attached device in the VMPS database.

Verifying VLAN Assignments

After configuring a port for VLAN assignments, use one of the following commands to verify the VLAN port assignments:

COS	`show port`
IOS	`(privileged)` `show interface` *type mod/port* `switchport`
	-OR-
	`(privileged)``show interface status`

NOTE	The command **show interface status** is not available on all switches that run IOS.

Feature Example

In this example, ports for the switches Access_1 and Distribution_1 are assigned as follows:

- Static assignments for ports 1 and 2 on the access switch and 3/1–48 on the distribution switch into VLAN 5

- Static assignments for ports 3 and 4 on the access switch and 4/1–48 on the distribution switch into VLAN 8

- Static assignments for ports 5 and 6 on the access switch and 5/1–12 and 5/18–24 on the distribution switch into VLAN 10

Distribution_1 will be assigned the IP address 10.1.1.1 and will serve as a VMPS server and get a file called *vmpsconfig.txt* (shown at the end of the example) from the server 10.1.1.101.

Ports 13–16 will be dynamic on the access switch, and ports 5/13-17 will be dynamic on the Distribution_1 server. Figure 6-1 shows the connections and assignments associated with this example.

Figure 6-1   *VLAN Port Assignments on Access_1 and Distribution_1*

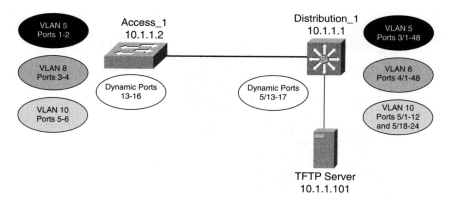

An example of the Catalyst OS configuration for Distribution_1 follows:

```
Distribution_1 (enable)>set vlan 5 3/1-48
Distribution_1 (enable)>set vlan 8 4/1-48
Distribution_1 (enable)>set vlan 10 5/1-12,5/18-24
Distribution_1 (enable)>set vmps downloadserver 10.1.1.101 vmpsconfig.txt
Distribution_1 (enable)>set int sc0 10.1.1.1/24
Distribution_1 (enable)>set vmps enable
Distribution_1 (enable)>set vmps server 10.1.1.1
Distribution_1 (enable)> set port membership 5/13-17 dynamic
```

An example of the Supervisor IOS configuration for Distribution_1 follows:

```
Distribution_1(config)#interface range fastethernet 3/1 - 48
Distribution_1(config-if)#switchport
Distribution_1(config-if)#switchport mode access
Distribution_1(config-if)#switchport access vlan 5
Distribution_1(config-if)#no shut
Distribution_1(config)#interface range fastethernet 2/1 - 48
Distribution_1(config-if)#switchport
Distribution_1(config-if)#switchport mode access
Distribution_1(config-if)#switchport access vlan 8
Distribution_1(config-if)#no shut
Distribution_1(config)#interface range fastethernet 5/1 - 12 , 5/18 - 24
Distribution_1(config-if)#switchport
Distribution_1(config-if)#switchport mode access
Distribution_1(config-if)#switchport access vlan 10
Distribution_1(config-if)#no shut
Distribution_1(config-if)# end
Distribution_1 #copy running-config startup-config
```

NOTE   For the Supervisor IOS running on a Catalyst 6000 or Catalyst 4000, dynamic VLAN services are currently not supported. These switches cannot be configured with dynamic access ports or to act as a VMPS server.

An example of the Layer 2 IOS configuration for Access_1 follows:

```
Access_1(config)#interface fastethernet 0/1
Access_1(config-if)#switchport access vlan 5
Access_1(config-if)#interface fastethernet 0/2
Access_1(config-if)#switchport access vlan 5
Access_1(config-if)#interface fastethernet 0/3
Access_1(config-if)#switchport access vlan 8
Access_1(config-if)#interface fastethernet 0/4
Access_1(config-if)#switchport access vlan 8
Access_1(config-if)#interface VLAN 1
Access_1(config-if)#ip address 10.1.1.2 255.255.255.0
Access_1(config-if)#vmps server 10.1.1.1
Access_1(config)#interface fastethernet 0/5
Access_1(config-if)#switchport access dynamic
Access_1(config-if)#interface fastethernet 0/6
Access_1(config-if)#switchport access vlan dynamic
Access_1(config-if)# end
Access_1 #copy running-config startup-config
```

An example of the VMPS database file *vmpsconfig.txt* follows:

```
vmps domain Switchblock1
vmps mode open
vmps fallback default
vmps no-domain-req allow
!
vmps-mac-addrs
!
!
address 0001.0387.0943 vlan-name Katie
address 0050.0491.F950 vlan-name Logan
address 0050.DA8F.1134 vlan-name Cameron
```

6-3: Trunking

- VLANs are local to each switch's database, and VLAN information is not passed between switches.

- Trunk links provide VLAN identification for frames traveling between switches.

- Cisco switches have two Ethernet trunking mechanisms: ISL and IEEE 802.1Q.

- Certain types of switches can negotiate trunk links.

- Trunks carry traffic from all VLANs to and from the switch by default but can be configured to carry only specified VLAN traffic.

- Trunk links must be configured to allow trunking on each end of the link.

Enabling Trunking

Trunk links are required to pass VLAN information between switches. A port on a Cisco switch is either an access port or a trunk port. Access ports belong to a single VLAN and do not provide any identifying marks on the frames that are passed between switches. Access ports also carry traffic that comes from only the VLAN assigned to the port. A trunk port is by default a member of *all* the VLANs that exist on the switch and carry traffic for all those VLANs between the switches. To distinguish between the traffic flows, a trunk port must mark the frames with special tags as they pass between the switches. Trunking is a function that must be enabled on both sides of a link. If two switches are connected together, for example, both switch ports must be configured for trunking, and they must both be configured with the same tagging mechanism (ISL or 802.1Q).

To enable trunking between the switches, use the following steps:

1 Enable trunking on a port.

a. Enable the trunk:

COS	`set trunk` *mod/port* `[auto	desirable	on	nonegotiate	off]`
IOS	`(global)` `interface` *type mod/port*
	`(`interface`)` `switchport mode dynamic [auto	desirable]`
	`(interface)` `switchport mode trunk`
	`(interface)` `switchport nonegotiate`

The most basic way to configure a trunk link is using the option **on**. This option enables the trunk and requires that you also specify a tagging mechanism for the trunk. For IOS devices, the command **switchport mode trunk** is equivalent to the **set trunk** *mod/port* **on** command. When specifying the option **on**, you must also choose a tagging mechanism (see Step 1b).

NOTE	Some IOS switches do not support Dynamic Trunking Protocol. For these switches, the only command that you can use to configure trunking is **switchport mode trunk**, which essentially turns trunking on.

Many Cisco switches employ an automatic trunking mechanism known as the *Dynamic Trunking Protocol* (DTP), which allows a trunk to be dynamically established between two switches. All COS switches and integrated IOS switches can use the DTP protocol to form a trunk link. The COS options **auto**, **desirable**, and **on** and the IOS options of **dynamic auto**, **dynamic desirable**, and **trunk** configure a trunk link using DTP. If one side of the link is configured to trunk and will send DTP signals, the other side of the link will dynamically begin to trunk if the options match correctly.

If you want to enable trunking and not send any DTP signaling, use the option **nonegotiate** for switches that support that function. If you want to disable trunking completely, use the **off** option for a COS switch or the **no switchport mode trunk** command on an IOS switch.

Table 6-2 shows the DTP signaling and the characteristics of each mode.

TIP	It is important to remember that not all switches support DTP and might not establish a trunk without intervention. Also remember that DTP offers no benefit when you are trunking with a non-Cisco switch. To eliminate any overhead associated with DTP, it is useful to use the **nonegotiate** option when DTP is not supported.

NOTE	When enabling trunking, it is not possible to specify a range of ports.

Table 6-2   *Trunking Mode Characteristics*

Trunking Mode	Characteristics
COS = **on** IOS = **mode trunk**	Trunking is on for these links. They will also send DTP signals that attempt to initiate a trunk with the other side. This will form a trunk with other ports in the states **on**, **auto**, or **desirable** that are running DTP. A port that is in **on** mode always tags frames sent out the port.

Table 6-2   *Trunking Mode Characteristics (Continued)*

Trunking Mode	Characteristics
COS = **desirable** IOS = **mode dynamic desirable**	These links would like to become trunk links and will send DTP signals that attempt to initiate a trunk. They will only become trunk links if the other side responds to the DTP signal. This will form a trunk with other ports in the states **on**, **auto**, or **desirable** that are running DTP. This is the default mode for the 6000 running Supervisor IOS.
COS = **auto** IOS = **mode dynamic auto**	These links will only become trunk links if they receive a DTP signal from a link that is already trunking or desires to trunk. This will only form a trunk with other ports in the states **on** or **desirable**. This is the default mode for COS switches.
COS = **nonegotiate** IOS = **mode nonegotiate**	Sets trunking on and disables DTP. These will only become trunks with ports in **on** or **nonegotiate** mode.
COS = **off** IOS = **no switchport mode trunk**	This option sets trunking and DTP capabilities off. This is the recommended setting for any access port because it will prevent any dynamic establishments of trunk links.

NOTE   Cisco 2950 and 3500XL switches do not support DTP and are always in a mode similar to **nonegotiate**. If you turn trunking on for one of these devices, it will not negotiate with the other end of the link and requires that the other link be configured to **on** or **nonegotiate**.

b. Specify the encapsulation method:

COS	`set trunk` *mod/port* `[negotiate	isl	dot1Q]`
IOS	`(global)` **interface** *type mod/port* `(interface)` **switchport trunk encapsulation** `[negotiate	isl	dot1Q]`

The other option when choosing a trunk link is the encapsulation method. For Layer 2 IOS switches, such as the 2900XL or the 3500XL, the default encapsulation method is **isl**. You can change from the default with the **switchport trunk encapsulation** command. For COS switches or integrated IOS switches, the default encapsulation is **negotiate**. This method signals between the trunked ports to choose an encapsulation method. (ISL is preferred over 802.1Q.) The **negotiate** option is valid for **auto** or **desirable** trunking modes only. If you choose **on** as the mode or if you want to force a particular method or if the other side of the trunk cannot negotiate the trunking type, you must choose the option **isl** or **dot1Q** to specify the encapsulation method.

Section 6-3

NOTE	Not all switches allow you to negotiate a trunk encapsulation setting. The 2900XL and 3500XL trunks default to **isl** and you must use the **switchport trunk encapsulation** command to change the encapsulation type. The 2950 and some 4000 switches support only 802.1Q trunking and provide no options for changing the trunk type.

c. *(Optional)* Specify the native VLAN:

COS	`set vlan` *number* `mod/port`
IOS	(global) `interface` *type mod/port* (interface) `switchport trunk native vlan` *number*

For switches running 802.1Q as the trunking mechanism, the native VLAN of each port on the trunk must match. By default all COS ports are in VLAN 1; and the native VLAN on the IOS devices is also configured for VLAN 1, so the native VLAN does match. If you choose to change the native VLAN, use the **set vlan** command for COS switches or the **switchport trunk native vlan** command for IOS switches to specify the native VLAN. Remember that the native VLAN *must* match on both sides of the trunk link for 802.1Q; otherwise the link will not work. If there is a native VLAN mismatch, *Spanning Tree Protocol* (STP) places the port in a *port VLAN ID* (PVID) inconsistent state and will not forward on the link.

NOTE	*Cisco Discovery Protocol* (CDP) version 2 passes native VLAN information between Cisco switches. If you have a native VLAN mismatch, you will see CDP error messages on the console output.

Specifying VLANs to Trunk

By default a trunk link carries all the VLANs that exist on the switch. This is because all VLANs are active on a trunk link; and as long as the VLAN is in the switch's local database, traffic for that VLAN is carried across the trunks. You can elect to selectively remove and add VLANs from a trunk link. To specify which VLANs are to be added or removed from a trunk link, use the following commands.

1 *(Optional)* Manually remove VLANs from a trunk link:

COS	`clear trunk` *mod/port vlanlist*
IOS	(global) `interface` *type mod/port* (interface) `switchport trunk allowed vlan remove` *vlanlist*

By specifying VLANs in the *vlanlist* field of this command, the VLANs will not be allowed to travel across the trunk link until they are added back to the trunk using the command **set trunk** *mod/port vlanlist* or **switchport trunk allowed vlan add** *vlanlist*.

Verifying Trunks

After configuring a port for trunking, use one of the following commands to verify the VLAN port assignments:

COS	`show trunk [mod] [mod/port]`
IOS	(privileged) `show interface type mod/port switchport`
	-OR-
	`show interfaces trunk`
	-OR-
	`show interface [mod] [interface_id] trunk`

NOTE   The commands **show interfaces trunk** and **show interface** [*mod*] [*interface_id*] **trunk** are not available on all switches that run IOS.

Feature Example

In this example the switches Access_1 and Distribution_1 and Core_1 are connected as shown in Figure 6-2. 802.1Q trunking is configured in the on mode between Access_1 and Distribution_1 switches. ISL is configured in desirable mode on the Distribution_1 switch to the link connecting to the core. The core is configured for autotrunking mode and encapsulation negotiate. The trunk connected between the access switch is configured to only trunk for VLANs 5, 8, and 10. The trunk between the Distribution_1 and Core_1 is configured to carry only VLAN 1 and VLAN 10.

Figure 6-2   *Network Diagram for Trunk Configuration on Access_1, Distribution_1, and Core_1*

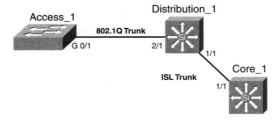

An example of the Catalyst OS configuration for Distribution_1 follows:

```
Distribution_1 (enable)>clear trunk 1/1 2-1001
Distribution_1 (enable)>set trunk 1/1 desirable isl 10
Distribution_1 (enable)>clear trunk 2/1 2-1001
Distribution_1 (enable)>set trunk 2/1 on dot1q 5,8,10
```

An example of the Catalyst OS configuration for Core_1 follows:

```
Core_1 (enable)>clear trunk 1/1 2-1001
Core_1 (enable)>set trunk 1/1 10
```

An example of the Supervisor IOS configuration for Core_1 follows:

```
Core_1(config)#interface gigabitethernet 1/1
Core_1(config-if)#switchport encapsulation negotiate
Core_1(config-if)#switchport mode dynamic auto
Core_1(config-if)#switchport trunk allowed vlan remove 2-1001
Core_1(config-if)#switchport trunk allowed vlan add 10
Core_1 (config-if)#end
Core_1#copy running-config startup-config
```

An example of the Layer 2 IOS configuration for Access_1 follows:

```
Access_1 (config)#interface gigabitethernet 0/1
Access_1 (config-if)#switchport mode trunk
Access_1 (config-if)#switchport trunk encapsulation dot1q
Access_1 (config-if)#switchport trunk allowed vlan remove 2-1001
Access_1 (config-if)#switchport trunk allowed vlan add 5,8,10
Access_1 (config-if)#end
Access_1#copy running-config startup-config
```

6-4: VLAN Trunking Protocol

- VTP sends messages between trunked switches to maintain VLANs on these switches in order to properly trunk.

- VTP is a Cisco proprietary method of managing VLANs between switches and runs across any type of trunking mechanism.

- VTP messages are exchanged between switches within a common VTP domain.

- VTP domains must be defined or VTP disabled before a VLAN can be created.

- Exchanges of VTP information can be controlled by passwords.

- VTP manages only VLANs 2 through 1002.

- VTP allows switches to synchronize their VLANs based on a configuration revision number.

- Switches can operate in one of three VTP modes: server, transparent, or client.

- VTP can prune unneeded VLANs from trunk links.

Enabling VTP for Operation

VTP exists to ensure that VLANs exist on the local VLAN database of switches in a trunked path. In addition to making sure the VLANs exist, VTP can further synchronize name settings and can be used to prune VLANs from trunk links that are destined for switches that do not have any ports active in that particular VLAN.

To manage and configure VTP, use the following steps.

1   Activate VTP on a switch.

a. Specify a VTP domain name:

COS	`set vtp domain` *name*
IOS	(privileged) `vlan database` (vlan_database) `vtp domain` *name* -OR- (global) `vtp domain` *name*

By default VTP is in server mode, which is an operational mode that enables you to manage VLANs on the local switch's database and use the information in the database to synchronize with other switches. To configure VTP for operation, you must specify a name. After you enable trunking, this name propagates to switches that have not been configured with a name. If you choose to configure names on your switches, however, remember that VTP names are case-sensitive and must match exactly. Switches that have different VTP names will not exchange VLAN information.

NOTE   The global configuration command **vtp domain** is not supported on all switches that run the IOS.

NOTE   VTP names are used only in the context of synchronizing VTP databases. VTP domain names do not separate broadcast domains. If VLAN 20 exists on two switches trunked together with different VTP domain names, VLAN 20 is still the same broadcast domain!

b. Enable the trunk:

COS	`set trunk` *mod/port* [**auto** | **desirable** | **on** | **nonegotiate** | **off**]
IOS	(global) `interface` *type mod/port* (interface) `switchport mode dynamic` [auto | desirable] (interface) `switchport mode trunk` (interface) `switchport nonegotiate`

Section 6-4

VTP information is passed only across trunk links. If you do not enable a trunk, VLAN information is not exchanged between the switches. See section "6-3: Trunking" for more details on trunking.

NOTE   Some IOS switches do not support DTP. For these switches, the only command that you can use to configure trunking is **switchport mode trunk**, which essentially turns trunking on.

Setting VTP Passwords

By default, there are no passwords in VTP informational updates, and any switch that has no VTP domain name will join the VTP domain when trunking is enabled. Also any switch that has the same VTP domain name configured will join and exchange VTP information. This could enable an unwanted switch in your network to manage the VLAN database on each of the switches. To prevent this from occurring, set a VTP password on the switches you want to exchange information.

1 *(Optional)* Set the VTP password:

COS	`set vtp passwd` *password*
IOS	(privileged) `vlan database` (vlan_database) `vtp password` *password* -OR- (global)`vtp password` *password*

The password is entered on each switch that will be participating in the VTP domain. The passwords are case-sensitive and must match exactly. If you want to remove the passwords, use the command **set vtp passwd 0** on a COS device or **no vtp password** in the VLAN database mode for the IOS device.

NOTE   If you choose to set a password for VTP, it must be between 8 and 32 characters in length.

NOTE   The global configuration command **vtp password** is not supported on all switches that run the IOS.

Changing VTP Modes

VTP operates in one of three modes: server, client, and transparent. The modes determine how VTP passes information, how VLAN databases are synchronized, and whether VLANs can be managed for a given switch.

1 *(Optional)* Set the VTP mode:

COS	`set vtp mode [server	client	transparent]`
IOS	(privileged) `vlan database` (vlan_database) `vtp [server	client	transparent]` -OR- (global)`vtp mode [server	client	transparent]`

By default Cisco switches are in VTP server mode. For a VTP server, you can create, delete, or modify a VLAN in the local VLAN database. After you make this change, the VLAN database changes are propagated out to all other switches in server or client mode in the VTP domain. A server will also accept changes to the VLAN database from other switches in the domain. You can also run the VTP in client mode. Switches in client mode cannot create, modify, or delete VLANs in the local VLAN database. Instead, they rely on other switches in the domain to update them about new VLANs. Clients will synchronize their databases, but they will not save the VLAN information and will loose this information if they are powered off. Clients will also advertise information about their database and forward VTP information to other switches. VTP transparent mode works much like server mode in that you can create, delete, or modify VLANs in the local VLAN database. The difference is that these changes are not propagated to other switches. In addition, the local VLAN database does not accept modifications from other switches. VTP transparent mode switches forward or relay information between other server or client switches. A VTP transparent mode switch does not require a VTP domain name.

NOTE   The global configuration command **vtp mode** is not supported on all switches that run the IOS.

NOTE   As of COS 7.1(1), Cisco introduced a VTP off mode (**set vtp mode off**). This mode is similar to transparent mode; but in VTP off mode, the switch does not relay VTP information between switches. This command is useful when you do not want to send or forward VTP updates—for example, if you are trunking with all non-Cisco switches or if you are using *Generic VLAN Registration Protocol* (GVRP) dynamic VLAN creation to manage your VLAN database.

Section 6-4

Enabling VTP Pruning

By default all the VLANs that exist on a switch are active on a trunk link. As noted in section "6-3: Trunking", you can manually remove VLANs from a trunk link and then add them later. VTP pruning allows the switch to not forward user traffic for VLANs that are not active on a remote switch. This feature dynamically prunes unneeded traffic across trunk links. If the VLAN traffic is needed at a later date, VTP will dynamically add the VLAN back to the trunk.

NOTE   Dynamic pruning removes only unneeded user traffic from the link. It does not prevent any management frames such as STP from crossing the link.

---

1 *(Optional)* Enable VTP pruning.

a. Enable pruning:

COS	`set vtp pruning enable`
IOS	`(privileged)` **`vlan database`** `(vlan_database)` **`vtp pruning`**

After VTP pruning is enabled on one VTP server in the domain, all other switches in that domain will also enable VTP pruning. VTP pruning can only be enabled on switches that are VTP version 2-capable, so all switches in the domain must be version 2-capable before you enable pruning.

NOTE   The switch must be VTP version 2-capable, but does not have to have version 2 enabled, to turn on pruning.

---

b. *(Optional)* Specify VLANs that are eligible for pruning:

COS	`clear vtp pruneeligible` *`vlanlist`*
IOS	`(global)` **`interface`** *`type mod/port`* `(interface)` **`switchport trunk pruning vlan remove`** *`vlanlist`*

By default all the VLANs on the trunk are eligible for pruning. You can remove VLANs from the list of eligible VLANs using these commands. After a VLAN has been removed from the eligible list, it cannot be pruned by VTP. To add the VLANs back, use the command **set vtp pruneeligible** *vlanlist* for COS switches or **switchport trunk pruning vlan add** *vlanlist* for IOS.

Changing VTP Versions

VTP supports two versions. By default all switches are in VTP version 1 mode, but most switches can support version 2 mode.

1 *(Optional)* Enable VTP version 2:

COS	`set vtp v2 enable`
IOS	(privileged) `vlan database`
	(vlan_database)`vtp v2-mode`
	-OR-
	(global)`vtp version 2`

VTP version 2 is disabled by default. After you have enabled version 2 on one switch, all other switches in the domain also begin to operate in version 2 mode.

NOTE   The global configuration command **vtp version 2** is not supported on all switches that run the IOS.

VTP version 2 offers the following support options not available with version 1:

— **Unrecognized *type-length-value* (TLV) support**—A VTP server or client propagates configuration changes to its other trunks, even for TLVs it is not able to parse. The unrecognized TLV is saved in NVRAM.

— **Version-dependent transparent mode**—In VTP version 1, a VTP transparent switch inspects VTP messages for the domain name and version and forwards a message only if the version and domain name match. Because only one domain is supported in the Supervisor engine software, VTP version 2 forwards VTP messages in transparent mode, without checking the version.

— **Consistency checks**—In VTP version 2, VLAN consistency checks (such as VLAN names and values) are performed only when you enter new information through the *command-line interface* (CLI) or *Simple Network Management Protocol* (SNMP). Consistency checks are not performed when new information is obtained from a VTP message or when information is read from NVRAM. If the digest on a received VTP message is correct, its information is accepted without consistency checks.

Verifying VTP Operation

After configuring VTP, use one of the following commands to verify the VLAN port assignments:

COS	`show vtp domain`
IOS	(privileged) `show vtp status`

Feature Example

In this example, Access_1, Distribution_1, and Distribution_2 will be assigned to a VTP domain named GO-CATS. Figure 6-3 shows that Access_1 will be in VTP client mode with an 802.1Q trunk connecting to Distribution_1. Distribution_1 will be configured in VTP server mode with an ISL trunk connecting it to Core_1, which is in VTP transparent mode. Core_1 has an ISL trunk to Distribution_2, which is also in VTP server mode. VTP pruning has also been enabled for the domain, and all switches are configured so that VLAN 10 is not prune-eligible on the trunk links. Because VTP runs across trunk links, it is not necessary to configure the VTP domain name on the Distribution_2 switch or the Access_1 switch. It is also not necessary to configure the pruning on each switch; this is also propagated by VTP.

Figure 6-3   *Network Diagram for VTP Configuration on Access_1, Distribution_1, Distribution_2, and Core_1.*

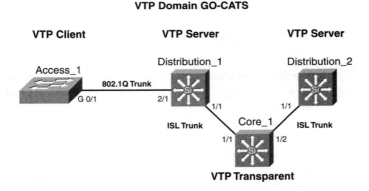

An example of the Catalyst OS configuration for Core_1 follows:

```
Core_1 (enable)>set vtp mode transparent
Core_1 (enable)>set trunk 1/1 on isl
Core_1 (enable)>set trunk 1/2 on isl
Core_1 (enable)>
```

An example of the Catalyst OS configuration for Distribution_1 follows:

```
Distribution_1 (enable)>set vtp domain  GO-CATS
Distribution_1 (enable)>set trunk 1/1 on isl
Distribution_1 (enable)>set trunk 2/1 on dot1Q
Distribution_1 (enable)>set vtp pruning enable
Distribution_1 (enable)>clear vtp pruneeligible 10
```

An example of the Catalyst OS configuration for Distribution_2 follows:

```
Distribution_2 (enable)>set trunk 1/1 on isl
Distribution_2 (enable)>clear vtp pruneeligible 10
```

An example of the Layer 2 IOS configuration for Access_1 follows:

```
Access_1#vlan database
Access_1 (vlan)#vtp client
Access_1 (vlan)#exit
Access_1 #config t
Access_1 (config)#interface gigabitethernet 0/1
Access_1 (config-if)#switchport mode trunk
Access_1 (config-if)#switchport trunk encapsulation dot1Q
Access_1 (config-if)#switchport trunk pruning vlan remove 10
Access_1 (config-if)#end
Access_1#copy running-config startup-config
```

6-5: GVRP

- *Generic Attribute Registration Protocol* (GARP) *VLAN Registration Protocol* (GVRP) is an application defined in the IEEE 802.1Q standard that allows for the control of VLANs.

- GVRP runs only on 802.1Q trunk links.

- GVRP prunes trunk links so that only active VLANs will be sent across trunk connections.

- GVRP expects to hear join messages from the switches before it will add a VLAN to the trunk.

- GVRP updates and hold timers can be altered.

- GVRP ports run in various modes to control how they will prune VLANs.

- GVRP can be configured to dynamically add and manage VLANS to the VLAN database for trunking purposes.

Section 6-5

Configuring GVRP

GVRP is supported only on COS switches. GVRP will run only on 802.1Q trunk ports and is used primarily to prune traffic from VLANs that does not need to be passed between trunking switches. Use the following steps to configure GVRP.

1 Enable GVRP globally:

COS	`set gvrp enable`

By default GVRP is not enabled for the switch. You must first enable GVRP on the switch before you can configure the 802.1Q ports for GVRP operation.

2 Configure the port for 802.1Q operation:

COS	`set trunk` *mod/port* [`auto` | `desirable` | `on`] `dot1q`

GVRP will run only on ports that are configured for 802.1Q trunking. See section "6-3: Trunking" for more information on trunking.

3 Configure the port GVRP:

COS	`set port gvrp` *mod/port* `enable`

This command enables GVRP on the individual 802.1Q trunk port. GVRP must be configured on both sides of the trunk to work correctly.

4 *(Optional)* Configure the port registration mode:

COS	`set gvrp registration` [`normal` | `fixed` | `forbidden`] *mod/port*

By default GVRP ports are in **normal** registration mode. These ports use GVRP join messages from neighboring switches to prune the VLANs running across the 802.1Q trunk link. If the device on the other side is not capable of sending GVRP messages, or if you do not want to allow the switch to prune any of the VLANs, use the **fixed** mode. Fixed mode ports will forward for all VLANs that exist in the switch database. Ports in **forbidden** mode forward only for VLAN 1.

Configuring GVRP for Dynamic VLAN Creation

Like VTP, GVRP can dynamically create VLANs on switches for trunking purposes. By enabling GVRP dynamic VLAN creation, a switch will add VLANs to its database when it receives GVRP join messages about VLANs it does not have.

1 (Optional) Enable dynamic VLAN creation:

COS	`set gvrp dynamic-vlan-creation enable`

Dynamic VLAN creation is configured on a switch-by-switch basis. GVRP does not synchronize between switches, but only adds VLANs on devices that have dynamic creation enabled in order to pass traffic between trunks. To enable dynamic VLAN creation, all the trunk ports on the switch have to be 802.1Q and they all must be GVRP-enabled ports. If the switch has any non-802.1Q trunk ports or if the 802.1Q ports that exist are not configured for GVRP, this feature will not be enabled. VLANs will be added only for join messages received across a normal registration port. You must also have configured VTP in transparent or off mode, because VTP and dynamic VLAN creation cannot both be enabled at the same time.

NOTE   The trunk ports 15/1 and 16/1 on a 5000 or 6000 series switch do not count as ISL trunks when enabling **dynamic-vlan-creation** and will not prevent the function from operating.

Verifying GVRP Operation

After you have configured GVRP, use the following command to verify operation:

COS	`show gvrp configuration`

Feature Example

In this example, the switch Access_1 is connected to Distribution_1 via an 802.1Q trunk shown in Figure 6-4. Distribution_1 is also connected to Core_1 via an 802.1Q trunk. GVRP is enabled on both the distribution and core switches and on each GVRP port on those switches. Dynamic VLAN creation has also been enabled on the switches, and the port from Distribution_1 to Access_1 has been set to GVRP fixed mode because the Access_1 device will not send join messages and the distribution switch would prune all VLANs if it were in the normal default mode.

Section 6-5

Figure 6-4   *Network Diagram for GVRP Configuration on Access_1, Distribution_1, and Core_1*

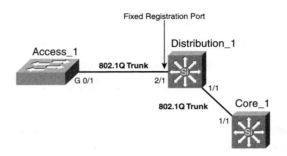

An example of the Catalyst OS configuration for Core_1 follows:

```
Core_1 (enable)>set vtp mode transparent
Core_1 (enable)>set trunk 1/1 on dot1Q
Core_1 (enable)>set gvrp enable
Core_1 (enable)>set port gvrp 1/1 enable
Core_1 (enable)>set gvrp dynamic-vlan-creation enable
```

An example of the Catalyst OS configuration for Distribution_1 follows:

```
Distribution_1 (enable)>set vtp mode transparent
Distribution_1 (enable)>set trunk 1/1 on dot1q
Distribution_1 (enable)>set trunk 2/1 on dot1q
Distribution_1 (enable)>set gvrp enable
Distribution_1 (enable)>set gvrp enable 1/1
Distribution_1 (enable)>set gvrp enable 2/1
Distribution_1 (enable)>set gvrp registration fixed 2/1
Distribution_1 (enable)>set gvrp dynamic-vlan-creation enable
```

An example of the Layer 2 IOS configuration for Access_1 follows:

```
Access_1 #config t
Access_1 (config)#interface gigabitethernet 0/1
Access_1 (config-if)#switchport mode trunk
Access_1 (config-if)#switchport trunk encapsulation dot1Q
Access_1 (config-if)#end
Access_1#copy running-config startup-config
```

6-6: Private VLANs

- Private VLANs allow for additional security between devices in a common subnet.

- Private edge VLANs can be configured to prevent connectivity between devices on access switches.

- Private VLANs can be configured on the Catalyst 6000 and Catalyst 4000 series products.

- Within a private VLAN, you can isolate devices to prevent connectivity between devices within the isolated VLAN.

- Within a private VLAN, communities can be created to allow connection between some devices and to prevent them from communicating with others.

- Promiscuous ports are mapped to private VLANs to allow for connectivity to VLANs outside of this network.

Configuring Private VLANs

Private VLANs provide a mechanism to control which devices can communicate within a single subnet. The private VLAN uses **isolated** and **community** secondary VLANs to control how devices communicate. The secondary VLANs are assigned to the primary VLAN, and ports are assigned to the secondary VLANs. Ports in an isolated VLAN cannot communicate with any device in the VLAN other than the promiscuous port. Ports configured in a community VLAN can communicate with other ports in the same community and the promiscuous port. Ports in different communities cannot communicate with one another. To configure private VLANs, use the following steps.

1 Set VTP transparent mode:

COS	`set vtp mode transparent`
IOS	`(privileged) vlan database` `(vlan_database) vtp transparent`

You must configure VTP to transparent mode before you can create a private VLAN. Private VLANs are configured in the context of a single switch and cannot have members on other switches. Private VLANs also carry TLVs that are not known to all types of Cisco switches.

2 Create the primary private VLAN:

COS	`set vlan primary_number pvlan-type primary`
IOS	`(global) vlan primary_number` `(vlan-config) private-vlan primary`

You must first create a primary private VLAN. The number of the primary VLAN is used in later steps for binding secondary VLANs and mapping promiscuous ports.

3 Create isolated and community VLANs:

COS	`set vlan secondary_number pvlan-type [isolated	community |` `twoway-community]`
IOS	`(global) vlan secondary_number` `(vlan-config) private-vlan [isolated	community]`

Configure isolated or community secondary VLANs for assignment of ports and control of the traffic. The secondary number for each of these VLANs must be unique from one another and the primary number. Members of an isolated VLAN can only communicate with the promiscuous port(s) mapped in Step 6, whereas members of a community VLAN can communicate with members of the same community and the promiscuous ports. A two-way community acts like a regular community, but has the additional aspect of allowing access control lists to check traffic going to and from (two ways) the VLAN and provides enhanced security within a private VLAN.

4   Bind isolated and community VLANs to the primary VLAN:

COS	`set pvlan` *primary_number secondary_number*
IOS	(global) `vlan` *primary_number* (vlan-config) `private-vlan association` *secondary_number_list* [**add** *secondary_number_list*]

This command associates or binds the secondary VLANs to the primary VLAN. For the IOS command, the **add** option allows other VLANs to be associated in the future.

5   Place ports into the isolated and community VLANs:

COS	`set pvlan` *primary_number secondary_number mod/port* [`sc0`]
IOS	(global) `interface` *type mod/port* (interface) `switchport` (interface) `switchport mode private-vlan host` (interface) `switchport mode private-vlan host-association` *primary_number secondary_number*

After you have created and associated the primary and secondary VLANs, you must assign ports to that VLAN. For COS switches, you can add the **sc0** interface to the private VLAN as well.

6   Map the isolated and community VLANs to promiscuous port(s):

COS	`set pvlan mapping` *primary_number secondary_number mod/port*
IOS	(global) `interface` *type mod/port* (interface) `switchport` (interface) `switchport mode private-vlan promiscuous` (interface) `switchport mode private-vlan mapping` *primary_number secondary_number*

After you have assigned ports to the secondary VLANs, you must map the VLANs to a promiscuous port for access outside of the isolated or community VLAN.

7 *(Optional)* Map the isolated and community VLANs a *Multilayer Switch Feature Card* (MSFC) interface:

COS	`set pvlan mapping` *primary_number secondary_number* `15/1`
	`session 15`
	`(privileged)`**`config t`**
	`(global)`**`interface vlan`** *primary_number*
	`(interface)`**`ip address`** *address mask*
IOS	`(global)` **`interface`** *primary_number*
	`(interface)` **`ip address`** *address mask*
	`(interface)` **`private-vlan mapping`** *primary_number secondary_number*

If your switch has an MSFC, you can map the private VLANs to the MSFC. For a switch running COS, you map the VLAN to port 15/1 (or 16/1 for the MSFC in slot 2), and then configure the IP address on the VLAN interface with the number of the primary VLAN. For an IOS switch, you go to the VLAN interface with the primary number, and then map the primary and secondary VLANs to that port.

Configuring Private Edge VLANs

The 3500XL switch uses the concept of a protected port to allow for control of traffic on the switch. A protected port on a 3500XL will not forward traffic to another protected port on the same switch. This behavior is similar to an isolated VLAN in that protected ports cannot communicate with one another. Use the following command to configure a protected port.

1 *(Optional)* Configure a protected port:

COS	—
IOS	`(global)` **`interface`** *type mod/port*
	`(interface)` **`port protected`**

To configure a private edge VLAN, select the interface and type the command **port protected**. To verify that a port is in protected mode, use the command **show port protected**.

Verifying Private VLAN Operation

After configuring private VLANs, use the following command to verify operation:

COS	**`show pvlan`** *number*
	`show pvlan mapping`
	`show pvlan capability` *mod/port*

IOS	**show vlan private-vlan** *[type]* show interface private-vlan mapping **show interface** *type mod/port* **switchport**

NOTE   A number of guidelines and restrictions apply to private VLANs. For a complete list of these items, go to www.cisco.com/univercd/cc/td/doc/product/lan/cat6000/sw_7_2/ confg_gd/vlans.htm#xtocid21.

Feature Example

Figure 6-5 shows the network diagram for a working private VLAN configuration example. In this example, the switch Access_1 is configured with ports 1 and 2 as protected ports both in VLAN 10. The VLAN 10 server on Distribution_1 is also in VLAN 10. This allows the PCs to connect to the server but not one another. Also on the distribution switch, private VLAN 90 has been created with a community VLAN 901 and an isolated VLAN 900. Server 2 in port 3/46 and Server 3 in port 3/48 are placed in the community VLAN, and servers connected to ports 3/1 and 3/2 are to be placed in the isolated VLAN. All these devices are mapped to the router connected to port 1/2 and the MSFC port 15/1 for interface VLAN 90.

Figure 6-5   *Network Diagram for Private VLAN Configuration*

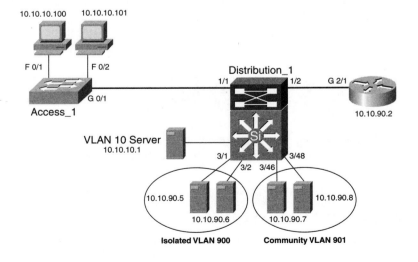

example of the Catalyst OS configuration for Distribution_1 follows:

```
Distribution_1 (enable)>set vtp mode transparent
stribution_1 (enable)>set vlan 90 pvlan-type primary
stribution_1 (enable)>set vlan 900 pvlan-type isolated
stribution_1 (enable)>set vlan 901 pvlan-type community
tribution_1 (enable)>set pvlan 90 900
Distribution_1 (enable)>set pvlan 90 901
Distribution_1 (enable)>set pvlan 90 900 3/1-2
Distribution_1 (enable)>set pvlan 90 901 3/46,3/48
Distribution_1 (enable)>set pvlan mapping 90 900 1/2,15/1
Distribution_1 (enable)>set pvlan mapping 90 901 1/2,15/1
Distribution_1 (enable)>session 15
MSFC_Dist1>enable
MSFC_Dist1#config t
MSFC_Dist1(config)#interface vlan 90
MSFC_Dist1(config-if)#ip address 10.10.90.1 255.255.255.0
MSFC_Dist1(config-if)#no shut
MSFC_Dist1(config-if)#end
MSFC_Dist1#copy running-config startup-config
```

An example of the Supervisor IOS configuration for Distribution_1 follows:

```
Distribution_1#vlan database
Distribution_1(vlan)#vtp transparent
Distribution_1(vlan)#exit
Distribution_1#conf t
Distribution_1(config)#vlan 90
Distribution_1(config-vlan)#private-vlan primary
Distribution_1(config-vlan)#vlan 900
Distribution_1(config-vlan)#private-vlan isolated
Distribution_1(config-vlan)#vlan 901
Distribution_1(config-vlan)#private-vlan community
Distribution_1(config-vlan)#vlan 90
Distribution_1(config-vlan)#private-vlan association 900,901
Distribution_1(config-vlan)#interface range fastethernet 3/1 - 2
Distribution_1(config-if)#switchport
Distribution_1(config-if)#switchport mode private-vlan host
Distribution_1(config-if)#switchport mode private-vlan host-association 90 900
Distribution_1(config-if)#no shut
Distribution_1(config-if)#interface range fastethernet 3/46 , 3/48
Distribution_1(config-if)#switchport
Distribution_1(config-if)#switchport mode private-vlan host
Distribution_1(config-if)#switchport mode private-vlan host-association 90 901
Distribution_1(config-if)#no shut
Distribution_1(config-if)#interface gigabitethernet 1/2
Distribution_1(config-if)#switchport
Distribution_1(config-if)#switchport mode private-vlan promiscuous
Distribution_1(config-if)#switchport mode private-vlan mapping 90 900,901
Distribution_1(config-if)#no shut
Distribution_1(config-vif)#interface vlan 90
Distribution_1(config-if)#ip address 10.10.90.1 255.255.255.0
Distribution_1(config-if)#private-vlan mapping 90 900,901
Distribution_1(config-if)#no shut
Distribution_1(config-if)#end
Distribution_1 #copy running-config startup-config
```

An example of the Layer 2 IOS configuration for Access_1 follows:

```
Access_1 #config t
Access_1 (config)#interface fastethernet 0/1
Access_1 (config-if)#switchport access vlan 10
Access_1 (config-if)#port protected
Access_1 (config)#interface fastethernet 0/2
```

Section 6-6

```
Access_1 (config-if)#switchport access vlan 10
Access_1 (config-if)#port protected
Access_1 (config)#interface gigabitethernet 0/1
Access_1 (config-if)#switchport mode trunk
Access_1 (config-if)#switchport trunk encapsulation dot1Q
Access_1 (config-if)#end
Access_1#copy running-config startup-config
```

Further Reading

Refer to the following recommended sources for further information about the topics covered in this chapter.

Cisco LAN Switching by Kennedy Clark and Kevin Hamilton, Cisco Press, ISBN 1-57870-094-9

Building Cisco Multilayer Switched Networks by Karen Webb, Cisco Press, ISBN 1-57870-093-0

CCNP Switching Exam Certification Guide by Tim Boyles and David Hucaby, Cisco Press, ISBN 1-57870-xxx-x

Securing Networks with Private VLANs and VLAN Access Control Lists at: www.cisco.com/warp/public/473/90.shtml

GVRP (802.1Q) Standard at: http://standards.ieee.org/reading/ieee/std/lanman/802.1Q-1998.pdf

CHAPTER 7

Spanning Tree Protocol (STP)

See the following sections for configuration information about these topics:

- **7-1: STP Operation**—Explains the spanning-tree algorithm in relation to the processes and decisions made by a switch.

- **7-2: STP Configuration**—Presents the basic steps needed to configure the *Spanning Tree Protocol* (STP).

- **7-3: STP Convergence Tuning**—Covers the more advanced steps needed to configure and tune STP convergence.

- **7-4: Navigating the Spanning-Tree Topology**—Offers suggestions on how to find the root of a spanning-tree topology and how to map out an active topology by hand.

7-1: STP Operation

- STP detects and prevents Layer 2 bridging loops from forming. Parallel paths can exist, but only one is allowed to forward frames.

- STP is based on the IEEE 802.1D bridge protocol standard.

- Switches run one instance of STP per VLAN with *Per-VLAN Spanning Tree* (PVST). PVST between switches requires the use of *Inter-Switch Link* (ISL) trunking.

- For IEEE 802.1Q trunks, only a single instance of STP is allowed for *all* VLANs. The *Common Spanning Tree* (CST) is communicated over VLAN 1.

- *PVST+* is a Cisco proprietary extension that allows switches to interoperate between CST and PVST. PVST *bridge protocol data units* (BPDUs) are tunneled over an 802.1Q trunk. Catalyst switches run PVST+ by default.

- *Multiple Instance Spanning Tree Protocol* (MISTP) is also a Cisco proprietary protocol that allows one instance of STP for one or more VLANs via a mapping function. This allows faster convergence with a lower CPU overhead and fewer BPDUs. MISTP discards PVST+ BPDUs.

- *MISTP-PVST+* is a hybrid STP mode used to transition between PVST+ and MISTP in a network. BPDUs from both modes are understood and not discarded.

- *Multiple Spanning Tree* (MST), based on the IEEE 802.1s standard, extends the 802.1w *Rapid Spanning Tree Protocol* (RSTP) to have multiple STP instances.
  - MST is backward-compatible with 802.1D, 802.1w, and PVST+ STP modes.
  - Switches configured with common VLAN and STP instance assignments form a single MST *region*.
  - MST can generate PVST+ BPDUs for interoperability.
  - MST supports up to 16 instances of STP.
- Switches send BPDUs out all ports every Hello Time interval (default 2 seconds).
- BPDUs are not forwarded by a switch; they are used only for further calculation and BPDU generation.
- Switches send two types of BPDUs:
  - Configuration BPDU
  - *Topology change notification* (TCN) BPDU

NOTE   BPDUs are sent to the well-known STP multicast address 01-80-c2-00-00-00, using each switch port's unique MAC address as a source address.

STP Process

1 **Root bridge election**—The switch with the lowest bridge ID becomes the root of the spanning tree. A *bridge ID* (BID) is made up of a 2-byte priority and a 6-byte MAC address. The priority can range from 0 to 65535 and defaults to 32768.

2 **Root port election**—Each nonroot switch elects a root port, or the port "closest" to the root bridge, by determining the port with the lowest root path cost. This cost is carried along in the BPDU. Each nonroot switch along the path adds its local port cost of the port that *receives* the BPDU. The root path cost becomes cumulative as new BPDUs are generated.

3 **Designated port election**—One switch port on each network segment is chosen to handle traffic for that segment. The port that announces the lowest root path cost in the segment becomes the designated port.

4 **Bridging loops are removed**—Switch ports that are neither root ports nor designated ports are placed in the blocking state. This step breaks any bridging loops that would form otherwise.

STP Tiebreakers

When any STP decision has identical conditions or a tie, the final decision is based on this sequence of conditions:

1 The lowest BID

2 The lowest root path cost

3 The lowest sender BID

4 The lowest port ID

Path Costs

By default, switch ports have the path costs defined in Table 7-1.

Table 7-1   *Switch Port Path Costs*

Port Speed	Default Port Cost "Short Mode"	Default Port Cost "Long Mode"
4 mbps	250	N/A
10 mbps	100	2,000,000
16 mbps	62	N/A
45 mbps	39	N/A
100 mbps	19	200,000
155 mbps	14	N/A
622 mbps	6	N/A
1 gbps	4	20,000
10 gbps	2	2000
100 gbps	N/A	200
1000 gbps (1 tbps)	N/A	20
10 tbps	N/A	2

By default, Catalyst switches in PVST+ mode use the "short mode" or 16-bit path or port cost values. When the port speeds in a network are less than 1 gbps, the short mode scale is sufficient. If you have any ports that are 10 gbps or greater, however, set *all* switches in the network to use the "long mode" or 32-bit path cost scale. This ensures that root path cost calculations are consistent on all switches. Switches using MISTP, MISTP-PVST+, or MST automatically use the long-mode values.

NOTE | The IEEE uses a nonlinear scale to relate the port bandwidth of a single link to its port cost value. STP treats bundled links, such as Fast EtherChannel and Gigabit EtherChannel, as a single link with an aggregate bandwidth of the individual links. As a result, remember that the port or path cost used for a bundled EtherChannel will be based on the bundled bandwidth. For example, a two-link Fast EtherChannel has 200 mbps bandwidth and a path cost of 12. A four-link Gigabit EtherChannel has 4 gbps bandwidth and a path cost of 2. Use Table 7-1 to see how these EtherChannel aggregate bandwidth and port costs relate to the values of single or individual links.

STP Port States

Each switch port progresses through a sequence of states:

1 **Disabled**—Ports that are administratively shut down or shut down due to a fault condition. (MST calls this state *discarding*.)

2 **Blocking**—The state used after a port initializes. The port cannot receive or transmit data, cannot add MAC addresses to its address table, and can receive only BPDUs. If a bridging loop is detected, or if the port loses its root or designated port status, it will be returned to the blocking state. (MST calls this state *discarding*.)

3 **Listening**—If a port can become a root or designated port, it is moved into the listening state. The port cannot receive or transmit data and cannot add MAC addresses to its address table. BPDUs can be received and sent. (MST calls this state *discarding*.)

4 **Learning**—After the Forward Delay timer expires (default 15 seconds), the port enters the learning state. The port cannot transmit data, but can send and receive BPDUs. MAC addresses can now be learned and added into the address table.

5 **Forwarding**—After another Forward Delay timer expires (default 15 seconds), the port enters the forwarding state. The port can now send and receive data, learn MAC addresses, and send and receive BPDUs.

STP Topology Changes

- If a switch port is moved into the forwarding state (except when PortFast is enabled), a topology change is signaled.

- If a switch port is moved from the forwarding or learning state into the blocking state, a topology change is signaled.

- To signal a topology change, a switch sends TCN BPDUs on its root port every hello time interval. This occurs until the TCN is acknowledged by the upstream designated bridge neighbor. Neighbors continue to relay the TCN BPDU on their root ports until it is received by the root bridge.

- The root bridge informs the entire spanning tree of the topology change by sending a configuration BPDU with the *topology change* (TC) bit set. This causes all down-stream switches to reduce their Address Table Aging timers from the default value (300 seconds) down to the Forward Delay (default 15 seconds). This flushes inactive MAC addresses out of the table faster than normal.

Improving STP Stability

- STP Root Guard can be used to help enforce the root bridge placement and identity in a switched network. When enabled on a port, Root Guard disables the port if a better BPDU is received. This prevents other unplanned switches from becoming the root.

- STP Root Guard should be enabled on all ports where the root bridge should not appear. This preserves the current choice of the primary and secondary root bridges.

- *Unidirectional Link Detection* (UDLD) provides a means to detect a link that is transmitting in only one direction, enabling you to prevent bridging loops and traffic black holes that are not normally detected or prevented by STP.

- UDLD operates at Layer 2, by sending packets containing the device and port ID to connected neighbors on switch ports. As well, any UDLD packets received from a neighbor are reflected back so that the neighbor can see it has been recognized. UDLD messages are sent at the *message interval* times, usually defaulting to 15 seconds.

- UDLD operates in two modes:

    — **Normal mode**—Unidirectional links are detected and reported as an error, but no other action is taken.

    — **Aggressive mode**—Unidirectional links are detected, reported as an error, and disabled after eight attempts (once a second for eight seconds) to reestablish the link. Disabled ports must be manually reenabled.

- STP Loop Guard detects the absence of BPDUs on the root and alternate root ports. Nondesignated ports are temporarily disabled, preventing them from becoming designated ports and moving into the forwarding state.

- STP Loop Guard should be enabled on the root and alternate root ports (both non-designated) for all possible active STP topologies.

STP Operation Example

As an example of STP operation, consider a network of three Catalyst switches connected in a triangle fashion as illustrated in Figure 7-1. RP labels the root ports, DP labels designated ports, F labels ports in the forwarding state, and X labels ports that are in the blocking state.

Figure 7-1 *Network Diagram for the STP Operation Example*

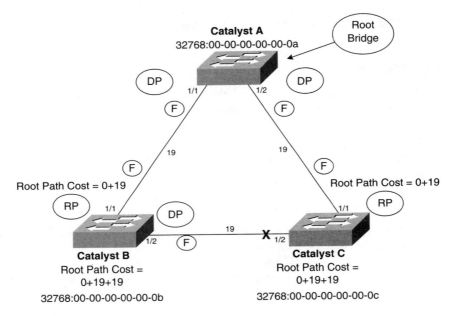

The spanning-tree algorithm proceeds as follows:

1. **The root bridge is elected**—All three switches have equal bridge priorities (32768, the default). However, Catalyst A has the lowest MAC address (00-00-00-00-00-0a), so it becomes the root bridge.

2. **The root ports are chosen**—The lowest root path costs are computed on each switch. These are Catalyst B port 1/1, which has a root path cost of 0+19, and Catalyst C port 1/1, which also has a root path cost of 0+19.

3. **The designated ports are chosen**—By definition, all ports on the root bridge become designated ports for their segments. Therefore, ports 1/1 and 1/2 on Catalyst A are designated. Catalyst B port 1/2 and Catalyst C port 1/2 share a segment, requiring that one of them become designated. The root path cost for each of these ports is 0+19+19 or 38, resulting in a tie. The lowest-sending BID breaks the tie, so Catalyst B (having the lowest MAC address of the two) port 1/2 becomes the designated port.

4 **All ports that are neither root nor designated ports are put in the blocking state**—The only remaining port that is neither root nor designated is Catalyst C port 1/2. This port is moved to the blocking state (as shown by the X in the figure).

7-2: STP Configuration

1 *(Optional)* Enable or disable STP:

COS	`set spantree [enable	disable] [vlan]`
IOS	`(global) [no] spanning-tree [vlan vlan]`

STP is enabled by default on VLAN 1 and any newly created VLANs. Without a specified VLAN, STP is enabled or disabled on all VLANs. Be aware that if STP is disabled, bridging loops are not detected and prevented. You should always enable STP.

2 *(Optional)* Set the STP mode for the switch (Catalyst 4000 and 6000 only):

COS	`set spantree mode {mistp	pvst+	mistp-pvst+	mst}`
IOS	N/A

By default, all Catalyst switches run PVST+ STP for one instance of STP on each VLAN. To configure other STP modes, use the keywords **mistp** (MISTP), **mistp-pvst+** (MISTP-PVST+ interoperability), or **mst** (MST).

3 *(MST only)* Activate an MST instance (Catalyst 4000 and 6000 only).

a. Identify the MST region:

COS	`set spantree mst config {name name} {revision number}`
IOS	N/A

The MST region is identified by *name* (a text string up to 32 characters). If no name is given, no region name is used. You can use a region revision number to indicate the number of times the region configuration has changed. The revision *number* (0 to 65535, default 1) must be explicitly set and is not automatically incremented with region changes.

b. Map one or more VLANs to the instance:

COS	`set spantree mst instance vlan vlan`
IOS	N/A

A *vlan* number (1 to 1005, 1025 to 4094) is mapped to the MST *instance* (0 to 15). This mapping is held in the MST region buffer until the changes are committed.

c. Commit the region mapping:

COS	`set spantree mst config commit`
IOS	N/A

MST region configuration changes are placed into an edit buffer, which is locked to the user making the change. These changes must be committed before they will become active. Committing the changes also unlocks the edit buffer so that another edit session can be initiated.

d. *(Optional)* Undo the last region configuration changes:

COS	`set spantree mst config rollback [force]`
IOS	N/A

If MST region configuration changes have been made in error, they can be retracted by using the **rollback** keyword. This can be done only on changes that have not yet been committed or applied. If another user has made changes and holds the edit buffer lock, you can add the **force** keyword to unlock the buffer and remove the changes.

4 *(Optional)* Placement of the root bridge switch.

NOTE	The root bridge (and secondary root bridges) should be placed near the "center" of the network, so that an optimum spanning-tree topology is computed. Typically, the root is located in the core or distribution layers of the network. If you choose not to manually configure the root placement, the switch with the lowest BID will win the root election. This almost always produces a spanning-tree topology that is inefficient.

COS	PVST+: **set spantree root** [**secondary**] [*vlans*] [**dia** *net-diameter*] [**hello** *hello-time*] MISTP: **set spantree root** [**secondary**] **mistp-instance** *instance* [**dia** *net-diameter*] [**hello** *hello-time*] MST: **set spantree root** [**secondary**] **mst** *instance* [**dia** *net-diameter*] [**hello** *hello-time*]
IOS	PVST+: (global) **spanning-tree vlan** *vlan* **root** {**primary** | **secondary**} [**diameter** *net-diameter* [**hello-time** *hello-time*]]

The switch is made to become the primary root bridge for the VLANs (a list of VLAN numbers 1 to 1005 and 1025 to 4094) or STP instances (1 to 16) specified (VLAN 1 if unspecified). The bridge priority value is modified as follows: If it is more than

8192, it is set to 8192; if it is already less than 8192, it is set to a value less than the current root bridge's priority. You can use the **secondary** keyword to place a secondary or backup root bridge, in case of a primary root failure. Here, the bridge priority is set to 16384. (For MST, the root priority is set to 24576, and the secondary priority to 28672.)

The **dia** keyword specifies the diameter or the maximum number of bridges or switches between two endpoints across the network (1 to 7, default 7). The BPDU Hello Time interval can also be set (default 2 seconds). Setting the network diameter causes other STP timer values to be automatically calculated and changed. You can adjust the timers explicitly with other commands, but adjusting the diameter hides the complexity of the timer calculations.

NOTE

This Supervisor IOS command is not available on the Catalyst 2900XL and 3500XL family switches.

5 *(Optional)* Adjust the bridge priority:

COS	PVST+: **set spantree priority** *priority vlans*
	MISTP: **set spantree priority** *priority* **mistp-instance** *instance-list*
	MST: **set spantree priority** *priority* **mst** *instance-list*
IOS	PVST+: (global) **spanning-tree vlan** *vlan* **priority** *priority*

You can also directly modify the bridge priority to achieve other values than the automatic root or secondary priorities. The priority can be set on a per-VLAN or -instance basis. Instances can be given as an *instance-list*, as one or more instance numbers separated by commas, or a hyphenated range of numbers.

To force a switch to become the root, the priority should be chosen such that the root bridge has a *lower* priority than all other switches on that VLAN or STP instance. The bridge priority ranges from 0 to 65535 (default 32768) for PVST+, or one of the values 0 (highest), 4096, 8192, 12288, 16384, 20480, 24576, 28672, 32768, 36864, 40960, 45056, 49152, 53248, 57344, and 61440 (lowest) for MISTP.

6 *(Optional)* Prevent other switches from becoming the STP root bridge:

COS	**set spantree guard {root	none}** *mod/port*
IOS	(interface) **spanning-tree guard {root	none}**
	-OR-
	(interface) **spanning-tree rootguard**

STP Root Guard will be enabled on the port or interface. If another bridge connected to that port tries to become the root, the port will be moved to *root-inconsistent* (listening) STP state. When BPDUs are no longer detected on the port, it will be moved back into normal operation.

On Catalyst 2900XL and 3500XL family switches, the **rootguard** keyword is used.

7 *(Optional)* Tune the root path cost.

a. *(Optional)* Set the port cost scale (Catalyst 4000 and 6000 only):

COS	`set spantree defaultcostmode {short	long}`
IOS	`(global) spanning-tree pathcost defaultcost-method {long	short}`

By default, PVST+ switches use the **short** (16-bit) port cost values. If you have any ports that are 10 gbps or greater, you should set the port cost scale to **long** (32-bit) values on *every* switch in your network. MISTP, MISTP-PVST+, and MST modes use long mode by default.

b. Set the port cost for all VLANs or instances:

COS	`set spantree portcost mod/port cost [mst]`
IOS	`(interface) spanning-tree cost cost`

The port cost can be set to *cost* (1 to 65535 short or MISTP mode, 1 to 2000000 long mode) for all VLANs or STP instances. The **mst** keyword signifies a port used in MST.

c. Set the port cost per VLAN or per instance:

COS	PVST+: `set spantree portvlancost mod/port [cost cost] [vlan-list]` MISTP: `set spantree portinstancecost mod/port [cost cost] [instances]` MST: `set spantree portinstancecost mod/port [cost cost] mst [instances]`
IOS	PVST+: `(interface) spanning-tree vlan vlan-id cost cost`

The port cost can be set to *cost* (1 to 65535 short mode, 1 to 2000000 long mode) for the VLAN *vlan-id* or the list of VLANs, *vlan-list,* or STP instance (0 to 15).

8 *(Optional)* Tune the port priority.

a. Set the port priority for all VLANs or instances:

COS	`set spantree portpri mod/port priority [mst]`
IOS	`(interface) spanning-tree port-priority port-priority`

The port priority can be set to *priority* (0 to 63 for COS, or 2 to 255 for IOS). Use the **mst** keyword to signify that the port is used for MST.

b. Set the port priority per VLAN or per instance:

COS	PVST+: **set spantree portvlanpri** *mod/port priority* [*vlans*]
	MISTP: **set spantree portinstancepri** *mod/port priority* [*instances*]
	MST: **set spantree portinstancepri** *mod/port priority* **mst** [*instances*]
IOS	PVST+: (interface) **spanning-tree vlan** *vlan-list* **port-priority** *priority*

The port priority can be set to *priority* (0 to 63 for COS, 0 to 255 for IOS) for the VLAN *vlan-id* or the list of VLANs, *vlan-list,* or STP instance (0 to 15).

9 *(MISTP only)* Activate a MISTP instance.

a. Enable a MISTP instance:

| COS | **set spantree enable mistp-instance** {*instance* | **all**} |
| IOS | N/A |

MISTP instance 1 is enabled by default. You can enable other instances by *instance* number (1 to 16) or the keyword **all**.

b. Map VLANs to a MISTP instance:

| COS | **set vlan** *vlan-list* **mistp-instance** {*instance* | **none**} |
| IOS | N/A |

One or more VLAN numbers can be given as *vlan-list*, to be mapped to a single MISTP instance. If you happen to assign a VLAN to more than one instance, all of that VLAN's ports will be set to STP blocking mode. You can use the keyword **none** to unmap the VLANs from any mapped instance.

10 *(Optional)* Detect unidirectional connections with UDLD.

a. Enable UDLD on the switch:

| COS | **set udld** {**enable** | **disable**} |
| IOS | (global) **udld** {**enable** | **aggressive**} |

By default, UDLD is disabled. It must be enabled before it can be used on specific ports. The Supervisor IOS allows the keyword **aggressive** to be used to globally enable UDLD aggressive mode on all Ethernet fiber-optic interfaces.

b. *(Optional)* Adjust the UDLD message interval timer:

COS	`set udld interval` *interval*
IOS	`(global)` `udld message time` *interval*

The UDLD message interval can be set to *interval* (7 to 90 seconds; COS default is 15 seconds, Supervisor IOS is 60 seconds).

c. Enable UDLD on specific ports:

COS	`set udld {enable	disable}` *mod/port*
IOS	`(interface)` `udld {enable	disable}`

After UDLD has been globally enabled on a switch, UDLD is also enabled by default on all Ethernet fiber-optic ports. UDLD is disabled by default on all Ethernet twisted-pair media ports.

d. *(Optional)* Enable UDLD aggressive mode on specific ports:

COS	`set udld aggressive-mode enable	disable` *mod/port*
IOS	`(interface)` `udld aggressive`

After aggressive mode has been enabled on a port, the port is disabled when a unidirectional connection is detected. It must be manually reenabled after the problem has been corrected. On the Supervisor IOS, use the EXEC command **udld reset** to reenable all ports that are disabled by UDLD.

11 *(Optional)* Improve STP stability with Loop Guard:

COS	`set spantree guard loop` *mod/port*
IOS	N/A

Loop Guard should be enabled only on the ports that you know are root or alternate root ports. For example, the uplink ports on an access layer switch would always be root or alternate root ports, because they are closest to the root bridge. (This assumes that you have placed the root bridge toward the center of your network.)

Displaying Information About STP

Table 7-2 lists the switch commands that you can use to display helpful information about STP.

Table 7-2   *Switch Commands to Display STP Information*

Display Function	Switch OS	Command
STP for a specific VLAN	COS	`show spantree` *vlan* `active`
	IOS	`(exec)` `show spanning-tree vlan` *vlan*
STP state for all VLANs on a trunk	COS	`show spantree` *mod/num*
	IOS	`(exec)` `show spanning-tree interface` *mod/num*
STP statistics for a VLAN on a port	COS	`show spantree statistics` *mod/num vlan*
	IOS	N/A
Ports in the blocking state	COS	`show spantree blockedports` [*vlan*]
	IOS	N/A
Log STP events	COS	`set logging level spantree` *severity*
	IOS	N/A

STP Configuration Examples

As a good practice, you should always configure one switch in your network as a primary root bridge for a VLAN and another switch as a secondary root. Suppose you build a network and forget to do this. What might happen if the switches are left to sort out a spanning-tree topology on their own, based on the default STP parameters?

Poor STP Root Placement

The top half of Figure 7-2 shows an example network of three Catalyst switches connected in a triangle fashion. Catalysts C1 and C2 form the core layer of the network, whereas Catalyst A connects to the end users in the access layer. (C1 and C2 might also be considered distribution layer switches if the overall campus network doesn't have a distinct core layer. In any event, think of them as the highest layer or the backbone of the network.)

As it might be expected, the links between the core and other switches are Gigabit Ethernet. The uplinks from Catalyst A into the core, however, are Fast Ethernet.

Figure 7-2 *Network Diagram Demonstrating Poor STP Root Placement*

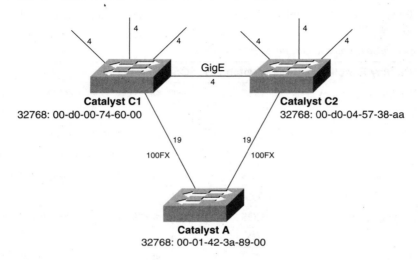

When the root bridge is elected, Catalyst A wins based on its lower MAC address. (All switches have their default bridge priorities of 32768.) Both of the uplink ports on switch A become designated ports, because it is now the root. The downlinks from C1 and C2 to switch A become root ports. Switch C1 makes its Gigabit Ethernet link to C2 a designated port because it has the lower sending BID. And sadly, switch C2 must move its Gigabit Ethernet link to C1 into the blocking state because it is neither a root nor a designated port. You can see this in the lower half of the figure.

Clearly, an inefficient topology has surfaced, because all the traffic passing across the network core must now pass across lower-speed links through switch A. Switch A, being an access layer switch, is also likely to have less horsepower than the core layer switches.

To remedy this situation, place the STP root bridge somewhere in the core or highest hierarchical layer of the network. You can do this with the following command for VLAN 10 on switch C1, for example:

COS	`set spantree root 10`
IOS	`(global)` `spanning-tree vlan 10 root primary`

Alternatively, you can explicitly set the bridge priorities with these commands (available on all Catalyst models):

COS	`set spantree priority 8192 10`
IOS	`(global)` `spanning-tree vlan 10 priority 8192`

STP Load Balancing

Figure 7-3 shows a network diagram consisting of three switches that are connected in a triangle fashion. Each of the links between switches is a trunk, carrying two VLANs. The switches will be configured so that the two VLANs are load balanced across the available trunks. The lower half of the figure shows the resulting spanning-tree topologies for VLAN 100 and VLAN 101.

Distribution switch Catalyst D1 will be chosen as the root bridge. Some users connected to access switch Catalyst A1 are on VLAN 100, whereas other users are on VLAN 101. The idea is to have VLAN 100 traffic forwarded to distribution switch Catalyst D1, while VLAN 101 traffic goes to Catalyst D2.

NOTE   Switch D1 has been selected as the root bridge for both VLANs for simplicity and to demonstrate the use of port cost adjustments in load balancing. You could also configure D1 as the root for VLAN 100 and D2 as the root for VLAN 101. The resulting STP topologies would be the same, but there would be no need to adjust the port costs in switch A1.

An additional benefit is that the two trunk links will failover to each other. Should one trunk link fail, the other moves from blocking into forwarding mode, forwarding both VLANs 100 and 101 across the same trunk. If the STP UplinkFast feature is also used on both switches, the link failover is almost instantaneous.

Figure 7-3   *Network Diagram for the STP Load-Balancing Example*

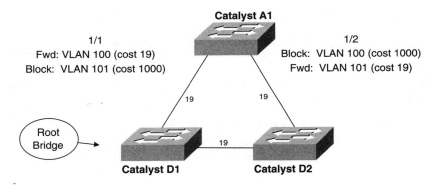

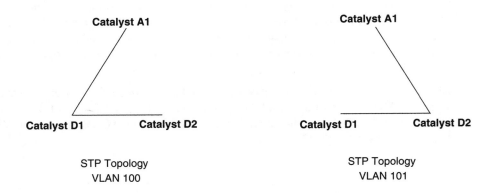

Switch Catalyst D1 will be configured as the primary root bridge for both VLANs, whereas Catalyst D2 will become the secondary root bridge. If D1 fails, D2 becomes the new root.

Catalyst D1 can be configured with these commands (if they are available on the switch OS):

COS	`set spantree root 100,101`
IOS	(global) `spanning-tree vlan 100 root primary` (global) `spanning-tree vlan 101 root primary`

Alternatively, you can explicitly set the bridge priorities with these commands (available on all Catalyst models):

COS	`set spantree priority 8192 100` `set spantree priority 8192 101`
IOS	(global) `spanning-tree vlan 100 priority 8192` (global) `spanning-tree vlan 101 priority 8192`

Catalyst D2 can be configured with these commands to become the secondary root:

COS	`set spantree root secondary 100,101`
IOS	(global) `spanning-tree vlan 100 root secondary` (global) `spanning-tree vlan 101 root secondary`

Alternatively, you can explicitly set D2's bridge priorities:

COS	`set spantree priority 8200 100` `set spantree priority 8200 101`
IOS	(global) `spanning-tree vlan 100 priority 8200` (global) `spanning-tree vlan 101 priority 8200`

Finally, Catalyst A1 will have the port cost adjusted for ports 1/1 and 1/2 for the two VLANs. Recall that the default port cost is shown as 19 in the diagram. We will be setting the new costs to 1000 on the undesirable paths so that those ports will be blocking. For example, VLAN 101 on port 1/1 will be blocked because it has a higher port cost of 1000:

COS	`set spantree portvlancost 1/1 cost 1000 101` `set spantree portvlancost 1/2 cost 1000 100`
IOS	(global) `interface fastethernet 1/1` (interface) `spanning-tree vlan 101 cost 1000` (global) `interface fastethernet 1/2` (interface) `spanning-tree vlan 100 cost 1000`

7-3: STP Convergence Tuning

- STP bases its operation on several timers. Usually, the default timer values are used for proper STP behavior. The defaults are based on a network diameter of seven switches but can be adjusted for faster convergence times.

  — The Hello Timer triggers periodic hello messages to neighboring switches.

  — The Forward Delay timer specifies the time a port stays in each of the listening and learning states.

  — The MaxAge timer specifies the lifetime of a stored BPDU received on a designated port. After the timer expires, other ports can become designated ports.

- BPDUs are expected at regular intervals. If they are delayed beyond the lapse of an STP timer, topology changes can be triggered in error. This condition can be detected with the *BPDU skewing* feature.

- *STP PortFast* allows ports that connect to hosts or nonbridging network devices to enter the forwarding mode immediately when the link is established. This bypasses the normal STP port states for faster startup, but allows the potential for bridging loops to form.

- *STP UplinkFast* is used only on leaf-node switches (the ends of the ST branches), usually located in the access layer. The switch keeps track of all potential paths to the root, which are in the blocking state.

  — When the root port fails, an alternate port is brought into the forwarding state without the normal STP port state progression and delays.

  — When UplinkFast is enabled, the bridge priority is raised to 49152, making it unlikely to become the root bridge. All switch ports have their port costs increased by 3000 so that they won't be chosen as root ports.

  — When an alternate root port comes up, the switch updates upstream switches with the new location of downstream devices. Dummy multicasts are sent to destination 01-00-0C-CD-CD-CD that contains the MAC addresses of stations in the bridging table.

- *STP BackboneFast* causes switches in the network core to actively look for alternate paths to the root bridge in case of an indirect failure.

  — When used, this feature should be enabled on *all* switches in the network. Switches use a request-and-reply mechanism to determine root path stability, so all switches must be able to participate.

  — BackboneFast can only reduce the convergence delay from the default 50 seconds (20 seconds for the MaxAge timer to expire, and 15 seconds in both listening and learning states) to 30 seconds.

Configuring STP Convergence Tuning

1 *(Optional)* Tune the STP timers to adjust convergence.

Section 7-3

NOTE   STP timer values should only be modified on the root bridge. The root will propagate the values to all other switches through its configuration BPDUs.

If you think that the STP timers must be adjusted, consider doing this by setting the network diameter on the STP root bridge. After the diameter has been set, all the other STP timer values are computed and adjusted automatically. Refer to Step 4 in section "7-2: STP Configuration" for more details.

a. *(Optional)* Adjust the STP Hello timer:

COS	PVST+: **set spantree hello** *interval* [*vlan-list*]
	MISTP: **set spantree hello** *interval* **mistp-instance** *instances*
	MST: **set spantree hello** *interval* **mst**
IOS	PVST+: (global) **spanning-tree** [**vlan** *vlan*] **hello-time** *interval*

The Hello timer can be set to *interval* (1 to 10 seconds, default 2 seconds). It can be set for specific VLANs or STP instances, or globally for VLAN 1 (COS) or all VLANs (IOS) if the VLAN number is not given.

b. (Optional) Adjust the STP Forward Delay timer:

COS	PVST+: **set spantree fwddelay** *delay* [*vlans*]
	MISTP: **set spantree fwddelay** *delay* **mistp-instance** [*instances*]
	MST: **set spantree fwddelay** *delay* **mst**
IOS	PVST+: **spanning-tree vlan** *vlan* **forward-time** *delay*

The Forward Delay interval can be set to *delay* (4 to 30 seconds, default 15 seconds) for specific VLANs, specific instances, or globally for VLAN 1 (COS) or all VLANs (IOS) if the VLAN number is not given.

c. (Optional) Adjust the STP MaxAge timer:

COS	PVST+: **set spantree maxage** *agingtime* [*vlan*]
	MISTP: **set spantree maxage** *agingtime* **mistp-instance** *instances*
	MST: **set spantree maxage** *agingtime* **mst**
IOS	PVST+: (global) **spanning-tree** [**vlan** *vlan*] **max-age** *agingtime*

The MaxAge timer can be set to *agingtime* (6 to 40 seconds, default 20 seconds) for specific VLANs, instances, or globally for VLAN 1 (COS) or all VLANs (IOS) if the VLAN number is not given.

2 *(Optional)* Detect BPDU skewing problems:

COS	`set spantree bpdu-skewing {enable	disable}`
IOS	N/A

For troubleshooting purposes, you can detect the delay or "skew" in BPDU reception by using the **enable** keyword (disabled by default). Any BPDU skewing events are logged on the switch. You can then use the **show spantree bpdu-skewing** *vlan* [*mod/port*] command to view the skew statistics that have been gathered.

3 *(Optional)* Use PortFast STP convergence for access layer nodes.

a. Use PortFast on specific ports:

COS	`set spantree portfast` *mod/port* `{enable [trunk]	disable	default}`
IOS	`(interface)` **`spanning-tree portfast`**

You can **enable** or **disable** PortFast on nontrunking ports. As well, you can use the keyword **trunk** to force PortFast to be used on a trunking link. The **default** keyword causes the port to be returned to its default behavior, configured by the optional command **set spantree global-default portfast** {**enable** | **disable**}.

NOTE   Enabling PortFast on a port also prevents TCN BPDUs from being generated due to a state change on the port. Although STP is still operating on the port to prevent bridging loops, topology changes are not triggered when the attached host goes up or down.

You should use the PortFast feature only on switch ports where single hosts are connected. In other words, don't enable PortFast on switch ports that connect to other switches or hubs, whether the ports or trunking or not.

b. *(Optional)* Enable PortFast BPDU Guard to improve STP stability:

COS	`set spantree portfast bpdu-guard` *mod/port* `{enable	disable	default}`
IOS	`(global)` **`spanning-tree portfast bpduguard`**

On a nontrunked port with PortFast enabled, BPDU Guard moves the port into the *Errdisable* state if a BPDU is detected. You can use **enable** or **disable** to control the BPDU filtering state on the port. Use the **default** keyword to return the port to the global default set by the optional command **set spantree global-default bpdu-guard** {**enable** | **disable**}.

On the Supervisor IOS, BPDU Guard is enabled globally on all ports that have PortFast enabled.

NOTE   This Supervisor IOS command is not available on the Catalyst 2900XL and 3500XL family switches.

c. *(Optional)* Enable PortFast BPDU Filtering to stop BPDU processing on a port:

COS	`set spantree portfast bpdu-filter` `mod/port` {`enable`	`disable`	`default`}
IOS	N/A

BPDU Filtering causes the switch to stop sending BPDUs on the specified port. As well, incoming BPDUs on that port will not be processed. You can use **enable** or **disable** to control the BPDU Filtering state on the port. Use the **default** keyword to return the port to the global default set by the optional command **set spantree global-default bpdu-filter** {**enable** | **disable**}.

4 *(Optional)* Use UplinkFast STP convergence for access layer uplinks:

COS	`set spantree uplinkfast` {`enable`	`disable`} [`rate` `station_update_rate`] [`all-protocols` {`off`	`on`}]
IOS	(global) `spanning-tree uplinkfast` [`max-update-rate` `packets-per-second`]

The switch can generate dummy multicasts at a rate up to *station-update-rate* per 100 milliseconds (Catalyst OS, default 15 per 100 ms) or *packets-per-second* (Supervisor IOS, default 150 packets per second). The **all-protocols** keyword can be used to generate multicasts for each protocol filtering group.

TIP   To disable UplinkFast and return the bridge priority and port costs to their original values, use the **clear spantree uplinkfast** COS command.

Section 7-3

TIP   If you are using GigaStack stacking GBIC modules on a Catalyst 2900XL, 3500XL, or 3550, you can connect more than one switch to a single *Gigabit Interface Converter* (GBIC) port. The stacking GBIC, having two physical connections, becomes a multidrop backbone, making the normal UplinkFast feature ineffective during a topology change.

You can enable *Cross-Stack UplinkFast* (CSUF) in addition to UplinkFast, allowing fast failover through the stacking GBIC connection. You can enable CSUF on only one stacking GBIC interface per switch and should enable it on all switches connected to the stack:

COS	N/A
IOS	(interface) **spanning-tree stack-port**

5 *(Optional)* Use BackboneFast STP convergence for redundant backbone links:

COS	**set spantree backbonefast {enable	disable}**
IOS	(global) **spanning-tree backbonefast**

When used, you should enable on all switches in the network. BackboneFast is enabled or disabled for all VLANs on the switch.

7-4: Navigating a Spanning-Tree Topology

Although navigating a spanning-tree topology is a rather tedious process, it is usually the only way to verify that the STP is operating as it was intended. Many times, you will have a diagram of the switches in the network showing the physical or logical interconnections. The spanning-tree topology, however, usually goes undocumented until there is a problem.

You might have to troubleshoot a network that is foreign to you, or one that is not completely documented. In this case, you need to get an idea of the current active STP topology—especially the root bridge location.

1 Find the root bridge.

a. Choose a switch to use as a starting point.

Ideally, you want to start out on the root bridge at the "top" of the STP hierarchy. If you don't know which switch is the root for a given VLAN, any switch will do as a starting point.

b. Display the root ID, local BID, and root port:

COS	**show spantree** *vlan* **active**
IOS	(exec) **show spanning-tree vlan** *vlan*

An example of the COS output follows. Notice that the designated root port consists of a list of switch ports (1/1, 1/2, 2/1, and 2/2). On this COS switch, the four ports have been bundled as an EtherChannel. STP treats this as a single logical link:

```
switch (enable) show spantree 534 active
VLAN 534
Spanning tree mode        PVST+
Spanning tree type        ieee
Spanning tree enabled

Designated Root           00-d0-04-57-3a-15
Designated Root Priority  8000
Designated Root Cost      2
Designated Root Port      1/1-2,2/1-2 (agPort 13/1)
Root Max Age   20 sec   Hello Time 2  sec   Forward Delay 15 sec

Bridge ID MAC ADDR        00-d0-ff-8a-2a-15
Bridge ID Priority        32768
Bridge Max Age 20 sec   Hello Time 2  sec   Forward Delay 15 sec

Port                      Vlan Port-State    Cost      Prio Portfast Channel_id
----------------------    ---- ------------  --------- ---- -------- ----------
1/1-2,2/1-2               534  forwarding          2    32 disabled 769
3/1,4/1                   534  forwarding         12    32 disabled 833
5/4                       534  forwarding          4    32 disabled 0
5/5                       534  forwarding          4    32 disabled 0
5/6                       534  forwarding          4    32 disabled 0
5/7                       534  forwarding          4    32 disabled 0
```

An example of the Supervisor IOS command follows:

```
switch#show spanning-tree vlan 534

Spanning tree 534 is executing the IEEE compatible Spanning Tree protocol
  Bridge Identifier has priority 49152, address 0005.32f5.45ef
  Configured hello time 2, max age 20, forward delay 15
  Current root has priority 8000, address 00d0.0457.3a15
  Root port is 67, cost of root path is 3006
  Topology change flag not set, detected flag not set, changes 132
  Times:  hold 1, topology change 35, notification 2
          hello 2, max age 20, forward delay 15
  Timers: hello 0, topology change 0, notification 0
  Fast uplink switchover is enabled
  Stack port is GigabitEthernet0/2

Interface Fa0/1 (port 13) in Spanning tree 534 is FORWARDING
   Port path cost 3019, Port priority 128
   Designated root has priority 8000, address 00d0.0457.3a15
   Designated bridge has priority 49152, address 0005.32f5.45ef
   Designated port is 14, path cost 3006
   Timers: message age 0, forward delay 0, hold 0
   BPDU: sent 2967446, received 0
   The port is in the portfast mode
...(output removed)...
Interface Gi0/1 (port 67) in Spanning tree 534 is FORWARDING
   Port path cost 3004, Port priority 128
   Designated root has priority 8000, address 00d0.0457.3a15
   Designated bridge has priority 32768, address 00d0.ff8a.2a15
   Designated port is 7, path cost 2
   Timers: message age 3, forward delay 0, hold 0
   BPDU: sent 3, received 2967537
```

Section 7-4

```
Interface Gi0/2 (port 75) in Spanning tree 534 is FORWARDING
   Port path cost 4, Port priority 128
   Designated root has priority 8000, address 00d0.0457.3a15
   Designated bridge has priority 49152, address 0005.32f5.45ef
   Designated port is 75, path cost 3006
   Timers: message age 0, forward delay 0, hold 0
   BPDU: sent 2967519, received 1
switch#
```

c. Follow the root port toward the root bridge.

Remember that a switch has only one root port, and that port leads toward the root bridge. A switch can have many designated ports, and those lead away from the root bridge. Our goal is to find the neighboring switch that is connected to the root port.

Notice in the example output of Step 1b that the COS displays the root port as a physical module and port number (1/1-2, 2/1-2—as a single bundled Gigabit EtherChannel), but the Supervisor IOS shows this as a logical port number (port 67). The port number is an index into the interfaces according to the STP. You can either page through the output until you find the interface with the port number or you can use the EXEC command **show spanning-tree brief | begin VLAN**_vlan_ to see only the port number associated with the specific VLAN number. An example of this follows:

```
switch# show spanning-tree brief | begin VLAN534
VLAN534
  Spanning tree enabled protocol IEEE
  ROOT ID    Priority 8000
             Address 00d0.0457.3a15
             Hello Time   2 sec  Max Age 20 sec  Forward Delay 15 sec

  Bridge ID  Priority   49152
             Address    0005.32f5.45ef
             Hello Time   2 sec  Max Age 20 sec  Forward Delay 15 sec

Port                            Designated
Name    Port ID Prio Cost Sts  Cost  Bridge ID       Port ID
------- ------- ---- ---- ---  ----  --------------- -------
Fa0/1   128.13  128  3100 BLK  3006  0005.32f5.45ef 128.13
Fa0/2   128.14  128  3019 FWD  3006  0005.32f5.45ef 128.14
...(output removed)...

Gi0/1   128.67  128  3004 FWD  2     00d0.ff8a.2a15 129.7
Gi0/2   128.75  128  4    FWD  3006  0005.32f5.45ef 128.75
```

Here, STP port 67 corresponds to the physical interface Gigabit0/1. The Supervisor IOS output also shows a bonus piece of information—the MAC address of the designated bridge on the root port.

d. Identify the designated bridge on the root port:

COS	**show cdp neighbor** _mod/num_ **detail**
IOS	(exec) **show cdp neighbor** _type mod/num_ **detail**

The neighboring switch can be found as a _Cisco Discovery Protocol_ (CDP) neighbor, if CDP is in use. Look for the neighbor's IP address in the output. An example follows:

```
switch#show cdp neighbor gigabitEthernet 0/1 detail
------------------------
Device ID: SCA03320048(Switch-B)
Entry address(es):
  IP address: 192.168.254.17
Platform: WS-C6509,  Capabilities: Trans-Bridge Switch
Interface: GigabitEthernet0/1,  Port ID (outgoing port): 5/7
Holdtime : 120 sec
```

After the IP address has been found, you can open a Telnet session to the neighboring switch.

e. Repeat Steps 1b, 1c, and 1d until you are at the root.

How will you know when you have reached the root bridge? The local BID will be identical to the root bridge ID, and the root cost will be 0. See the following example from a Catalyst OS switch:

```
switch (enable) show spantree 534 active
VLAN 534
Spanning tree mode         PVST+
Spanning tree type         ieee
Spanning tree enabled

Designated Root            00-d0-04-57-3a-15
Designated Root Priority   8000
Designated Root Cost       0
Designated Root Port       1/0
Root Max Age   20 sec   Hello Time 2  sec   Forward Delay 15 sec

Bridge ID MAC ADDR         00-d0-04-57-3a-15
Bridge ID Priority         8000
Bridge Max Age 20 sec   Hello Time 2  sec   Forward Delay 15 sec

Port                     Vlan Port-State   Cost      Prio Portfast Channel_id
-----------------------  ---- -----------  --------- ---- -------- ----------
1/1-2,2/1-2              534  forwarding          2   32 disabled 769
3/1-2,4/1-2              534  forwarding          2   32 disabled 833
 3/3                     534  forwarding          4   32 disabled 0
```

Notice that the root bridge and local BID MAC addresses are the same and that the root priorities are also the same. (Recall that the BID is made up of both the MAC address and the bridge priority.) This must be the root bridge for VLAN 534.

2 Draw out the active topology from the top down.

Beginning at the root bridge, look for other switches that are participating in the spanning tree for a specific VLAN.

a. Identify other neighboring switches:

COS	**show cdp neighbor detail**
IOS	(exec) **show cdp neighbor detail**

Every neighbor can be identified by name, IP address, and connecting port. There will usually be more neighbors listed on switches that are toward the core layer and fewer neighbors on the access layer.

b. Identify the BID, the root and designated ports, and their costs:

COS	`show spantree` `vlan` `active`
IOS	`(exec)` `show spanning-tree brief	begin VLAN`*vlan*

The BID and the root port will be listed first. The switch ports on VLAN number *vlan* will be listed, along with their STP states and port costs. The designated ports are the ones marked in the *forwarding* state.

c. Identify the blocking ports:

COS	`show spantree blockedports` *vlan*
IOS	`(exec)` `show spanning-tree vlan` *vlan* `| include BLOCKING`

d. Move to a neighboring switch and repeat Steps 2a through 2c.

Further Reading

Refer to the following recommended sources for further information about the topics covered in this chapter.

Cisco LAN Switching by Kennedy Clark and Kevin Hamilton, Cisco Press, ISBN 1-57870-094-9

Building Cisco Multilayer Switched Networks by Karen Webb, Cisco Press, ISBN 1-57870-093-0

CCNP Switching Exam Certification Guide by Tim Boyles and David Hucaby, Cisco Press, ISBN 1-58720-000-7

Interconnections: Bridges, Routers, Switches, and Internetworking Protocols by Radia Perlman, Addison-Wesley, ISBN 0-20163-448-1

Understanding and Configuring the Cisco Uplink Fast Feature at: www.cisco.com/warp/customer/473/51.html

Understanding Spanning Tree Protocol's Backbone Fast Feature at: www.cisco.com/warp/customer/473/18.html

802.1D MAC Bridges, IEEE, at: www.ieee802.org/1/pages/802.1D.html

802.1s Multiple Spanning Trees, IEEE, at: www.ieee802.org/1/pages/802.1s.html

CHAPTER 8

Multilayer Switching

See the following sections to configure and use these features:

- **8-1: Multilayer Switching**—Discusses the configuration of Layer 3 switching on platforms that support *multilayer switching* (MLS) and have separate route processor and switching engines.

- **8-2: Cisco Express Forwarding**—Covers the steps that tune Layer 3 switching on the platforms that support *Cisco Express Forwarding* (CEF).

- **8-3: NetFlow Data Export**—Explains how to use *NetFlow Data Export* (NDE) to send Layer 3 flow statistics for collection and analysis.

- **8-4: MSFC Redundancy with Single Router Mode**—Explains how to configure dual *Multilayer Switching Feature Card* (MSFC) modules for failover when only one is active.

- **8-5: MSFC Redundancy with Configuration Synchronization**—Covers the steps needed to allow dual MSFC modules to both be active, while maintaining a common configuration.

- **8-6: Router Redundancy with HSRP**—Discusses the configuration steps required for Layer 3 switches to share a common IP address for gateway redundancy.

Table 8-1 shows the Cisco Catalyst switch platforms that are capable of Layer 3 switching. To configure Layer 3 switching, find your switch model and the type of Layer 3 switching that it supports (MLS or CEF). Then go to the appropriate section.

Table 8-1 *Catalyst Switch Platforms with Layer 3 Switching Capabilities*

Catalyst Model	Module	Supported Layer 3 Switching	See Section
2900XL	N/A	N/A	N/A
2948G-L3	N/A	CEF in hardware	8-2
3500XL	N/A	N/A	N/A
3550	N/A	CEF in hardware	8-2
4000	Sup II	MLS[1]	N/A

continues

Table 8-1 *Catalyst Switch Platforms with Layer 3 Switching Capabilities (Continued)*

Catalyst Model	Module	Supported Layer 3 Switching	See Section
4000	Sup III	CEF in hardware	8-2
4908G-L3	N/A	CEF in hardware	8-2
5000	Sup IIg	MLS[1]	N/A
	Sup III + NFFC	MLS[1]	N/A
6000	No MSFC	None	N/A
	MSFC + Policy Feature Card (PFC)	Internal MLS automatically used	8-1
	MSFC2 + PFC2	CEF in hardware automatically used	8-2

[1] MLS is supported by using an external router or an installed Layer 3 routing (RSM, RSFC, or Layer 3 services) module. Both the switch (SE) and the router (RP) must be independently configured.

8-1: Multilayer Switching

- *Multilayer switching* (MLS) performs Layer 3 switching by combining separate routing and switching functions on different switch modules.

- MLS is supported on the Catalyst 6000 by the MSFC (route processor) and the PFC (Layer 3 switching engine). On the Catalyst 4000 and 5000 platforms, the route processor can be an external router.

- MLS can perform Layer 3 switching for IP, IP multicast (also known as *IP Multicast MLS* or *MMLS*), and IPX traffic.

- MLS operation consists of these steps:

  — The *route processor* (RP) routs the first packet in a traffic flow.

  — The *switching engine* (SE) sets up an MLS cache entry for the flow based on the first packet (a "candidate" packet).

  — When the SE sees the return packet from the RP, the MLS cache entry is completed with source and destination information. For the duration of the traffic flow, subsequent packets are switched at the SE.

  — When the SE switches flow packets, the SE also rewrites the source and destination MAC addresses, the IP *time-to-live* (TTL), and both Layer 2 and Layer 3 checksum values. This is done in hardware, as if a traditional router had forwarded the packets.

  — The MLS cache entry for a flow is deleted when the connection is closed or after an aging timer expires.

- MLS builds its flow cache based on the following:
  - **IP**—Destination address, source and destination addresses, or source and destination address and port numbers ("full flow")
  - **IP multicast**—Source address, source VLAN number, and destination multicast group
  - **IPX**—Destination address
- MLS can report on traffic flow statistics through the use of NDE. Refer to section "8-3: NetFlow Data Export" for more information.

Configuration

1 *(Optional)* Tune MLS on the RP.

TIP

This chapter covers MLS as it is integrated between SE and RP in the Catalyst 6000 with an MSFC and PFC. MLS is automatically enabled between the RP and SE modules, and Step 1a is not required.

To configure the RP portion of MLS for a Catalyst 4000 (Supervisor I or II) or a Catalyst 5000, which require an external RP, begin with Step 1a.

---

a. *(Optional; external RP only)* Configure MLS.

— Enable MLS on the router:

COS	N/A
IOS	(global) **mls rp ip**

— *(Optional)* Identify the VTP domain:

COS	N/A
IOS	(interface) **mls rp vtp-domain** *name*

If the RP communicates with a switch in a VTP domain, that domain *name* must be identified. The RP can then learn VLAN configuration information from the VTP server.

— *(Optional)* Identify the VLAN number for VLAN or non-ISL interfaces:

COS	N/A
IOS	(interface) **mls rp vlan-id** *vlan-id*

— Enable this interface for MLS management:

COS	N/A
IOS	(interface) **mls rp management-interface**

This interface is used to send and receive MLS management information (MLSP packets). You should use the VLAN interface that connects to the switches using MLS. Often, this will be the management VLAN.

b. *(Optional)* Use unicast MLS on specific VLAN interfaces:

COS	N/A
IOS	(interface) **[no] mls {ip	ipx}**

By default, IP unicast MLS is enabled on all interfaces and IPX MLS is not. Use the **no** keyword to disable MLS on the interface.

c. *(Optional)* Set the flow mask:

COS	N/A
IOS	(global) **mls flow ip {destination	destination-source	full}** -OR- (global) **mls flow ipx {destination	destination-source}**

The MLS flow mask can be set to use destination addresses (**destination**; the default), both source and destination addresses (**destination-source**), or source and destination addresses and port numbers (**full**).

d. *(Optional)* Exclude specific protocols from MLS:

COS	N/A
IOS	(global) **mls exclude protocol {tcp	udp	both} [port** *port-number*]

By default, all protocols and port numbers are used to generate MLS flow entries. Specific protocols can be excluded by identifying the protocol (**tcp**, **udp**, or **both** TCP and UDP) and the *port-number* (1 to 65535).

2 *(Optional)* Tune MLS on the SE.

a. *(Optional; Catalyst 5000 only)* Enable MLS for IP or IPX:

COS	`set mls {enable	disable} {ip	ipx}`
IOS	N/A

By default, IP MLS is enabled and IPX MLS is not.

b. *(Catalyst 5000 only)* Identify the external MLS RPs:

COS	`set mls include {ip	ipx}` *ip-addr1* `[`*ip-addr2...*`]`
IOS	N/A

External routers that work with the switch for MLS are located at IP address *ip-addr1*, *ip-addr2*, and so on. These routers must be connected to the switch over a single trunk port. Router modules such as the RSM and RSFC that are integrated in the Catalyst 5000 chassis are added as MLS RPs automatically.

c. *(Optional)* Tune the MLS cache aging times:

COS	`set mls agingtime [ip	ipx]` *agingtime* `set mls agingtime fast` *fastagingtime pkt-threshold* `set mls agingtime long-duration` *longagingtime*
IOS	N/A

When created, an MLS entry is kept in the cache for an *agingtime* period (8 to 2024 seconds, multiple of 8, default 256 seconds) if no packets are being switched using that entry.

MLS entries can be aged out of the cache sooner for very short flows like DNS requests with the **fast** keyword. An entry is aged out if no more than *pkt-threshold* packets (0, 1, 3, 7, 15, 31, 63, or 127 packets, default 0 packets) are switched using that entry in a *fastagingtime* period (0 to 128 seconds, multiple of 8, default 0 or no fast aging).

MLS cache entries for active switched flows can also be aged out before they become idle, by using the **long-duration** keyword. After the MLS entry is created, it is removed when the *longagingtime* period (64 to 1920 seconds, multiples of 64, default 1920 seconds) expires.

TIP	Cisco recommends that the number of entries in the MLS cache be kept below 32K. Flows that exceed the cache size are sent to the route processor for normal routing, rather than being switched through MLS. You can monitor the cache size with the **show mls** (COS) and **show mls ip count** (IOS) commands.

If the number of cache entries is more than 32,768, you can begin to adjust the MLS timers. Begin by reducing the aging time by 8 seconds to affect normal flows. Periodically monitor the cache size again. If the cache size continues to exceed 32K, reduce the aging time in 64-second increments.

If you suspect a large number of short duration flows, you can also tune the fast aging timer. By default, the fast aging timer is 0 or not used. Start with a fast aging time of 128 seconds. If the cache size grows to over 32K entries, decrease the fast aging time.

d. *(Optional)* Set the minimum MLS flow mask:

COS	`set mls flow {destination	destination-source	full}`
IOS	N/A

The flow mask used for MLS is actually negotiated between the RP and SE devices, as the most specific or longest mask needed. By default, the SE uses a **destination** mask at a minimum, as the RP also does. If the RP has been configured for a longer mask or has extended access lists applied to its interfaces, a longer mask is negotiated.

3 *(Optional)* Tune IP *Multicast MLS* (MMLS) on the RP.

a. Enable IP multicast routing.

— Start multicast routing on the RP:

COS	N/A
IOS	(global) `ip multicast-routing`

— Enable IP *Protocol Independent Multicast* (PIM) on each multicast interface:

COS	N/A
IOS	(interface) `ip pim {dense-mode	sparse-mode	sparse-dense-mode}`

By default, multicast routing uses PIM **sparse-dense-mode**. Refer to *Cisco Field Manual: Router Configuration*, ISBN 1-58705-024-2, section "7-7: IP Multicast Routing", for complete configuration information.

b. Enable IP MMLS on the RP:

COS	N/A
IOS	(global) **mls ip multicast**

By default IP MMLS is disabled, even if IP multicast is active. After MMLS is enabled, it is used only on the interfaces that have IP PIM multicast enabled.

c. *(Optional)* Use a threshold to control the rate of MMLS cache entries:

COS	N/A
IOS	(global) **mls ip multicast threshold** *pps*

You can use a threshold to prevent the MMLS cache from becoming filled with short-lived flows. If the rate of new multicast packets exceeds the *pps* threshold (10 to 10000 packets per second, no default), the packets are switched via MMLS. If the rate is below the threshold, the multicast packets are sent to the RP for normal (non-MMLS) processing.

4 *(Optional)* Tune IP MMLS on the SE.

TIP   IP MMLS is automatically enabled on the SE side, if IP multicast has been configured and enabled. See Chapter 9, "Multicast," for complete configuration information.

MLS Example

MLS is configured on a switch with integrated RP and SE modules (a Catalyst 6000 with a Supervisor 1, PFC, and MSFC, for example). Interfaces VLAN 100 and VLAN 200 are configured to use MLS to switch Layer 3 flows. A "full" MLS flow mask is to be used, as governed by the RP configuration.

The SE portion is configured to use the standard 256-second MLS cache aging time. However, the fast aging time is adjusted so that cache entries are dropped if more than 31 packets are switched within an 8-second fast aging period.

IP multicast is supported through IP MMLS on the RP. The SE portion is automatically configured to support multicast MLS:

COS	**set mls agingtime fast 8 31**
IOS	(global) **interface vlan 100**
	(interface) **mls ip**
	(global) **interface vlan 200**
	(interface) **mls ip**
	(global) **mls flow ip full**
	(global) **ip multicast-routing**
	(global) **mls ip multicast**

Displaying Information About MLS

Table 8-2 lists RP commands with the "IOS" switch OS, and SE commands with the "COS" switch OS.

Table 8-2 *Commands to Display MLS Information*

Display Function	Switch OS	Command
IP MLS status	COS	**show mls** [**ip** | **ipx**] [*module*]
	IOS	(exec) **show mls rp** [**ip** | **ipx** | **interface** *interface interface-number* | **vtp-domain** *domain*]
IP MLS information	COS	**show mls**
	IOS	(exec) **show mls ip** [**any** | **destination** {*hostname* | *ip-address*} | **detail** | **flow** {**tcp** | **udp**} | {**interface** {*interface interface-number*}} | {**Vlan** *vlan*} | {**macd** *destination-mac-address*} | {**macs** *source-mac-address*} | {**module** *number*} | **source** {*hostname* | *ip-address*}]
MLS statistics	COS	**show mls statistics protocol**
		show mls statistics entry [*mod*]
		show mls statistics entry ip [*mod*] [**destination** *ip_addr_spec*] [**source** *ip_addr_spec*] [**protocol** *protocol* [**src-port** *src_port*] [**dst-port** *dst_port*]]
	IOS	(exec) **show mls statistics**
Protocols excluded from IP MLS	COS	**show mls exclude protocol**
	IOS	N/A
IP MLS cache entries	COS	**show mls entry ip** [*mod*] [**destination** *ip_addr_spec*] [**source** *ip_addr_spec*] [**protocol** *protocol*] [**src-port** *src_port*] [**dst-port** *dst_port*] [**short** | **long**]
	IOS	N/A

Table 8-2 *Commands to Display MLS Information (Continued)*

Display Function	Switch OS	Command
IPX MLS information	COS	**show mls statistics entry ipx** [*mod*] [**destination** *ipx_addr_spec*] [**source** *ipx_addr_spec*]
	IOS	(exec) **show mls ipx** [{**destination** *ipx-network*} | {**interface** {*interface interface-number*}} | {**Vlan** *vlan-id*} | {**macd** *destination-mac-address*} | {**macs** *source-mac-address*} | {**module** *number*} | {**source** {*hostname* | *ipx-network*}}] [**detail**]
IPX MLS cache entries	COS	**show mls entry ipx** [*mod*] [**destination** *ipx_addr_spec*] [**short** | **long**]
	IOS	N/A
Size of MLS cache	COS	**show mls**
	IOS	(exec) **show mls ip count** (exec) **show mls ipx count**
IP MMLS	COS	**show mls multicast** **show mls multicast statistics** {*mod*}
	IOS	(exec) **show mls ip multicast** [{{**connected** | **group**} {*hostname* | *ip-address*} [*ip-mask*]} | {**interface** {*interface interface-number*}} | {**module** *number*} | {**source** {*hostname* | *ip-address*}} | **statistics** | **summary**}]
IP MMLS cache entries	COS	**show mls multicast entry** {[**all**] [**short** | **long**]} **show mls multicast** entry {[*mod*] [**vlan** *vlan_id*] [**group** *ip_addr*]} [**source** *ip_addr*] [**long** | **short**]
	IOS	N/A

8-2: Cisco Express Forwarding

- *Cisco Express Forwarding* (CEF) handles all packet forwarding in hardware, for all packets in a flow.

- CEF is implemented on the Catalyst 2948G-L3, 4908G-L3, 4000 Supervisor III, and 3550 series switches. It is also implemented on the Catalyst 6000 as a cooperation between the PFC2 Layer 3 switching engine and the MSFC2 route processor module.

- A route processor runs routing protocols and populates the following tables:

  — **The normal routing table**—A table of routes and next-hop destinations as determined by the routing protocols, administrative distances, metrics, and so on.

  — **The *Forwarding Information Base (FIB)***—Every known route is represented in the FIB as a hierarchical tree structure. Longest-match routes can then be quickly looked up in hardware, pointing to the next-hop entry in the adjacency table.

— The *adjacency table*—Every next-hop router address and *Address Resolution Protocol* (ARP) reply that is discovered is entered into the adjacency table, giving an efficient Layer 3-to-Layer 2 forwarding lookup.

- CEF supports high-performance switching of IP, IP multicast, and IPX traffic.

- CEF can switch packets over up to six equal-cost paths to a common destination.

- CEF can use *Reverse Path Forwarding* (RPF) to make sure packets arrive on interfaces that are the best return paths to the source. This can be used to detect forged or spoofed addresses in received packets, in the case of some malicious activity.

- IP multicast traffic is switched by CEF only for multicast groups within 225.0.0.* through 239.0.0.* and 224.128.0.* through 239.128.0.*. CEF will not switch anything in 224.0.0.* because those addresses are reserved for routing protocols and must be flooded to all ports that are forwarding in a VLAN.

- When the route processor creates the FIB, the FIB information is downloaded and used by the switching engine hardware. On a Catalyst 6000, the FIB is downloaded from the MSFC2 to the PFC2 module, as well as any *distributed forwarding cards* (DFCs) that are present.

- In addition to the CEF tables, a NetFlow forwarding table (identical to that of MLS) is independently generated just to provide flow-based accounting information. This information can be exported to external applications. See section "8-3: NetFlow Data Export" for more information.

CEF Configuration

TIP   CEF is automatically enabled on the switch platforms that support it, and cannot be disabled.

1 *(Optional)* Use RPF to detect forged or malformed packets:

COS	N/A
IOS	(interface) **ip verify unicast reverse-path** [*list*]

By default, RPF is globally disabled on the switch. RPF can be enabled on specific VLAN interfaces.

For each packet received on the interface, CEF checks to see that a valid route back to the source address is present in the FIB. The return route must use the receiving interface as one possible path back to the source. If multiple equal-cost paths exist to the source, any of them are valid.

By default, CEF drops all inbound packets that fail the RPF test on the interface. A standard or extended IP access list *list* (number or name) can be given to conditionally drop these packets. Packets that meet the **permit** condition are forwarded even if they fail RPF, whereas the ones that meet the **deny** condition are dropped.

2   *(Optional; Catalyst 6000 only)* Tune CEF load balancing:

COS	`set mls cef load-balance {full	source-destination-ip}`
IOS	N/A

Traffic flows are load-balanced flows across parallel paths according to a hash function based on source and destination addresses (**source-destination-ip**, the default) or source and destination addresses and port numbers (**full**). CEF does not support per-packet load balancing.

3   *(Optional; Catalyst 6000 only)* Control the rate of CEF packets returned to the RP:

COS	N/A
IOS	(global) `mls ip cef rate-limit` *pps*

Some packets cannot be fully forwarded by CEF and must be returned to the RP (MSFC2) for processing. These include packets requiring an ARP request and packets destined for an RP interface. Although these are normal activities, they can be exploited as a denial-of-service attack against the RP.

You can limit the rate that packets are sent to the RP to *pps* (0 to 1,000,000 packets per second, default 0 or no rate limiting).

Displaying Information About CEF

You can use the switch commands in Table 8-3 to display helpful information about CEF. These labels are used to differentiate the commands for different switch platforms:

- **COS**—Catalyst operating system, used by Catalyst 6000 Supervisor.

- **IOS**—Cisco IOS Software, used by Catalyst 6000 MSFC2, Catalyst 2948G-L3, 4908G-L3, 4000 Supervisor III, and 3550.

- **Sup IOS**—"Supervisor IOS." Cisco IOS Software for the Catalyst 6000 Supervisor 2.

TIP	Remember that a Catalyst 6000 switch splits the CEF function across the MSFC2 and PFC2. If you display information about CEF on the MSFC2, you will see only the portion that creates the FIB and adjacency tables. Although the MSFC2 can use its own CEF to forward packets that are not Layer 3 switched by the PFC2, it generally only creates, downloads, and updates the FIB and adjacency tables for the PFC2.
	To view the CEF information that performs the Layer 3 switching, you must issue commands on the Catalyst Supervisor module where the PFC2 resides.
	Naturally, if you have a switch running native IOS code, you will see one set of integrated CEF information that is created on the MSFC2 and used by the PFC2 module.

Table 8-3 *Commands to Display CEF Information*

Display Function	Switch OS	Command
FIB created by MSFC2 or RP	COS	N/A
	IOS	(exec) **show ip cef** [[**unresolved** [**detail**]]	[**detail**	**summary**]] (exec) **show ip cef** [*network* [*mask*]] [**longer-prefixes**] [**detail**] (exec) **show ip cef** [**vlan** *number*] [**detail**]
	Sup IOS	**show mls cef** [*prefix*] [*mask*] **show mls cef** [**module** *number*	**summary**]
FIB used by PFC2	COS	**show mls cef** **show mls entry cef ip** [[*ip-addr/*]*mask-len*] **show mls entry cef ipx** [[*ipx-addr/*]*mask-len*]
	IOS	N/A
	Sup IOS	**show mls cef** [**module** *number*	**summary**] **show mls cef ip** [{*prefix* [*mask*	**module** *number*]}	{**module** *number*}] **show mls cef ipx** [{*prefix* [*mask*	**module** *number*]}	{**module** *number*}]
Adjacency table	COS	**show mls entry cef adjacency** **show mls entry cef ip** [[*next-hop-addr/*]*32*] **adjacency** **show mls entry cef ipx** [[*next-hop-addr/*]*mask-len*] **adjacency**
	IOS	(exec) **show adjacency** [*type number*] [**detail**] [**summary**] (exec) **show ip cef adjacency** *type number ip-prefix* [**detail**] (exec) **show ip cef adjacency** {**discard**	**drop**	**glean**	**null**	**punt**} [**detail**]
	Sup IOS	(exec) **show mls cef adjacency** [**count**	**mac-address** *number*] [**module** *number*]

Table 8-3   *Commands to Display CEF Information (Continued)*

Display Function	Switch OS	Command
CEF multicast entries	COS	`show mls multicast entry` [`all`] [`short` | `long`] `show mls multicast` entry [*mod*] [`vlan` *vlan-id*] [`group` *ip-addr*] [`source` *ip-addr*] [`long` | `short`]
	IOS	`(exec)` `show mls ip multicast group` *group-address* [`interface` *type number* | `statistics`]
	Sup IOS	`show mls cef ip multicast` [{*prefix* [*mask* | `module` *num*]}]]
Active VLAN interfaces used by MSFC2 CEF	COS	`show mls cef interface` [*vlan*] `show mls cef mac`
	IOS	N/A
	Sup IOS	`show mls cef mac`

When the FIB table contents are displayed, each entry is shown with a "FIB-type" field:

- *Receive*—The destination is associated with an MSFC interface (mask of length 32).
- *Connected*—The destination is associated with a connected network.
- *resolved*—The destination is associated with a valid next-hop address and adjacency.
- *drop*—Drop packets associated with this destination.
- *wildcard*—Match-all entry (drop or MSFC redirect), when no default route is present.
- *default*—Default route. (Wildcard will point to default route.)

When the adjacency table contents are displayed, each entry is shown with an "AdjType" field:

- *drop, null, loopbk*—Drop packets (don't forward).
- *frc drp*—Drop adjacency because of ARP throttling.
- *punt*—Redirect to MSFC for further processing.
- *no r/w*—Redirect to MSFC because packet rewrite is incomplete.

8-3: NetFlow Data Export

- Traffic statistics from Layer 3 switching can be gathered and sent to an external application for collection and analysis. This is done through the *NetFlow Data Export* (NDE) facility.
- Switches using MLS for Layer 3 switching can send data about expired flows using NDE. This is a natural extension of MLS because the switch uses flow cache data.

- Switches using CEF do not inherently use a flow cache, and therefore can't offer statistics through NDE. The Catalyst 6000 PFC2/MSFC2, however, keeps a NetFlow cache independent of the CEF process, strictly for exporting flow data with NDE.

- NetFlow data can be sent as several versions:

  — **NDE version 1**—Used in legacy systems; data record includes specific information about the IP traffic flow and the interfaces used to forward it.

  — **NDE version 5**—Adds a sequence number to prevent lost UDP datagrams, and the *Border Gateway Protocol* (BGP) *autonomous system* (AS) number for the flow.

  — **NDE version 7**—Used to report flow data from Catalyst switches. Version 7 is not supported on a Catalyst 6000 MSFC.

  — **NDE version 8**—Used to report aggregate flow data from routers, Catalyst 5000 with NFFC, and Catalyst 6000 running MLS or CEF. Version 8 is not supported on a Catalyst 6000 MSFC.

- NDE will export flow statistics according to the MLS flow mask that is used by the switch. To see detailed flow records, use a "full" flow mask.

NDE Configuration

1 Start NDE on the RP.

MLS must first be configured on the RP. Refer to section "8-1: Multilayer Switching" (Step 1) for further details.

2 Start NDE on the SE.

a. Identify the flow data collector:

COS	**set mls nde** *collector udp-port*
IOS	(global) **ip flow-export destination** *collector udp-port*

The host running the collector application is identified by *collector* (IP address or name). In addition, the NDE UDP port must be assigned as *udp-port* to match the port number used by the collector application.

b. Identify the NDE source:

COS	N/A
IOS	(global) **ip flow-export source** [{*interface interface-number*} | {**null 0**} | {**port-channel** *number*} | {**vlan** *vlan-id*}]

NDE packets receive a source IP address from the interface specified. For a COS switch, the source address is taken from the sc0 management interface. You should always use a loopback interface as the source because the loopback interface is always up and available. You can use the null 0 interface if the source address of the NDE information is not needed in the exported data.

c. Enable NDE:

COS	**set mls nde version** {**1** | **7** | **8**} **set mls nde** {**enable** | **disable**}
IOS	(global) **mls nde sender** [**version** *version*] -OR- (global) **ip flow-export** *version* {**1** | {**5** [**origin-as** | **peer-as**]} | {**6** [**origin-as** | **peer-as**]}}

The NDE *version* can be **1**, **7** (the default), or **8**. On an IOS switch, the **mls nde sender** command sets the NDE version used by the Catalyst 6000 PFC2 (native or Supervisor IOS), whereas the **ip flow-export** command configures the NDE version for routed flows on an MSFC/MSFC2 (MSFC IOS).

3 Filter the exported data:

COS	**set mls nde flow** {**include** | **exclude**} [**destination** *ip-addr-spec*] [**source** *ip-addr-spec*] [**protocol** *protocol* [**src-port** *src-port*] [**dst-port** *dst-port*]]
IOS	(global) **mls nde flow** {**include** | **exclude**} {{**dest-port** *port-num*} | {**destination** *ip-addr ip-mask*}} | {**protocol** {**tcp** | **udp**}} | {**source** *ip-addr ip-mask*} | {**src-port** *port-num*}}

Traffic flows can be exported only if the **include** keyword and matching criteria are given. If the **exclude** keyword is used, flows to that host are not reported. The **include** and **exclude** filters are mutually exclusive, in that only one of them can be active at a time. However, you can use multiple commands to configure an **include** or an **exclude** filter.

Flows can be matched by **destination** address, **source** address, destination port **dst-port** (0 matches any value), source port **src-port** (0 matches any value), and **protocol** (IOS: **tcp** or **udp**; COS: 0 to 255 or **ip**, **ipinip**, **icmp**, **igmp**, **tcp**, or **udp**; 0 matches any value). Addresses are given as *ip-addr ip-mask* for IOS switches. For COS switches, addresses can be given as either *ip-addr*, *ip-addr/ip-mask*, or *ip-addr/maskbits*.

Notice that the IOS command allows only one of the criteria to be given, whereas the COS command allows any combination of those parameters.

NDE Example

NDE is configured on a switch with integrated RP and SE modules. The NetFlow Collector is located at 192.168.177.10, and uses UDP port 5000 for NDE exchanges. The switch sends NDE data using a source address of 192.168.40.1, which comes from the management interface sc0 (COS) or VLAN interface 900 (IOS).

The switch will only include flow data for TCP port 80 traffic when it sends NDE data to the NetFlow Collector:

| COS | ```
set mls nde 192.168.177.10 5000
set mls nde version 7
set mls nde enable
set mls nde flow include protocol tcp dst-port 80

set interface sc0 900 192.168.40.1 255.255.255.0
``` |
|-----|-----|
| IOS | ```
(global) ip flow-export destination 192.168.177.10 5000
(global) ip flow-export source vlan 900
(global) mls nde sender version 7
(global) mls nde flow include dest-port 80

(global) interface vlan 900
(interface) ip address 192.168.40.1 255.255.255.0
``` |

Displaying Information About NDE

You can use the switch commands in Table 8-4 to display helpful information about NDE.

Table 8-4 *Commands to Display NDE Information*

Display Function	Switch OS	Command
NDE version and activity	COS	`show mls nde`
	IOS	`(exec) show mls netflow`

8-4: MSFC Redundancy with Single Router Mode

- Only the Catalyst 6000 supports redundant supervisor engines with redundant route processors (MSFC/MSFC2).
- Only one MSFC is designated and active; the other is booted up, synchronizes its configuration with the active MSFC, starts any routing protocol processes, but keeps all interfaces in the "line down" state so that no network traffic is exchanged.

- Only the designated and active MSFC is involved in creating MLS flow cache entries for the switching engine and in creating and downloading the CEF FIB and adjacency tables to the PFC2 switching engine.

- In the event of a failure, *single router mode* (SRM) causes the nondesignated MSFC to bring its interfaces up and allow its routing protocols to converge. During this time, the existing Layer 3 switching information supplied by the failed MSFC continues to be used by the designated Supervisor PFC until the new MSFC can provide an update.

- Both MSFC modules must run the same Cisco IOS Software image—Software Release 12.1(8a)E2 or later.

- The Supervisor modules must run in high-availability mode to support SRM, using Supervisor Engine Software Release 6.3(1) or later.

- *Hot Standby Router Protocol* (HSRP) is not necessary in SRM, because only one MSFC is active in the chassis at any one time. However, you should use HSRP if you have other MSFC or Layer 3 devices that have a presence on the same VLANs as the SRM MSFC. These other devices can then act as redundant gateways on those VLANs.

Configuration

1 Enable Supervisor high availability:

COS	`set system highavailability enable`
IOS	N/A

High availability is required on the redundant Supervisor engines so that the Layer 3 switching information can be properly maintained across a Supervisor or PFC failure. This information is used during an MSFC failure, while the nondesignated MSFC waits for its routing information to converge.

2 Enable SRM on the designated MSFC:

COS	N/A
IOS	(global) `redundancy` (redundancy) `high-availability` (highavailability) `single-router-mode`

The MSFC that has SRM configured first will become designated. SRM will not become active until both MSFCs have SRM enabled.

3 *(Optional)* Adjust the failover convergence delay time:

COS	N/A
IOS	(highavailability) **single-router-mode failover table-update-delay** *seconds*

When a nondesignated MSFC detects a failure and becomes active, it waits for *seconds* (default 120 seconds) before sending any new Layer 3 switching information to the switching engine (PFC/PFC2). You can tune this delay time to allow any configured routing protocols to properly converge.

4 Enable SRM on the nondesignated MSFC:

COS	N/A
IOS	(global) **redundancy** (redundancy) **high-availability** (highavailability) **single-router-mode**

The nondesignated MSFC will now accept its configuration from the designated MSFC.

5 Save the running configuration on the designated MSFC:

COS	N/A
IOS	**copy running-config startup-config**

The designated MSFC configuration will automatically be saved to the nondesignated MSFC.

6 Reload the nondesignated MSFC:

IOS	(exec) **reload**

After the reload, the nondesignated MSFC enters SRM mode with its interfaces in the "line down" state.

Displaying Information About SRM

You can use the switch commands in Table 8-5 to display helpful information about SRM redundancy.

Table 8-5   *Commands to Display SRM Information*

Display Function	Switch OS	Command
SRM status	COS	N/A
	IOS	(exec) **show redundancy**

8-5: MSFC Redundancy with Configuration Synchronization

- In config-sync mode, both MSFCs are active at all times; all interfaces and routing processes are available and active on both modules.

- One MSFC is "designated" and maintains the master copies of startup and running configurations. The other is "nondesignated" and receives its configurations from the designated module.

- The nondesignated MSFC can be monitored through an EXEC session, but doesn't allow the configuration mode.

- Config-sync mode allows an immediate failover because both MSFCs are always active. All VLAN interfaces are up, and any configured routing protocols are active on both modules.

- For MLS, either of two redundant MSFC modules can be involved in setting up a flow cache entry. The PFC is aware of both RP modules.

- For CEF, only the designated MSFC downloads the FIB and adjacency table information to the other modules. The designated MSFC is the one that initializes first, in the lowest module slot position.

- HSRP should be used to provide a redundant gateway address on each VLAN. Both MSFCs share a common gateway address, while operating their own unique interface addresses. (See section "8-6: Router Redundancy with HSRP" for more information about HSRP.)

- After config-sync mode has been enabled and is active, any configuration changes that are made on the designated MSFC are automatically synchronized with the nondesignated module:

  — Whenever you enter the **write mem** or **copy** *source* **startup-config** commands, the startup configuration is updated across MSFCs.

  — Whenever you enter the **copy** *source* **running-config** command, the running configuration is updated across MSFCs.

  — As you enter commands in configuration mode, they are also sent to and executed on the nondesignated MSFC.

Section 8-5

Config-sync Redundancy Configuration

1 Enable config-sync mode on the designated MSFC:

COS	N/A
IOS	(global) **redundancy** (redundancy) **high-availability** (highavailability) **config-sync**

The designated MSFC can be arbitrarily chosen and is the first module to be initialized with config-sync enabled. Generally, it is easier to start with the MSFC located in chassis slot 1 (session 15).

TIP

The config-sync mode will be administratively enabled at this point. However, config-sync mode requires that the designated MSFC have configuration information for *both* MSFCs because it keeps the master configuration. This requires some commands to have the **alt** keyword to specify parameters for the nondesignated MSFC.

The operational config-sync state will not become active until the alternate information is configured and the nondesignated MSFC has config-sync enabled.

---

2 Configure any alternate parameters on the designated MSFC.

TIP

If you have already configured the designated MSFC for some features, you will have to enter some commands again to provide alternate values for the nondesignated MSFC. Remember that the designated MSFC keeps the master configuration for both MSFCs. The command syntax for some commands is changed to allow both the slot 1 MSFC (before the **alt** keyword) and the slot 2 MSFC (after the **alt** keyword) values to be given in the same command line.

If you begin with the slot 1 MSFC as the designated module, it will be intuitive that the command parameters are laid out as "designated **alt** nondesignated."

Notice that in most cases the whole command is repeated after the **alt** keyword—not just the command parameters.

---

a. *(Optional)* MSFC host name:

COS	N/A
IOS	(global) **hostname** *hostname* **alt hostname** *hostname*

b. *(Optional)* Default IP gateway:

COS	N/A
IOS	(global) **ip default-gateway** *ip-address* **alt ip default-gateway** *ip-address*

c. *(Optional)* BGP router ID:

COS	N/A
IOS	(global) **router bgp** *as-number*
	(router-bgp) **bgp router-id** *ip-address* [**alt** *ip-address*]

d. *(Optional)* OSPF router ID:

COS	N/A
IOS	(global) **router ospf** *process-id*
	(router-ospf) **router-id** *ip-address* [**alt** *ip-address*]

e. *(Optional)* Interface IP address:

COS	N/A
IOS	(interface) **ip address** *ip-address mask* [**secondary**] **alt** [**no**] **ip address** *ip-address mask* [**secondary**]

This command must be repeated for every interface. If the slot 2 MSFC doesn't have a corresponding active interface, use the **no** keyword.

TIP

Be careful when you are entering this command for secondary addresses. It is very easy to remember the **secondary** keyword on the designated portion but forget to type the **secondary** keyword for the alternate portion. If you forget the **secondary** keyword, the IP address you enter displaces any previously assigned primary address.

f. *(Optional)* HSRP group number and IP address:

COS	N/A
IOS	(interface) **standby** [*group*] **ip** [*ip-address* [**secondary**]] **alt** [**no**] **standby** [*group*] **ip** [*ip-address* [**secondary**]]

Section 8-5

Again, if you are using secondary addresses, make sure you enter the **secondary** keyword for both MSFC interfaces.

g. *(Optional)* HSRP priority and delay:

COS	N/A
IOS	(interface) **standby** [*group*] **priority** *priority* [**preempt** [**delay** *delay*]] **alt standby** [*group*] **priority** *priority* [**preempt** [**delay** *delay*]]

The HSRP priorities (1 to 255, default 100) should be set to different values for the two MSFC interfaces. Choose a higher value for the interface that will become the active HSRP address.

h. *(Optional)* IPX network:

COS	N/A
IOS	(interface) **ipx network** *network* [**encapsulation** *encap-type* [**secondary**]] **alt ipx network** *network* [**encapsulation** *encap-type* [**secondary**]]

3   Save the configuration on the designated MSFC:

COS	N/A
IOS	(exec) **copy running-config startup-config**

4   Enable config-sync mode on the nondesignated MSFC:

COS	N/A
IOS	(global) **redundancy** (redundancy) **high-availability** (highavailability) **config-sync**

Config-sync mode will not become operational until both MSFC modules have it configured and enabled. As soon as both modules have config-sync mode enabled, a 1-minute timer starts to allow the modules to stabilize and communicate. When this period ends, the designated MSFC copies its running configuration to the non-designated MSFC.

Displaying Information About Config-sync Redundancy

You can use the switch commands in Table 8-6 to display helpful information about config-sync redundancy.

Table 8-6   *Commands to Display the Config-sync Redundancy Status*

Display Function	Switch OS	Command
Config-sync status	COS	N/A
	IOS	(exec) **show redundancy**

8-6: Router Redundancy with HSRP

- Route processors in the same or another chassis can share redundant gateway addresses on a VLAN by using the *Hot Standby Router Protocol* (HSRP).

- Route processors sharing a common HSRP IP address must belong to the same HSRP group number.

- The HSRP address appears on the network with a special virtual MAC address— 00-00-0C-07-AC-*XX*, where *XX* is the HSRP group number (0 to 255). The hosts on the HSRP VLAN use this MAC address as the default gateway.

- Although HSRP is enabled on an interface, each route processor still maintains its own unique IP and MAC addresses on the VLAN interface. These addresses are used by other routers for routing protocol traffic.

- When an HSRP group is enabled, the highest-priority HSRP device at that time becomes the active router, whereas the second-highest-priority stays in the standby state. All other HSRP devices in the group maintain a "listening" state, waiting for the active device to fail. A new active router election occurs only when the active device fails. The previous active router (having the highest priority) may reclaim its active role by preempting the other HSRP routers in the group.

- HSRP devices communicate by sending a hello message over UDP at multicast address 224.0.0.2. These messages are sent every 3 seconds by default.

- Devices on a VLAN use the HSRP address as their default gateway. If one of the HSRP devices fails, there will always be another one to take its place as the default gateway address.

Configuration

1   Specify the HSRP group number and IP address:

COS	N/A
IOS	(interface) **standby** [*group-number*] **ip** [*ip-address* [**secondary**]]

The VLAN interface participates in HSRP group *group-number* (0 to 255, default 0) as HSRP IP address *ip-address*. Use the **secondary** keyword if this address corresponds to a secondary address on the actual VLAN interface. This allows HSRP addresses to be activated for both primary and secondary interface addresses.

The group number and the IP address should be the same across all Layer 3 devices participating in HSRP on the VLAN. This also makes the HSRP virtual MAC address identical on all the HSRP devices.

TIP   It is common practice to use the VLAN number as the HSRP group number, for convenient reference. However, the Catalyst 6000 PFC2/MSFC2 combination supports only up to 16 different HSRP groups (each numbered 1 to 255). You can, however, reuse a group number on several VLAN interfaces as long as no bridging exists between the VLANs.

2 *(Optional)* Set the HSRP priority:

COS	N/A
IOS	(interface) standby [group-number] priority *priority* [**preempt** [**delay minimum** *delay*]]

The interface negotiates with other HSRP devices in the group to become the active device. Assign a *priority* (1 to 255, default 100) value to each HSRP device so that the one with the highest priority (255 is the highest) becomes active. Adjust the priorities of all other devices to achieve expected elections if the active device fails.

If the active device (highest priority) fails, it waits until the new active device (lower priority) fails before becoming active again. Use the **preempt** keyword to allow the device to immediately take over the active role again. You can add the **delay minimum** keywords to cause preemption to wait until *delay* (0 to 3600 seconds, default 0 or no delay) time after the Layer 3 switch has been restarted. This allows a period of time for the routing protocols to converge.

3 *(Optional)* Use HSRP authentication:

COS	N/A
IOS	(interface) **standby** [*group-number*] **authentication** *string*

By default, any device can participate in HSRP communications. You can use the **authentication** keyword to force HSRP devices to authenticate with one another by using *string* (text string, up to eight characters) as a clear-text key.

4 *(Optional)* Tune the HSRP timers:

COS	N/A
IOS	(interface) **standby** [*group-number*] **timers** [**msec**] *hellotime* [**msec**] *holdtime*

You can adjust the time between HSRP hello messages to *hellotime* (1 to 254 seconds, default 3 seconds, or 50 to 999 milliseconds, by using **msec**.

HSRP devices listen for hellos from the active device until a holdtime period expires. After this, the active device is declared dead and the next-highest-priority device becomes active. You can adjust this to *holdtime* (up to 255 seconds, default 10 seconds, or up to 3000 milliseconds) by using **msec**. Make sure the holdtime is set consistently across all HSRP devices in the group.

TIP   To be notified of HSRP active device changeovers, you can enable SNMP traps from the HSRP MIB. Use the **snmp-server enable traps hsrp** command. See section "12-2: SNMP" for more information about SNMP configuration.

HSRP Example

Two Layer 3 switches have interfaces on VLAN 199. These devices could be two MSFC modules in a single Catalyst 6000 chassis or in two separate chassis, or two Catalyst 3550 switches, and so on.

Here, HSRP group 1 is used. In fact, HSRP group 1 can be used on every VLAN interface, provided that no Layer 2 bridging is configured. The HSRP devices will share the 192.168.104.1 IP address so that the hosts on VLAN 199 will always have a default gateway available. Note that IP address 192.168.104.1 will appear as the virtual MAC address 00-00-0C-07-AC-01 (01 signifying HSRP group 1).

The devices are set with an HSRP hello time of 3 seconds and a holdtime of 40 seconds. Device A is configured with priority 210, making it the active device over device B's priority of 200. Device A is configured to preempt all other lower-priority HSRP devices that might become active, but only if this is at least 60 seconds after it has been restarted. This will allow it to immediately take over its active role if needed. (This is not necessary in a two-router HSRP scenario because the two devices will always trade off the active role. Preemption can be useful when more than two HSRP devices participate in a group.)

Finally, the HSRP devices use the string *myhsrpkey* in all HSRP communication as a simple form of authentication. If a host attempts to use HSRP messages without the authentication key, none of the other devices will listen to it.

Layer 3 Device A configuration:

COS	N/A
IOS	(global) **interface vlan 199**
	(interface) **standby 1 ip 192.168.104.1**
	(interface) standby **1 priority 210 preempt delay 60**
	(interface) **standby 1 authentication myhsrpkey**
	(interface) **standby 1 timers 3 40**

Layer 3 Device B configuration:

COS	N/A
IOS	(global) **interface vlan 199**
	(interface) **standby 1 ip 192.168.104.1**
	(interface) standby **1 priority 200 preempt**
	(interface) **standby 1 authentication myhsrpkey**
	(interface) **standby 1 timers 3 40**

Displaying Information About HSRP

You can use the switch commands in Table 8-7 to display helpful information about HSRP on interfaces.

Table 8-7 *Commands to Display HSRP Information*

Display Function	Switch OS	Command
Concise HSRP status	COS	N/A
	IOS	(exec) **show standby brief**
HSRP on a specific VLAN interface	COS	N/A
	IOS	(exec) **show standby Vlan** *vlan-number* [*hsrp-group*] [**brief**]

Further Reading

Refer to the following recommended sources for further information about the topics covered in this chapter.

MLS

Cisco LAN Switching by Kennedy Clark and Kevin Hamilton, Cisco Press, ISBN 1-57870-094-9

CCNP Switching Exam Certification Guide by Tim Boyles and David Hucaby, Cisco Press, ISBN 1-58720-000-7

CEF

Inside Cisco IOS Software Architecture by Bollapragada, Murphy, and White, Cisco Press, ISBN 1-57870-181-3, pages 58 to 65

How-To Troubleshoot Unicast IP Routing CEF on Catalyst 6000s with a Supervisor 2 in Hybrid Mode at: www.cisco.com/warp/public/473/128.html

NetFlow Data Export

Cisco IOS NetFlow at: www.cisco.com/warp/public/732/Tech/netflow/

NetFlow Services Solutions Guide at: www.cisco.com/univercd/cc/td/doc/cisintwk/intsolns/netflsol/nfwhite.htm

Router Redundancy

Gigabit Campus Network Design—Principles and Architecture at: www.cisco.com/warp/public/cc/so/neso/lnso/cpso/gcnd_wp.htm

Understanding and Troubleshooting HSRP Problems in Catalyst Switch Networks at: www.cisco.com/warp/public/473/62.shtml

Using HSRP for Fault-Tolerant IP Routing at: www.cisco.com/univercd/cc/td/doc/cisintwk/ics/cs009.htm

Section 8-6

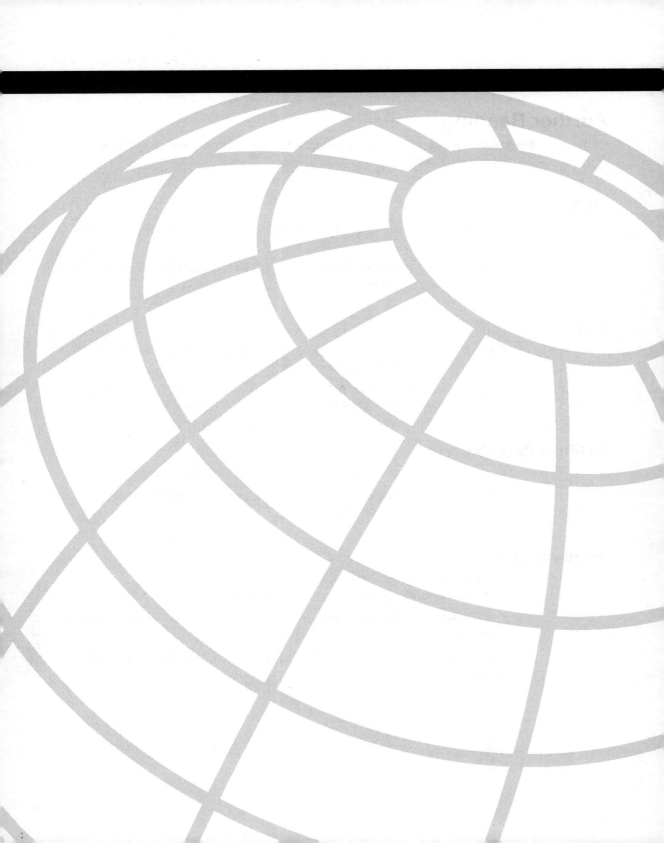

CHAPTER 9

Multicast

Refer to the following sections to configure and use these features:

- **9-1: IGMP Snooping**—Explains how to configure a switch to constrain multicast traffic by listening to *Internet Group Management Protocol* (IGMP) messages.

- **9-2: CGMP**—Discusses the steps needed to allow a switch and a router to constrain multicast traffic by exchanging *Cisco Group Management Protocol* (CGMP) messages.

- **9-3: GMRP**—Covers the configuration steps needed for a switch to use the *GARP Multicast Router Protocol* (GMRP) to communicate with multicast hosts.

- **9-4: RGMP**—Explains how a switch and a router can use the *Router-port Group Management Protocol* (RGMP) to constrain multicast traffic toward routers in the network.

TIP

Choose the multicast features for your network based on the type of switches that are used. IP multicast routing using *Protocol Independent Multicast* (PIM) is usually required and is configured only on a router or Layer 3 platforms. Configure other multicast features based on the following guidelines and the information in Table 9-1.

- Use IGMP snooping on all but the low-end switch models. IGMP snooping doesn't require any other interaction with routers.

- Use CGMP for the lower-end switch models that can't use IGMP snooping. Be sure to configure CGMP on any directly connected router interfaces so that CGMP information is fed to the switches.

- Use GMRP to control multicast traffic only if your multicast-capable hosts can use both IGMP and GMRP. The switch platform must also be GMRP-capable.

- Use RGMP to prune multicast traffic to routers even further, eliminating ports to routers that don't need multicast groups. Both routers and switches must support RGMP.

Table 9-1 *Switch Multicast Features*

Catalyst Model	PIM Routing	IGMP Snooping	CGMP	GMRP	RGMP
2900XL	N	N	Y	N	N
3500XL	N	N	Y	N	N
3550	Y	Y	N	N	N
5000	N	Y	Y	Y	Y
4000 Sup I, II	N	Y	Y	Y	N
4000 Sup III	Y	Y	Y	N	N
6000 w/ PFC	N	Y	N	N	N
6000 w/ PFC/MSFC	Y	Y	N	Y (COS)	Y
6000 w/ PFC2/MSFC2	Y	Y	N	Y (COS)	Y

Multicast Addressing

- IP multicast flows can be designated by these notations:

   — **(S,G)**—A unique shortest path tree structure between the source and the multicast destinations, pronounced "S comma G." S is an IP unicast source address, and G is the IP multicast destination address or group.

   — **(*,G)**—A common shared tree structure, where a multicast *rendezvous point* (RP) accepts multicast traffic from the source and then forwards it on to the destinations, pronounced "Star comma G." The star or asterisk (*) represents the RP, because it is a wildcard source that accepts input from any real multicast source. The G represents the IP multicast destination address or group.

- IP multicast or Class D addresses begin with 1110 in the most significant address bits—Addresses within the range 224.0.0.0 to 239.255.255.255.

- Hosts anywhere in the network can register to join a multicast group defined by a specific multicast IP address. Registration is handled through the IGMP.

- IP multicast addresses 224.0.0.1 (all hosts on a subnet) and 224.0.0.2 (all routers on a subnet) are well-known and don't require registration. You can find other well-known multicast addresses listed in Appendix B, "Well-known Protocol, Port, and other Numbers."

- Multicast also uses Ethernet or MAC addresses beginning with 01-00-5e. (The least-significant bit of the high-order byte is always 1.) The multicast IP addresses must be translated into multicast MAC addresses in this fashion, following the structure shown in Figure 9-1:

    — The 25 most-significant bits in the MAC address are always 01-00-5e.

    — The 23 lowest-significant bits are copied from the 23 lowest-significant bits of the IP address.

    — The address translation is not unique; 5 bits of the IP address are not used. Therefore, 32 different IP addresses can all correspond to a single multicast MAC address.

Figure 9-1   *Multicast Address Translation*

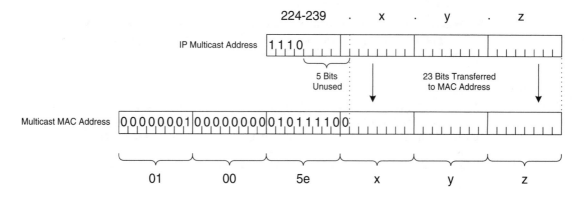

9-1: IGMP Snooping

- Some Catalyst switches can be configured to intercept IGMP join requests as hosts ask to join IP multicast groups.

- IGMP join requests can occur as the following happen:

    — Hosts send unsolicited membership reports to join specific multicast groups.

    — Multicast routers acting as *IGMP queriers* send IGMP membership query messages to the all-hosts multicast group 224.0.0.1 every 60 seconds. Interested hosts respond with membership reports to join specific multicast groups.

- The switch keeps a record of the IP multicast group, its Layer 2 MAC address, and the switch ports that connect to the requesting host and the multicast router.

- Multicast routers cannot keep a detailed list of all hosts belonging to a multicast group. Rather, a router knows only which multicast groups are active on specific subnets.

- The switch also relays the initial join request for a multicast group to all its known multicast routers.

- If no multicast routers are present in the network, the switch can be configured to act as an IGMP querier.

- When a host wants to leave a multicast group, IGMPv1 detects only the absence of its membership reports. IGMPv2, however, allows the host to send an IGMP leave group message to the "all-routers" multicast group 224.0.0.2 at any time.

- When the switch intercepts an IGMP leave group message on a switch port, it normally sends a query to that multicast group back out the same switch port. If no hosts respond to the query and no multicast routers have been discovered on the switch port, that port is removed from the multicast group. *IGMP Fast-Leave Processing* can be used to allow the switch to immediately remove a port from a multicast group after a Leave Group message is received.

- Spanning tree topology changes that occur in a VLAN also cause the switch to purge any multicast group information learned through IGMP snooping. That information must be relearned.

TIP   IGMP snooping is supported on all Catalyst switch platforms except the 2900XL and 3500XL families. IGMP snooping requires specialized hardware to intercept and inspect every IGMP multicast packet—hardware that is not available on the lower-end switch models.

Configuration

1 *(Optional)* Enable IGMP snooping:

COS	**set igmp {enable	disable}**
IOS	(interface) **ip igmp snooping**

IGMP snooping is enabled by default, except on the Catalyst 5000 family.

2 *(Optional; Catalyst 6000 IOS only)* Allow snooping to learn from another source:

COS	N/A
IOS	(interface) **ip igmp snooping mrouter learn {cgmp	pim-dvmrp}**

In addition to normal IGMP snooping, the switch can also learn by listening to CGMP messages (**cgmp**) or PIM-DVMRP messages (**pim-dvmrp**).

3 *(Optional)* Use IGMP Fast-Leave Processing:

COS	`set igmp fastleave {enable	disable}`
IOS	`(interface) ip igmp snooping fast-leave`

By default, Fast-Leave Processing is disabled. Fast-Leave improves the latency of multicast group removal, but should be used only on VLANs where single hosts are connected to each switch port.

4 *(Optional)* Statically identify a multicast router port:

COS	`set multicast router mod/port`
IOS	`(interface) ip igmp snooping mrouter {interface {interface interface-number}	{Port-channel number}}`

IGMP snooping automatically detects ports where multicast routers are connected. You can also give a static definition of a multicast router port.

5 *(Optional)* Define a static multicast host entry:

COS	`set cam {static	permanent} {mac-address} {mod/port}`
IOS	`(interface) ip igmp snooping static {mac-address} {interface {interface interface-number}}	{Port-channel number}}`

The host connected to the specified interface is statically joined to multicast group *mac-address* (dotted-triplet format) on the current VLAN interface. On the COS switch, the static entry can be used until the next reboot (**static**) or even across the next reboot (**permanent**).

6 *(Optional)* Act as an IGMP querier.

a. Enable the querier:

COS	`set igmp querier {enable	disable} vlan`
IOS	`(interface) ip igmp snooping querier`

By default, the IGMP querier function is disabled. If no other multicast routers are available and there is no need to route multicast packets on the local network, the switch can provide the IGMP querier function. Use the **enable** keyword and specify the *vlan* number where the querier will be used.

b. *(Optional)* Adjust the query interval:

COS	`set igmp querier vlan qi seconds`
IOS	`(global) ip igmp query-interval seconds`

The time between general IGMP queries or the query interval, on the *vlan* number can be set to *seconds*. (The default is 125 seconds.)

c. *(Optional)* Adjust the self-election interval:

COS	`set igmp querier` *vlan* `oqi` *seconds*
IOS	`(global) ip igmp query-timeout` *seconds*

If more than one querier is present on a VLAN, only one of them is elected to remain the querier. If no other general IGMP queries are overheard on the *vlan* number for *seconds* (default 300 seconds), the switch will elect itself as the querier.

TIP   Querier election takes place by using the source IP address in the general query messages. For a specific VLAN, switches use the IP address from their VLAN interface as the IGMP source address. The lowest IP address wins the querier election.

IGMP Snooping Example

IGMP snooping is enabled globally on the COS switch and on specific interfaces on the IOS switch. IGMP Fast-Leave Processing is allowed. A static entry for IP multicast group address 224.100.1.35 (MAC address 01-00-5e-64-01-23) is configured that lists switch ports 2/1 and 2/3 as permanent members. These switch ports are assigned to a common VLAN 199.

COS	`set igmp enable`
	`set igmp fastleave enable`
	`set vlan 199 2/1-48`
	`set cam permanent 01-00-5e-64-01-23 2/1,2/3`

IOS	`(global) interface fastethernet 2/1`
	`(interface) ip igmp snooping`
	`(interface) ip igmp snooping fast-leave`
	`(interface) switchport access vlan 199`
	`(global) interface fastethernet 2/3`
	`(interface) ip igmp snooping`
	`(interface) ip igmp snooping fast-leave`
	`(interface) switchport access vlan 199`
	
	`(global) interface vlan 199`
	`(interface) ip igmp snooping static 0100.5364.0123 interface`
	`    fastethernet 2/1`
	`(interface) ip igmp snooping static 0100.5364.0123 interface`
	`    fastethernet 2/3`

Displaying Information About IGMP Snooping

Table 9-2 lists some switch commands that you can use to display helpful information about IGMP snooping.

Table 9-2   *Switch Commands to Display IGMP Snooping Information*

Display Function	Switch OS	Command
Multicast protocols in use	COS	`show multicast protocols status`
	IOS	N/A
IGMP statistics	COS	`show igmp statistics` [*vlan-id*]
	IOS	(exec) `show ip igmp interface` *interface interface-number*
Multicast routers discovered	COS	`show multicast router igmp` [*mod/port*] [*vlan-id*]
	IOS	(exec) `show ip igmp snooping mrouter interface vlan` *vlan-id*
Number of multicast groups in a VLAN	COS	`show multicast group count` [*vlan-id*]
	IOS	(exec) `show mac-address-table multicast` *vlan-id* `count`
Multicast group information	COS	`show multicast group` [*mac-addr*] [*vlan-id*] -or- `show mac multicast` [{**Vlan** *vlan-id* | *grp-mac-addr*}]
	IOS	(exec) `show mac-address-table multicast` {*mac-group-address* [*vlan-id*]}
IGMP snooping on an interface	COS	N/A
	IOS	(exec) `show ip igmp interface` *vlan-id*

9-2: CGMP

- CGMP is a cooperative protocol between Cisco routers and switches used to constrain multicast traffic.

- CGMP on a Catalyst switch relies on a CGMP router to provide it with multicast join or leave requests. This allows efficient multicast group registration without requiring the switch to inspect IGMP messages.

- CGMP uses destination multicast MAC address 01-00-0c-dd-dd-dd for all its messages. These messages are flooded to all switch ports so that even non-CGMP switches will relay CGMP information.

- CGMP requires that IGMP snooping be disabled. The two features are mutually exclusive. However, a router can be configured for both IGMP and CGMP to support a variety of switch platforms.

- CGMP is supported on all Catalyst switch platforms except the Catalyst 6000.

Configuration

1   *(Router only)* Enable CGMP on a router:

IOS	(interface) **ip cgmp**

CGMP must be enabled on a router that also performs multicast routing. Once enabled, the router can send CGMP messages to Catalyst switches.

2   Enable CGMP on the switch:

COS	**set cgmp {enable	disable}**
IOS	(global) **[no]** **cgmp**

By default, CGMP is disabled on COS switches but is enabled on IOS switches. Therefore, this command must be used on COS switches to enable CGMP.

3   *(Optional)* Statically identify a CGMP router:

COS	**set multicast router** *mod/port*
IOS	N/A

By default, routers using CGMP announce themselves to CGMP switches. You can also give a static definition of a multicast router port if needed.

4   *(Optional)* Use CGMP Fast-Leave:

COS	**set cgmp leave {enable	disable}**
IOS	(global) **cgmp leave-processing**

Fast-Leave is disabled by default. If enabled, the switch will listen to IGMPv2 leave group messages. When a leave message is intercepted on a port and there are no subsequent join messages, the port is pruned from the multicast group with no CGMP intervention from the router.

CGMP Example

First, a router is configured to support CGMP on its VLAN 199 interface, as follows:

IOS	(global) **interface vlan 199**
	(interface) **ip cgmp**

A switch connected to VLAN 199 is configured to enable CGMP support. CGMP Fast-Leave Processing is also enabled for efficient handling of multicast leave requests, as follows:

COS	`set cgmp enable`
	`set cgmp leave enable`
IOS	`(global) cgmp`
	`(global) cgmp leave-processing`

Displaying Information About CGMP

Table 9-3 lists switch commands that you can use to display helpful information about CGMP.

Table 9-3   *Switch Commands to Display CGMP Information*

Display Function	Switch OS	Command
CGMP status	COS	`show cgmp leave`
	IOS	`(exec) show cgmp state`
CGMP statistics	COS	`show cgmp statistics [`*vlan_id*`]`
	IOS	N/A
CGMP routers	COS	`show multicast router cgmp [`*mod/port*`] [`*vlan-id*`]`
	IOS	`(exec) show cgmp router [`*address*`]`
CGMP groups	COS	`show multicast group [`*mac-addr*`] [`*vlan-id*`]`
	IOS	`(exec) show cgmp {vlan` *vlan-id* `|` `group [`*address*`]}`

9-3: GMRP

- GMRP is an industry standard multicast flooding control protocol defined in IEEE 802.1p.

- A host uses both IGMP (Layer 3) and GMRP (Layer 2) to coordinate its multicast activities. When it wants to join a multicast group, it sends an IGMP join request along with a GMRP join request.

- The switch forwards IGMP control packets on to the multicast router. GMRP traffic is used by the switch to determine which switch ports to add to a multicast group.

- The switch periodically queries hosts with a GMRP leave-all message. Hosts that want to continue participating in a multicast group must respond with a join request. If not, they can either send a GMRP leave message or just not respond at all.

Configuration

1   Enable GMRP.

a. Enable GMRP on all VLANs and switch ports:

COS	`set gmrp {enable	disable}`
IOS	N/A

b. Enable or disable GMRP on specific ports:

COS	`set port gmrp mod/ports... {enable	disable}`
IOS	N/A

After GMRP has been enabled on the switch, it is enabled on all VLANs and switch ports. You can disable it on ports where it is not needed.

2   Identify ports where routers are connected:

COS	`set gmrp fwdall enable mod/port...`
IOS	N/A

The switch must know where any multicast routers are connected so that it can forward all multicast traffic there. GMRP traffic is not forwarded because it is only used by hosts and switches to constrain multicast traffic.

3   Specify the GMRP registration type:

COS	`set gmrp registration {normal	fixed	forbidden} mod/port...`
IOS	N/A

The registration type controls how a switch port will participate in registering hosts to multicast groups. In normal mode (the default), hosts are free to dynamically register and leave multicast groups on the port. In fixed mode, the current multicast registrations are frozen; no further joins or leaves are allowed. In forbidden mode, all multicast registrations on the port are released and no further joins are allowed.

4   *(Optional)* Tune the GARP/GMRP timers.

TIP   The GARP timers are used to define when control messages, such as join and leave requests, can be sent or accepted. If you decide to adjust these timers, be sure to adjust them consistently on all switches and host devices.

---

a. *(Optional)* Adjust the join timer:

COS	`set gmrp timer join` *timer-value*
IOS	N/A

The join timer is used to pace GARP control message transmissions (join requests, for example). These messages can only be sent every *timer-value* (1 to 2,147,483,647 milliseconds, default 200 ms).

b. *(Optional)* Adjust the leave timer:

COS	`set gmrp timer leave` *timer-value*
IOS	N/A

When a host sends a leave request, the switch port could potentially be removed from a multicast group. The switch waits for a leave time to listen for any join requests on the port before removing the registration. The leave timer is set to *timer-value* (1 to 2,147,483,647 milliseconds, default 600 ms). The leave timer must be at least three times greater than the join timer.

c. *(Optional)* Adjust the leave-all timer:

COS	`set gmrp timer leaveall` *timer-value*
IOS	N/A

If the switch doesn't receive a response from a registered host within *timer-value* (1 to 2,147,483,647 milliseconds, default 10,000 ms or 10 seconds), the host is removed from any multicast groups. The leave-all timer must be greater than the leave timer.

Displaying Information About GMRP

Table 9-4 lists some switch commands that you can use to display helpful information about GMRP.

Table 9-4   *Switch Commands to Display GMRP Information*

Display Function	Switch OS	Command
GMRP status	COS	`show gmrp configuration`
	IOS	N/A
GMRP statistics	COS	`show gmrp statistics` [*vlan*]
	IOS	N/A
GARP timers	COS	`show garp timer`
	IOS	N/A

Section 9-3

9-4: RGMP

- RGMP is a dynamic protocol that controls multicast traffic to multicast routers.
- With RGMP, a switch must still use IGMP snooping to constrain multicast traffic to interested hosts.
- RGMP can communicate only with routers that also run RGMP. Routers periodically send RGMP hello messages to switches.
- Routers that are interested in receiving traffic for a multicast group send an RGMP join request to the switch. Otherwise, the switch will not forward multicast traffic to the router.
- RGMP supports the use of PIM sparse mode only on multicast routers.

Configuration

1 Enable IGMP snooping on the switch.

   See section "9-1: IGMP Snooping" for the necessary switch configuration steps.

2 Enable PIM sparse mode multicast routing on a router.

   Refer to *Cisco Field Manual: Router Configuration* (ISBN 1-58705-024-2), section "7-7: IP Multicast Routing" for the router configuration steps.

3 *(Router only)* Enable RGMP on the router:

IOS	(interface) **ip rgmp**

   RGMP must be enabled on the router interfaces that connect to RGMP-capable switches.

4 Enable RGMP on the switch:

COS	**set rgmp {enable	disable}**
IOS	N/A

   By default, RGMP is disabled.

Displaying Information About RGMP

Table 9-5 lists some switch commands that you can use to display helpful information about RGMP.

Table 9-5   *Switch Commands to Display RGMP Information*

Display Function	Switch OS	Command
RGMP statistics	COS	`show rgmp statistics [vlan]`
	IOS	N/A
Multicast groups requested by RGMP router	COS	`show rgmp group [mac-addr] [vlan-id]`
	IOS	N/A
Number of multicast groups requested by RGMP router	COS	`show rgmp group count [vlan-id]`
	IOS	N/A

Further Reading

Refer to the following recommended sources for further information about the topics covered in this chapter.

IGMP and CGMP, Multicast Routing

Internet Protocol (IP) Multicast Technology Overview at www.cisco.com/warp/public/cc/pd/iosw/prodlit/ipimt_ov.htm

Developing IP Multicast Networks Volume 1 by Beau Williamson, Cisco Press, ISBN 1-57870-077-9

Cisco LAN Switching by Kennedy Clark and Kevin Hamilton, Cisco Press, ISBN 1-57870-094-9

GMRP

IEEE Standard 802.1Q – Virtual Bridged Local Area Networks at http://standards.ieee.org/getieee802/802.1.html

RGMP

Configuration Note: RGMP - Router-port Group Management Protocol at ftp://ftpeng.cisco.com/ipmulticast/config-notes/rgmp.txt

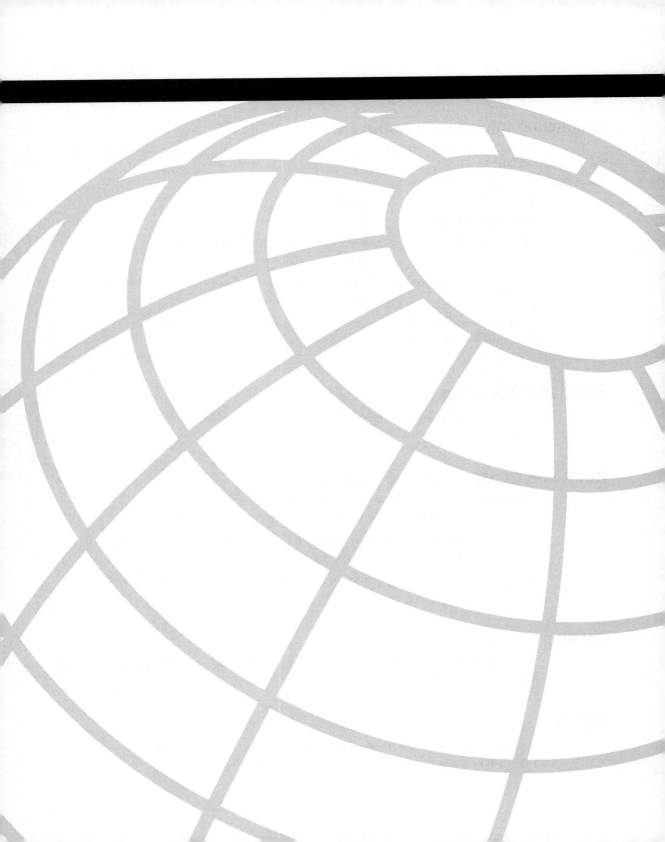

CHAPTER 10

Server Load Balancing (SLB)

See the following sections to configure and use these features:

- **10-1: SLB**—Covers the configuration steps needed to provide load balancing of traffic to one or more server farms.

- **10-2: SLB Firewall Load Balancing**—Discusses the configuration steps necessary to load balance traffic to one or more firewall farms.

- **10-3: SLB Probes**—Explains the configuration steps needed to define probes that test server and firewall farm functionality.

10-1: SLB

- SLB provides a virtual server IP address to which clients can connect, representing a group of real physical servers in a server farm. Figure 10-1 shows the basic SLB concept. A client accesses a logical "virtual" server (IP address v.v.v.v), which only exists within the Catalyst 6000 SLB configuration. A group of physical "real" servers (IP addresses x.x.x.x, y.y.y.y, and z.z.z.z) is configured as a server farm. Traffic flows between clients and the virtual server are load balanced across the set of real servers, transparent to the clients.

Figure 10-1 *SLB Concept*

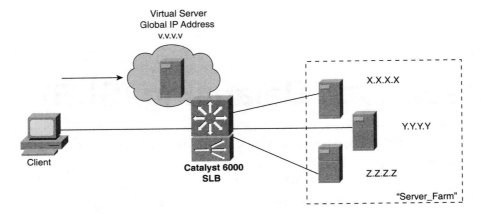

- As clients open new connections to the virtual server, SLB decides which real server to use based on a load-balancing algorithm.
- Server load balancing is performed by one of these methods:
  - **Weighted round-robin**—Each real server is assigned a weight that gives its ability to handle connections, relative to the other servers. For a weight n, a server is assigned n new connections before SLB moves on to the next server.
  - **Weighted least connections**—SLB assigns new connections to the real server with the least number of active connections. Each real server is assigned a weight m, where its capacity for active connections is m divided by the sum of all server weights. SLB assigns new connections to the real server with the number of active connections farthest below its capacity.
- With weighted least connections, SLB controls the access to a new real server, providing a slow start function. New connections are rate limited and allowed to increase gradually to keep the server from becoming overloaded.
- The virtual server can masquerade as the IP address for all TCP and UDP ports of the real server farm. As well, the virtual server can appear as the IP address of a single port or service of a server farm.
- *Sticky* connections allow SLB to assign new connections from a client to the last real server the client used.
- SLB can detect a real server failure by monitoring failed TCP connections. SLB can take the failed server out of service and return it to service as soon as it is working again.

- SLB can use *server Network Address Translation* (NAT) to translate between the real and virtual server addresses if they reside on different Layer 3 subnets.

- SLB can use *client NAT* to translate the source addresses of client requests into addresses on the server side of the SLB device. This is used when several SLB devices are operating so that return traffic can be sent to the correct SLB device.

- SLB provides a control mechanism over incoming TCP SYN floods to the real servers. This can prevent certain types of denial-of-service attacks.

- SLB can coexist with *Hot Standby Router Protocol* (HSRP) to provide a "stateless backup." If one SLB router fails, a redundant router can take over the SLB function. However, existing SLB connections will be lost and will have to be reestablished from the client side.

- IOS SLB can also operate as a *Dynamic Feedback Protocol* (DFP) load-balancing manager. The DFP manager collects capacity information from DFP agents running on the real servers.

Configuration

NOTE   This chapter presents SLB commands as "IOS" for Catalyst 6000 native IOS and "CSM" for Catalyst 6000 Content Switching Module. SLB is not available on any COS platform, so that type of command format has been omitted.

The CSM commands are actually used from the native IOS *command-line interface* (CLI), in the CSM configuration mode. The IOS and CSM commands are presented side-by-side here for comparison purposes. The CSM commands are based on the CSM 2.1 software image.

1   *(CSM only)* Define client-side and server-side *virtual LANs* (VLANs).

   a. Start configuring a CSM module:

IOS	N/A
CSM	(global) **module csm** *slot-number*

   The native IOS CLI begins CSM configuration mode for the CSM located at *slot-number* in the switch chassis. To end this mode, use the **exit** command. To find the appropriate slot number, use the **show module all** command.

b. Define the VLAN type:

IOS	N/A
CSM	`(csm)` **`vlan`** `vlan-id` **`{client	server}`**

The VLAN number is given as *vlan-id* (2 to 4095; VLAN 1 cannot be used). This VLAN must already be defined on the switch in the VLAN database. The VLAN type, **client** or **server**, defines where the clients or servers (server farms of real servers) are located as seen by the CSM. You must define *both* client-side and server-side VLANs before the CSM can be used properly. Clients and servers must be located in different VLANs.

c. *(Optional)* Assign a primary IP address:

IOS	N/A
CSM	`(csm-vlan)` **`ip address`** `ip-address netmask`

One IP address can be defined per VLAN on the CSM. This address is used for management traffic (probes, for example) and ARP requests.

d. *(Optional)* Assign an additional secondary IP address:

IOS	N/A
CSM	`(csm-vlan)` **`alias`** `ip-address netmask`

Additional IP addresses allow the CSM to communicate with servers on a different IP network without using a router.

e. *(Optional)* Select a default gateway:

IOS	N/A
CSM	`(csm-vlan)` **`gateway`** `ip-address`

A next-hop default gateway or router address is given by *ip-address*. This command can be repeated to define up to 7 gateways per VLAN, or 255 gateways per CSM. Gateways are usually used on the client-side VLAN, although they can be used on the server-side if needed.

f. *(Optional)* Define static routes to reach distant networks:

IOS	N/A
CSM	`(csm-vlan)` **`route`** `ip-address netmask` **`gateway`** `gw-ip-address`

A static route can be defined when the CSM needs to know how to reach servers that are more than one router hop away. Define the route by the network *ip-address* and *netmask*, using gateway address *gw-ip-address*. The gateway must reside on the same local network as the CSM VLAN.

g. Repeat Steps 1b to 2f for each client-side and server-side VLAN.

h. *(Optional)* Define a fault-tolerant VLAN for redundant CSMs.

— Identify the fault-tolerant VLAN:

IOS	N/A
CSM	(csm) **vlan** *vlan-number* **ft**

This VLAN should be defined on both redundant CSMs. It should be a private VLAN that connects the two modules so that they can share connection and redundancy traffic. Each pair of redundant CSMs must use a different private fault-tolerant VLAN number.

— Define the fault-tolerant group:

IOS	N/A
CSM	(csm) **ft group** *group-id* **vlan** *vlan-id*

Each of the redundant CSMs must be given a common fault-tolerance *group-id* (1 to 254). The fault-tolerance VLAN is *vlan-id* (2 to 4095).

— *(Optional)* Set the CSM priority:

IOS	N/A
CSM	(csm-ft) **priority** *value*

The CSM with the highest priority *value* (1 to 254; default 10) becomes the primary CSM.

— *(Optional)* Allow a restored CSM to become primary again:

IOS	N/A
CSM	(csm-ft) **preempt**

By default, a primary CSM that fails cannot become the primary again when it is restored to service. Use the **preempt** command to allow a restored CSM to take over as the primary. This command must be entered on both of the redundant CSMs so that they agree on the preempt strategy.

— *(Optional)* Set the heartbeat interval:

IOS	N/A
CSM	(csm-ft) **heartbeat-time** *heartbeat-time*

— Heartbeat messages are exchanged between redundant CSMs over the fault-tolerant VLAN at regular *heartbeat-time* intervals (1 to 65,535 seconds; default 1 second).

— *(Optional)* Set the failover time:

IOS	N/A
CSM	(csm-ft) **failover** *failover-time*

The standby CSM will wait for *failover-time* (1 to 65,535 seconds; default 3 seconds) after the last heartbeat message was received before taking over as the primary CSM.

2 Define a server farm.

a. Assign a name to the server farm:

IOS	(global) **ip slb serverfarm** *serverfarm-name*
CSM	(csm) **serverfarm** *serverfarm-name*

The server farm is identified by *serverfarm-name* (text string up to 15 characters).

b. *(Optional)* Select a load-balancing algorithm for the server farm:

IOS	(server-farm) **predictor {roundrobin	leastconns}**
CSM	(server-farm) **predictor {roundrobin	leastconns	hash url	hash address [source	destination]** [*ip-netmask*] **| forward}]**

SLB selects a real server using **roundrobin** (weighted round-robin the default) or **leastconns** (weighted least connections).

A CSM can also load balance based on **hash url** (hash value from the URL; used along with the **url-hash** command in Step 5, substep l), **hash address** (hash value from the **source** address or **destination** address; *ip-netmask* can specify the address bits used for hashing; 255.255.255.255 or "all bits" is the default), or **forward** (forward traffic according to CSM routing tables).

c. *(Optional)* Use server NAT:

IOS	(server-farm) **nat server**
CSM	(server-farm) **nat server**

By default, the virtual server and real server addresses must be Layer 2-adjacent. In other words, SLB forwards packets between the virtual server and a real server by substituting the correct MAC addresses. Server NAT can be used instead, allowing the virtual and real servers to have addresses from separate IP subnets. SLB then substitutes the Layer 3 IP addresses to forward packets between the virtual and real servers, allowing the servers to be separated by multiple routing hops.

d. *(Optional)* Use client NAT.

— Define a NAT pool of addresses:

IOS	(global) **ip slb natpool** *pool-name start-ip end-ip* {**netmask** *netmask* | **prefix-length** *leading-1-bits*} [**entries** *init-addr* [*max-addr*]]
CSM	(global) **natpool** *pool-name start-ip end-ip* {**netmask** *netmask* | **prefix-length** *leading-1-bits*}

A pool of IP addresses is given the name *pool-name* (text string up to 15 characters), consisting of addresses bounded by *start-ip* and *end-ip*. The subnet mask associated with the pool can be given as a regular subnet mask, *netmask* (x.x.x.x format), or as the number of leading 1 bits in the mask, *leading-1-bits* (1 to 32).

For IOS SLB, client NAT allocates a number of entries as IP addresses and port numbers, *init-addr* (1 to 1,000,000; default 8000) as an initial set to use. When the number of dynamically allocated entries reaches half of the initial number, more entries are allocated. The maximum number of NAT entries can be defined as *max-addr* (1 to 8,000,000; default is the pool size times the number of ports available, or 65,535 − 11,000, or 54,535). Port numbers for translation begin at 11,000.

— Enable client NAT with a pool:

IOS	(server-farm) **nat client** *pool-name*
CSM	(server-farm) **nat client** *pool-name*

The SLB NAT pool is identified by *pool-name* (up to 15 characters).

e. *(Optional)* Assign a unique identifier for DFP:

IOS	(server-farm) **bindid** [*bind-id*]
CSM	(server-farm) **bindid** [*bind-id*]

Sometimes, a real server is assigned to multiple server farms. The *bind-id* (0 to 65533; default 0) is an arbitrary identification value given to a server farm. Each instance of a real server references this value, allowing DFP to assign a unique weight to it.

f. *(Optional)* Test the server with a probe:

IOS	(server-farm) **probe** *name*
CSM	(server-farm) **probe** *name*

The probe defined as *name* (text string, up to 15 characters) periodically tests for server connectivity and operation. IOS SLB offers ping, HTTP, and *Wireless Session Protocol* (WSP) probes. The CSM also offers TCP, FTP, SMTP, Telnet, and DNS probes. See section "10-3: SLB Probes" for more information about configuring probes.

g. *(Optional; CSM only)* Purge connections to a failed server:

IOS	N/A
CSM	(server-farm) **failaction purge**

By default, connections are not purged when a server fails (**no failaction purge**). When a CSM is used to load balance VPN connections, this command must be used so that existing tunnel connections to a failed server will be torn down automatically. Otherwise, the connections must time out before the remote end will become aware of a failure.

h. *(Optional; CSM only)* Define a redirect virtual server that will receive redirected traffic.

— Name the redirect virtual server:

IOS	N/A
CSM	(server-farm) **redirect-vserver** *name*

The redirect virtual server is named *name* (text string, up to 15 characters).

— Specify the address and port for the virtual server:

IOS	N/A
CSM	(redirect-virtual) **virtual** *ip-address* **tcp** *port*

The redirect virtual server is bound to *ip-address* (default 0.0.0.0, or no packet forwarding) and the TCP *port* number.

— *(Optional)* Restrict access by client:

IOS	N/A
CSM	(redirect-virtual) **client** *ip-address* [*network-mask*] [**exclude**]

Clients having IP addresses within the range given by *ip-address* (default 0.0.0.0, or all addresses) and *network-mask* (default 255.255.255.255, or all networks) will be allowed to connect to the virtual server. The *network-mask* in this case resembles the mask of an access list, where a 1 bit ignores and a 0 bit matches. On a CSM, you can use the **exclude** keyword to exclude clients with matching IP addresses instead.

— *(Optional)* Restrict access by VLAN:

IOS	N/A
CSM	(redirect-virtual) **vlan** {*vlan-number* | **all**}

If desired, only hosts from *vlan-number* (2 to 4095) or **all** VLANs (the default) can access the virtual server.

— *(Optional)* Advertise the virtual server:

IOS	N/A
CSM	(redirect-virtual) **advertise** [**active**]

By default, SLB creates a static host route (netmask 255.255.255.255) for the virtual server address to the Null0 logical interface. This static route can then be redistributed and advertised by a routing protocol. The **active** keyword causes the route to be advertised only when at least one real server is available. You can disable the advertisement with **no advertise**, preventing the static route from being created.

— *(Optional)* Enable connection redundancy between multiple CSMs:

IOS	N/A
CSM	(redirect-virtual) **replicate csrp**

Connection information is replicated to other CSMs that are configured for redundancy.

— *(Optional)* Hold connections open after no activity:

IOS	N/A
CSM	(redirect-virtual) **idle** *duration*

When SLB detects an absence of packets for a connection, it keeps the connection open for *duration* (4 to 65,535 seconds, default 3600 seconds or 1 hour) before sending a TCP *Reset* (RST).

— *(Optional)* Redirect and forward SSL:

IOS	N/A
CSM	(redirect-virtual) **ssl** {**https** | **ftp** | *ssl-port-number*}

— By default, HTTP requests are not forwarded to SSL servers. You can forward these as **https** (port 443), **ftp**, or as an *ssl-port-number* (1 to 65535).

— *(Optional)* Send a relocation string to redirected HTTP requests:

IOS	N/A
CSM	(redirect-virtual) **webhost relocation** *relocation-string* [**301** | **302**]

The *relocation-string* (text string up to 127 characters) is sent in response when an HTTP request is redirected. The original URL path can be appended to the *relocation-string* by ending the string with **%p**. The status code that is returned can be **301** ("The requested resource has been assigned a new permanent URL.") or **302** (the default; "The requested resource resides temporarily under a different URL.").

— *(Optional)* Send a relocation string when the redirect server is not in service:

IOS	N/A
CSM	(redirect-virtual) **webhost backup** *backup-string* [**301** | **302**]

The *backup-string* is sent in response when an HTTP request is redirected, but no real servers are available. The original URL path can be appended to the *relocation-string* by ending the string with **%p**. The status code that is returned can be **301** ("The requested resource has been assigned a new permanent URL.") or **302** (the default; "The requested resource resides temporarily under a different URL.").

— Enable the redirect virtual server for use:

IOS	N/A
CSM	(redirect-virtual) **inservice**

3 Specify one or more real servers in the server farm.

a. Identify the real server:

IOS	(server-farm) **real** *ip-address*
CSM	(server-farm) **real** *ip-address* [*port*]

The real server has the IP address given by *ip-address*. The CSM allows port translation for the server by specifying the *port* number (1 to 65,535; default no port translation).

b. *(Optional)* Specify a connection threshold.

— Set the maximum number of connections:

IOS	(real-server) **maxconns** *number*
CSM	(real-server) **maxconns** *number*

At any given time, the real server will be limited to *number* (1 to 4,294,967,295 connections; default 4,294,967,295) active connections.

— *(Optional; CSM only)* Set the minimum connection threshold:

IOS	N/A
CSM	(real-server) **minconns** *number*

If used, the **minconns** *number* (1 to 4,294,967,295 connections) is the threshold that the number of active connections must fall to before new connections are allowed again.

c. *(Optional)* Assign a relative capacity weight:

IOS	(real-server) **weight** *weighting-value*
CSM	(real-server) **weight** *weighting-value*

The real server is assigned a *weighting-value* (1 to 255 for IOS, 1 to 100 for CSM; default 8) that indicates its capacity relative to other real servers in the server farm. For weighted round-robin, *weighting-value* defines the number of consecutive connections the server will receive before SLB moves to the next server. For weighted least connections, the next connection is given to the server whose number of active connections is furthest below its capacity. The capacity is computed as the *weighting-value* divided by the sum of all real server weighting values in the server farm.

d. *(Optional; IOS SLB only)* Reassign connections when a server doesn't answer:

IOS	(real-server) **reassign** *threshold*
CSM	N/A

SLB attempts to assign a new connection to a real server by forwarding the client's initial SYN. If the server doesn't answer with a SYN handshake before the client retransmits its SYN, an unanswered SYN is recorded. After *threshold* (1 to 4, default 3) unanswered SYNs occur, SLB reassigns the connection to the next server.

e. *(Optional; IOS SLB only)* Define a failed server threshold:

IOS	(real-server) **faildetect numconns** *number-conns* [**numclients** *number-clients*]
CSM	N/A

A server is determined to have failed if *number-conns* (1 to 255, default 8 connections) TCP connections have been reassigned to another server. You can also use the **numclients** keyword to specify the *number-clients* (1 to 8, default 2) of unique clients that have had connection failures.

f. *(Optional; IOS SLB only)* Specify the amount of time before retrying a failed server:

IOS	(real-server) **retry** *retry-value*
CSM	N/A

After a real server has been declared "failed," SLB attempts to assign a new connection to it after *retry-value* (1 to 3600 seconds, default 60 seconds) time has elapsed. You can also use a value of 0 to indicate that new connections should not be attempted.

g. *(Optional; CSM only)* Accept redirected HTTP traffic:

IOS	N/A
CSM	(real-server) **redirect-vserver** *name*

The real server can receive traffic that has been redirected to the redirect virtual server *name* (text string, up to 15 characters). The virtual server is configured in Step 2.

h. Allow SLB to begin using the real server:

IOS	(real-server) **inservice**
CSM	(real-server) **inservice**

By default, the real server is not used by SLB unless it is placed in service. To remove a server from service, use **no inservice**.

4 *(CSM only)* Match specific traffic with load-balancing policies.

   a. *(Optional)* Define a map to match URLs.

   — Name the map:

IOS	N/A
CSM	(csm) **map** *url-map-name* **url**

   The map named *url-map-name* (text string up to 15 characters) contains matching conditions for URL contents.

   — Match URLs based on a regular expression:

IOS	N/A
CSM	(map-url) **match protocol http url** *urln*

The regular expression *urln* (up to 255 characters) matches against URL contents. You can enter up to 1023 **match** statements in a single map.

Regular expressions can contain the following symbols for matching: ***** (zero or more characters), **?** (exactly one character), **** (an escaped character), **[ ]** (a bracketed range of characters separated by a dash), **^** (don't match any in the range, when followed by a range), **\a** (alert or ASCII 7), **\b** (backspace or ASCII 8), **\f** (form-feed or ASCII 12), **\n** (newline or ASCII 10), **\r** (carriage return or ASCII 13), **\t** (tab or ASCII 9), **\v** (vertical tab or ASCII 11), **\0** (null or ASCII 0), **** (a backslash), and **\x##** (any character denoted by two hex digits for ASCII value).

b. *(Optional)* Define a map to match cookies.

— Name the map:

IOS	N/A
CSM	(csm) **map** *cookie-map-name* **cookie**

The map named *cookie-map-name* (text string up to 15 characters) contains one or more matching conditions for cookies.

— Match a cookie:

IOS	N/A
CSM	(map-cookie) **match protocol http cookie** *cookie-name* **cookie-value** *cookie-value-expression*

Cookies are matched by name *cookie-name* (text string, up to 63 characters) and a regular expression *cookie-value-expression* (text string, up to 255 characters). Regular expression symbols are defined in Step 4a. Multiple **match** commands can appear in a cookie map, but they all must be met before the cookie can be matched.

c. *(Optional)* Define a map to match header strings.

— Name the map:

IOS	N/A
CSM	(csm) **map** *header-map-name* **header**

The map named *header-map-name* (text string up to 15 characters) contains one or more matching conditions for HTTP headers.

— Match an HTTP header:

IOS	N/A
CSM	(map-header) **match protocol http header** *field* **header-value** *expression*

HTTP headers are matched by literal field name *field* (text string up to 63 characters) and a regular *expression* (text string, up to 127 characters). Regular expression symbols are defined in Step 4a. Multiple **match** commands can appear in a header map, but they all must be met before the header can be matched.

d. *(Optional)* Match successive connections from a client:

IOS	N/A
CSM	(csm) **sticky** *sticky-group-id* {**netmask** *netmask* | **cookie** *name* | **ssl**} [**timeout** *sticky-time*]

Connections from a client that match a policy can be made "sticky," so that they all use the same real server. Group common **sticky** commands into a sticky group instance, *sticky-group-id* (1 to 255). You can permit sticky connections based on the masked client IP address (**netmask** *netmask*, a standard subnet mask), a cookie name (**cookie** *name*), or SSL (**ssl**). The connection stickiness allows the last used real server to be remembered for a time period *sticky-time* (0 to 65,535 minutes; default 1440 minutes or 24 hours; 0 disables stickiness).

e. *(Optional)* Match client source addresses.

— Create a named standard IP access list:

IOS	N/A
CSM	(csm) **ip access-list standard** *access-list-name*

The access list is named *access-list-name* (text string).

— Permit or deny source addresses:

IOS	N/A
CSM	(access-list) {**permit** | **deny**} *source-address* [*source-wildcard*]

You can **permit** or **deny** client source addresses based on the
source-address (IP address format) and an address mask *source-wildcard* (subnet mask format, but 1 bits are used as wildcards).
One or more **permit** and **deny** commands can be listed in an access
list. They are evaluated in the order that they are entered.

f. Create one or more load-balancing policies.

— Name the policy:

IOS	N/A
CSM	(csm) **policy** *policy-name*

The policy is named *policy-name* (text string up to 15 characters).
You can configure up to 12,287 different policies on a CSM.

TIP

A policy can consist of one or more of the **map** and **group** commands that follow. If
multiple policy maps and groups are used in a single policy, matching traffic must match
all of them.

— *(Optional)* Use a URL map:

IOS	N/A
CSM	(policy) **url-map** *url-map-name*

URLs matched by the URL map *url-map-name* are handled by the
policy. URL maps are created in Step 4a.

— *(Optional)* Use a cookie map:

IOS	N/A
CSM	(policy) **cookie-map** *cookie-map-name*

Cookies matched by the cookie map *cookie-map-name* are handled
by the policy. Cookie maps are created in Step 4b.

— *(Optional)* Use a header map:

IOS	N/A
CSM	(policy) **header-map** *header-map-name*

Headers matched by the header map *header-map-name* are handled by the policy. Header maps are created in Step 4c.

— *(Optional)* Use a sticky group:

IOS	N/A
CSM	(policy) **sticky-group** *group-id*

Connections matching the sticky group number *group-id* (1 to 255; default 0 or no sticky connections) in this policy are sent to the same real server. Sticky groups are created in Step 4d.

— *(Optional)* Use a client filter group:

IOS	N/A
CSM	(policy) **client-group** {*acl-number*	*acl-name*}

Traffic that matches the standard IP access list *acl-number* (1 to 99) or *acl-name* are handled by the policy. Client filter access lists are created in Step 4e.

— *(Optional)* Mark traffic with a DSCP value:

IOS	N/A
CSM	(policy) **set ip dscp** *dscp-value*

Packets matching the policy have their *Differentiated Services Code Point* (DSCP) values set to *dscp-value* (0 to 63; no default). For more information about the DSCP values, refer to section "13-1: QoS Theory."

— Associate a server farm to the policy:

IOS	N/A
CSM	(policy) **serverfarm** *serverfarm-name*

A policy is used by virtual servers, but it must first be associated with only one server farm. This allows the policy to control load balancing to the real servers in the server farm named *serverfarm-name* (text string).

5 Define a virtual server for the server farm.

a. Name the virtual server:

IOS	(global) **ip slb vserver** *virtual-server-name*
CSM	(csm) **vserver** *virtual-server-name*

The virtual server is given the name *virtual-server-name* (text string up to 15 characters).

b. Assign the virtual server to a server farm:

IOS	(virtual-server) **serverfarm** *serverfarm-name*
CSM	(virtual-server) **serverfarm** *serverfarm-name*

SLB will use the virtual server as the front end for the server farm named *serverfarm-name* (text string up to 15 characters).

c. Define the virtual server capabilities:

IOS	(virtual-server) **virtual** *ip-address* [*network-mask*] {**tcp** | **udp**} [*port* | **wsp** | **wsp-wtp** | **wsp-wtls** | **wsp-wtp-wtls**] [**service** *service-name*]
CSM	(virtual-server) **virtual** *ip-address* [*network-mask*] {**tcp** | **udp** | **any** | *protocol-number*} *port* [**service ftp**]

The virtual server will appear as IP address *ip-address* (default 0.0.0.0 or "all networks") with *network-mask* (default 255.255.255.255).

With IOS SLB, it provides load balancing for the specified **tcp** or **udp** *port*: **dns** or **53** (Domain Name System), **ftp** or **21** (File Transfer Protocol), **https** or **443** (HTTP over Secure Socket Layer), **www** or **80** (HTTP), **telnet** or **23** (Telnet), **smtp** or **25** (SMTP), **pop3** or **110** (POPv3), **pop2** or **109** (POPv2), **nntp** or **119** (Network News Transport Protocol), or **matip-a** or **350** (Mapping of Airline Traffic over IP, type A). A port number of 0 can be given to indicate that the virtual server accepts connections on all ports.

Other alternatives to a port number are **wsp** (connectionless WSP, port 9200), **wsp-wtp** (connection-oriented WSP, port 9201 with WAP FSM), **wsp-wtls** (connectionless secure WSP, port 9202), and **wsp-wtp-wtls** (connection-oriented secure WSP, port 9203).

With a CSM, the protocol can be **tcp**, **udp**, **any** (any protocol, no port number is required; the default), or *protocol-number* (0 to 255). Any valid *port* number or name (0 to 65535) can be specified.

The **service** keyword can be given to force SLB to assign all connections associated with a given *service-name* (**ftp** or **wsp-wtp**) to the same real server. On a CSM, only **ftp** connections are allowed to be coupled to the originating control session.

d. *(Optional)* Control access to the virtual server.

— *(Optional)* Allow only specific clients to use the virtual server:

IOS	(virtual-server) **client** *ip-address* *network-mask*
CSM	(virtual-server) **client** *ip-address* [*network-mask*] [**exclude**]

Clients having IP addresses within the range given by *ip-address* (default 0.0.0.0, or all addresses) and *network-mask* (default 255.255.255.255, or all networks) are allowed to connect to the virtual server. The *network-mask* in this case resembles the mask of an access list, where a 1 bit ignores and a 0 bit matches. On a CSM, you can use the **exclude** keyword to disallow the IP addresses specified.

— *(Optional; CSM only)* Allow only specific source VLANs to use the virtual server:

IOS	N/A
CSM	(virtual-server) **vlan** *vlan-number*

By default, a virtual server accepts connections coming from any VLAN. To restrict the access, specify a *vlan-number* (2 to 4095) that is to be allowed. After it has been defined, all other VLANs are restricted from accessing the virtual server.

e. *(Optional)* Assign connections from the same client to the same real server:

IOS	(virtual-server) **sticky** *duration* [**group** *group-id*] [**netmask** *netmask*]
CSM	(virtual-server) **sticky** *duration* [**group** *group-id*] [**netmask** *netmask*]

For a given client, connections are assigned to the last-used real server for *duration* in seconds (IOS: 0 to 65,535, and CSM: 1 to 65,535). Virtual servers can be assigned to a *group-id* (0 to 55; default 0), associating them as a single group. A *netmask* (default 255.255.255.255) can be given such that all client source addresses within the mask are assigned to the same real server.

f. *(Optional; IOS SLB only)* Hold connections open after they are terminated:

IOS	(virtual-server) **delay** *duration*
CSM	N/A

After a TCP connection is terminated, SLB can maintain the connection context for *duration* (1 to 600 seconds, default 10 seconds). This can be useful when packets arrive out of sequence, and the connection is reset before the last data packet arrives.

g. *(Optional)* Hold connections open after no activity:

IOS	(virtual-server) **idle** *duration*
CSM	(virtual-server) **idle** *duration*

When SLB detects an absence of packets for a connection, it keeps the connection open for *duration* in seconds (IOS: 10 to 65,535, and CSM: 4 to 65,535, default 3600 seconds or 1 hour) before sending an RST.

h. *(Optional; IOS SLB only)* Prevent a SYN flood to the real servers:

IOS	(virtual-server) **synguard** *syn-count* [*interval*]
CSM	N/A

SLB monitors the number of SYNs that are received for the virtual server. If more than *syn-count* (0 to 4294967295, default 0 or no SYN monitoring) SYNs are received within the *interval* (50 to 5000 milliseconds, default 100 ms), any subsequent SYNs are dropped.

i. *(Optional)* Control the advertisement of the virtual server:

IOS	(virtual-server) **advertise** [**active**]
CSM	(virtual-server) **advertise** [**active**]

By default, SLB creates a static route for the virtual server address to the Null0 logical interface. This static route can then be redistributed and advertised by a routing protocol. The **active** keyword causes the route to be advertised only when at least one real server is available. You can disable the advertisement with **no advertise**, preventing the static route from being created.

j. *(Optional; CSM only)* Set the depth that URLs and cookies are parsed:

IOS	N/A
CSM	(virtual-server) **parse-length** *bytes*

The CSM parses up to *bytes* (1 to 4000 bytes; default 600 bytes) when looking for URL and cookie information.

k. *(Optional; CSM only)* Enable HTTP 1.1 connection persistence:

IOS	N/A
CSM	(virtual-server) **persistent rebalance**

By default, persistent connections for HTTP 1.1 are not maintained. Use this command to enable connection persistence.

l. *(Optional; CSM only)* Tune URL hashing for load balancing:

IOS	N/A
CSM	(virtual-server) **url-hash {begin-pattern	end-pattern}** *pattern*

With the "predictor hash URL" load-balancing algorithm, the entire URL is hashed by default. To specify a portion of the URL to be hashed, define the bounding text: **begin-pattern** *pattern* (text string that starts the hashed portion) or **end-pattern** *pattern* (text string that ends the hashed portion). The hashed portion includes the beginning pattern and goes up to the ending pattern. To define both a beginning and ending pattern, use this command twice.

m. *(Optional; CSM only)* Use an SLB policy to control Layer 7 traffic:

IOS	N/A
CSM	(virtual-server) **slb-policy** *policy-name*

You can use one or more **slb-policy** commands to define policies that control how higher layer traffic is load balanced. The *policy-name* (text string) is the name of a policy that has been assigned in Step 4f. When multiple policies are listed, they are evaluated in sequential order. The highest-priority policy should be entered first.

n. Allow SLB to begin using the virtual server:

IOS	(virtual-server) **inservice** [**standby** *group-name*]
CSM	(virtual-server) **inservice**

By default, the virtual server is not used by SLB unless it is placed in service. To remove a virtual server from service, use **no inservice**.

TIP

You can use multiple IOS SLB devices to provide redundancy for virtual servers. *IOS SLB stateless backup* allows each SLB device to listen to HSRP messages from Layer 3 interfaces on redundant switches. When one switch (and its IOS SLB) fails, another HSRP interface becomes the primary gateway. When the other IOS SLB also detects the failure, the virtual servers that are associated with the HSRP *group-name* (defined above) become active. No SLB state information is kept, however, so existing connections are dropped and must be reestablished.

Stateless backup requires that HSRP be configured on all the redundant Layer 3 devices on the *server-side* VLAN. Be sure that the *group-name* matches between the HSRP and virtual server configurations. See section "8-6: Router Redundancy with HSRP" for further HSRP configuration information.

o. *(Optional)* Use SLB stateful backup:

IOS	(virtual-server) **replicate casa** *listening-ip remote-ip port-number* [*interval*] [**password** [**0**|**7**] *password* [*timeout*]]
CSM	(virtual-server) **replicate csrp** {**sticky** | **connection**}

IOS SLB replicates and exchanges its load-sharing decision tables with other stateful backup devices using the *Cisco Appliance Services Architecture* (CASA) mechanism. When a failure occurs, the backup SLB device already has the current state information and can immediately take over.

This information is sent from the *listening-ip* address (an interface on the local device) to the *remote-ip* address (an interface on the backup device), using TCP port *port-number* (1 to 65,535). Replication messages are sent at *interval* seconds (1 to 300, default 10).

A *password* (text string; use **0** if unencrypted, the default, or **7** if encrypted) can be used for MD5 authentication with the backup device. The optional *timeout* (0 to 65,535 seconds; default 180 seconds) defines a time period when the password can be migrated from an old value to a new one. During this time, both old and new passwords are accepted.

CSM replicates its connection information using the *Content Switching Replication Protocol* (CSRP). The **sticky** connection database or the regular **connection** database can be replicated. To replicate both, choose each one in a separate **replicate csrp** command.

6 *(Optional)* Use SLB *Dynamic Feedback Protocol* (DFP).

a. *(Optional)* Use the DFP manager to communicate with DFP agents on servers.

— Enable the DFP manager:

IOS	(global) **ip slb dfp** [**password** [**0**|**7**] *password* [*timeout*]]
CSM	(csm) **dfp** [**password** *password* [*timeout*]]

The router can become a DFP load-balancing manager. DFP can be configured with a *password* (text string; use **0** if unencrypted, the default, or **7** if encrypted) for MD5 authentication with a host agent. The optional *timeout* (0 to 65,535 seconds; default 180 seconds) defines a time period when the password can be migrated from an old value to a new one. During this time, both old and new passwords are accepted.

— Specify a DFP agent:

IOS	(slb-dfp) **agent** *ip-address port-number* [*timeout* [*retry-count* [*retry-interval*]]]
CSM	(dfp) **agent** *ip-address port-number* [*timeout* [*retry-count* [*retry-interval*]]]

A DFP agent on a real server is identified by its *ip-address* and the *port-number* number used. The DFP agent (the server) must contact the DFP manager (the IOS SLB device) at *timeout* intervals (0 to 65,535 seconds; default 0 seconds or no timeout period). The DFP manager attempts to reconnect to the agent *retry-count* (0 to 65,535 retries; default 0 retries or an infinite number) times, at intervals of *retry-interval* (1 to 65,535 seconds; default 180 seconds).

b. *(Optional)* Use a DFP agent to provide DFP reports.

— Define the agent:

IOS	(global) **ip dfp agent** *subsystem-name*
CSM	N/A

The DFP agent sends periodic reports to its manager, a distributed-director device. The *subsystem-name* (text string up to 15 characters) allows the manager to associate the server reports with a subsystem (controlled by the SLB device) for global load balancing. To see what *subsystem-name* values are available from the global manager, use the **ip dfp agent ?** command.

— *(Optional)* Set a DFP agent password:

IOS	(dfp) **password** [**0**|**7**] *password* [*timeout*]
CSM	N/A

A *password* (text string; use **0** if unencrypted, the default, or **7** if encrypted) can be used for MD5 authentication with a DFP manager. The optional *timeout* (0 to 65,535 seconds; default 180 seconds) defines a time period when the password can be migrated from an old value to a new one. During this time, both old and new passwords are accepted.

— Set the DFP port number:

IOS	(dfp) **port** *port-number*
CSM	(dfp) **manager** *port-number*

The DFP manager and agents communicate over a common port number, *port-number* (1 to 65535, no default). DFP managers discover their agents dynamically, requiring the port number to be identical between the manager (distributed director) and the agents (IOS SLB).

— *(Optional)* Set the interval for recalculating weights:

IOS	(dfp) **interval** *seconds*
CSM	N/A

DFP server weights are recalculated at an interval of *seconds* (5 to 65,535 seconds; default 10 seconds) before they are supplied to the DFP manager.

— Enable the DFP agent:

IOS	(dfp) **inservice**
CSM	N/A

By default, the DFP agent is disabled.

SLB Example

See Figure 10-2 for a network diagram. SLB is configured to provide load balancing for two server farms: FARM1 and FARM2.

FARM1 is a server farm of three real web servers having IP addresses 192.168.250.10, 192.168.250.11, and 192.168.250.12. The real servers are considered in a "failed" state if four consecutive TCP connections cannot be established with the server. SLB waits 30 seconds before attempting another connection to a failed server. (The number of failed TCP connections and the retry interval are only supported in the IOS command set.) An HTTP probe is configured to try a connection to each real server in the server farm every 120 seconds.

The virtual server VSERVER1 at 10.10.10.101 uses the weighted least connections algorithm for load balancing between the real servers. New connections are made sticky (passed to the real server last used by the same client) for 60 seconds.

The CSM version of this example also includes the client and server-side VLAN numbers (10 and 20) and IP addresses (10.10.10.2 and 192.168.250.1).

One server is given a weight of 32, one server has a weight of 16, and one server has a weight of 8. New connections are assigned to the server with the least number of active connections, as measured by the server capacities. For example, server 192.168.254.10 has a weight of 32, and a capacity of 32/(32+16+8) or 32/56. Server 192.168.254.11 has a weight of 16 and a capacity of 16/(32+16+8) or 16/56. Server 192.168.254.12 has a weight of 8 and a capacity of 8/(32+16+8) or 8/56. At any given time, the server with the number of active connections furthest below its capacity is given a new connection.

Figure 10-2 *Network Diagram for the SLB Example*

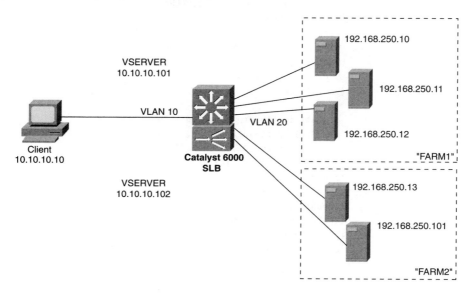

The configuration that follows shows the commands that are necessary for server farm FARM1 and virtual server VSERVER1. The same configuration is shown for an IOS-based switch and a CSM module.

IOS	
(global)	`ip slb serverfarm FARM1`
(server-farm)	`predictor leastconns`
(server-farm)	`nat server`
(server-farm)	`probe HTTP1`
(server-farm)	`real 192.168.250.10`
(real-server)	`weight 32`
(real-server)	`faildetect numconns 4`
(real-server)	`retry 30`
(real-server)	`inservice`
(real-server)	`exit`
(server-farm)	`real 192.168.250.11`
(real-server)	`weight 16`
(real-server)	`faildetect numconns 4`
(real-server)	`retry 30`
(real-server)	`inservice`
(real-server)	`exit`
(server-farm)	`real 192.168.250.12`
(real-server)	`weight 8`
(real-server)	`faildetect numconns 4`
(real-server)	`retry 30`
(real-server)	`inservice`
(real-server)	`exit`
(global)	`ip slb vserver VSERVER1`
(virtual-server)	`serverfarm FARM1`
(virtual-server)	`virtual 10.10.10.101 tcp www`
(virtual-server)	`sticky 60 group 1`
(virtual-server)	`advertise active`
(virtual-server)	`inservice`
(virtual-server)	`exit`
(global)	`ip slb dfp password 0 test123`
(slb-dfp)	`agent 192.168.250.10 2000`
(slb-dfp)	`agent 192.168.250.11 2000`
(slb-dfp)	`agent 192.168.250.12 2000`
(slb-dfp)	`exit`
(global)	`probe HTTP1 http`
(probe)	`interval 120`
(probe)	`port 80`
(probe)	`request method get`
(probe)	`exit`

```
CSM        (global) module csm 3
           (csm) vlan 10 client
           (csm-vlan) ip address 10.10.10.2 255.255.255.0
           (csm-vlan) gateway 10.10.10.1
           (csm-vlan) exit
           (csm) vlan 20 server
           (csm-vlan) ip address 192.168.250.1 255.255.255.0
           (csm-vlan) exit

           (csm) serverfarm FARM1
           (server-farm) predictor leastconns
           (server-farm) nat server
           (server-farm) probe HTTP1
           (server-farm) real 192.168.250.10
           (real-server) weight 32
           (real-server) inservice
           (real-server) exit
           (server-farm) real 192.168.250.11
           (real-server) weight 16
           (real-server) inservice
           (real-server) exit
            (server-farm) real 192.168.250.12
           (real-server) weight 8
           (real-server) exit

           (csm) vserver VSERVER1
           (virtual-server) serverfarm FARM1
           (virtual-server) virtual 10.10.10.101 tcp www
           (virtual-server) sticky 60 group 1
           (virtual-server) advertise active
           (virtual-server) inservice
           (virtual-server) exit

           (csm) dfp password test123
           (dfp) agent 192.168.250.10 2000
           (dfp) agent 192.168.250.11 2000
           (dfp) agent 192.168.250.12 2000
           (dfp) exit

           (csm) probe HTTP1 http
           (probe) interval 120
           (probe) request method get
           (probe) exit
```

FARM2, the second server farm, is made up of two real servers at 192.168.250.13 and 192.168.250.101. The IOS SLB device is configured for the default round-robin load balancing. The CSM, however, offers more options. The URL hash load-balancing algorithm is used instead. HTTP probe HTTP2 tests GET operations to the real servers every 60 seconds. A server is moved to the failed state if five probes fail.

The virtual server VSERVER2 is assigned to 10.10.10.102 for HTTP traffic. The CSM is configured to use two load-balancing policies for the virtual server. Policy1 uses URL map URL1 to match against URLs that have either /signup/* or /support/*. Sticky SSL connections are also matched. Policy2 uses cookie map Cart to match against the cookie name mystore containing the cookie value Shop*. Policy2 also matches against sticky connections that have cookies named test.

The configuration that follows shows the commands that are necessary for server farm FARM2 and virtual server VSERVER2.

IOS	`(global) ip slb serverfarm FARM2`
	`(server-farm) predictor roundrobin`
	`(server-farm) nat server`
	`(server-farm) probe HTTP2`
	`(server-farm) real 192.168.250.13`
	`(real-server) inservice`
	`(real-server) exit`
	`(server-farm) real 192.168.250.101`
	`(real-server) inservice`
	`(real-server) exit`
	`(global) ip slb vserver VSERVER2`
	`(virtual-server) serverfarm FARM2`
	`(virtual-server) virtual 10.10.10.102 tcp 80`
	`(virtual-server) inservice`
	`(virtual-server) exit`
	`(csm) probe HTTP2 http`
	`(probe) credentials testuser test123`
	`(probe) request method get /home`
	`(probe) interval 60`
	`(probe) faildetect 5`
CSM	`(csm) serverfarm FARM2`
	`(server-farm) predictor hash url`
	`(server-farm) nat server`
	`(server-farm) probe HTTP2`

```
CSM          (server-farm) real 192.168.250.13
(Cont.)      (real-server) inservice
             (real-server) exit
             (server-farm) real 192.168.250.101
             (real-server) inservice
             real-server) exit

             (csm) vserver VSERVER2
             (virtual-server) serverfarm FARM2
             (virtual-server) virtual 10.10.10.102 tcp 80
             (virtual-server) slb-policy Policy1
             (virtual-server) slb-policy Policy2
             (virtual-server) inservice
             (virtual-server) exit

             (csm) map Cart cookie
             (map-cookie) match protocol http cookie mystore cookie-value Shop*
             (map-cookie) exit
             (csm) map URL1 url
             (map-url) match protocol http url /signup/*
             (map-url) match protocol http url /support/*
             (map-url) exit
             (csm) sticky 1 ssl
             (csm) sticky 2 cookie test

             (csm) policy Policy1
             (policy) url-map URL1
             (policy) sticky-group 1
             (policy) serverfarm FARM2
             (policy) exit

             (csm) policy Policy2
             (policy) cookie-map Cart
             (policy) sticky-group 2
             (policy) serverfarm FARM2
             (policy) exit

             (csm) probe HTTP2 http
             (probe) credentials testuser test123
             (probe) request method get /home
             (probe) interval 60
             (probe) retries 5
             (probe) exit
```

Displaying Information About SLB

Table 10-1 lists some switch commands that you can use to display helpful information about SLB configuration and status.

Table 10-1 *Commands to Display Server Load-Balancing Configuration and Status Information*

Display Function	Switch OS	Command
VLAN assignment	IOS	N/A
	CSM	(exec) **show module csm** *slot* **vlan** [**client** | **server** | **ft**] [**id** *vlan-id*] [**detail**]
Server farms	IOS	(exec) **show ip slb serverfarms** [**name** *serverfarm-name*] [**detail**]
	CSM	(exec) **show module csm** *slot* **serverfarms** [**name** *serverfarm-name*] [**detail**]
Real servers	IOS	(exec) **show ip slb reals** [**vserver** *virtual-server-name*] [**detail**]
	CSM	(exec) **show module csm** *slot* **real** [**sfarm** *sfarm-name*] [**detail**]
CSM policies	IOS	N/A
	CSM	(exec) **show module csm** *slot* **policy** [**name** *policy-name*]
Virtual servers	IOS	(exec) **show ip slb vserver** [**name** *virtual-server-name*] [**detail**]
	CSM	(exec) **show module csm** *slot* **vserver** [**detail**]
Virtual redirect servers	IOS	N/A
	CSM	(exec) **show module csm** *slot* **vserver redirect**
SLB connections	IOS	(exec) **show ip slb conns** [**vserver** *virtual-server-name* | **client** *ip-address*] [**detail**]
	CSM	(exec) **show module csm** *slot* **conns** [**vserver** *virtserver-name*] [**client** *ip-address*] [**detail**]
DFP status	IOS	(exec) **show ip slb dfp** [**agent** *agent-ip-address port-number* | **manager** *manager-ip-address* | **detail** | **weights**]
	CSM	(exec) **show module csm** *slot* **dfp** [**agent** [**detail** | *ip-address port*] | **manager** [*ip-addr*] | **detail** | **weights**]
SLB redundancy	IOS	(exec) **show ip slb replicate**
	CSM	(exec) **show module csm** *slot* **ft** [**detail**]
Probes	IOS	(exec) **show ip slb probe** [**name** *probe_name*] [**detail**]
	CSM	(exec) **show module csm** *slot* **probe** [**http** | **icmp** | **telnet** | **tcp** | **ftp** | **smtp** | **dns**] [**name** *probe_name*] [**detail**]
SLB statistics	IOS	(exec) **show ip slb stats**
	CSM	(exec) **show module csm** *slot* **stats**

10-2: SLB Firewall Load Balancing

- Firewall load balancing balances traffic flows to one or more firewall farms.

- A firewall farm is a group of firewalls that are connected in parallel or that have their "inside" (protected) and "outside" (unprotected) interfaces connected to common network segments.

- Firewall load balancing requires a load-balancing device (IOS SLB) to be connected to each side of the firewall farm. A firewall farm with "inside" and "outside" interfaces would then require two load-balancing devices—each making sure that traffic flows are directed toward the same firewall for the duration of the connection. Figure 10-3 illustrates the basic firewall load-balancing concept.

Figure 10-3 *Firewall Load-Balancing Concept*

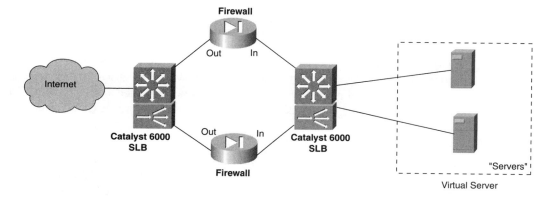

- Firewall load balancing is performed by computing a hash value of each new traffic flow (source and destination IP addresses and ports). This is called a *route lookup*.

- The firewall load-balancing device then masquerades as the IP address for all firewalls in the firewall farm.

- Firewall load balancing can detect a firewall failure by monitoring probe activity.

- The HSRP can be used to provide a "stateless backup" redundancy for multiple firewall load-balancing devices. If one device fails, a redundant device can take over its function.

- Multiple firewall load-balancing devices can also use "stateful backup" for redundancy. Backup devices keep state information dynamically and can take over immediately if a failure occurs.

Configuration

1 *(CSM only)* Define client-side and server-side VLANs.

a. Start configuring a CSM module:

IOS	N/A
CSM	(global) **module csm** *slot-number*

The native IOS CLI begins CSM configuration mode for the CSM located at *slot-number* in the switch chassis. To end this mode, use the **exit** command. To find the appropriate slot number, use the **show module all** command.

b. Define each of the VLAN types:

IOS	N/A
CSM	(csm) **vlan** *vlan-id* {**client** | **server**}

The VLAN number is given as *vlan-id* (2 to 4095; VLAN 1 cannot be used). This VLAN must already be defined on the switch in the VLAN database. The VLAN type, **client** or **server**, defines where the clients or servers are located as seen by the CSM. You must define *both* client-side and server-side VLANs before the CSM can be used properly.

TIP   The CSM doesn't have a special configuration mode for firewall farms or firewall load balancing. Instead, the same concept of client-side and server-side load balancing is used. When configuring a CSM for firewall load balancing, always consider the client-side VLAN of the CSM to be away from the firewalls. The server-side VLAN of the CSM is always closest or directly connected to the firewall farms.

---

c. *(Optional)* Assign a primary IP address:

IOS	N/A
CSM	(csm-vlan) **ip address** *ip-address netmask*

One IP address can be defined per VLAN on the CSM. This address is used for management traffic (probes, for example) and ARP requests.

d. *(Optional)* Assign an additional secondary IP address:

IOS	N/A
CSM	(csm-vlan) **alias** *ip-address netmask*

Additional IP addresses allow the CSM to communicate with servers on a different IP network without using a router.

e. *(Optional)* Select a default gateway:

IOS	N/A
CSM	(csm-vlan) **gateway** *ip-address*

A next-hop default gateway or router address is given by *ip-address*. This command can be repeated to define up to 7 gateways per VLAN or 255 gateways per CSM. Gateways are usually used on the client-side VLAN, although they can be used on the server-side if needed.

f. *(Optional)* Define static routes to reach distant networks:

IOS	N/A
CSM	(csm-vlan) **route** *ip-address netmask* **gateway** *gw-ip-address*

A static route can be defined when the CSM needs to know how to reach servers that are more than one router hop away. Define the route by the network *ip-address* and *netmask*, using gateway address *gw-ip-address*. The gateway must reside on the same local network as the CSM VLAN.

g. Repeat Steps b to f for each client-side and server-side VLAN.

2 Define a firewall farm.

a. Assign a name to the firewall farm:

IOS	(global) **ip slb firewallfarm** *firewallfarm-name*
CSM	(csm) **serverfarm** *serverfarm-name*

In IOS SLB, the collection of firewalls is referenced by *firewallfarm-name* (text string up to 15 characters). A CSM, however, views a firewall farm as just another form of a server farm, referenced by *serverfarm-name* (text string up to 15 characters).

TIP

Recall that firewall load balancing requires two load-balancing devices—one on each side of the firewall farm. For IOS SLB, the firewall farm is configured as a **firewallfarm**, consisting of real servers or firewalls. Load balancing is then based on the firewall "routes" that are configured into each load-balancing device. SLB has no concept of virtual servers with firewall load balancing.

The CSM, however, views firewall load balancing as an extension of regular load balancing. You should configure the firewall farm as a **serverfarm** of real servers. Virtual servers are configured to load balance traffic toward the firewall farm. Traffic away from the firewall farm must also be configured for load balancing, with a generic **serverfarm** having no real servers. Instead, a generic virtual server forwards all traffic through the generic server farm according to the CSM's internal routing tables.

b. Identify one or more firewalls in the farm.

— Specify the firewall's IP address:

IOS	(firewall-farm) **real** *ip-address*
CSM	(server-farm) **real** *ip-address*

The firewall is directly connected (same logical subnet) to the load-balancing device with an interface at IP address *ip-address*.

— *(Optional; IOS SLB only)* Assign a relative capacity weight:

IOS	(real-firewall) **weight** *weighting-value*
CSM	N/A

The real firewall is assigned a *weighting-value* (1 to 255; default 8) that indicates its capacity relative to other real firewalls in the firewall farm. These values are statically defined and are based on what you think the firewall can handle, relative to the others. The weight values are only used for round-robin or least-connections algorithms.

— *(Optional; IOS SLB only)* Define one or more probes to detect a firewall failure:

IOS	(real-firewall) **probe** *probe-name*
CSM	N/A

The probe that is defined by *probe-name* (text string) is used
periodically to determine whether the firewall has failed. Even if
more than one probe is defined, the firewall is declared down if it
fails just one probe. A firewall must pass all probes in order to be
recovered again.

TIP	You must also define the probes separately, as described in section "10-3: SLB Probes." Ping probes are the most useful for firewall load balancing. For each firewall in the firewall farm, configure a probe to send ping packets that pass completely through the firewall, destined for the firewall load-balancing device on the other side. This tests both "inside" and "outside" interfaces of the firewall, requiring them to be active and operational so that the ping probe is reflected from the other side. Be sure that the firewall is configured to allow ICMP ping packets to pass through.

— Allow load balancing to begin using the firewall:

IOS	`(real-firewall)` **`inservice`**
CSM	`(real-server)` **`inservice`**

By default, the real firewall is not used by SLB unless it is placed
in service. To remove a firewall from service, use **no inservice**.

c. *(Optional; IOS SLB only)* Define one or more flows that will be sent to the firewall
farm:

IOS	`(firewall-farm)` **`access`** `[`**`source`** `source-ip-address network-mask]` `[`**`destination`** `destination-ip-address network-mask]`
CSM	N/A

When multiple firewall farms exist, traffic can be identified by address and sent through
the appropriate firewall farm. A traffic flow is defined by its source and destination
addresses and subnet masks. If either **source** or **destination** keywords are omitted,
they default to 0.0.0.0 with a mask of 0.0.0.0 — signifying all addresses and networks.
This is the default behavior.

With a CSM, traffic is load balanced to a firewall farm by using a virtual server and
load-balancing algorithms.

d. *(Optional)* Choose a firewall load-balancing method:

IOS	`(firewall-farm)` **`predictor hash address [port]`**
CSM	`(server-farm)` **`predictor hash address source 255.255.255.255`** -OR-
	`(server-farm)` **`predictor hash address destination 255.255.255.255`**

By default IOS SLB uses the source and destination IP addresses of a flow to select a destination firewall. Use the **port** keyword to use the source and destination addresses, and the source and destination TCP or UDP port numbers, in the selection decision.

On a CSM located "outside" relative to the firewall farm (unsecure side), the algorithm should use only the **source** addresses. Here, the netmask option is set to **255.255.255.255** so that all address bits are used in the hash algorithm. On a CSM located "inside" relative to the firewall farm (secure side), you should use **destination** addresses with a **255.255.255.255** address mask. The hash algorithm provides the best load-balancing distribution when it is based on the large population of addresses furthest away from the firewall farm. (This assumes that the size of the network and the number of hosts and IP addresses increase as you move out from the firewall farm.)

e. *(CSM only)* Disable server NAT:

IOS	N/A
CSM	`(server-farm)` **`no nat server`**

By default, server NAT is enabled for a CSM server farm. In the case of firewall load balancing, the firewall farm is considered a server farm. However, NAT is never required when load balancing to firewalls.

f. *(Optional; CSM only)* Define one or more probes to detect failures within the firewall farm:

IOS	N/A
CSM	`(server-farm)` **`probe`** *`probe`*`-name`

The probe that is defined by *probe-name* (text string) periodically checks each firewall (real server) within the firewall farm. The probe inherits each real server IP address to use as a target address. Even if more than one probe is defined, a firewall is declared down if it fails just one probe. A firewall must pass all probes in order to be recovered again.

TIP

You must also define the probes separately, as described in section "10-3: SLB Probes." Ping probes are the most useful for firewall load balancing.

Unlike IOS SLB firewall load balancing, the CSM only offers probes that can be used on a server farm as a whole. In other words, you cannot define probes with unique target addresses. Ideally, probes should be configured so that a ping packet passes completely through the firewall, destined for the firewall load-balancing device on the other side. This would test both "inside" and "outside" interfaces of the firewall, requiring them to be active and operational so that the ping probe is reflected from the other side.

CSM probes can only inherit the target addresses from each real server defined in a server farm. This is always the nearest firewall interface, so total firewall operation can't be determined from a probe.

g. *(Optional)* Use stateful backup to recover from a failure:

IOS	(firewall-farm) **replicate casa** *listening-ip remote-ip port-number* [*interval*] [**password** [**0**|**7**] *password* [*timeout*]]
CSM	N/A

The redundant load-balancing devices use CASA structure to exchange and replicate state information. This is sent from the *listening-ip* address (an interface on the local device) to the *remote-ip* address (an interface on the backup device), using *port-number* (1 to 65535). Replication messages are sent at *interval* seconds (1 to 300, default 10).

A *password* (text string; use **0** if unencrypted, the default, or **7** if encrypted) can be used for MD5 authentication with the backup device. The optional *timeout* (0 to 65,535 seconds; default 180 seconds) defines a time period when the password can be migrated from an old value to a new one. During this time, both old and new passwords are accepted.

h. *(Optional; IOS SLB only)* Adjust the TCP or UDP connection parameters.

— Enter the TCP or UDP configuration mode:

IOS	(firewall-farm) {**tcp**	**udp**}
CSM	N/A

You might need to make adjustments to both TCP and UDP. In this case, this command can be repeated to configure each independently.

Section 10-2

— *(Optional; TCP only)* Hold connections open after they are terminated:

IOS	(firewall-farm-protocol) **delay** *duration*
CSM	N/A

After a TCP connection is terminated, the connection context can be maintained for *duration* (1 to 600 seconds, default 10 seconds). This can be useful when packets arrive out of sequence, and the connection is reset before the last data packet arrives.

— *(Optional)* Hold connections open after no activity:

IOS	(firewall-farm-protocol) **idle** *duration*
CSM	N/A

When an absence of packets is detected for a connection, the connection is kept open for *duration* (10 to 65,535 seconds, default 3600 seconds or 1 hour) before an RST is sent.

— *(Optional)* Specify the maximum number of connections:

IOS	(firewall-farm-protocol) **maxconns** *number*
CSM	N/A

At any given time, the real server is limited to *number* (1 to 4,294,967,295; default 4,294,967,295) active connections.

— (Optional) Assign connections from the same IP address to the same firewall:

IOS	(firewall-farm-protocol) **sticky** *duration* [**netmask** *netmask*]
CSM	N/A

For a given IP address, connections are assigned to the last-used firewall for *duration* (0 to 65,535 seconds). A *netmask* can be given such that all source addresses within the mask are assigned to the same firewall.

i. *(IOS SLB only)* Allow firewall load balancing to begin using the firewall:

IOS	(firewall-farm) **inservice**
CSM	N/A

By default, the firewall is not used by firewall load balancing unless it is placed in service. To remove a firewall from service, use **no inservice**. A CSM server farm is inherently in service.

3 *(CSM only)* Define a virtual server to handle traffic toward the firewall farm.

a. Name the virtual server:

IOS	N/A
CSM	(csm) **vserver** *virtual-server-name*

The virtual server is given the name *virtual-server-name* (text string up to 15 characters).

b. Assign the virtual server to a firewall server farm:

IOS	N/A
CSM	(virtual-server) **serverfarm** *serverfarm-name*

SLB uses the virtual server as the front end for the server farm named *serverfarm-name* (text string up to 15 characters).

c. Define the virtual server capabilities:

IOS	N/A
CSM	(virtual-server) **virtual** *ip-address* [*network-mask*] **any**

The virtual server appears as IP address *ip-address* (default 0.0.0.0) with *network-mask* (default 255.255.255.255; 1-bit matches, 0 is wildcard). In the case of a firewall farm, you can set the *ip-address* and *network-mask* to be that of an entire internal network of servers. This allows the virtual server to represent many real machines, while actually load balancing the traffic to the firewalls (real servers). The **any** keyword allows all protocols to be load balanced.

d. *(Optional)* Allow traffic only from a source VLAN to use the virtual server:

IOS	N/A
CSM	(virtual-server) **vlan** *vlan-number*

By default traffic from all VLANs is allowed to reach the firewalls through the virtual server. To restrict the access, specify a *vlan-number* (2 to 4095) that is to be allowed. This is usually the CSM VLAN that connects the "outside" network, farthest away from the firewalls. After this has been defined, all other VLANs are restricted from accessing the virtual server.

e. Allow SLB to begin using the virtual server:

IOS	N/A
CSM	(virtual-server) **inservice**

By default the virtual server is not used by SLB unless it is placed in service. To remove a virtual server from service, use **no inservice**.

f. *(Optional)* Use SLB stateful backup:

IOS	N/A
CSM	(virtual-server) **replicate csrp {sticky	connection}**

CSM replicates its connection information using the CSRP. The **sticky** connection database or the regular **connection** database can be replicated. To replicate both, choose each one in a separate **replicate csrp** command.

4 *(CSM only)* Define a generic server farm for traffic away from the firewall farm.

a. Assign a name to the generic server farm:

IOS	N/A
CSM	(csm) **serverfarm** *serverfarm-name*

The CSM sees the network away from the firewall farm as a server farm. On the CSM "outside" of the firewall farm, this is usually toward the Internet or public network. On the CSM "inside" the firewall farm, this might be other internal networks or actual server farms.

TIP   Traffic away from the firewall farm must also be configured for load balancing, with a generic **serverfarm** having no real servers. Instead, a generic virtual server forwards all traffic through the generic server farm according to the CSM's internal routing tables.

---

b. *(Optional)* Choose a load-balancing method:

IOS	N/A
CSM	(server-farm) **predictor forward**

On a CSM located "outside" relative to the firewall farm (unsecure side), the algorithm should use only the **forward** mode. This mode forwards traffic destined away from the firewall farm according to the CSM's internal routing table.

On a CSM located "inside" relative to the firewall farm (secure side), traffic is usually destined toward an internal network or actual server farm. In this case, normal server farm load balancing can be used.

c. Disable server NAT:

IOS	N/A
CSM	(server-farm) **no nat server**

By default server NAT is enabled for a CSM server farm. In the case of firewall load balancing, the firewall farm is considered a server farm. However, NAT is never required when load balancing to firewalls.

5 *(CSM only)* Define a generic virtual server to handle traffic away from the firewall farm.

a. Name the virtual server:

IOS	N/A
CSM	(csm) **vserver** *virtual-server-name*

The virtual server is given the name *virtual-server-name* (text string up to 15 characters).

b. Assign the virtual server to a firewall server farm:

IOS	N/A
CSM	(virtual-server) **serverfarm** *serverfarm-name*

SLB uses the virtual server as the front end for the generic server farm named *serverfarm-name* (text string up to 15 characters).

Section 10-2

c. Define the virtual server capabilities:

IOS	N/A
CSM	(virtual-server) **virtual** *ip-address [network-mask]* **any**

The virtual server appears as IP address *ip-address* (default 0.0.0.0) with *network-mask* (default 255.255.255.255; 1-bit matches, 0 is wildcard). To represent the outer public network (the Internet, for example), use **virtual 0.0.0.0 0.0.0.0 any**.

d. *(Optional)* Allow traffic only from a source VLAN to use the virtual server:

IOS	N/A
CSM	(virtual-server) **vlan** *vlan-number*

By default, traffic from all VLANs is allowed to reach the firewalls through the virtual server. To restrict the access, specify a *vlan-number* (2 to 4095) that is to be allowed. This is usually the CSM VLAN that connects to the firewall farm. After this has been defined, all other VLANs are restricted from accessing the virtual server.

e. Allow SLB to begin using the virtual server:

IOS	N/A
CSM	(virtual-server) **inservice**

By default the virtual server is not used by SLB unless it is placed in service. To remove a virtual server from service, use **no inservice**.

Firewall Load-Balancing Example

To perform firewall load balancing, two load-balancing devices are needed—one located externally and one located internally with respect to the firewall farm. Figure 10-4 shows a network diagram for this example.

The firewall farm consists of two real firewalls. Their "outside" (unprotected) interfaces are at 192.168.1.2 and 192.168.1.3. Their "inside" (protected) interfaces are at 192.168.100.2 and 192.168.100.3. On the outside, the default gateway is 10.5.1.1, and the external SLB device is at 10.5.1.2.

The internal SLB device performs firewall load balancing for outbound traffic to the firewall farm. As well, it provides normal server load balancing for an internal server farm. The real servers are 10.70.1.10 and 10.70.1.20, and the virtual server appears as 10.5.1.80.

Ping probes are used by both external and internal SLB devices to test for firewall operation. An HTTP probe tests each of the real servers in the server farm. These use the default GET method and are sent every 240 seconds.

Figure 10-4 *Network Diagram for the Firewall Load-Balancing Example*

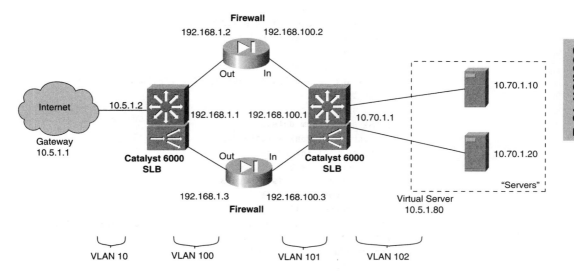

The configuration for the external load-balancing device is shown first:

```
IOS        (global) ip slb firewallfarm Outside
           (firewall-farm) real 192.168.1.2
           (real-firewall) weight 8
           (real-firewall) probe Ping1
           (real-firewall) inservice
           (real-firewall) exit
           (firewall-farm) real 192.168.1.3
           (real-firewall) weight 8
           (real-firewall) probe Ping2
           (real-firewall) inservice
           (real-firewall) exit
           (firewall-farm) inservice
           (firewall-farm) exit

           (global) ip slb probe Ping1 ping
           (probe) address 192.168.100.1
           (probe) interval 10
           (probe) faildetect 4
           (global) ip slb probe Ping2 ping
           (probe) address 192.168.100.1
           (probe) interval 10
           (probe) faildetect 4
           (probe) exit
```

CSM

```
(global) module csm 3
(csm) vlan 10 client
(csm-vlan) ip address 10.5.1.2 255.255.255.0
(csm-vlan) gateway 10.5.1.1
(csm-vlan) exit
(csm) vlan 100 server
(csm-vlan) ip address 192.168.1.1 255.255.255.0
(csm-vlan) exit

(csm) serverfarm Outside
(server-farm) real 192.168.1.2
(real-server) inservice
(real-server) exit
(server-farm) real 192.168.1.3
(real-server) inservice
(real-server) exit
(server-farm) predictor hash address source 255.255.255.255
(server-farm) no nat server
(server-farm) probe Ping1
(server-farm) exit

(csm) vserver Voutside
(virtual-server) serverfarm Outside
(virtual-server) virtual 10.5.1.0 255.255.255.0 any
(virtual-server) vlan 10
(virtual-server) inservice
(virtual-server) exit

(csm) serverfarm Internet
(server-farm) predictor forward
(server-farm) no nat server
(server-farm) exit

(csm) vserver Vinternet
(virtual-server) serverfarm Internet
(virtual-server) virtual 0.0.0.0 0.0.0.0 any
(virtual-server) vlan 100
(virtual-server) inservice
(virtual-server) exit

(csm) probe Ping1 ping
(probe) address 192.168.1.1
(probe) retries 4
(probe) exit
```

Now the configuration for the internal load-balancing device is shown:

IOS	
	(global) `ip slb firewallfarm Inside`
	(firewall-farm) `real 192.168.100.2`
	(real-firewall) `weight 8`
	(real-firewall) `probe Ping1`
	(real-firewall) `inservice`
	(real-firewall) `exit`
	(firewall-farm) `real 192.168.100.3`
	(real-firewall) `weight 8`
	(real-firewall) `probe Ping2`
	(real-firewall) `inservice`
	(real-firewall) `exit`
	(firewall-farm) `inservice`
	(firewall-farm) `exit`
	(global) `ip slb serverfarm Servers`
	(server-farm) `nat server`
	(server-farm) `probe HTTP1`
	(server-farm) `real 10.70.1.10`
	(real-server) `inservice`
	(real-server) `exit`
	(server-farm) `real 10.70.1.20`
	(real-server) `inservice`
	(real-server) `exit`
	(global) `ip slb vserver Vservers`
	(virtual-server) `serverfarm Servers`
	(virtual-server) `virtual 10.5.1.80 tcp 0`
	(virtual-server) `inservice`
	(virtual-server) `exit`
	(global) `ip slb probe Ping1 ping`
	(probe) `address 192.168.1.1`
	(probe) `interval 10`
	(probe) `faildetect 4`
	(probe) `exit`
	(global) `ip slb probe Ping2 ping`
	(probe) `address 192.168.1.1`
	(probe) `interval 10`
	(probe) `faildetect 4`
	(probe) `exit`
	(global) `ip slb probe HTTP1 http`
	(probe) `port 80`
	(probe) `interval 240`
	(probe) `request`

```
CSM     (global) module csm 3
        (csm) vlan 102 client
        (csm-vlan) ip address 10.70.1.1 255.255.255.0
        (csm-vlan) exit
        (csm) vlan 101 server
        (csm-vlan) ip address 192.168.100.1 255.255.255.0
        (csm-vlan) exit

        (csm) serverfarm Inside
        (server-farm) real 192.168.100.2
        (real-server) inservice
        (real-server) exit
        (server-farm) real 192.168.100.3
        (real-server) inservice
        (real-server) exit
        (server-farm) predictor hash address destination 255.255.255.255
        (server-farm) no nat server
        (server-farm) probe Ping1
        (server-farm) exit

        (csm) vserver Vinside
        (virtual-server) serverfarm Inside
        (virtual-server) virtual 0.0.0.0 0.0.0.0 any
        (virtual-server) vlan 102
        (virtual-server) inservice
        (virtual-server) exit

        (csm) serverfarm Servers
        (server-farm) real 10.70.1.10
        (real-server) inservice
        (real-server) exit
        (server-farm) real 10.70.1.20
        (real-server) inservice
        (real-server) exit
        (server-farm) probe HTTP1
        (server-farm) exit

        (csm) vserver Vservers
        (virtual-server) serverfarm Servers
        (virtual-server) virtual 10.5.1.80 tcp 0
        (virtual-server) vlan 101
        (virtual-server) inservice
        (virtual-server) exit

        (csm) probe Ping1 ping
        (probe) address 192.168.1.1
        (probe) retries 4
        (probe) exit
        (csm) probe HTTP1 http
        (probe) interval 240
        (probe) request
```

Displaying Information About Firewall Load Balancing

Table 10-2 lists some switch commands that you can use to display helpful information about SLB firewall load-balancing configuration and status.

Table 10-2   *Commands to Display SLB Firewall Load-Balancing Configuration and Status Information*

Display Function	Switch OS	Command
Status of firewalls in a farm	IOS	(exec) **show ip slb reals**
	CSM	(exec) **show module csm** *slot* **real** [**sfarm** *sfarm-name*]
Firewall weight and connection counters	IOS	(exec) **show ip slb reals detail**
	CSM	(exec) **show module csm** *slot* **real** [**sfarm** *sfarm-name*] **detail**
Firewall farm status	IOS	(exec) **show ip slb firewallfarm**
	CSM	(exec) **show module csm** *slot* **serverfarms** [**name** *serverfarm-name*] [**detail**] -OR- (exec) **show module csm** *slot* **vserver** [**detail**]
Load-balancing connections to firewalls	IOS	(exec) **show ip slb conns** [**firewall** *firewallfarm-name*] [**detail**]
	CSM	(exec) **show module csm** *slot* **conns** [**vserver** *virtserver-name*] [**client** *ip-address*] [**detail**]
Probes	IOS	(exec) **show ip slb probe** [**name** *probe_name*] [**detail**]
	CSM	(exec) **show module csm** *slot* **probe** [**http** | **icmp** | **telnet** | **tcp** | **ftp** | **smtp** | **dns**] [**name** *probe_name*] [**detail**]
Sticky connections	IOS	(exec) **show ip slb sticky**
	CSM	(exec) **show module csm** *slot* **sticky** [**groups** | **client** *ip_address*]

10-3: SLB Probes

- Probes can be used to test for server or firewall connectivity and proper operation.
- Probes can be defined to simulate requests for these protocols:
    - **ICMP**—Sends ICMP echo (ping) requests to a real server.
    - **HTTP**—Sends HTTP requests to a real server, using TCP port 80.
    - **WSP**—Requests and verifies the replies using *Wireless Access Protocol* (WAP), port 9201.
    - **Telnet**—Opens and closes a Telnet connection (TCP port 23) to a real server.

— **TCP**—Establishes and resets TCP connections to a real server. This can be used to support any TCP port, including HTTPS or SSL, port 443.

— **FTP**—Opens and closes an FTP connection (TCP ports 20 and 21) to a real server.

— **SMTP**—Opens and closes an SMTP connection (TCP port 25) to a real server.

— **DNS**—Sends requests to and verifies the replies from a real DNS server.

Configuration

1 Define the probe:

IOS	(global) **ip slb probe** *name* {**ping** | **http** | **wsp**}
CSM	(csm) **probe** *probe-name* {**http** | **icmp** | **telnet** | **tcp** | **ftp** | **smtp** | **dns**}

The probe is named *name* (text string up to 15 characters) and can be referenced by other SLB server and firewall farm commands. IOS SLB allows these probe types: **ping** (ICMP), **http**, or **wsp** (WAP port 9201). In addition, the CSM allows **http**, **icmp** (Ping), **telnet**, **tcp** (TCP connection), **ftp**, **smtp**, and **dns**.

2 *(Optional)* Define the target address:

IOS	(probe) **address** [*ip-address*]
CSM	(probe) **address** *ip-address*

For a server farm, this command is not used. The *ip-address* used by the probe is inherited from each real server in the server farm. However, a CSM allows an address to be configured for a ping or DNS probe type.

With IOS SLB, addresses are not inherited when the probe is used for a firewall farm. You must use this command to define the address of a target firewall.

3 Set the probe behavior:

a. *(Optional)* Set the time between probes:

IOS	(probe) **interval** *seconds*
CSM	(probe) **interval** *seconds*

Probes are sent toward the target at intervals of *seconds* (IOS SLB: 1 to 65,535 seconds, default 1 second; CSM: 5 to 65,535 seconds, default 120 seconds).

b. *(Optional; CSM only)* Set the time to wait for a non-TCP probe reply:

IOS	N/A
CSM	(probe) **receive** `receive-timeout`

The CSM waits *receive-timeout* (1 to 65,535 seconds; default 10 seconds) for data to be received in response to probes other than TCP.

c. *(Optional; CSM only)* Set the time to wait for a TCP probe connection:

IOS	N/A
CSM	(probe) **open** `open-timeout`

For HTTP, TCP, FTP, Telnet, and SMTP probes, the CSM waits *open-timeout* (1 to 65,535 seconds; default 10 seconds) for a TCP connection to be opened in response to the probe.

d. *(Optional)* Define the criteria for a failure:

IOS	(probe) **faildetect** `retry-count`
CSM	(probe) **retries** `retry-count`

With IOS SLB, a server or firewall is considered to have failed if *retry-count* (1 to 255; default 10) consecutive ping probes are unanswered. With a CSM, the target has failed if *retry-count* (0 to 65,535; default 3) probes of any type are unanswered.

e. *(Optional; CSM only)* Wait to retry a failed server:

IOS	N/A
CSM	(probe) **failed** `failed-interval`

When a CSM has determined that a server has failed, it waits *failed-interval* (5 to 65,535 seconds; default 300 seconds) before sending another probe.

4 *(Optional; HTTP probe only)* Define the HTTP probe operation:

a. *(Optional; IOS SLB only)* Set the port number:

IOS	(probe) **port** `port-number`
CSM	N/A

Usually, an HTTP probe uses *port-number* 80. If the *port-number* is unspecified, however, it is inherited from the virtual server. For a firewall probe, the *port-number* must be given (1 to 65,535). The target device must be able to answer an HTTP request for the probe to work.

b. *(Optional)* Define the HTTP probe method:

IOS	(probe) **request** [**method** {**get** | **post** | **head** | **name** *name*}] [**url** *path*]
CSM	(probe) **request** [**method** {**get** | **head**}] [**url** *path*]

The probe requests information from the server using the **get** (the default), **post**, **head** (request a header data type)**,** or **name** (request the data named *name*) method. A URL can also be given, specifying the server *path* (text string URL; default /).

c. *(Optional)* Specify the probe header information:

IOS	(probe) **header** *field-name* [*field-value*]
CSM	(probe) **header** *field-name* [*field-value*]

The probe header name is set to *field-name* (text string up to 15 characters), with a value of *field-value*. A colon is automatically inserted between the name and value. By default, the request contains these headers:

```
Accept: */*
Connection: close
User-Agent: cisco-slb-probe/1.0
Host: virtual-IP-address
```

d. *(Optional)* Specify the HTTP authentication values:

IOS	(probe) **credentials** *username* [*password*]
CSM	(probe) **credentials** *username* [*password*]

If HTTP authentication is required, a *username* (text string, up to 15 characters) and a *password* (text string up to 15 characters) can be given for the probe.

e. *(Optional)* Expect a specific status code to be returned:

IOS	(probe) **expect** [**status** *status-code*] [**regex** *regular-expression*]
CSM	(probe) **expect status** *min-number* [*max-number*]

A real server or a firewall is considered to have failed if it either does not respond to an HTTP probe or if it returns a *status-code* (100 to 599, default 200) other than the one specified. For firewalls, the *status-code* should be set to 401. For a CSM, the status code must be within the range *min-number* (default 0) and *max-number* (optional, default 999).

With IOS SLB, you can also expect a regular expression along with the status code. Use the **regex** keyword and specify a *regular-expression* (text string, no default). Only the first 2920 bytes of the probe reply are searched for a match.

5 *(Optional; WSP probe only)* Define the target URL:

IOS	(probe) **url** [*path*]
CSM	N/A

A URL can also be given, specifying the server *path* (text string URL; default /).

6 *(Optional; DNS probe only)* Define the domain name:

IOS	N/A
CSM	(probe) **name** *domain-name*

A DNS probe requires a *domain-name* (text string) that can be resolved by a DNS server target.

Displaying Information About SLB Probes

Table 10-3 lists some switch commands that you can use to display helpful information about SLB probes.

Table 10-3 *Commands to Display SLB Probe Information*

Display Function	Switch OS	Command
Probe configuration and status	IOS	(exec) **show ip slb probe** [**name** *probe_name*] [**detail**]
	CSM	(exec) **show module csm** *slot* **probe** [**http** | **icmp** | **telnet** | **tcp** | **ftp** | **smtp** | **dns**] [**name** *probe_name*] [**detail**]

Section 10-3

Further Reading

Refer to the following recommended sources for further information about the topics covered in this chapter.

Cisco IOS Server Load Balancing and the Catalyst 6000 Family of Switches, Cisco white paper at:
www.cisco.com/warp/customer/cc/pd/si/casi/ca6000/tech/ios6k_wp.htm

The Cisco Dynamic Feedback Protocol, Cisco white paper at:
www.cisco.com/warp/public/cc/pd/ibsw/mulb/tech/dfp_wp.htm

CHAPTER 11

Controlling Traffic and Switch Access

See the following sections for configuration information about these topics:

- **11-1: Broadcast Suppression**—Describes the method for preventing the switch from forwarding excessive broadcasts received on a port.

- **11-2: Protocol Filtering**—Explains how to configure a port to prevent forwarding of flood packets of a particular protocol out a port.

- **11-3: Port Security**—Provides the information required to configure a port for use only by a specified list of clients based on MAC addresses.

- **11-4: VLAN Access Control Lists**—Describes how to control the traffic that passes through a Layer 2 switch using access control lists applied to a VLAN.

- **11-5: Switch Authentication**—Explains how to configure the switch for use of a RADIUS, TACACS, or TACACS+ for authentication into the switch.

- **11-6: Permit Lists**—Shows how to create a list of hosts that are permitted to access the switch for management purposes (Telnet, SNMP, and HTTP).

- **11-7: SSH Telnet Configuration**—Provides the information needed to configure the switch for Secure Shell Telnet logins.

- **11-8: 802.1X Port Authentication**—Describes how to configure a port to require a login or certificate for user authentication before granting access to the network.

NOTE   Many of the traffic-control features covered in this chapter are very dependent on the hardware and products. As you read through this chapter, note that many of the commands differ between the product lines and that some of the features discussed are not supported.

11-1: Broadcast Suppression

- A network protocol can create a large amount of broadcast traffic.

- In Layer 2 networks, broadcasts must be forwarded on all ports except the receiving port; because of this, a large or excessive number of broadcasts can have an impact on network and device performance.

- Broadcast suppression enables you to control how a receiving port handles excessive broadcast traffic.

- By configuring a threshold, a port can be configured to stop flooding broadcasts for a predefined period or until the broadcasts fall below a certain level.

- Suppressing these broadcasts will prevent them from being forwarded out other switch ports and limit the effect they have on the network.

- Suppression of the broadcasts does not have any effect on the multicast or unicast traffic received by the port.

- Broadcast suppression is supported by both the COS and IOS operating systems on most Catalyst platforms.

- In addition to broadcast suppression, unicast and multicast suppression can also be configured for some platforms.

Configuring Broadcast Suppression

By default broadcast suppression is disabled on all platforms and on all operating systems. Broadcast suppression is applied to individual ports on a switch. When configuring broadcast suppression, keep in mind that it is the number of broadcasts received by a port. When the threshold is reached, the port stops passing broadcast packets to the backplane until the condition is corrected. To configure broadcast suppression, use the following steps.

1 Enable broadcast suppression:

COS	`set port broadcast` *mod/port* *threshold%*
3500XL IOS	(interface) `port storm-control broadcast threshold rising` *ppsrisingthreshold#* `falling` *ppsfallingthreshold#*
2950 IOS	(interface) `storm-control broadcast level` *risingthreshold%* [*fallingthreshold%*]
3550 IOS	(interface) `storm-control broadcast level` *threshold%*
Supervisor IOS (Catalyst 6000)	(interface) `broadcast suppression` *threshold%*

The syntax for broadcast suppression, and the action, varies greatly by platform. For the COS switches, setting a *threshold%* on the interface to less than 100 percent enables broadcast suppression. The threshold limits the amount of bandwidth on an interface that can be used for broadcast packets. For example, a value of 50 percent means that the interface is required to take action on all broadcast packets that were above 50 percent of the total bandwidth. A value of 100 percent disables broadcast suppression because it lets the broadcast take up to 100 percent of the available bandwidth. For the 2950, 3550, and Supervisor IOS on the 6000 series switch, the concept is the same. The *threshold%* or *risingthreshold%* specifies the percentage of bandwidth limit that would have to be reached by broadcast traffic before action would be taken.

For the 2900/3500XL switches, the rising value that causes broadcasts to be suppressed is a *packet per second* (pps) value. When the *ppsrisingthreshold#* is reached, action is taken against the packets. For these switches a *ppsfallingthreshold#* must also be configured. This is the value the broadcast must fall below before the action is removed from the port. You might want to keep in mind that a 100 mbps Ethernet port has a maximum forwarding capability of 148,000 pps in full-duplex mode. Any value of 148,000 pps or more would have no effect on controlling broadcasts.

On the COS switches, on all operating systems on the 6000 series, and on the 3550 switch, the suppression is a time-based action—that is, broadcasts are suppressed over a 1-second interval. On the 2950 and 2900XL switches, the suppression is based on an absolute value or a falling value. The *fallingthreshold* is an optional value that can be set to specify when the action is removed. If the *risingthreshold* is 50 percent and the *fallingthreshold* is 45 percent, for example, when 50 percent of the traffic is broadcast, action is taken until the value falls below 45 percent. Because the falling value is not required, and if no falling value is set, the default is to remove the action when the percentage of broadcast traffic falls below the rising value.

NOTE	Broadcast suppression is not supported on the Catalyst 4000 series switch.

2 Specify action to be taken:

COS	`set port broadcast` *mod/port threshold%* `[violation {drop-packets	errdisable}]`
3500XL IOS	`(interface)` `port storm-control broadcast action {filter	shutdown}`
2950 IOS	`(interface)` `storm-control broadcast action {shutdown	trap}`
3550 IOS	N/A
Supervisor IOS (Catalyst 6000)	N/A

When broadcast suppression occurs, the default action is to suppress or filter the packets. This means that packets are dropped and do not make it onto the backplane of the switch. You can, on some of the platforms, configure the switch to take another action. For example, on COS switches you can place the port in an *Errdisable* state. This means that the port will stay in this state as long as the threshold is reached and even after that until an administrator has corrected the problem. For the 3500XL switch, you can change the device from the default action of **filter** to the **shutdown** option. When the port is placed in shutdown mode, it remains there until an administrator has reenabled the port with the **no shutdown** command. Each time the threshold is crossed, the administrator must reenable the port. For the 2950 broadcast, frames are dropped unless the action has changed to **shutdown**; this works the same as it does on the 3500XL. To revert to filtering the frames, the administrator must issue the command **no port storm-control broadcast action shutdown**. Another option that can be configured on the 2950 is for the switch to generate an SNMP **trap**. The action is not configurable for the 3550 or the Catalyst 6000 running Supervisor IOS.

NOTE	You can have the switch automatically try to enable a port that has been placed in an Errdisable state because of a broadcast storm using the command **set errdisable-timeout enable bcast-suppression**.

3 *(Optional)* Control unicast or multicast:

COS	`set port broadcast` *mod/port threshold%* `[multicast {enable | disable}] [unicast {enable | disable}]`
3500XL IOS	`(interface)` **port storm-control {multicast | unicast} threshold rising** *ppsrisingthreshold#* **falling** *ppsfallingthreshold#*
2950 IOS	`(interface)` **storm-control {multicast | unicast} level** *risingthreshold%* `[fallingthreshold%]`
3550 IOS	`(interface)` **storm-control {multicast | unicast} level** *threshold%*
Supervisor IOS (Catalyst 6000)	N/A

In addition to configuring the switch to control broadcast floods, you can also configure a port to drop frames or become disabled when it encounters a large number of unicast or multicast packets. To configure this option, use the **multicast** and **unicast** keywords in the commands to enable the control of the frames.

Verifying Configuration

After you have configured broadcast suppression, use the following commands to verify the configuration and operation on the switch:

COS	**show port broadcast** `[mod][/port]`
3500XL IOS	`(privileged)` **show port storm-control** `[interface]`
2950/3550 IOS	`(privileged)` **show storm-control** `[interface]` `[{broadcast | multicast | unicast | history}]`
Supervisor IOS (Catalyst 6000)	`(privileged)` **show interfaces switchport** `[module` number`]`

Feature Example

This example shows a typical configuration for setting broadcast suppression on port 3/1 of a COS switch using a threshold of 33 percent. When the threshold is met, the port is errdisabled and the switch is configured to attempt to reenable the port automatically.

An example of the Catalyst OS configuration follows:

```
Catalyst (enable)> set port broadcast 3/1 33% violation errdisable
Catalyst (enable)> set errdisable-timeout enable bcast-suppression
```

For a 2950, this example shows a configuration that enables broadcast suppression when the traffic reaches 55 percent on interface Fast Ethernet 0/9 and resumes normal broadcast propagation when the broadcast falls below 44 percent.

An example of the Supervisor IOS configuration follows:

```
2950(config)#interface fastethernet 0/9
2950(config-if)#storm-control broadcast level 55 44
2950(config-if)#end
2950#copy running-config startup-config
```

11-2: Protocol Filtering

- Protocol filtering can be configured on Catalyst 4000, 5000, or 6000 series switches.

- Protocol filtering does not require any special feature cards on the switch to operate.

- Protocol filtering enables you to configure a port to filter or block flood (broadcast, multicasts, and unknown unicasts) traffic based on protocols.

- Protocol filtering is only supported on Layer 2 access ports and cannot be configured on trunk links or Layer 3 ports.

- Protocol filtering supports blocking of IP, IPX, AppleTalk, VINES, and DECnet traffic. All other protocols are not affected by protocol filtering.

- Administrative protocols such as *Spanning Tree Protocol* (STP), *Cisco Discovery Protocol* (CDP), and *VLAN Trunking Protocol* (VTP) are not blocked by protocol filtering.

Configuration

By configuring protocol filtering on a switch, you are preventing the port from flooding traffic of that type received from other ports in the VLAN out the given port. This can be useful in controlling traffic from clients within the same VLAN running different and "chatty" protocols. To configure protocol filtering, use the following steps.

1 Enable protocol filtering for the switch:

COS	`set protocolfilter enable`
IOS	`(global) protocol-filter`

Protocol filtering is disabled by default. For the ports to control the traffic, you must first enable protocol filtering for the switch. After enabling the process, you can set up the ports to react to a given protocol.

2   Enable protocol filtering on an access port:

COS	`set port protocol` *mod/port* `{ip	ipx group} {on	off	auto}`
IOS	`(interface) switchport protocol {ip	ipx	group} {on	off	auto}`

For each port on which you want to control traffic, you must specify the protocol and how traffic is to be handled. The **protocol** option specifies the given type of protocol. You can choose from among the following options: **ip** (IP), **ipx** (IPX), and **group** (AppleTalk, DECnet, and Banyan VINES). The options specify how traffic is to be handled. The option **on** specifies that a port is to receive traffic for the protocol and forward flood traffic for that protocol. The option **off** specifies that the port cannot receive or flood traffic for a given protocol. The option **auto** indicates that the port will not flood traffic for a given protocol until it first receives a packet of that protocol on the port. Table 11-1 lists the default actions if the ports are not configured.

Table 11-1   *Protocol Filtering Defaults*

Protocol	Mode
IP	on
IPX	auto
Group	auto

Verification

To verify the configuration of protocol filtering, use the following commands:

COS	`show port protocol` *mod/port(s)*

IOS	`(privileged) show protocol-filtering`
	 -OR-
	 `(privileged) show protocol-filtering interface {type` *slot/port*`}`

These **show** commands display the configuration for the specified ports. In IOS, the command **show protocol-filtering** without any port designations will only show ports that have at least one protocol that is in the nondefault mode.

Feature Example

This example shows the configuration for protocol filtering. This example enables protocol filtering. It then sets the Fast Ethernet ports 5/1 through 5/6 to allow IP traffic to pass without being filtered and blocks all other traffic. This example also configures ports 5/7 to 5/8 to allow only IPX traffic. In this example, ports 5/9 to 5/10 allow IP and IPX traffic only if the ports detect an IP or IPX client on the specific port and allow all other traffic to be forwarded.

An example of the Catalyst OS configuration follows:

```
Catalyst(enable)>set protocolfilter enable
Catalyst(enable)>set port protocol 5/1-6 ip on
Catalyst(enable)>set port protocol 5/1-6 ipx off
Catalyst(enable)>set port protocol 5/1-6 group off
Catalyst(enable)>set port protocol 5/7-8 ip off
Catalyst(enable)>set port protocol 5/7-8 ipx on
Catalyst(enable)>set port protocol 5/7-8 group off
Catalyst(enable)>set port protocol 5/9-10 ip auto
Catalyst(enable)>set port protocol 5/9-10 ipx auto
Catalyst(enable)>set port protocol 5/9-10 group on
```

An example of the Supervisor IOS configuration follows:

```
Switch(config)#protocol-filter
Switch(config)#interface fastethernet 5/1
Switch(config-if)#switchport protocol ip on
Switch(config-if)#switchport protocol ipx off
Switch(config-if)#switchport protocol group off
Switch(config-if)#interface fastethernet 5/2
Switch(config-if)#switchport protocol ip on
Switch(config-if)#switchport protocol ipx off
Switch(config-if)#switchport protocol group off
Switch(config-if)#interface fastethernet 5/3
Switch(config-if)#switchport protocol ip on
Switch(config-if)#switchport protocol ipx off
Switch(config-if)#switchport protocol group off
Switch(config-if)#interface fastethernet 5/4
Switch(config-if)#switchport protocol ip on
Switch(config-if)#switchport protocol ipx off
Switch(config-if)#switchport protocol group off
Switch(config-if)#interface fastethernet 5/5
Switch(config-if)#switchport protocol ip on
Switch(config-if)#switchport protocol ipx off
Switch(config-if)#switchport protocol group off
Switch(config-if)#interface fastethernet 5/6
Switch(config-if)#switchport protocol ip on
Switch(config-if)#switchport protocol ipx off
Switch(config-if)#switchport protocol group off
Switch(config-if)#interface fastethernet 5/7
Switch(config-if)#switchport protocol ip off
Switch(config-if)#switchport protocol ipx on
Switch(config-if)#switchport protocol group off
Switch(config-if)#interface fastethernet 5/8
Switch(config-if)#switchport protocol ip off
Switch(config-if)#switchport protocol ipx on
```

Section 11-2

```
Switch(config-if)#switchport protocol group off
Switch(config-if)#interface fastethernet 5/9
Switch(config-if)#switchport protocol ip auto
Switch(config-if)#switchport protocol ipx auto
Switch(config-if)#switchport protocol group off
Switch(config-if)#interface fastethernet 5/10
Switch(config-if)#switchport protocol ip auto
Switch(config-if)#switchport protocol ipx auto
Switch(config-if)#switchport protocol group off
Switch(config-if)#end
Switch(config)#copy running-config startup-config
```

11-3: Port Security

- Port security enables you to configure a port to only allow a given device or devices access to the switch port.

- Port security defines the allowed devices by MAC address.

- MAC addresses for allowed devices can be manually configured and/or "learned" by the switch.

- There are limits to how many MAC addresses can be secured on a port. These numbers vary between platforms.

- When an unauthorized MAC attempts to access the port, the switch can suspend or disable the port.

- Port security cannot be configured on a trunk port, a *Switched Port Analyzer* (SPAN) port, or a port that is dynamically assigned to a VLAN.

- Port security is supported on the 5000, 4000, and 6000 switches running COS. It is supported on the 3500XL, 3550, and 2950 switches running IOS.

Configuration

When a port is active on a switch, any user can plug into the port and access the network. Because many networks use *Dynamic Host Configuration Protocol* (DCHP) to assign user addresses, it would be very easy for someone with physical access to a network port to plug in his own device, such as a laptop, into the port and become a user on the network. From there, a person could proceed to generate traffic or cause other problems within the network. Port security enables you to specify the MAC address(es) of the devices that are allowed to connect to the port. Use the following steps to configure port security.

1 Enable port security:

COS	`set port security` *mod/port* `enable`
IOS	`(interface)` `switchport port-security`
3500XL IOS	`(interface)`**port security**

By default anyone can plug into a port and access network services. To protect a port, you must first enable port security on the individual port. Use the command that is appropriate for your device.

NOTE

At the time of this writing, you cannot configure port security on the 4000 or 6000 series switches running Supervisor IOS code. If and when Cisco offers support for those platforms, it is expected that the syntax will be similar to the IOS configuration (not the 3500XL IOS) listed in these steps.

2 Specify the number of MAC addresses:

COS	`set port security` *mod/port* `maximum` *value*
IOS	`(interface) switchport port-security maximum` *value*
3500XL IOS	`(interface)port security max-mac-count` *value*

After you have enabled port security, you need to determine how many different devices will be accessing the ports and how many addresses will need to be secured. The *value* option specifies the number of addresses to be secured. The default value is one address. Each hardware platform has a limited number of addresses that can be secured; so if you expect to secure more than 250 total addresses on the switch, check the specific documentation for that hardware.

3 Manually enter MAC addresses to be secured:

COS	`set port security` *mod/port* `enable` [*mac_address*]
IOS	`(interface) switchport port-security mac-address` *mac_address*
3500XL IOS	N/A

By default, the switches will "learn" the MAC addresses of the devices that are plugged into that port. If you want to control which devices can access the switch, use these commands to specify which MAC addresses are secured on a port.

4 Specify the action to be taken by the port:

COS	`set port security` *mod/port* `violation {shutdown	restrict}`
IOS	`(interface) switchport port-security violation {protect	restrict	shutdown}`
3500XL IOS	`(interface)port security action {shutdown	trap}`

When a violation occurs, the switch generally protects the port by dropping the traffic that comes from unauthorized MAC addresses. This means that the switch does not allow those frames through the device; if a frame comes from a device that is configured as secure, however, those frames are allowed through. This is the default configuration for each of the devices and is specified by the **protect** option for IOS switches and the **restrict** option for COS switches—the default when you enable port security on a 3500XL (unless you specify a different option). Another option that you can configure is for the interface to move to a **shutdown** state. If you configure this option, the port remains in the administratively down state until an administrator reenables the port with a **no shutdown** command. A third option is to generate an SNMP trap. If a violation occurs, the **restrict** option for IOS and the **trap** option for the 3500XL IOS perform this function.

Verification

To verify the configuration of port security on the switch, use one of the following commands:

COS	`show port security [statistics]` *mod/port*
	`show port security statistics [system]` [*mod/port*]
IOS	(privileged) `show port security [interface` *interface-id*] [*address*]
3500XL IOS	`show port security` [*interface-id*]

Feature Example

This example shows the configuration for port security. In this example, ports Fast Ethernet 2/1 are configured to allow a single MAC address 00-01-03-87-09-43 to have access to the port and will shut down if the security is violated. Ports 2/2 and 2/3 are configured to allow 10 addresses each, which the switch will learn as devices plug into the ports, and will drop unauthorized packets.

An example of the Catalyst OS configuration follows:

```
Catalyst (enable)>set port security 2/1 enable
Catalyst (enable)>set port security 2/1 enable 00-01-03-87-09-43
Catalyst (enable)>set port security 2/1 violation shutdown
Catalyst (enable)>set port security 2/2-3 enable
Catalyst (enable)>set port security 2/2-3 maximum 10
```

An example of the Supervisor IOS configuration follows:

```
Switch(config)#interface fastethernet 2/1
Switch(config-if)#switchport port-security
Switch(config-if)#switchport port-security mac-address 00-01-03-87-09-43
Switch(config-if)#switchport port-security violation shutdown
Switch(config-if)#interface fastethernet 2/2
Switch(config-if)#switchport port-security
```

```
Switch(config-if)#switchport port-security maximum 10
Switch(config-if)#interface fastethernet 2/3
Switch(config-if)#switchport port-security
Switch(config-if)#switchport port-security maximum 10
Switch(config-if)#end
Switch(config)#copy running-config startup-config
```

11-4: VLAN Access Control Lists

- *Access control lists* (ACLs) define how traffic is to be handled as it passes through a network device.

- ACLs use addressing and port information to control conversations.

- ACLs are typically implemented in routers, but new hardware allow Layer 2 and Layer 3 switches to consult the list before passing the packet.

- ACLs enable users to configure any switch to control traffic based on Layer 3 and above of the OSI reference model.

- These ACLs are mapped to a VLAN or a Layer 2 port to control traffic flows.

- VACLs are controlled in hardware and are not supported on all platforms.

- Currently VACLs are supported on the 6000 (with a *Policy Feature Card* [PFC] or PFC2), the 3550, and the 2950 series switches.

The *VLAN ACL* (VACL) is an ACL that specifies traffic parameters based on Layer 3 and above information that is applied to a Layer 2 VLAN or in some instances a Layer 2 interface. These lists offer a benefit over traditional router access lists of being applied in hardware and therefore being faster than traditional ACLs. They also add the capability to filter traffic within an IP subnet and beyond the IP subnet. Although the functionality is the same between operating systems, the configuration differs. This section is divided into two parts. The first set of commands specifies the VACL configuration on COS devices that support VACLs, and the second portion specifies the IOS VACLs. Use the steps in each section to configure and apply VACLs on your switch. These steps apply to only IP VACLs because this is a protocol that is supported for all the platforms listed. It is possible to configure IPX VACLs for some platforms. Although the syntax and process are the same, the protocol options differ for IPX.

Section 11-4

NOTE   ACLs behave in the same manner on both routers and switches. This section does not discuss every option and configuration principal. For more on access list configuration, consult the Cisco Press titles *Interconnecting Cisco Network Devices* and *Cisco Field Manual: Router Configuration*.

COS VACL Configuration

These configuration steps apply to the Catalyst 6000 series switch with a PFC or PFC2 running the COS software.

1 Configure the access list:

COS	`set security acl ip {acl_name} {permit	deny	redirect mod/port} {protocol} {sourceaddress mask} [op] [srcport] {dest mask} [op] [destport] [before editbuffer_index	modify editbuffer_index] [log]`

To control the traffic, you must first specify which traffic it is you want to control and how you want to deal with that traffic. A *VACL* is a sequential list of entries that specify which traffic is controlled and how that traffic is controlled. To create the list, you type the command listed here for every set of conditions that you want to test. When a frame meets the criterion of an entry in the list (from the top down), that action is taken on the frame. If no entries are matched to the frame, the frame is dropped.

The command **set security acl ip** *name* specifies the name of an IP ACL that you are configuring. After you have specified a name, all entries that are to be checked against will have the same name. After the name is specified, the protocol specifications and actions follow. The first item after the name is the action. The **permit** option allows traffic that meets the specifications to be passed across the switch. The **deny** option drops packets that meet the specifications. The **redirect** option sends traffic to a specified *mod/port* on the switch instead of using the content addressable memory (CAM) table entry.

The *protocol*, *address/mask*, *ports*, and *operator* options enable you to specify the traffic flow by IP address and port information. You can use the keyword **all** in the place of the *address/mask* option.

By default all entries created in an ACL go at the bottom of the list; for a COS device, however, the ACL is written to a special edit buffer and are not part of the switch operation until they are **committed**. You can, using the **before** or **modify** keywords, either place the item before a particular entry in the edit buffer or modify (replace) an entry. To view the entries in an edit buffer that has not been committed to memory, use the command **show security acl ip** *name* **editbuffer**. You then use the edit buffer index numbers listed to modify or place the entries. The final option is to **log** the entries, which allows the switch to log only frames that have been denied by the access list.

2 Commit the ACL to the *ternary content addressable memory* (TCAM):

COS	`commit security acl {name	all}`

After you have configured the VACL, it is only resident in the edit buffer and cannot be used by the switch until it has been written to the TCAM tables. Use the **commit security acl** command to place the information into the TCAM table for use by the switch. The **all** option commits all uncommitted VACLs, and the *name* option commits only the list specified.

3 Map the ACL to a VLAN:

COS	**set security acl map** *acl_name vlan*

After you have created and committed the VACL, you need to map it to a VLAN before it will control traffic for the switch. To map the VACL, use the command **set security acl map** followed by the VACL name and the VLAN to which it will be mapped. A VLAN can only have one VACL mapped to it for the control of traffic, but a VACL can be mapped to many VLANs.

Verification

To verify the configuration and mapping of COS VACLs on the switch, use one of the following commands:

COS	**show security acl info** [*name* | **all**]
	show security acl map [*name* | *vlan* | **all**]

IOS VACL Configuration

IOS VACLs are configured as standard or extended IP access lists. Then those lists are mapped to a port or a VLAN. Currently, only the 6000 running Supervisor IOS, the 3550, and the 2950G switches support VACLs. Use these commands to configure the VACL option.

1 Configure the access list.

The first parameter that has to be configured is the list, which identifies traffic to be controlled by the list. For IOS ACLs, the list is either a number or a name. There are also various types of ACLs—for example, standard lists that specify source information and extended lists that specify source and destination. Use the commands in these steps to configure the access lists.

a. Configure a numbered standard access list:

IOS	(global) **access-list** *access-list-number* {**deny** | **permit** | **remark**} {*source source-wildcard* | **host** *source* | **any**}

The command creates a standard ACL. The number range for standard ACLs is 1 to 99 and 1300 to 1999. The parameter **permit** allows traffic, and **deny** drops traffic. The **remark** parameter enables you to insert remarks into the list that provide information about the list and why parameters are added. For the **permit** or **deny** option, the *address/mask* enables you to control traffic from specified source addresses. You can use the keyword **any** to specify all source addresses.

b. Configure a numbered extended access list:

IOS	(global) **access-list** *access-list-number* {**deny** | **permit** | **remark**} *protocol* {*source source-wildcard* | **host** *source* | **any**} [*operator port*] {*destination destination-wildcard* | **host** *destination* | **any**} [*operator port*]

The command creates a standard ACL. The number range for standard ACLs is 100 to 199 and 2000 to 2699. The parameter **permit** allows traffic, and **deny** drops traffic. The **remark** parameter enables you to insert remarks into the list that provide information about the list and why parameters are added.

The *protocol* parameter specifies which type of protocol within IP you are looking to match. Examples include **udp** or **tcp**. The protocol **ip** in this field would specify all IP traffic. The *address/mask* pair specifies the source and destination of the sending and receiving devices for which you are trying to control traffic. You can use the keyword **any** to specify all source or destination addresses. The operator and port options enable you to specify protocol- and application-specific ports.

c. Configure a named standard access list:

IOS	(global) **ip access-list standard** {*name*}
	(std-acl) {**deny** | **permit**} {*source source-wildcard* | **host** *source* | **any**}

For a standard-named ACL, the command **ip access-list standard** *name* indicates that you want to enter a configuration mode on the list specified by the name given. From there the switch will enter a mode that enables you to enter the options a line at a time until you exit the ACL configuration mode.

The parameter **permit** allows traffic, and **deny** drops traffic. For the **permit** or **deny** option, the *address/mask* pair specifies which source address will be controlled. You can use the keyword **any** to specify all source addresses.

d. Configure a named extended access list:

IOS	(global) **ip access-list extended** {*name*}
	(extd-acl) {**deny** | **permit**} *protocol* {*source source-wildcard* | **host** *source* | **any**} [*operator port*] {*destination destination-wildcard* | **host** *destination* | **any**} [*operator port*]

For an extended-named ACL, the command **ip access-list extended** *name* indicates that you want to enter a configuration mode on the list specified by the name given. From there the switch will enter a mode that enables you to enter the options a line at a time until you exit the ACL configuration mode.

The parameter **permit** allows traffic, and **deny** drops traffic. The *protocol* parameter specifies which type of protocol within IP you are looking to match. Examples include **udp** and **tcp**. The protocol **ip** in this field would specify all IP traffic. The *address/ mask* pair specifies the source and destination of the sending and receiving devices for which you are trying to control traffic. You can use the keyword **any** to specify all source or destination addresses. The operator and port options enable you to specify protocol and application-specific ports.

2 Create a VLAN map.

If the list you have created is going to be mapped to a VLAN, you must configure a **vlan access-map** to specify an access map name and the action to be taken for a specific matched entry, as follows:

IOS	(global) **vlan access-map** *name* [*number*]
	(vlan-map) **match ip address** {*aclname* | *aclnumber*}
	(vlan-map) **action** {**drop** | **forward**}

An *access map* is a list of map clauses that specify what action is to be taken for packets on the VLAN. When creating the access map, it is given a name and then subsequent clauses are given numbers. Each clause is checked to find a match for the packets, and then the action specified for that clause is taken. If no clauses are found, the packets are dropped. To create an access map, use the **vlan access-map** command followed by a *name*. The *number* option is used for subsequent clauses in the access map.

After you have entered a map name, you will be placed in access map configuration mode, where you will specify an ACL name or number to identify the traffic to be acted upon for a clause. For ACLs that are included in this access map, a **permit** statement in the ACL is a match and a **deny** is not a match for the given clause. After a match has been identified by an ACL, the **action** command specifies whether to drop or permit the traffic. If none of the clauses match a given frame, the frame is dropped.

3 Apply the access lists.

After you have created an access list, you need to apply the list to the switch. The list is applied differently depending on the platform. For the 6000 running IOS or the 3550, use option *a* to map the list to a VLAN. If you are configuring an access list on a 2950, use option *b* to apply the list to an interface.

a. Apply a VLAN map to a VLAN:

IOS	(global) **vlan filter** *mapname* **vlan-list** *list*

Section 11-4

To apply an access map to a VLAN for the IOS switches that support VACLs, use the **vlan filter** command. The *mapname* option specifies the name of the map created in Step 2. The **vlan-list** parameter is followed by a VLAN number or a list of VLAN numbers to which the ACL will be applied.

b. Apply an access list to an interface:

IOS	(interface) **ip access-group** {*access-list-number* | *name*} **in**

For the 2950, ACLs are applied to the Layer 2 interface. For these ACLs, traffic is permitted or denied by the entries of the ACL and not the clauses in the map statements. Use the **ip access-group** command followed by a number or ACL name to apply the list to an interface. The parameter **in** specifies the direction that the ACL is applied to an interface for Layer 2 ACLs. The packets can only be checked as they are entering the switch.

Verification

To verify configuration of IOS VACLs, use the following commands:

IOS	**show ip access-lists** [*number* | *name*]
	show vlan access-map [*mapname*]
	show vlan filter [access-map *name* | vlan *vlan-id*]
	show ip interface *type number*

Feature Example

This example shows the configuration for VACL filtering. In the list configured on this switch, you want to meet the following conditions:

- Permit all IP traffic from subnet 10.101.0.0 to host 10.101.1.1.
- Permit ICMP echo request from all hosts.
- Permit ICMP echo reply from all host.
- Deny all other ICMP traffic.
- Permit all TCP traffic.
- Deny all UDP traffic not specified above.
- Permit all other IP traffic.

You want to apply this list to VLAN 101 on the switch.

An example of the Catalyst OS configuration follows:

```
Catalyst (enable)>set security acl ip watchlist permit ip 10.101.0.0 0.0.255.255
    host 10.101.1.1
Catalyst (enable)>set security acl ip watchlist permit icmp any any echo
Catalyst (enable)>set security acl ip watchlist permit icmp any any echo
Catalyst (enable)>set security acl ip watchlist permit icmp any any echo-reply
Catalyst (enable)>set security acl ip watchlist deny icmp any any echo
Catalyst (enable)>set security acl ip watchlist permit tcp any any
Catalyst (enable)>set security acl ip watchlist deny udp any any
Catalyst (enable)>set security acl ip watchlist permit ip any any
Catalyst (enable)>commit security acl ip watchlist
Catalyst (enable)>set security acl ip map watchlist 101
```

An example of the Supervisor IOS configuration follows:

```
Switch(config)#ip access-list extended ip_subnet2host
Switch(config-ext-acl)#permit ip 10.101.0.0 0.0.255.255 host 10.101.1.1
Switch(config)#ip access-list extended ping
Switch(config-ext-acl)#permit icmp any any echo
Switch(config-ext-acl)#permit icmp any any echo-reply
Switch(config-ext-acl)#exit
Switch(config)#ip access-list extended_icmp
Switch(config-ext-acl)#permit icmp any any
Switch(config-ext-acl)#exit
Switch(config)#ip access-list extended_tcp
Switch(config-ext-acl)#permit tcp any any
Switch(config-ext-acl)#exit
Switch(config)#ip access-list extended_udp
Switch(config-ext-acl)#permit udp any any
Switch(config-ext-acl)#exit
Switch(config)#vlan access-map watchlist
Switch(config-access-map)#match ip address ip_subnet2host
Switch(config-access-map)#action forward
Switch(config-access-map)#vlan access-map watchlist 10
Switch(config-access-map)#match ip address ping
Switch(config-access-map)#action forward
Switch(config-access-map)#vlan access-map watchlist 20
Switch(config-access-map)#match ip address ip_icmp
Switch(config-access-map)#action drop
Switch(config-access-map)#vlan access-map watchlist 30
Switch(config-access-map)#match ip address ip_tcp
Switch(config-access-map)#action forward
Switch(config-access-map)#vlan access-map watchlist 40
Switch(config-access-map)#match ip address ip_udp
Switch(config-access-map)#action drop
Switch(config-access-map)#vlan access-map watchlist 50
Switch(config-access-map)#action forward
Switch(config-access-map)#exit
Switch(config)#vlan filter watchlist vlan-list 101
Switch(config)#end
Switch(config)#copy running-config startup-config
```

Section 11-5

11-5: Switch Authentication

- Switch authentication enables you to control how people access the switch.

- By default switch authentication is controlled locally by the user password and the enable password.

- You can configure the switch to use an authentication server, such as a RADIUS or TACACS+ server, for authentication.

- After you have configured RADIUS or TACACS+, it is important to have local authentication enabled to log in to the switch if the authentication server is down.

- Configuration for authentication is sometimes required for options such as *Secure Shell* (SSH) Telnet and 802.1X port authorization.

Configuration

Switch authentication specifies how users are verified before being allowed to access the user or privileged mode command-line interface prompts. Authentication can be configured by local passwords on the switch or it can be configured so users are authorized by a TACACS or RADIUS server. Use the following commands to control authentication of users on the switch.

1 Configure local authentication.

Default authorization is handled by passwords on the switch. The commands listed in this section show how to enable or disable this default authentication. Local authentication should not be disabled even if you are using a server for authentication—because it provides a "back door," or a secondary option, for authentication if the server fails. A switch has two levels of authentication: user level and privileged level. These commands show how to control authentication for each level.

a. Configure user-level authentication:

COS	`set authentication login local {enable	disable} [all	console |` `telnet	http]`

Use this command to enable or disable user-level local authentication for the **console**, **telnet**, **http**, or **all** services on a COS switch.

b. Configure privileged-level authentication:

COS	`set authentication enable local {enable	disable} [all	console |` `telnet	http]`

Use this command to enable or disable privileged-level local authentication for the **console**, **telnet**, **http**, or **all** services on a COS switch.

2 Configure TACACS authentication.

It is also possible to configure the switch to authenticate users from a database on a TACACS server. For this to work, a username and password must be configured on the TACACS server. After the server has been configured, you use the following commands to provide TACACS authentication.

a. Configure the TACACS server:

COS	`set tacacs server` *address* `[primary]`

This command specifies the address of the TACACS server. This assumes that the switch has been configured for an IP address and has a gateway if necessary to reach the server. You can specify multiple servers, in case one of the devices is not functioning. The **primary** option specifies which server is queried first.

b. Enable TACACS authentication for user level:

COS	`set authentication login tacacs {enable	disable} [all	console	telnet	http] [primary]`

After you have specified the server address, you set the user-level authentication process to use the **tacacs** option for the **console**, **telnet**, **http**, or **all** services. The **primary** option for this command specifies that TACACS is the first authentication method. If that fails, other authentication methods, such as local login, are attempted.

c. Enable TACACS authentication for privileged level:

COS	`set authentication enable tacacs {enable	disable} [all	console	telnet	http] [primary]`

After you have specified the server address, you set the privileged-level authentication process to use the **tacacs** option for the **console**, **telnet**, **http**, or **all** services. The **primary** option for this command specifies that TACACS is the first authentication method. If that fails, other authentication methods, such as local login, are attempted.

d. Specify the TACACS key:

COS	`set tacacs key` *key*

Because the information between the TACACS device and the switch is encrypted, you must also supply the TACACS process with the *key* that is used by the server. This command specifies the key used.

3 Configure RADIUS authentication.

In addition to local or TACACS, you can configure the switch to authenticate users from a database on a RADIUS server. For this to work, a username and password must be configured on the RADIUS server. After the server has been configured, you use the following commands to provide RADIUS authentication.

a. Configure the RADIUS server:

COS	`set radius server` *address* `[auth-port` *port*`] [primary]`

Section 11-5

This command specifies the address of the RADIUS server. This assumes that the switch has been configured for an IP address and has a gateway if necessary to reach the server. You can specify multiple servers, in case one of the devices is not functioning. The **primary** option specifies which server is queried first.

b. Enable RADIUS authentication for user level:

COS	`set authentication login radius {enable	disable} [all	console	telnet	http] [primary]`

After you have specified the server address, you set the user-level authentication process to use the **radius** option for the **console**, **telnet**, **http**, or **all** services. The **primary** option for this command specifies that RADIUS is the first authentication method. If that fails, other authentication methods, such as local login, are attempted.

c. Enable RADIUS authentication for privileged level:

COS	`set authentication enable radius {enable	disable} [all	console	telnet	http] [primary]`

After you have specified the server address, you set the privileged-level authentication process to use the **radius** option for the **console**, **telnet**, **http**, or **all** services. The **primary** option for this command specifies that RADIUS is the first authentication method. If that fails, other authentication methods, such as local login, are attempted.

d. Specify the RADIUS key:

COS	`set radius key` *key*

Because the information between the RADIUS device and the switch is encrypted, you must also supply the RADIUS process with the *key* that is used by the server. This command specifies the key used.

Verification

To verify configuration of authentication, use the following commands:

COS	`show authentication`
	`show tacacs`
	`show radius`

Feature Example

This example shows the configuration for a switch that will use a RADIUS server with the address 192.168.1.10 as the primary authentication method for Telnet users and a TACACS server with the address 192.168.1.8 for the primary authentication method for console users. The TACACS key will be abc123, and the radius key will be 789xyz.

An example of the Catalyst OS configuration follows:

```
Catalyst (enable)> set radius server 192.168.1.10
Catalyst (enable)> set authentication login radius enable telnet primary
Catalyst (enable)> set authentication enable radius enable telnet primary
Catalyst (enable)> set radius key 789xyz
Catalyst (enable)> set tacacs server 192.168.1.8
Catalyst (enable)> set authentication login tacacs enable console primary
Catalyst (enable)> set authentication enable tacacs enable console primary
Catalyst (enable)> set tacacs key abc123
```

11-6: Permit Lists

- Permit lists are used on COS switches to specify which devices are allowed to access a switch via Telnet, HTTP, or SNMP.

- You can configure entries in the list to be applied for SNMP or Telnet access, or you can make a list for both.

- You can enter up to 100 addresses in the permit list.

- Entries in the lists are matched against a wildcard mask. If no mask is specified, all the bits of the address are matched.

- Permit lists have no effect on outbound Telnet or management traffic.

- SNMP traps can be generated when an unauthorized access attempt is made.

Configuration

To configure a permit list on a COS switch, use the following commands.

1 Add addresses to a permit list:

COS	`set ip permit` *address mask* `[snmp	telnet]`

To control which devices are allowed to access the switch, you must first configure the IP permit list. The *address* parameter specifies the IP address of the device that is allowed to access the network. The *mask* parameter is an option. The mask is in dotted-decimal format, where a 1 means match the address and a 0 means ignore the address. For example, the address 172.16.101.1 with a mask of 255.255.255.0 would match all the addresses that start with 172.16.101. The address of 172.16.101.1 with a mask of 255.255.255.255 would match only the host 172.16.101.1. If you do not specify a mask, a mask of all 1s or the host mask is used. The options **snmp** and **telnet** specify which processes will use a specific list entry. If you do not specify a process, it is applied to each process.

Section 11-6

2 Activate the permit list:

COS	`set ip permit enable [snmp	telnet]`

After you have configured a list of devices that are permitted, use this command to enable the permit list. The **snmp** and **telnet** options specify for which processes the permit list will be activated.

3 *(Optional)* Enable SNMP trap generation:

COS	`set snmp trap enable ip permit`

This command enables the **ip permit** process to send SNMP traps when there is an unauthorized attempt to access the switch.

Verification

Use the **show ip permit** command to verify the configuration of the IP permit list:

COS	`show ip permit`

Feature Example

This example shows a permit list configuration. This list allows any user from the network 192.168.5.0 to access the device for SNMP and Telnet. This example also allows any user from the 192.168.1.0 subnet to access the device via Telnet. In addition, this example has an entry that allows the host 192.168.255.1 to reach the device via SNMP. This list is also enabled for Telnet and SNMP.

An example of the Catalyst OS configuration follows:

```
Console (enable)>set ip permit 192.168.5.0 255.255.255.0
Console (enable)>set ip permit 192.168.1.0 255.255.255.0 telnet
Console (enable)>set ip permit 192.168.255.1 255.255.255.255 snmp
Console (enable)>set ip permit telnet
Console (enable)>set ip permit snmp
```

TIP   When creating an IP permit list, you should add the address of your management station first to avoid locking yourself out of the switch.

11-7: SSH Telnet Configuration

- Telnet connections to the switch take place over TCP port 23 and are transmitted in plain text.

- If someone with a network analyzer captures packets going to a server, he can see the data transmitted in plain text, including the passwords.

- *Secure Shell* (SSH) is a method of communicating through Telnet that encrypts packets before they are transmitted between devices.

- SSH runs on TCP port 22 between a SSH-compatible client and a device configured to accept SSH connections.

- Cisco switches support SSH version 1 only.

- To implement SSH on your switch, it must be Crypto-compatible code.

- By default SSH is disabled on the switch and must be enabled before clients can connect.

Configuration

To provide secure Telnet communications between the switch and a SSH Telnet client, you must configure the switch to allow SSH connectivity. The following commands outline the configuration steps to activate SSH.

1 Set the Crypto key:

COS	`set crypto key rsa` *number*
IOS	`(global)` `crypto key generate rsa`

Before you can configure SSH, you must allow the switch to generate a key for encoding the data. The **crypto key rsa** command generates that key. For COS switches, the *number* option specifies the modulus length. For IOS you are prompted for a value. The greater the length, the stronger the encryption. The recommended modulus is 1024 or greater.

2 Specify the devices allowed to SSH:

COS	`set ip permit` *address mask* `ssh`
IOS	N/A

For the COS switches, SSH is enabled using IP permit lists. To enable the process, you must first specify who will be allowed to Telnet to the switch using SSH. If you don't want to specify any particular address or range of addresses using this command, enter any address with a mask of 0.0.0.0 to allow anyone to use the SSH process.

3 Enable the SSH permit list:

COS	`set ip permit enable ssh`
IOS	`(global) ip ssh`

To actually enable the SSH process, use the command **set ip permit ssh** for a COS switch. This command allows the IP addresses specified in Step 2 to attach to the SSH Telnet process. For an IOS switch, turn on SSH with the global command **ip ssh**.

Verification

To verify configuration of SSH, use the following commands:

IOS	`show ip ssh`
	`show ip permit`

Feature Example

This example shows the configuration that allows any device to access the switch using SSH. The RSA modulus for the switch will be set to 1024.

An example of the Catalyst OS configuration follows:

```
Catalyst (enable)>set crypto key rsa 1024
Catalyst (enable)>set ip permit 0.0.0.0 0.0.0.0 ssh
Catalyst (enable)>set ip permit ssh
```

An example of the Supervisor IOS configuration follows:

```
Switch(config)#crypto key generate rsa
Enter modulus:1024
Switch(config)#ip ssh
Switch(config)#end
Switch(config)#copy running-config startup-config
```

11-8: 802.1X Port Authentication

- On most switches, ports are enabled by default and anyone who can plug into the port gains access to the network.

- Port security using MAC addresses can control which devices can access a network on a given port but must be reconfigured if a device is moved.

- 802.1X provides a standard method for authorizing ports using client certificates or usernames.

- 802.1X uses a RADIUS server to provide authorization of a port for use.

- Until an 802.1X port is authorized, it cannot be used to pass user traffic.
- In 802.1X, the switch acts as a proxy between the client and the server to pass authentication information.

Configuration

To configure 802.1X port authentication, use the following steps.

1 Enable 802.1X authentication globally:

COS	`set dot1x system-auth-control enable`
IOS	N/A

On a COS switch, you must first enable the 802.1X authentication process globally on the switch before you can configure the ports for authorization.

2 Specify the RADIUS server and key:

COS	`set radius server` *address*
	`set radius key` *string*
IOS	(global) `radius-server host` *address* `key` *string*

Because the 802.1X process relies on a RADIUS server, you must configure the switch with the address of the RADIUS server and the key used on the server.

3 Create an *authentication, authorization, accounting* (AAA) model:

COS	N/A
IOS	(global) `aaa new-model`
	(global) aaa authentication dot1x default group radius

For the IOS switch, you will enable 802.1X authentication by creating an AAA model using the commands listed.

4 Enable 802.1x on the port:

COS	`set port dot1x` *mod/port* `port-control auto`
IOS	(interface) `dot1x port-control {auto	force-authorized	force-unauthorized}`

After completing the previous steps, you can configure a port for 802.1X authorization. When a port is configured for 802.1X authentication, it will not pass user traffic until a RADIUS server sends authorization for the port.

Feature Example

This example shows the configuration for Ethernet port 3/6 to provide 802.1X authentication for a client using the RADIUS server 10.1.1.1 with a key string of funhouse.

An example of the Catalyst OS configuration follows:

```
Catalyst (enable)>set dot1x system-auth-control enable
Catalyst (enable)>set radius server 10.1.1.1
Catalyst (enable)>set radius key funhouse
Catalyst (enable)>set port dot1x 3/6 port-control auto
```

An example of the Supervisor IOS configuration follows:

```
Switch(config)#radius-server host 10.1.1.1 key funhouse
Switch(config)#aaa new-model
Switch(config)#aaa authentication dot1x default group radius
Switch(config)#interface fastethernet 3/6
Switch(config-if)#dot1x port-control auto
Switch(config-if)#end
Switch(config)#copy running-config startup-config
```

Further Reading

Refer to the following recommended sources for further information about the topics covered in this chapter.

Cisco LAN Switching by Kennedy Clark and Kevin Hamilton, Cisco Press, ISBN 1-57870-094-9

Building Cisco Multilayer Switched Networks by Karen Webb, Cisco Press, ISBN 1-57870-093-0

CCNP Switching Exam Certification Guide by Tim Boyles and David Hucaby, Cisco Press, ISBN 1-57870-xxx-x

Cisco Field Manual: *Router Configuration* by Dave Hucaby and Steve McQuerry, Cisco Press, ISBN 1-58705-024-2

Switch Management

See the following sections to configure and use these topics:

- **12-1: Logging**—Covers the steps needed to configure a variety of methods to log messages from a switch.

- **12-2: Simple Network Management Protocol**—Presents information on how to configure a switch to use network management protocols.

- **12-3: Switched Port Analyzer**—Explains how to mirror switch traffic for network analysis, either locally or from a remote switch.

- **12-4: Power Management**—Covers the Catalyst 6000 commands for managing power to the chassis and modules.

- **12-5: Environmental Monitoring**—Covers the Catalyst 6000 commands for displaying switch temperature information.

- **12-6: Packet Tracing**—Discusses several methods for tracing both Layer 2 and Layer 3 packets through a network. From a switch, you can test connectivity to a remote host.

12-1: Logging

- Logging is used by the switch to send system messages to a logging facility.

- Logging messages can be sent to any of four different facilities: the switch console, a file on the switch, Telnet sessions, or a syslog server.

- Logging history can be maintained in a file to ensure that a record of the messages being sent to *Simple Network Management Protocol* (SNMP) or syslog servers are kept in case a packet is lost or dropped.

- Logging displays all error and debug messages by default. The logging level can be set to determine which messages should be sent to each of the facilities.

- Time stamping logging messages or setting the syslog source address can help in real-time debugging and management. If the time and date are set on a switch, the switch can provide time stamps with each syslog message. The clocks in all switches can be synchronized so that it becomes easier to correlate syslog messages from several devices.

- System messages are logged with the following format:

  timestamp %function-severity-MNEMONIC:description

  where the *timestamp* denotes the time of the event, *%function* is the switch function (also called facility) generating the event, *severity* is the severity level (0 to 7, lower is more severe) of the event, and *MNEMONIC* is a text string that briefly describes the event. A more detailed *description* text string completes the message.

  An example of a severity level 3 Supervisor IOS system message is as follows:

  11w1d: %LINK-3-UPDOWN: Interface FastEthernet0/10, changed state to up

  An example of a severity level 5 Catalyst OS system message is as follows:

  2001 Dec 20 11:44:19 %DTP-5-NONTRUNKPORTON:Port 5/4 has become non-trunk

---

NOTE   Logging to a syslog server uses UDP port 514.

Configuration

1 *(Optional)* Enable or disable logging:

COS	N/A
IOS	(global) [**no**] **logging on**

Logging is enabled by default. Use the **no** keyword to disable all logging on the switch, except for logging to the console.

2 *(Optional)* Log messages to a syslog server.

a. Identify the syslog server:

COS	**set logging server** *syslog-host*
IOS	(global) **logging** *syslog-host*

Text messages are sent to the syslog server at *syslog-host* (host name or IP address). The messages are captured and can be reviewed on the syslog server.

b. Send messages to a syslog facility:

COS	`set logging server facility facility-type`
IOS	`(global) logging facility facility-type`

When the syslog server receives a message, it forwards the message to a log file or destination based on the originating system facility. In this fashion, syslog servers can collect and organize messages by using the facility as service area or type. All syslog messages from switches can be collected together, if the facility is set identically in each switch.

Syslog servers are based around UNIX operating system concepts and have facility types that are named after various system services. The facility used in switch syslog messages is defined as *facility-type*, given as one of **local0**, **local1**, **local2**, **local3**, **local4**, **local5**, **local6**, **local7** (the default), which all represent locally defined services. Usually, one or more local facilities are used for messages from network devices.

The Supervisor IOS also allows these additional facility types: **auth** (user authentication services), **cron** (job scheduling services), **daemon** (system background or daemon services), **kern** (system kernel services), **lpr** (line printer spooler services), **mail** (system mail services), **news** (Usenet newsgroup services), **syslog** (syslog services), **sys9**, **sys10**, **sys11**, **sys12**, **sys13**, **sys14** (all reserved for system services), **user** (system user processes), or **uucp** (UNIX-to-UNIX copy file transfer services).

c. Limit the severity of the logged messages:

COS	`set logging server severity level`
IOS	`(global) logging trap level`

System messages are assigned a severity level based on the type and importance of the error condition. Only messages that are less than or equal to (at least as severe as) the severity level are sent to the syslog server. The *level* is a number (0 to 7, default 6) defined in Table 12-1.

Table 12-1   *System Message Severity Levels*

Level	Name	Description
0	**emergencies**	System is unusable.
1	**alerts**	Immediate action is needed.
2	**critical**	Critical conditions.
3	**errors**	Error conditions.
4	**warnings**	Warning conditions.

continues

Table 12-1 *System Message Severity Levels (Continued)*

Level	Name	Description
5	**notifications**	Normal but significant conditions.
6	**informational**	Informational messages.
7	**debugging**	Debugging messages.

The Supervisor IOS also enables you to enter the *level* as a name. Most physical state transitions (ports and modules up or down) are logged at level 5, whereas hardware or software malfunctions are reported at level 3.

d. *(Optional; IOS only)* Use a specific source address for syslog messages:

COS	N/A
IOS	(global) **logging source-interface** *type number*

An IOS switch can use the IP address of a specific interface as the source address in syslog packets. This can be useful if there are many interfaces, but you want to see all syslog messages from a switch appear as a single switch address. (A COS switch always uses the sc0 interface address for this purpose.)

e. *(COS only)* Start logging to the syslog server:

COS	**set logging server enable**
IOS	N/A

f. *(Optional; IOS only)* Limit the messages logged to the SNMP history table:

COS	N/A
IOS	(global) **logging history** *level* (global) **logging history size** *number*

Messages sent as traps to an SNMP management station can be lost. Therefore, messages that are less than or equal to the specified severity level can also be saved to a history table for future review. The *level* is a number (0 to 7) defined in Table 12-1. By default, only one message is kept in the history table. You can change this by specifying the **size** keyword with the *number* of message entries (1 to 500).

3 *(Optional)* Log messages to the switch buffer:

COS	**set logging buffer** *size*
IOS	(global) **logging buffered** [*size*]

All system messages are saved in a section of switch memory. The message buffer remains intact until the switch is powered off or the buffer is cleared with the **clear logging** command. The maximum buffer size can be given as *size* (COS: 1 to 500 messages, default 500; Supervisor IOS: 4096 to 2,147,483,647 bytes, default 4096 bytes).

CAUTION   The buffer size varies between Catalyst switch platforms. By logging to a buffer on a Supervisor IOS switch, you are using system resources that can also be needed for the operational aspects of the switch. Be prudent when setting the maximum buffer size so that you don't waste system memory.

---

4 *(Optional; IOS only)* Log messages to a file on the switch:

COS	N/A
IOS	(global) **logging file** [**flash:**]*filename* [*max-file-size*] [*min-file-size*] *level*

System messages are stored to a file named *filename* (text string) located on the system **flash:** device. The file can be constrained to a maximum size *max-file-size* (4096 to 2,147,483,647 bytes, default 4096) and a minimum size *min-file-size* (1024 to 2,147,483,647 bytes, default 2048). Messages with a severity level less than or equal to *level* (0 to 7 or a name from Table 12-1, default 7 or **debugging**) are appended to the file.

5 *(Optional)* Log messages to terminal sessions.

a. *(Optional)* Log messages to the switch console:

COS	**set logging console {enable	disable}**
IOS	(global) **logging console** *level*

By default, system messages are logged to the console. You can disable logging with the **disable** keyword. On an IOS switch, only messages with a severity level less than or equal to *level* (0 to 7 or a name from Table 12-1, default 7 or **debugging**) are sent to the console.

b. *(Optional)* Log messages to a Telnet or line session:

COS	**set logging telnet {enable	disable}**
IOS	(global) **logging monitor** *level*

By default system messages are logged to all Telnet and terminal line sessions. On a COS switch, you can also disable logging, but only for the current session, by using the **set logging session disable** command. On an IOS switch, only messages with a severity level less than or equal to *level* (0 to 7 or a name from Table 12-1, default 7 or **debugging**) are sent to the session.

NOTE   To view system messages during a Telnet session to a vty line on an IOS switch, you must issue the **terminal monitor** EXEC command.

c. *(Optional; IOS only)* Control the output of messages to terminal sessions:

COS	N/A
IOS	(line) **logging synchronous** [**level** *level* | **all**] [**limit** *buffers*]

When synchronous logging is enabled, logging messages are queued until solicited output (regular output from **show** or configuration commands, for example) is displayed. When a command prompt is displayed, logging output will be displayed. Synchronization can be used on messages at or below a specific severity *level* (0 to 7 or a name from Table 12-1; default 2) or **all** levels. With the **limit** keyword, the switch can queue up to *buffers* (default 20) messages before they are dropped from the queue.

TIP   Although synchronous logging keeps switch messages from interfering with your typing or reading other displayed text, it can also be confusing. When synchronous logging is enabled on the switch console line and no one is currently logged in to the switch, for example, the switch will queue all messages until the next person logs in. That person will see a flurry of messages scroll by—possibly from hours or days before.

6 *(Optional)* Record a time stamp with each system message:

COS	**set logging timestamp** {**enable** | **disable**}
IOS	(global) **service timestamps log** {**uptime** | **datetime**}

By default a COS switch records a date and time time stamp with system messages, whereas an IOS switch records the system uptime. To use the date and time, use the **datetime** keyword. This can prove useful if you need to reference an error condition to the actual time that it occurred.

TIP   You should configure and set the correct time, date, and time zone on the switch before relying on the message logging time stamps. Refer to section "3-8: Time and Calendar" for further information.

7 *(Optional; IOS only)* Control the rate of system message generation:

COS	N/A
IOS	(global) **logging rate-limit** *number* [**all** | **console**] [**except** *level*]

To avoid flooding system messages to a logging destination, you can limit the rate that the messages are sent to *number* (1 to 10,000 messages per second, no default). The **all** keyword rate limits all messages, whereas the **console** keyword rate limits only messages that are sent to the console. You can use the **except** keyword to rate-limit messages at or below the specified *level* (0 to 7 as given in Table 12-1).

8 *(Optional; COS only)* Set the severity level for specific switch functions:

COS	**set logging level** {**all** | *function*} *level* [**default**]
IOS	N/A

System messages can be logged if they have a severity level that is at or below a configured level. You can also tune the severity level for predefined switch functions to determine whether and when they will be logged. You can use the keyword **all** to set all switch functions to the same *level* (0 to 7 or a name, as defined in Table 12-1).

Otherwise, a level can be assigned to one of the following functions: **acl** (access control lists), **cdp** (*Cisco Discovery Protocol*, CDP), **cops** (*Common Open Policy Server*, COPS), **dtp** (*Dynamic Trunking Protocol*, DTP), **dvlan** (Dynamic VLAN), **earl** (*Enhanced Address Recognition Logic*, EARL), **filesys** (file system), **gvrp** (*GARP VLAN Registration Protocol*, GVRP), **ip** (*Internet Protocol*, IP), **kernel** (switch kernel), **ld** (*Accelerated Server Load Balancing*, ASLB), **mcast** (multicast), **mgmt** (management), **mls** (*MultiLayer Switching*, MLS), **pagp** (*Port Aggregation Protocol*, PAgP), **protfilt** (protocol filtering), **pruning** (VLAN pruning), **privatevlan** (private VLANs), **qos** (*Quality of Service*, QoS), **radius** (*Remote Access Dial-In User Service*, RADIUS), **rsvp** (*Resource Reservation Protocol*, RSVP), **security** (security), **snmp** (*Simple Network Management Protocol*, SNMP), **spantree** (*Spanning Tree Protocol*, STP), **sys** (system), **tac** (*Terminal Access Controller*, TAC), **tcp** (*Transmission Control Protocol*, TCP), **telnet** (*Terminal Emulation Protocol*, Telnet), **tftp** (*Trivial File Transfer Protocol*, TFTP), **udld** (*Unidirectional Link Detection*, UDLD), **vmps** (*VLAN Membership Policy Server*, VMPS), or **vtp** (*VLAN Trunking Protocol*, VTP).

COS switches have these functions and severity levels set as a default: **sys** (5), **dtp** (5), **pagp** (5), **mgmt** (5), **mls** (5), **cdp** (4), **udld** (4), **ip** (3), **qos** (3), and all other functions (2).

Severity levels set are modified only for the current session. To modify the levels for all sessions, use the **default** keyword.

Logging Example

A switch is configured for logging to a syslog server at 192.168.254.91. By default, the local7 facility is used, with messages that are at level 6, or informational, or less. The COS switch is also configured to log up to 500 messages to its internal buffer, whereas the IOS switch buffers up to 64 Kb characters of message text. On the COS switch, system messages are disabled on the current Telnet session.

The switch prepends date and time time stamps to each logged message. The COS switch has an additional tweak: VTP messages are logged if they are at or below severity level 5 (notifications):

COS	`set logging server 192.168.254.91`
	`set logging server enable`
	`set logging buffer 500`
	`set logging session disable`
	`set logging timestamp enable`
	`set logging level vtp 5 default`

IOS	`(global) logging 192.168.254.91`
	`(global) logging buffered 65536`
	`(global) service timestamps log datetime`

Displaying Information About Logging

Table 12-2 lists some switch commands that you can use to display helpful information about system logging.

Table 12-2　*Switch Commands to Display System Logging Information*

Display Function	Switch OS	Command
Logging configuration	COS	`show logging [noalias]`
	IOS	`(exec) show logging`
System messages	COS	`show logging buffer [-] [number-of-messages]`
	IOS	`(exec) show logging`

12-2: Simple Network Management Protocol

- *Simple Network Management Protocol* (SNMP) is a protocol that allows the monitoring of information about and management of a network device.

- A *Management Information Base* (MIB) is a collection of variables stored on a network device. The variables can be updated by the device or queried from an external source.

- MIBs are structured according to the SNMP MIB module language, which is based on the *Abstract Syntax Notation One* (ASN.1) language.

- An SNMP agent runs on a network device and maintains the various MIB variables. Any update or query of the variables must be handled through the agent.

- An SNMP agent can also send unsolicited messages, or *traps*, to an SNMP manager. Traps are used to alert the manager of changing conditions on the network device.

- An SNMP manager is usually a network management system that queries MIB variables, can set MIB variables, and receives traps from a collection of network devices.

- SNMP agents can send either *traps* or *inform requests*. Traps are sent in one direction, and are unreliable. Inform requests are reliable in the sense that they must be acknowledged or be re-sent.

- *SNMP version 1* (SNMPv1) is the original version. It is based on RFC 1157 and has only basic clear text community strings for security. Access can also be limited to the IP address of the SNMP manager.

- *SNMP version 2* (SNMPv2) is an enhanced version, based on RFCs 1901, 1905, and 1906. It improves on bulk information retrieval and error reporting, but uses the clear-text community strings and IP addresses to provide security.

- *SNMP version 3* (SNMPv3) is based on RFCs 2273 to 2275 and offers robust security. Data integrity and authentication can be provided through usernames, *Message Digest 5* (MD5), and *Security Hash Algorithm* (SHA) algorithms, and encryption through *Data Encryption Standard* (DES).

NOTE   SNMP requests and responses are sent using UDP port 161. Notifications or traps are sent using UDP port 162.

- *Remote Monitoring* (RMON) provides a view of traffic flowing through a switch port. IOS switches can also provide RMON alarms and events. RMON support provides nine management groups as defined in RFC 1757: Statistics (group 1), History (group 2),

Alarms (group 3), Hosts (group 4), hostTopN (group 5), Matrix (
(group 7), Capture (group 8), and Event (group 9)). RMON2 sup
adds two groups: UsrHistory (group 18) and ProbeConfig (group

- When RMON is enabled, a switch collects data internally. Therefo   a
  cannot be viewed from the switch *command-line interface* (CLI)
  through a *network management system* (NMS).

Configuration

1 Configure the SNMP identity.

a. Define the contact information:

COS	`set system contact [`*contact-string*`]`
IOS	(global) `snmp-server contact` *contact-string*

The *contact-string* contains text information that the router can provide about the network administrator. If the string is omitted, it is cleared.

b. Define the device location:

COS	`set system location [`*location-string*`]`
IOS	(global) `snmp-server location` *location-string*

The *location-string* is text information that the router can provide about its physical location. If the string is omitted, it is cleared.

c. *(IOS only)* Define the device serial number:

COS	N/A
IOS	(global) `snmp-server chassis-id` *id-string*

The *id-string* is text information that the router can provide about its own serial number. If the hardware serial number can be read by the IOS software, this number is the default chassis ID.

2 Configure SNMP access.

a. *(Optional)* Define SNMP views to restrict access to MIB objects:

COS	`set snmp view [`**-hex**`]{`*view-name*`}{`*oid-tree*`}[`**mask**`] [`**included** | **excluded**`] [`**volatile** | **nonvolatile**`]`
IOS	(global) `snmp-server view` *view-name oid-tree* {**included** | **excluded**}

If necessary, an SNMP manager can be limited to view only specific parts of the switch's MIB tree. You can define a view with the name *view-name*. The *oid-tree* value is the object identifier of the MIB subtree in ASN.1 format. This value is a text string with numbers or words representing the subtree, separated by periods (that is, *system*, *cisco*, *system.4*, *1.*.2.3*). You can use wildcards (asterisks) with any component of the subtree. Viewing access of the subtree is either permitted or denied with the **included** and **excluded** keywords.

Multiple views can be defined, each applied to a different set of users or SNMP managers.

COS switches require the –**hex** keyword and a hexadecimal *view-name* if the view name contains nonprintable characters. The view can be stored in either **volatile** or **nonvolatile** (preserved across power cycles) memory.

b. Define access methods for remote users.

— *(SNMPv1 or SNMPv2c only)* Define community strings to allow access:

COS	`set snmp community {read-only	read-write	read-write-all}` `[string]`
IOS	`(global)` **`snmp-server community`** `string` [**`view`** `view`] [**`ro`**	**`rw`**] `acc-list`

A community string value *string* permits access to SNMP information on the switch. Any SNMP manager that presents a matching community string is permitted access. You can specify an optional view with the **view** keyword (IOS only). Access is then limited to only the MIB objects permitted by the view definition.

Access is granted as read-only or read-write with the **ro** / **read-only** (default community, "public," can't read the community strings), **rw** / **read-write** (default community, "private," can write any MIB object except community strings), and **read-write-all** (default community, "secret," can write any MIB object) keywords.

On IOS switches, optional standard IP access list *acc-list* can be given to further limit access only to SNMP managers with permitted IP addresses. Access can be defined for read-only and read-write SNMP modes. On COS switches, access can only be controlled to SNMP in general. You do this through the use of **set ip permit** commands. Refer to section "11-6: Permit Lists" for more information about the IP permit command.

TIP   You should strongly consider changing the default SNMP community strings on all switches. Leaving the default values active can make it easier for unauthorized people to gain access to your switch's activity and configuration. After you have changed the community strings to unique values, restrict SNMP access to only the IP addresses of the network management hosts under your control.

— *(SNMPv3 only)* Define names for the engine IDs.

To specify the local engine ID name, enter the following command(s):

COS	`set snmp engineid` *id-string*
IOS	(global) `snmp-server engineID` [`local` *id-string*] | [`remote` *ip-address* `udp-port` *port id-string*]

SNMPv3 uses authentication and encryption based on several parameters. Each end of the SNMP trust relationship must be defined, in the form of engine ID text strings, *id-string*. These values are 24-character strings, but can be specified with shorter strings that are filled to the right with zeros. The local switch running SNMP must be defined with the **local** keyword and *id-string* (IOS only).

— *(IOS only)* To specify the remote SNMP engine ID name, enter the following command:

(global) `snmp-server engineID remote` *ip-address* [`udp-port` *port*] *id-string*

The remote SNMP engine (an SNMP instance on a remote host or management station) is defined with an *ip-address* and a text string name *id-string*. An optional UDP port to use for the remote host can be given with the **udp-port** keyword (default 161).

NOTE   If either local or remote engine ID names change after these commands are used, the authentication keys become invalid and users must be reconfigured. MD5 and SHA keys are based on user passwords and the engine IDs.

— *(Optional)* Define a group access template for SNMP users:

COS	**set snmp group** [**-hex**] *groupname* **user** [**-hex**] *username* **security-model** {**v1** | **v2c** | **v3**} [**volatile** | **nonvolatile**]
IOS	(global) **snmp-server group** [*groupname* {**v1** | **v2c** | **v3** {**auth** | **noauth**}}] [**read** *readview*] [**write** *writeview*] [**notify** *notifyview*] [**access** *acc-list*]

The template *groupname* defines the security policy to be used for groups of SNMP users. The SNMP version used by the group is set by the **v1**, **v2c**, and **v3** keywords. For SNMPv3 (IOS only), the security level must also be specified as **auth** (packet authentication, no encryption), **noauth** (no packet authentication), or **priv** (packet authentication with encryption).

On an IOS switch, you can also specify SNMP views to limit MIB access for the group, using the keywords **read** (view *readview* defines readable objects; defaults to all Internet 1.3.6.1 OID space), **write** (view *writeview* defines writeable objects; no default write access), and **notify** (view *notifyview* defines notifications that can be sent to the group; no default). You can use an optional standard IP access list *acc-list* to further limit SNMP access for the group.

On a COS switch, an SNMP user must be defined as a member of the group.

— *(Optional; IOS only)* Define SNMP users and access methods.

For SNMPv1 or SNMPv2c, apply a user to a group by entering the following:

COS	N/A
IOS	(global) **snmp-server user** *username* *groupname* [**remote** *ip-address*] {**v1** | **v2c**} [**access** *acc-list*]

A user *username* is defined to belong to the group template *groupname*. The IP address of the remote SNMP manager where the user belongs can be specified with the **remote** keyword. The version of SNMP must be specified with the **v1** or **v2c** keywords. You can use a standard IP access with the **access** keyword to allow only specific source addresses for the SNMP user.

For SNMPv3, apply a user to a group and security policies by entering the following:

COS	N/A
IOS	(global) **snmp-server user** *username groupname* [**remote** *ip-address*] **v3** [**encrypted**] [**auth** {**md5** | **sha**} *auth-password*] [**access** *acc-list*]

A user *username* is defined to belong to the group template *group-name*. The IP address of the remote SNMP manager where the user belongs can be specified with the **remote** keyword. SNMP version 3 must be specified with the **v3** keyword. You can use a standard IP access list with the **access** keyword to allow only specific source addresses for the SNMP user.

By default passwords for the user are input as text strings. If the **encrypted** keyword is given, passwords must be input as MD5 digests (already encrypted). An authentication password for the user is specified with the **auth** keyword, the type of authentication as keywords **md5** (HMAC-MD5-96 Message Digest 5) or **sha** (HMAC-SHA-96), and a text string *auth-password* (up to 64 characters).

c. *(Optional; IOS only)* Limit the switch operations controlled by SNMP.

— Enable use of the SNMP reload operation:

COS	N/A
IOS	(global) **snmp-server system-shutdown**

By default, you cannot use SNMP to issue a reload operation to the switch. If this function is desired, you can use this command to enable reload control.

— Specify the TFTP server operations controlled by SNMP:

COS	N/A
IOS	(global) **snmp-server tftp-server-list** *acc-list*

SNMP can be used to cause the switch to save or load its configuration file to a TFTP server. You can use the standard IP access list *acc-list* to permit only a limited set of TFTP server IP addresses.

3 *(Optional)* Configure SNMP notifications.

a. Define a global list of notifications to send:

COS	`set snmp trap {enable	disable}` *`type`*
IOS	`(global)` `snmp-server enable {traps` [*`type`*] [*`option`*] `| informs}`

Notifications (both traps and informs) are enabled for the types specified. Because only one type can be given with this command, you can issue the command as many times as necessary. On an IOS switch, if the *type* keyword is not specified, all available notifications are enabled. In addition, if this command is not issued at least once, none of the notifications that it controls are enabled.

On an IOS switch, the possible choices for *type* are **c2900** (notifications based on the Catalyst 2900 series), **cluster** (cluster management changes), **config** (configuration changes), **entity** (entity MIB changes), **hsrp** (HSRP state changes), **vlan-membership** (changes in a port's VLAN membership), and **vtp** (VLAN Trunking Protocol events). For the *type* **snmp** (basic router status changes), the *option* keyword can also be given as **authentication** (authentication failures), **linkup** (interface has come up), **linkdown** (interface has gone down), or **coldstart** (router is reinitializing). If none of these keywords are given, all of them are enabled.

On a COS switch, the possible choices for *type* are **all** (enable all trap types), **auth** (authentication failures), **bridge** (STP root and topology changes), **chassis** (chassis alarms), **config** (configuration changes), **entity** (entity MIB traps), **entityfru** (field-replaceable unit traps), **envfan** (fan failure), **envpower** (power-supply events), **envshutdown** (environmental shutdown), **ippermit** (denials from IP permit), **module** (switch module up/down), **repeater** (RFC 1516 Ethernet repeater events), **stpx** (STPX traps), **syslog** (syslog notifications), **system, vmps** (VLAN membership changes), or **vtp** (VPT events).

b. Define recipients of notifications:

COS	SNMPv1 and SNMPv2c: `set snmp trap` *`host community-string`*
	SNMPv3: `set snmp targetaddr` [`-hex`] *`host`* `param` [`-hex`] `{`*`paramsname`*`}{`*`ipaddr`*`}`[`udpport {`*`port`*`}`] [`timeout {`*`value`*`}`] [`retries` `{`*`value`*`}`] [`volatile	nonvolatile`][`taglist {`[`-hex`] *`tag`*`}`] [[`-hex`] `tag` *`tagvalue`*]  `set snmp targetparams` [`-hex`] `{`*`paramsname`*`}` `user` [`-hex`] `{`*`username`*`}` `{security-model v3} {message-processing v3 {noauthentication |` `authentication	privacy}} [volatile	nonvolatile]`
IOS	`(global)` `snmp-server host` *`host`* [`traps	informs`] [`version {1	2c |` `3 [auth	noauth]}]` *`community-string`* [`udp-port` *`port`*] [*`type`*]

A single host (*host* is either IP address or host name) is specified to receive SNMP notifications (either **traps** or **informs**). The SNMP version can optionally be given as SNMPv1 (**1**, the default), SNMPv2c (**2c**), or SNMPv3 (**3**). If SNMPv3, a keyword can be given to select the type of security: **auth** (use MD5 and SHA authentication), or **noauth** (no authentication or privacy; the default).

The *community-string* keyword specifies a "password" that is shared between the SNMP agent and SNMP manager. The UDP port used can be given as *port* (default 162).

On an IOS switch, the possible choices for *type* are **c2900** (notifications based on the Catalyst 2900 series), **cluster** (cluster management changes), **config** (configuration changes), **entity** (entity MIB changes), **hsrp** (HSRP state changes), **vlan-membership** (changes in a port's VLAN membership), and **vtp** (VLAN Trunking Protocol events). For the *type* **snmp** (basic switch status changes), the *option* keyword can also be given as **authentication** (authentication failures), **linkup** (interface has come up), **linkdown** (interface has gone down), or **coldstart** (switch is reinitializing). If none of these keywords are given, all of them are enabled.

c. *(Optional; IOS only)* Tune notification parameters.

— Specify trap options:

COS	N/A
IOS	(global) **snmp-server trap-timeout** *seconds*
	(global) **snmp-server queue-length** *length*

SNMP traps are not sent reliably, because no acknowledgement is required. Traps can be queued and re-sent only when no route to the trap recipient is present. In that case, the router waits *seconds* (default 30 seconds) before retransmitting the trap. In addition, 10 traps can be queued for each recipient by default. You can use the **queue-length** command to set the queue size to *length* traps each.

— Specify the source address to use for notifications:

COS	N/A
IOS	(global) **snmp-server trap-source** *interface*

SNMP traps can be sent from any available switch interface. To have the switch send all traps using a single source IP address, specify the *interface* to use. In this way, traps can be easily associated with the source switch.

d. *(Optional)* Enable SNMP link traps on specific interfaces:

COS	`set port trap` *mod/port* `{enable	disable}`
IOS	`(interface) [no] snmp trap link-status`

IOS switches, by default, generate SNMP link traps on all interfaces when they go up or down. If this is not desired, use the **no** keyword to disable traps on specific interfaces. The default for COS switches is to **disable** traps on all ports.

4 *(Optional)* Enable RMON support.

a. *(Optional)* Collect RMON statistics:

COS	`set snmp rmon {enable	disable}`
IOS	`(interface) rmon collection stats index [owner name]`

On a COS switch, RMON statistics are collected for all Ethernet, Fast Ethernet, Gigabit Ethernet, and EtherChannel ports. An IOS switch, however, collects RMON statistics only on the configured interfaces. Statistics are gathered in "collections," each uniquely identified by a collection number or *index* (1 to 65535). An optional owner *name* (text string) can be given to associate a username with the collection.

b. *(Optional; IOS only)* Collect RMON history statistics:

COS	N/A
IOS	`(interface) `**`rmon collection history`**` index `**`[owner `***`name`***`] [buckets`**` nbuckets] `**`[interval `***`seconds`***`]`

An IOS switch can collect history statistics on the configured interfaces. Statistics are gathered in "collections," each uniquely identified by a collection number or *index* (1 to 65535). An optional owner *name* (text string) can be given to associate a username with the collection. The **buckets** keyword defines the number of collection buckets to be used (default 50). The **interval** keyword specifies the number of seconds (default 1800 seconds) during the polling cycle.

c. *(Optional; IOS only)* Define an RMON alarm:

COS	N/A
IOS	`(global) `**`rmon alarm`**` number object interval {`**`delta`**`	`**`absolute`**`}` **`rising-threshold`**` rise [event] `**`falling-threshold`**` fall [event]` `[`**`owner`**` string]`

An alarm indexed by *number* (1 to 65535) is configured to monitor a specific MIB variable *object*. The object is given as a dotted-decimal value, in the form of *entry.integer.instance*. The *interval* field specifies the number of seconds (1 to 4294967295) that the alarm will monitor the object. The **delta** keyword watches a change between MIB variables, whereas **absolute** watches a MIB variable directly. You can configure the alarm to test the object against a **rising-threshold** and a **falling-threshold**, where *rise* and *fall* are the threshold values that trigger the alarm. The *event* field specifies an event number in an event table to trigger for the rising and falling thresholds. An optional **owner** text string can be given, as the owner of the alarm.

d. *(Optional; IOS only)* Define an RMON event:

COS	N/A
IOS	(global) **rmon event** *number* [**description** *string*] [**owner** *name*] [**trap** *community*] [**log**]

An RMON event is identified by an arbitrary *number* (1 to 65535). The **description** keyword gives the event a descriptive *string* (text string). An optional event **owner** can be assigned as *name* (text string). If the **trap** keyword is given, an SNMP trap is generated with the *community* string (text string). The **log** keyword causes the event to generate an RMON log entry on the switch.

SNMP Example

A switch is configured for SNMP, using community *public* for read-only access, and community *noc-team* for read-write access. SNMP access is limited to any host in the 172.30.0.0 network for read-only, and to network management hosts 172.30.5.91 and 172.30.5.95 for read-write access. (This is possible with access lists on an IOS switch. However, the COS switch is limited to IP permit statements for all types of SNMP access. Specific hosts will have to be added to the IP permit list.)

SNMP traps are sent to an SNMP agent machine at 172.30.5.93, using community string *nms*. All possible traps are sent, except for switch configuration change traps. Also SNMP link up/down traps are disabled for port 3/1:

COS	`set system contact John Doe, Network Operations`
	`set system location Building A, closet 123`
	`set snmp community read-only public`
	`set snmp community read-write noc-team`

COS	`set snmp trap 172.30.5.93 nms`
(Cont.)	`set snmp trap enable all`
	`set snmp trap disable config`
	`set ip permit 172.30.5.91`
	`set ip permit 172.30.5.95`
	`set ip permit enable snmp`
	`set port trap 3/1 disable`
IOS	`(global) snmp-server contact John Doe, Network Operations`
	`(global) snmp-server location Building A, closet 123`
	`(global) snmp-server community public ro 5`
	`(global) snmp-server community noc-team rw 6`
	`(global) snmp-server host 172.30.5.93 traps nms`
	`(global) snmp-server enable traps`
	`(global) no snmp-server enable config`
	`(global) access-list 5 permit 172.30.0.0 0.0.255.255`
	`(global) access-list 6 permit host 172.30.5.91`
	`(global) access-list 6 permit host 172.30.5.95`
	`(global) interface gig 3/1`
	`(interface) no snmp trap link-status`

Displaying Information About SNMP

Table 12-3 lists some switch commands that you can use to display helpful information about SNMP.

Table 12-3   *Switch Commands to Display SNMP Information*

Display Function	Switch OS	Command
SNMP configuration	COS	`show snmp`
	IOS	`(exec) show snmp`
RMON collections	COS	N/A
	IOS	`(exec) show rmon [alarms	events	history	statistics]`

12-3: Switched Port Analyzer

- *Switched Port Analyzer* (SPAN) mirrors traffic from one or more source switch ports or a source VLAN to a destination port. This allows a monitoring device such as a network analyzer to be attached to the destination port for capturing traffic.

- SPAN source and destination ports must reside on the same physical switch.

- Multiple SPAN sessions can be configured to provide several simultaneous monitors.

- *Remote SPAN* (RSPAN) provides traffic mirroring from a source on one switch to a destination on one or more remote switches.

- RSPAN is carried from source to destination over a special RSPAN VLAN.

- RSPAN is only available on the Catalyst 4000 and 6000 switch families.

NOTE What happens if a speed mismatch occurs between the SPAN source and destination ports? During a SPAN session, a switch merely copies the packets from the source and places them into the output queue of the destination port. If the destination port becomes congested, the SPAN packets are dropped from the queue and are not seen at the destination. Traffic from the SPAN source then is not affected by any congestion at the SPAN destination.

SPAN Configuration

1 Create a SPAN session.

 — *(COS and IOS Catalyst 2900/3500 only)* Select the source and destination:

COS	**set span** *src-mod/src-ports* | *src-vlans* | **sc0**} {*dest-mod/dest-port*} [**rx** | **tx** | **both**] [**inpkts** {**enable** | **disable**}] [**learning** {**enable** | **disable**}] [**multicast** {**enable** | **disable**}] [**filter** *vlans...*] [**create**]
IOS	(global) **interface** *dest-interface* (interface) **port monitor** [*src-interface* | **vlan** *src-vlan*]

The source of traffic for the SPAN session can be either switch ports, VLANs, or the switch management interface (COS only). If switch ports are to be monitored, they are identified as *src-mod/src-ports* (COS; can be one or a range of ports) or as *src-interface* (IOS; only a single interface type and number).

If VLANs are to be monitored, they are identified as *src-vlans* (COS allows one or a range of VLAN numbers; IOS allows only a single VLAN number). COS switches also allow the sc0 management interface to be used as a source if desired.

The SPAN destination port, where the monitoring device is connected, is identified as *dest-mod/dest-port* (COS). For IOS switches, the destination interface is selected by the **interface** *dest-interface* command before the **port monitor** command is applied. On IOS switches, the destination port must belong to the same VLAN as the source.

The direction of source traffic to be monitored can also be selected, as **rx** (traffic received at the source), **tx** (traffic transmitted from the source), or **both** (default). IOS switches inherently monitor traffic in both directions.

By default multicast traffic is monitored as it exits from the source. To disable this behavior, use the **multicast enable** keywords.

The destination port is normally used for a traffic-capturing device, so inbound traffic on the destination port is not allowed by default. If needed, you can enable normal switching of inbound traffic at the destination with the **inpkts enable** keywords.

Section 12-3

CAUTION   Remember that the destination port always belongs to an active VLAN, whether it is monitoring for a SPAN session or not. As well, a SPAN destination port does not run the STP so that STP *bridge protocol data units* (BPDUs) can be monitored. Therefore, if **inpkts** is enabled and the destination port is connected to another network device, a spanning-tree loop can easily be formed.

By default the MAC addresses from inbound packets on the destination port are learned, as they are on any switch port. You can disable address learning on the destination with the **learning disable** keywords.

If a trunk is being used as a source port, you can filter out specific VLANs to be monitored. On a COS switch, use the **filter** *vlans* (one or a range of VLAN numbers) keywords. An IOS switch has no SPAN option to do this. However, you can assign the destination port to the same VLAN you want to monitor in the trunk source.

TIP   If you are monitoring sources that belong to several VLANs, you might want to have a record of the source VLANs for the packets appearing on the destination port. To do this, enable trunking on the destination port. The source packets are tagged with the VLAN numbers from which they originated.

TIP	COS switches allow more than one active SPAN session. You can configure the first session as shown in the full syntax for the **set span** COS command. To create subsequent sessions, use the **create** keyword. If **create** is omitted, the newly configured session overwrites the first session.

— *(IOS; Catalyst 6000 only)* Select the source and destination.

a. Select the session source:

COS	N/A
IOS	(global) **monitor session** *session* {**source** {**interface** *interface*} | {**vlan** *vlan-id*}} [, | - | **rx** | **tx** | **both**]

The SPAN session is uniquely identified by *session* (**1** or **2**). The source can be an *interface* (an interface type and number or a port-channel number) or a VLAN number *vlan-id* (1 to 1005). Multiple source VLANs can be given by using the **vlan** keyword followed by *vlan-id* numbers separated by commas (,). To specify a range of VLAN numbers, use the **vlan** keyword followed by the first and last *vlan-id* numbers, separated by a dash (-).

— Source traffic to be monitored can be one of **rx** (traffic received at the source), **tx** (traffic transmitted from the source), or **both** (the default).

b. Select the session destination:

COS	N/A
IOS	(global) **monitor session** *session* {**destination** {**interface** *interface*} [, | -] | {**vlan** *vlan-id*}}

The destination for the SPAN *session* (session number **1** or **2**) can be an *interface* (interface type and number) or a VLAN number *vlan-id* (1 to 1005). Multiple destinations can also be specified, if needed. These can be given with the **interface** keyword, followed by a list of *interface* numbers separated by commas (,). To specify a range of interfaces, use the **interface** keyword followed by the first and last *interface* numbers, separated by a dash (-).

c. *(Optional)* Filter VLANs on a trunk source:

COS	N/A
IOS	(global) **monitor session** *session* **filter vlan** *vlan-id*} [, | -]

If a trunk is being used as a source port, you can filter the trunk to select specific VLANs to be monitored. A VLAN number is identified as *vlan-id* (1 to 1005). Multiple source VLANs can be given with the **vlan** keyword, followed by a list of *vlan-id* numbers separated by commas (,). To specify a range of VLANs, use the **vlan** keyword followed by the first and last *vlan-id* numbers, separated by a dash (-).

2 *(Optional)* Disable a SPAN session:

COS	**set span disable** [*dest-mod/dest-port* | **all**]
IOS	(global) **no monitor session** *session* -OR- (interface) **no port monitor**

SPAN sessions can be disabled individually, referenced by their destination *dest-mod/dest-port* (COS) or by *session* number (IOS). For Catalyst 2900/3500 IOS switches, SPAN sessions are disabled on the destination interfaces with the **no port monitor** command.

RSPAN Configuration

1 Create one or more VLANs to be used by RSPAN:

COS	**set vlan** *vlan-id* **rspan**
IOS	N/A

The VLAN number *vlan-id* (1 to 1000, 1025 to 4094) should be created on all switches from the RSPAN source to the RSPAN destination. As well, the RSPAN VLAN should be trunked end-to-end, because it carries the remotely monitored traffic. Create a different RSPAN VLAN for each RSPAN session that you will be using. See Chapter 6, "VLANs and Trunking," for more configuration information related to VLANs and VTP.

NOTE   Notice the use of the **rspan** keyword when the RSPAN VLAN is created. This must be used so that the VLAN can correctly carry the RSPAN traffic. An RSPAN-capable switch floods the RSPAN packets out all of its ports belonging to the RSPAN VLAN, in an effort to send

Section 12-3

them toward the RSPAN destination. This is because a switch participating in RSPAN has no idea where the destination is located.

Otherwise, if the switch were using a regular VLAN, it would try to forward the RSPAN packets on ports where the packet destination addresses were detected—something quite different from RSPAN altogether! This is why all switches involved in the end-to-end RSPAN path must be RSPAN-capable. Currently, this is limited to the Catalyst 4000 and 6000 families.

TIP	Create and maintain the RSPAN VLAN for the special monitoring purpose. Don't allow any normal hosts to join the RSPAN VLAN.

Ideally, all the switches will belong to a common VTP domain so that the VLAN can be created on a VTP server and propagated to all other switches. VTP pruning also prunes the RSPAN VLAN from unnecessary trunks, limiting the traffic impact in unrelated areas of the network.

Be aware that RSPAN traffic can increase the traffic load on a trunk, even though RSPAN is restricted to one special VLAN in the trunk. If the additional load is significant, the normal and monitored traffic contends with each other for available bandwidth and both could suffer.

---

2 *(Source switches only)* Select the monitor sources:

COS	`set rspan source {`*src-mod/src-ports...* `|` *vlans...* `|` `sc0}` `{`*rspan-vlan*`}` `[rx	tx	both] [multicast {enable	disable}] [filter` *vlans...*`] [create]`
IOS	N/A

The RSPAN source is identified as one or more physical switch ports *src-mod/src-ports*, as one or more VLAN numbers *vlans*, or as the management port sc0. This is performed only on the switch where the source is connected. The RSPAN VLAN number to be used is *rspan-vlan* (1 to 1000, 1025 to 4094). The direction of the monitored traffic can be **rx** (traffic received at the source), **tx** (traffic transmitted from the source), or **both** (the default).

By default multicast traffic is monitored as it exits from the source. To disable this behavior, use the **multicast disable** keywords.

If a trunk is being used as a source port, you can filter the trunk to select specific VLANs to be monitored by using the **filter** *vlans* (one or a range of VLAN numbers) keywords.

TIP   You can configure more than one active RSPAN session at the source switch. The first session is created as shown above. To create subsequent sessions, use the   **create** keyword. If **create** is omitted, the newly configured session overwrites the first session. You should use a different RSPAN VLAN for each session.

3 *(Destination switches only)* Select the destinations:

COS	`set rspan destination` *mod/port* `{rspan-vlan}` `[inpkts {enable | disable}]` `[learning {enable | disable}]` `[create]`
IOS	N/A

The RSPAN destination port, where the monitoring device is connected, is identified as *mod/port*. This is performed only on the switch where the destination port resides.

The destination port is normally used for a traffic-capturing device, so inbound traffic on the destination port is not allowed by default. If needed, you can enable normal switching of inbound traffic at the destination with the   **inpkts enable** keywords.

NOTE   RSPAN differs from SPAN in that the destination port always has the STP enabled. This prevents bridging loops from accidentally forming if other network devices are connected to the destination port. However, this also means that you can't monitor STP BPDUs with RSPAN.

By default the MAC addresses from inbound packets on the destination port are learned, as they are on any switch port. You can disable address learning on the destination with the   **learning disable** keywords.

TIP   You can also configure more than one active RSPAN session at the destination switch. The first session is created as shown previously. To create subsequent sessions, use the **create** keyword. If **create** is omitted, the newly configured session overwrites the first session. You should use a different RSPAN VLAN for each session.

4 *(Intermediate switches only)* No further configuration is needed.

The switches in the path from RSPAN source to destination do not need to know about any specific RSPAN configuration. After all the RSPAN VLANs have been created end-to-end, the intermediate switches flood the RSPAN traffic correctly toward the destinations. Remember that all the intermediate switches must be RSPAN-capable.

5 *(Optional)* Disable an RSPAN session:

COS	`set rspan disable source [`*`rspan-vlan`*`	`**`all`**`]`
	-OR-
	`set rpsan disable destination [`*`mod/port`*`	`**`all`**`]`
IOS	N/A

You can disable an RSPAN session when it is no longer needed. Source sessions are identified by the *rspan-vlan* (VLAN number) or the **all** keyword. Destination sessions are identified by the destination port as *mod/port* or the **all** keyword.

SPAN Examples

Network analyzer A (a "sniffer") is connected to a Catalyst switch port 5/1 and will monitor all traffic on VLAN 58.

A PC is connected to port 4/39 and a file server to port 2/4 of a Catalyst switch. Network analyzer B is connected to port 5/48. The switch is configured for a SPAN session that will allow the analyzer to capture all traffic to and from the server. Figure 12-1 shows a network diagram of the two SPAN sessions.

Figure 12-1 *Network Diagram for the SPAN Example*

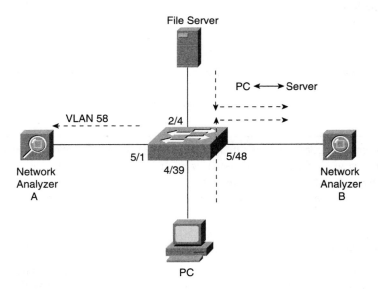

COS	`set span 58 5/1 both`
	`set span 2/4 5/48 both create`
IOS	`(global) interface fast 5/1`
	`(interface) port monitor vlan 58`
	`(global) interface fast 5/48`
	`(interface) port monitor fast 2/4`
IOS 6000	`(global) monitor session 1 source vlan 58 both`
	`(global) monitor session 1 destination interface fast 5/1`
	`(global) monitor session 2 source interface fast 5/48 both`
	`(global) monitor session 2 destination interface fast 2/4`

Figure 12-2 shows a network of three switches. A file server is connected to Catalyst B port 3/1. A network analyzer is connected to Catalyst C port 5/48. Catalyst A connects Catalysts B and C by two trunk ports. RSPAN VLAN 901 carries all the RSPAN traffic from the source to the destination. (Assume for this example that Catalyst B is the VTP server for the domain of three switches.)

Figure 12-2 *Network Diagram for the RSPAN Example*

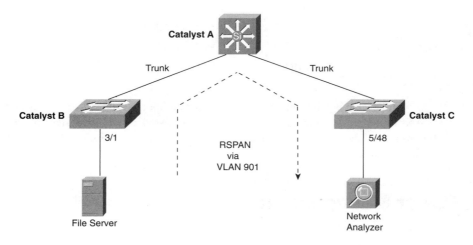

The configuration needed for Catalyst B follows:

COS	`set vlan 901 rspan`
	`set rspan source 3/1 901 both`
IOS	N/A

The configuration needed for Catalyst C follows:

COS	`set rspan destination 5/48 901`
IOS	N/A

No additional configuration is needed for Catalyst A because it merely transports RSPAN traffic over the RSPAN VLAN 901.

Displaying Information About SPAN

Table 12-4 lists some switch commands that you can use to display helpful information about SPAN.

Table 12-4   *Switch Commands to Display SPAN Information*

Display Function	Switch OS	Command
SPAN session activity	COS	`show span`

	IOS	`show monitor [session session-number]`
		-OR-
		`show port monitor`

RSPAN session activity	COS	`show rspan`
	IOS	N/A

COS switches display the source ports with "Admin Source" and "Oper Source" labels. All VLANs or ports that are configured as sources are listed as administrative sources. However, only the ports that are being actively monitored (not disabled) are listed as operational sources.

12-4: Power Management

- Power management is available on the Catalyst 6000 switch family only.

- Power supplies can be put into a redundancy mode such that multiple supplies share the total power load. If one supply fails, another supply carries the entire system load.

- Power supplies not in redundancy mode can combine their capacities to power the system. This proves useful when the total load of all switch modules is greater than the capacity of a single power supply. If one power supply fails and the other supply does not have the capacity to carry the entire system load, some switch modules are powered down to reduce the load.

Configuration

1 *(Catalyst 6000 only)* Configure power-supply redundancy:

COS	`set power redundancy {enable	disable}`
IOS	`(global) power redundancy-mode {combined	redundant}`

Power-supply redundancy (**enable** or **redundant**) is enabled by default.

2 *(IOS Catalyst 6000 only)* Control power-supply operation:

COS	N/A
IOS	`(global) [no] power enable power-supply` *number*

By default power is enabled to all power supplies. Supplies are identified by *number* (1 or 2). Use the **no** keyword to disable a power supply.

3 *(Catalyst 6000 only)* Control power to switch modules:

COS	`set module power up	down` *mod*
IOS	`(global) [no] power enable module` *mod*

By default all switch modules receive power. To disable power to a module, use the **down** (COS) or **no** (IOS) keywords with the module number *mod* (1 to the maximum number of slots in the chassis).

Displaying Information About Power Management

Table 12-5 lists some switch commands that you can use to display helpful information about power management.

Table 12-5 *Switch Commands to Display Power Management Information*

Display Function	Switch OS	Command
System power	COS	`show environment power`
	IOS	`(exec) show power [{available	redundancy-mode	{power-supply` *number*`}	total	used}]`
Module power state	COS	`show module`
	IOS	`(exec) show power status all`

12-5: Environmental Monitoring

NOTE Temperature monitoring commands are currently available only on the Catalyst 6000 and 4000 switch families.

Table 12-6 lists some switch commands that you can use to display helpful information about environmental monitoring.

Table 12-6 *Switch Commands to Display Environmental Monitoring Information*

Display Function	Switch OS	Command
Module temperatures	COS	`show environment temperature`
	IOS	`(exec) show environment temperature`

The output from the **show environment temperature** command lists the temperatures measured at the intake and exhaust of each module, with the warning and critical alarm temperatures in parentheses. To operate normally, a switch temperature should not exceed the levels shown within the parentheses.

"Device 1" and "Device 2" temperatures refer to additional sensors within the modules. "VTT" modules are located on the chassis backplane.

12-6: Packet Tracing

- The **ping** (Packet Internet Groper) command can be used to test end-to-end connectivity from a switch to a remote host. The IP ping uses ICMP type 8 requests and ICMP type 0 replies.

- The **traceroute** or Layer 3 traceroute command can be used to discover the routers along the path that packets are taking to a destination. An IP traceroute uses UDP probe packets on port 33434.

- The **l2trace** or Layer 2 traceroute command can be used to discover the physical path that a packet will take through a switched network.

- **l2trace** looks up the destination in the forwarding table, and then contacts the next neighboring switch via CDP. Each switch hop is queried in a similar fashion.

- **l2trace** is only supported on Catalyst 4000, 5000, and 6000 (COS only) switches. If other switches are encountered along the path to the destination, they won't know how to respond to the **l2trace** request, and the **l2trace** will time out.

Configuration

1 Use ping packets to check reachability:

COS	**ping -s** *host* [*packet-size*] [*packet-count*]
IOS	(exec) **ping** [*host*]

The IP ping sends ICMP type 8 (echo request) packets to the target *host* (IP address or host name), and ICMP echo replies are expected in return. A COS switch sends a single ping packet unless the –s option is used, causing ping packets to be continually sent until the switch is interrupted with a **^-C** (control-C) key sequence. The ping packet size, *packet-size* (bytes), and the number of packets, *packet-count*, can also be specified.

An IOS switch sends five ping packets toward the destination, by default. Each ping is displayed by one of these characters: ! (successful reply packet received), . (no reply seen within the timeout period, 2 seconds), U (a destination unreachable error was received), M (a could-not-fragment message was received), C (a congestion-experienced packet was received), I (the ping test was interrupted on the switch), ? (an unknown packet type was received), or & (the packet lifetime or *time-to-live* [TTL] was exceeded).

When the test completes, the success rate is reported along with a summary of the round-trip minimum, average, and maximum in milliseconds.

NOTE For the regular **ping** command, only the destination address can be given. The source address used in the ping packets comes from the switch management interface.

The IOS switch also provides a more flexible echo test called an *extended ping*. The EXEC-level command **ping** is given, with no options. You will be prompted for all available **ping** options, including the source address to be used. You can specify the following options:

- Protocol (default **ip**)—Can also be **appletalk**, **clns**, **novell**, **apollo**, **vines**, **decnet**, or **xns** on Catalyst 6000 IOS and other Layer 3 switches.

- Target address.

- Repeat count (default 5 packets)—The number of echo packets to send.

- Datagram size (default 100 bytes)—The size of the echo packet; choose a size larger than the *maximum transfer unit* (MTU) to test packet fragmentation.

- Timeout (default 2 seconds)—The amount of time to wait for a reply to each request packet.

Section 12-6

- Extended commands.

  — Source address or interface—Any source address can be given; however, the address must be the address of the management interface on the switch if the reply packets are to be seen.

  — Type of service (default 0).

  — Set DF bit in IP header (default no)—If set, the packet is not fragmented for a path with a smaller MTU; you can use this to detect the smallest MTU in the path.

  — Validate reply data (default no)—The data sent in the echo request packet is compared to the data echoed in the reply packet.

  — Data pattern (default 0xABCD)—The data pattern is a 16-bit field that is repeated throughout the data portion of the packet; this can prove useful for testing data integrity with CSU/DSUs and cabling.

  — Loose, strict, record, timestamp, verbose (default none)—**loose** (loose source route with hop addresses), **strict** (strict source route with hop addresses), **record** (record the route with a specified number of hops), **timestamp** (record time stamps at each router hop), and **verbose** (toggle verbose reporting). The **record** option can be useful to see a record of the router addresses traversed over the round-trip path.

- Sweep range of sizes (default no)—Sends echo requests with a variety of packet sizes.

  — Sweep min size (default 36)

  — Sweep max size (default 18024)

  — Sweep interval (default 1)

2 *(Optional)* Use Layer 3 traceroute to discover routers along a path:

COS	**traceroute** [**-n**] [**-w** *wait-time*] [**-i** *initial-ttl*] [**-m** *max-ttl*] [**-p** *dest-port*] [**-q** *nqueries*] [**-t** *tos*] *host* [*data-size*]
IOS	(exec) **traceroute** [*protocol*] [*host*]

The **traceroute** command sends successive probe packets to *host* (either a network address or a host name). The *protocol* field can be **appletalk**, **clns**, **ip**, or **vines** on Catalyst 6000 IOS and other Layer 3 switches.

For IP, the first set of packets (default 3) is sent with a TTL of one. The first router along the path decrements the TTL, detects that it is zero, and returns ICMP TTL-exceeded error packets. Successive sets of packets are then sent out, each one with a TTL value incremented by one. In this fashion, each router along the path responds with an error, allowing the local router to detect successive hops.

The following fields are output as a result of traceroute probes:

- Probe sequence number—The current hop count.
- Host name of the current router.
- IP address of the current router.
- Round-trip times (in milliseconds) of each of the probes in the set.
- *—The probe timed out.
- U—Port unreachable message was received.
- H—Host unreachable message was received.
- P—Protocol unreachable message was received.
- N—Network unreachable message was received.
- ?—An unknown packet type was received.
- Q—Source quench was received.

The traceroute probes continue to be sent until the maximum TTL value (30 by default for IP) is exceeded or until you interrupt the router with the escape sequence (Ctrl-Shift-6).

You can also invoke traceroute with no options. This allows the switch to prompt for the parameters from the following list:

- Protocol (default IP)—Can also be **appletalk**, **clns**, or **vines** on Catalyst 6000 IOS and other layer 3 switches.
- Target address.
- Source address—An IP address of a router interface; if not specified, the interface closest to the destination is used.
- Numeric display (default no)—By default, both the host name and IP address of each hop display; if set to yes, only the IP addresses display. This is handy if DNS is not available.
- Timeout in seconds (default 3)—The amount of time to wait for a response to a probe.
- Probe count (default 3)—The number of probes to send to each TTL (or hop) level.
- Minimum TTL (default 1)—The default of one hop can be overridden to begin past the known router hops.
- Maximum TTL (default 30)—The maximum number of hops to trace; traceroute ends when this number of hops or the destination is reached.
- Port number (default 33434)—The UDP destination port for probes.

- Loose, strict, record, timestamp, verbose (default none)—**loose** (loose source route with hop addresses), **strict** (strict source route with hop addresses), **record** (record the route with a specified number of hops), **timestamp** (record time stamps at each router hop), and **verbose** (toggle verbose reporting). The **record** option can be useful to see a record of the router addresses traversed over the round-trip path.

NOTE   Some routers do not respond to traceroute probes correctly. In this case, some or all of the probes sent are reported with asterisks (*) in the display.

---

3 *(Optional)* Use Layer 2 traceroute to discover switches along a path:

COS	**l2trace** *src-mac dest-mac* [*vlan*] [**detail**]
	-OR-
	l2trace *src-ip dest-ip* [**detail**]
IOS	N/A

NOTE   The **l2trace** command is currently available only on the Catalyst 4000, 5000, and 6000 COS switch families. You can use **l2trace** to trace a path containing other types of switches. However, these switches do not know how to interpret and reply to the CDP l2trace message. At these switch hops, **l2trace** timeouts display.

Layer 2 traces are performed from the source MAC address *src-mac* (in dash-separated hexadecimal pairs) to the destination MAC address *dest-mac*. Both source and destination must be present in the address table on the switch. As well, both source and destination must be in the same VLAN. If the hosts belong to more than one VLAN, you can specify the desired VLAN number as *vlan*. The **detail** keyword displays additional information about the switch port media at each hop along the path.

If the MAC addresses are not readily known, you can give the source and destination as IP addresses *src-ip* and *dest-ip*. However, both hosts must be present in the switch's ARP table so that their MAC addresses can be found.

Packet-Tracing Example

On a Catalyst 4000 switch, a Layer 2 trace is performed from source 00-b0-d0-40-01-d1 to destination 00-10-a4-c6-b4-b7. These two hosts are on the same VLAN and are both present in the switch's address table.

The source address is found on port 2/12 of the local switch. The first Layer 2 hop is at IP address 192.168.1.16, where the destination address is found in the address table for port 3/1 on that switch.

Notice that the second Layer 2 hop is the switch at 192.168.1.253, which was identified via CDP. However, either the switch model or its OS does not support the l2trace protocol. As a result, the Layer 2 traces time out and no response is returned from the neighboring switch at 192.168.1.253:

COS	`cat4000 (enable) `**`l2trace 00-b0-d0-40-01-d1 00-10-a4-c6-b4-b7`**
	`Starting L2 Trace`
	` 2/12 : 192.168.1.16 :  3/1`
	`l2trace: no response from neigh 192.168.1.253`
	`l2trace: no response from neigh 192.168.1.253`
	`Error in l2trace.`
	`cat4000 (enable)`
IOS	N/A

This time, a Layer 2 trace is performed on a Catalyst 6000 switch running COS. All switches in the path to the destination are l2trace-capable. The source is 00-05-9b-fb-b8-80, and the destination is 00-04-9b-57-3c-c0.

During the first trace, the source is found on port 6/3 of the local switch, 192.168.1.4. The first Layer 2 hop is the local switch, departing on ports 1/1-2,2/1-2 (a four-port Fast EtherChannel bundle). The second hop is found entering on ports 3/1-2,4/1-2 (the other end of the FEC bundle), at switch 192.168.1.252. The third hop is found departing on port 3/3 of 192.168.1.252, and arriving at port 7/1 on switch 192.168.1.7. The fourth hop is the destination at port 7/3 on 192.168.1.7.

Next, the same Layer 2 trace is performed again, with the **detail** keyword added. Notice how this provides added information at each hop. The hardware platform, host name (if available), and the IP address of each switch hop is shown. As well, each link to the next hop is shown with its port number and media type.

| COS | ```
Cat6000-A (enable) l2trace 00-05-9b-fb-b8-80 00-04-9b-57-3c-c0
Starting L2 Trace
 6/3 : 192.168.1.4 : 1/1-2,2/1-2
3/1-2,4/1-2 : 192.168.1.252 :  3/3
 7/1 : 192.168.1.7 :  7/3
Cat6000-A (enable)


Cat6000-A (enable) l2trace 00-05-9b-fb-b8-80 00-04-9b-57-3c-c0
detail
Starting L2 Trace


l2trace vlan number is 901.


00-05-9b-fb-b8-80 found in WS-C6509 named Cat6000-A on port  6/3
1000MB full duplex
WS-C6509 : Cat6000-A : 192.168.1.4:  6/3 1000MB full duplex ->
1/1-2,2/1-2 1000MB full duplex
WS-C6509 :    : 192.168.1.252: 3/1-2,4/1-2 1000MB full duplex ->
3/3 1000MB full duplex
WS-C6509 :    : 192.168.1.7:  7/1 1000MB full duplex ->  7/3 1000MB
full duplex
Destination 00-04-9b-57-3c-c0 found in WS-C6509 on port  7/3 1000MB
full duplex
Cat6000-A (enable)
``` |
| IOS | N/A |

Further Reading

Refer to the following recommended sources for further information about the topics covered in this chapter.

CCNP Switching Exam Certification Guide by Tim Boyles and David Hucaby, Cisco Press, ISBN 1-58720-000-7

Building Cisco Multilayer Switched Networks by Karen Webb, Cisco Press, ISBN 1-57870-093-0

Cisco LAN Switching by Kennedy Clark and Kevin Hamilton, Cisco Press, ISBN 1-57870-094-9

Performance and Fault Management by Maggiora, Elliott, Pavone, Phelps, and Thompson; Cisco Press, ISBN 1-57870-180-5
```

CHAPTER **13**

Quality of Service

See the following sections to configure and use these features:

- **13-1: QoS Theory**—Discusses the various operations and mechanisms that make up *quality of service* (QoS) as a whole.

- **13-2: QoS Configuration**—Explains the sequence of steps necessary to configure and monitor QoS on a Catalyst switch.

- **13-3: QoS Data Export**—Presents the configuration steps needed to gather and send QoS statistics information to external collection devices.

- **13-4: QoS Management**—Discusses how switches can be configured to support *Common Open Policy Service* (COPS) and *Resource Reservation Protocol* (RSVP) management protocols.

13-1: QoS Theory

- QoS defines policies on how switches and routers deliver different types of traffic. A *QoS domain* is the entire collection of network devices that are administered so that they adhere to the QoS policies.

- To guarantee that QoS policies are met, QoS must be configured on all switches and routers end-to-end across the network.

- Traffic should be classified at the edges of the QoS domain. Where this isn't possible, classify traffic as close as possible to the source. Classification can occur at Layer 2 or Layer 3, depending on the network functions available at the edge.

- The top portion of Figure 13-1 shows QoS operations on a Catalyst switch, including the following:

  - **Classification**—Selects specific traffic to which a QoS policy can be applied. The priority values of inbound frames can also be trusted or reclassified.

  - **Policing**—Limits the bandwidth used by a traffic flow. Policers can control aggregate or individual flows, and can also mark or drop traffic.

  - **Marking**—Assigns a value to either the Layer 3 *Differentiated Services Code Point* (DSCP), the Layer 2 *class of service* (CoS), or both for each frame.

  - **Scheduling**—Assigns traffic to a specific switch port queue, for either ingress or egress traffic.

  - **Congestion Avoidance**—Reserves bandwidth in the switch port queues. Traffic that exceeds a threshold can be dropped or reduced in priority, making space for other traffic in the queues.

- All Catalyst QoS operations are based around the concept of an *internal DSCP* value. This value is determined by an ingress port's trust state, and is carried throughout the QoS process with each frame. Upon egress, the internal DSCP can be used to mark other QoS values within the frame. The bottom portion of Figure 13-1 shows the internal DSCP operations.

Figure 13-1 *Catalyst Switch QoS Operations and Internal DSCP*

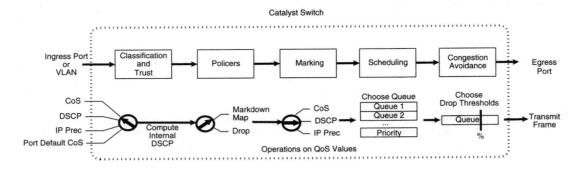

As a summary, Table 13-1 lists QoS capabilities of the various Cisco Catalyst switch families.

Table 13-1 *Cisco Catalyst Switches: QoS Capabilities*

Switch Family	Classification	Policing	Scheduling	Congestion Avoidance	Marking
6000 w/ Policy Feature Card (PFC) or PFC2	Based on CoS, DSCP, IP precedence, access lists (Layers 3 and 4)	Aggregate and microflow (1023 policers)	Configurable queues	Configurable w/ drop thresholds	CoS, DSCP
6000 w/o PFC	Based on CoS, MAC addresses	N/A	Configurable queues	Configurable w/ drop thresholds	CoS
4000 w/ Supervisor III	Based on CoS, DSCP, IP precedence, access lists (Layers 3 and 4)	Aggregate and microflow (1023 policers)	Configurable queues	Configurable w/ drop thresholds	CoS, DSCP
4000 w/o Supervisor III	Based on CoS, MAC address	N/A	Configurable queues	Fixed thresholds	Default CoS
5000	Based on CoS, MAC address	N/A	Fixed	Configurable w/ drop thresholds	CoS
3550	Based on CoS, DSCP, IP precedence, access lists (Layers 3 and 4)	Aggregate and microflow (128 policers)	Configurable queues	Configurable w/ drop thresholds	CoS, DSCP
3500XL/2900XL	Based on CoS	N/A	Fixed	N/A	CoS

Layer 2 QoS Classification and Marking

At Layer 2, individual frames have no mechanism for indicating the priority or importance of their contents. Therefore, the delivery of Layer 2 frames must be on a "best effort" basis.

When *virtual LANs* (VLANs) are trunked over a single link, however, the trunk provides a means to carry priority information along with each frame. Layer 2 CoS is transported as follows:

- **IEEE 802.1Q trunk**—Frames are tagged with a 12-bit VLAN ID. The CoS is contained in the three 802.1p priority bits in the User field. Frames in the native VLAN are not tagged at all; they are given the default CoS or priority for the switch port. Figure 13-2 shows the format of the 802.1Q encapsulation tag.

Figure 13-2 *802.1Q Trunk Encapsulation Format*

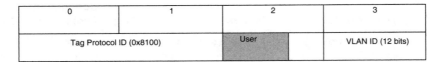

- *Inter-Switch Link* **(ISL) trunk**—Frames are tagged with a 15-bit VLAN ID. The CoS is contained in the lower three bits of the User field. Although this is not standardized, Catalyst switches copy the 802.1p CoS bits from a frame in an 802.1Q trunk into the User field of frames in an ISL trunk. Figure 13-3 shows the format of the ISL tag.

Figure 13-3 *ISL Trunk Encapsulation Format*

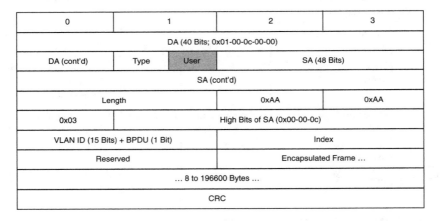

Layer 3 QoS Classification and Marking

QoS is also built around the concept of *Differentiated Service* (DiffServ), where the QoS specification is carried within each Layer 3 packet. IP packets have a *type of service* (ToS) byte that is formatted according to the top row of Figure 13-4. Bits P2, P1, and P0 form the IP precedence value. Bits T3, T2, T1, and T0 form the ToS value.

For DiffServ, the same byte is called the *Differentiated Services* (DS) byte, and is also formatted according to the bottom row of Figure 13-4. Bits DS5 through DS0 form the *Differentiated Services Code Point* (DSCP). The DSCP is arranged to be backward-compatible with the IP precedence bits because the two quantities share the same byte in the IP header.

Figure 13-4 *ToS and DSCP Byte Formats*

ToS Byte:	P2	P1	P0	T3	T2	T1	T0	Zero
DS Byte:	DS5	DS4	DS3	DS2	DS1	DS0	ECN1	ECN0
	(Class Selector)			(Drop Precedence)				

Bits DS5, DS4, and DS3 form the DSCP class selector. Classes 1 through 4 are termed the *Assured Forwarding* (AF) service levels. Higher class numbers indicate a higher-priority traffic. Each class or AF service level has three *drop precedence* categories:

- Low (1)
- Medium (2)
- High (3)

Traffic in the AF classes can be dropped, with the most likelihood of dropping in the Low category and the least in the High category. In other words, service level AF class 4 with drop precedence 3 is delivered before AF class 4 with drop precedence 1, which is delivered before AF class 3 with drop precedence 3, and so on.

Class 5 is also called the *Expedited Forwarding* (EF) class, offering premium service and the least likelihood of packet drops. The *Default* class selector (DSCP 000 000) offers only best-effort forwarding.

Class 6, *Internetwork Control*, and Class 7, *Network Control*, are both set aside for network control traffic. This includes the Spanning Tree Protocol and routing protocols—traffic that is not user-generated but usually considered high-priority.

Table 13-2 shows how the IP precedence names and bits have been mapped to DSCP values. DSCP is broken down by *per-hop behavior* (PHB), class selector, and drop precedence. Many times, DSCP values are referred to by the codepoint name (AF23, for example), which are also listed in the table. The DSCP bits are shown along with their decimal equivalent. In many DSCP-related commands, you need to enter a decimal DSCP value, even though it is difficult to relate the decimal numbers with the corresponding DSCP service levels and PHBs. Use this table as a convenient cross-reference.

Table 13-2 *Mapping of IP Precedence and DSCP Fields*

IP Precedence (3 Bits)			DSCP (6 Bits)				
Name	Value	Bits	Per-Hop Behavior	Class Selector	Drop Precedence	Codepoint Name	DSCP Bits (Decimal)
Routine	0	000	Default			Default	000 000 (0)
Priority	1	001	AF	1	1: Low	AF11	001 010 (10)
					2: Medium	AF12	001 100 (12)
					3: High	AF13	001 110 (14)
Immediate	2	010	AF	2	1: Low	AF21	010 010 (18)
					2: Medium	AF22	010 100 (20)
					3: High	AF23	010 110 (22)
Flash	3	011	AF	3	1: Low	AF31	011 010 (26)
					2: Medium	AF32	011 100 (28)
					3: High	AF33	011 110 (30)
Flash Override	4	100	AF	4	1: Low	AF41	100 010 (34)
					2: Medium	AF42	100 100 (36)
					3: High	AF43	100 110 (38)
Critical	5	101	EF	N/A	N/A	EF	101 110 (46)[1]
Internetwork Control	6	110	N/A	N/A	N/A	N/A	N/A[2]
Network Control	7	111	N/A	N/A	N/A	N/A	N/A[2]

[1] IP precedence value 5 (DSCP EF) corresponds to the range of DSCP bits 101000 through 101111, or 40–47. However, only the value 101110 or 46 is commonly used, and is given the EF designation.

[2] IP precedence values 6 and 7 consume the DSCP ranges 48–55 and 56–63, respectively. However, these values are normally used by network control traffic and are not shown in the table for simplicity.

TIP　　Layer 2 CoS and Layer 3 DSCP/ToS are completely independent concepts. As such, the two QoS values do not intermingle or automatically translate to each other. A switch must map between CoS and DSCP values at a Layer 2 and Layer 3 boundary.

　　The Layer 3 DSCP/ToS is carried within each IP packet, allowing the QoS information to be propagated automatically. The Layer 2 CoS is not contained in Layer 2 frames, however, and can only be carried across a trunk. To propagate the CoS values, you must use a trunk between switches.

Catalyst Switch Queuing

Catalyst switch ports have both ingress and egress queues. These buffer frames as they are received or before they are transmitted. Each port usually has multiple queues, each configured for a relative traffic priority. For example, the lowest-priority queue is serviced only after the higher-priority queues.

Most switch platforms have a strict-priority queue that is used for time-critical traffic. This queue is always serviced before any other queue on the port.

Each port queue usually has one or more thresholds that indicate when traffic can or cannot be dropped. When the queue is less full than a threshold, frames are not dropped. If the queue is filled over a threshold, the likelihood that frames can be dropped increases.

During QoS configuration, you must reference the queues by number. The lowest-priority standard queue is always queue 1. The next-higher priority standard queues follow, beginning with 2. The strict-priority queue always receives the highest queue index number.

Cisco Catalyst switch ports are described with the following queue type notation: x**p**y**q**z**t**, where the notations indicate the following:

- **p**—The number of strict-priority queues, given by x
- **q**—The number of standard queues, given by y
- **t**—The number of configurable thresholds per queue, given by z

For example, a switch port of type **1p1q4t** has one strict-priority queue, one standard queue, and four thresholds per queue. The low-priority standard queue is called queue 1, whereas the strict-priority queue is called queue 2.

13-2: QoS Configuration

- QoS operations and policies can be applied as follows:

    - **Port-based**—All data passing through a specific port. This is usually used on a switch with a Layer 3 switching engine.

    - **VLAN-based**—All data passing through a specific VLAN on the switch. This is usually used on a switch with a Layer 2 switching engine or when QoS policies are common for all traffic on a VLAN.

- Classification can be performed at ingress switch ports. Inbound CoS, IP precedence, or DSCP values can be trusted by accepting the values that were assigned by an attached device. This is acceptable when the source of the values is known and under administrative control. If these values cannot be trusted as they enter a switch, they can be mapped to new values. An internal DSCP value is derived from the classification for each frame.

- Ingress switch port queues and scheduling can be tuned to support advanced QoS needs.

- Policers can be used to control ingress traffic:

  — Policers use a *token bucket* algorithm to monitor the bandwidth utilization of a traffic flow. The lengths of inbound frames are added to the token bucket as they arrive. Every 0.25 ms (1/4000th of a second), a value of the *committed information rate* (CIR) or average policed rate is subtracted from the token bucket. The idea is to keep the token bucket equal to zero for a sustained data rate.

  — The policer allows the traffic rate to burst a certain amount over the average rate. Valid burst amounts are allowed as the token bucket rises up to the level of the burst value (in bytes). This is also called *in-profile traffic*.

  — When the token bucket size exceeds the burst value, the policer considers the traffic flow to be "excessive." With a PFC2 module, a *peak information rate* (PIR) can be defined. When traffic flows exceed the maximum burst size over the PIR, the policer considers the flow to be "in violation." This type of traffic is also called *out-of-profile traffic*.

  — Aggregate policers monitor and control a cumulative flow that travels through one or more ingress ports or a VLAN. Up to 1023 aggregate policers can be defined on a Catalyst 6000 switch.

  — Microflow policers monitor and control one specific traffic flow, or a *microflow*. An IP microflow is defined by source and destination IP addresses, Layer 4 protocol, and source and destination port numbers. An IPX microflow has common source and destination networks and a common destination node. A MAC layer microflow has a common protocol and common source and destination MAC addresses. Up to 63 microflow policers can be defined on a Catalyst 6000 switch.

- *Access control entries* (ACEs) match traffic based on address and Layer 4 port information. ACEs are grouped into *access control lists* (ACLs) or QoS policies that are applied to specific switch ports.

- Congestion avoidance is configured by assigning thresholds to the various egress queues. Traffic is dropped when the queue level rises above the appropriate threshold, reserving queue space for other traffic.

- Egress switch port queue scheduling can be tuned to assign classes of traffic to queues and thresholds with relative service priorities.

Catalyst 2900XL/3500XL Configuration

TIP   The QoS operations on a Catalyst 2900XL or 3500XL switch are limited to QoS trust and fixed-queue scheduling. Therefore, these switches are presented here separately.

1 *(Optional)* Classify traffic based on a port.

a. *(Optional)* Set the default ingress CoS value:

COS	N/A
IOS	(interface) **switchport priority default** *cos*

Frames that are untagged receive CoS value *cos* (0 to 7).

b. *(Optional)* Don't trust any inbound information:

COS	N/A
IOS	(interface) **switchport priority override**

For a Catalyst 3500XL, the CoS value is set to the default CoS value configured in Step 1a. By default, all switch ports override inbound untagged or static access CoS values with 0.

c. *(Optional)* Instruct a connected appliance to handle CoS:

COS	N/A
IOS	(interface) **switchport priority extend {cos** *cos* **| none	trust}**

CoS trust can be extended to a Cisco IP Phone or other appliance that is connected to a Catalyst 3500XL switch port. The switch can instruct the appliance on how to trust CoS values from other devices connected to it. CoS trust can be **cos** (override the CoS in frames from other devices with value *cos*, 0 to 7), **none** (the appliance doesn't do anything with the CoS, the default), or **trust** (the appliance trusts and forwards the CoS in frames from other devices). See Chapter 14, "Voice," for more IP Phone configuration information.

2 Port queue scheduling:

— Catalyst 2900XL and 3500XL switches have a single ingress queue. This queue cannot be configured.

— These switches have 2q0t egress ports. Frames with a CoS 0 to 3 are assigned to the lower-priority queue (queue 1). Frames with CoS 4 to 7 are assigned to the higher-priority queue (queue 2).

— The egress queue scheduling is not configurable. As well, the congestion-avoidance thresholds are fixed at 100 percent.

All Other Catalyst Configuration

<table>
<tr><td>**NOTE**</td><td>Some configuration steps are applicable only to switches with a Layer 2 or Layer 3 switching engine. These are denoted by the following:

• **(Layer 2 only)**—Catalyst 6000 *without* a PFC or PFC2, or Catalyst 5000

• **(Layer 3 only)**—Catalyst 6000 *with* a PFC or PFC2, Catalyst 4000 with Supervisor III, or Catalyst 3550

The IOS commands shown often begin with the **mls** keyword. Although these commands are supported on the Catalyst 4000 Supervisor III IOS, the syntax is identical but the **mls** keyword is omitted.</td></tr>
</table>

1 Enable QoS functionality:

COS	`set qos enable	disable`
IOS	`(global)` **`mls qos`**

By default, QoS is disabled. All traffic is switched in a "pass-through" mode, where only "best effort" delivery is offered.

2 *(Layer 3 only)* Apply QoS to ports or VLANs:

COS	`set port qos` *mod/port* `{`**`port-based`** `|` **`vlan-based`**`}`
IOS	`(interface)` **`mls qos vlan-based`**

By default, QoS is **port-based** (**no mls qos vlan-based**) or applied to individual Layer 2 ports. QoS policies can be applied to a port's VLAN instead. When the application is changed, any port-based QoS policies are detached from the port.

3 Classify traffic based on a port.

TIP	A switch port can be configured to always trust selected inbound QoS parameters in this step. Otherwise, a QoS policy can be defined to trust QoS parameters conditionally. This is done in Step 6 (COS) and Step 8 (IOS). On an IOS switch, the trust state can be set only on physical switch ports and not on VLAN interfaces.

a. *(Optional)* Set the default ingress CoS value:

COS	`set port qos` *mod/ports* `cos` *cos-value*
IOS	`(interface)` `mls qos cos` *cos-value*

The CoS value is set to *cos-value* (0 to 7, default 0) for frames received on untrusted ports and for unmarked frames received on trusted ports (frames in the 802.1Q native VLAN).

b. *(Optional)* Don't trust any inbound information:

COS	`set port qos` *mod/port* `trust untrusted`
IOS	`(interface)` `no mls qos trust`

The inbound CoS, DSCP, and IP precedence values are not trusted. All of these values are reclassified based on any matching QoS policies or maps. If no policies are present, both the CoS and DSCP are set to 0.

When QoS is enabled, the default state for each port is **untrusted**.

c. *(Optional; Catalyst 6000 only)* Extend the trust boundary to an IP Phone.

— Set the phone access port trust:

COS	`set port qos` *mod/ports* `trust-ext {trusted	untrusted}`
IOS	N/A

A Cisco IP Phone has its own access layer switch port, where a PC can be connected. This port is **untrusted** by default, causing the CoS and IP precedence values for inbound frames to be set to 0. To allow the PC to mark its own packets with IP precedence values, set the mode to **trusted**.

— Set the default phone access port CoS value:

COS	`set port qos` *mod/ports* `cos-ext` *cos-value*
IOS	N/A

— When the phone's access port is set to untrusted mode, the CoS value for all inbound frames will be set to *cos-value* (0 to 7, default 0) by the phone. See Chapter 14 for more IP Phone information.

d. *(Optional; Layer 3 only)* Trust the inbound CoS value by default.

— Map CoS values to internal DSCP values:

COS	`set qos cos-dscp-map` *dscp1* ... *dscp8*
IOS	(global) `mls qos map cos-dscp` *dscp1* ... *dscp8*

The CoS values (0 to 7) from inbound frames are mapped to the corresponding 8 *dscp1* through *dscp8* values (0 to 63). The resulting internal DSCP values are then used by the QoS processes in the switch. The default mapping is as follows:

CoS	DSCP
0	0 ("best effort")
1	8 (AF class 1 "best effort")
2	16 (AF class 2 "best effort")
3	24 (AF class 3 "best effort")
4	32 (AF class 4 "best effort")
5	40 (EF "best effort")
6	48 (Internetwork control "best effort")
7	56 (Network control "best effort")

Note that no drop precedences are used by default. This gives DSCP values that differ slightly from those shown in Table 13-2 because the drop precedence bits are all 000. When you need to map CoS to DSCP values in a switch, alter the default mapping so that distinct drop precedences are used instead. To return to the default mapping, use the **clear qos cos-dscp-map** or **no mls qos map cos-dscp** command.

— Enable CoS trust on one or more ports:

COS	`set port qos` *mod/port* `trust trust-cos`
IOS	`(interface)` `mls qos trust cos`

Trust only the inbound CoS value, from which the ToS or DSCP values will be derived.

TIP

On 10/100 COS switch ports, the **trust-cos** state only enables the receive-drop thresholds. To apply a trust state to these ports, you must also define a matching **trust-cos** ACL. This is described in Step 6.

---

e. *(Optional; Layer 2 only)* Set a CoS value based on destination MAC address:

COS	`set qos mac-cos` *dest-mac vlan cos*
IOS	N/A

For all frames destined to the *dest-mac* MAC address on VLAN number *vlan*, you can set the CoS value to *cos* (0 to 7). This can be useful for reclassifying traffic to a specific destination host.

f. *(Optional; Layer 3 only)* Trust the inbound IP precedence value by default.

— Map IP precedence to internal DSCP values:

COS	`set qos ipprec-dscp-map` *dscp1 ... dscp8*
IOS	`(global)` `mls qos map ip-prec-dscp` *dscp1 ... dscp8*

The IP precedence values (0 through 7, or **routine**, **priority**, **immediate**, **flash**, **flash-override**, **critical**, **internet**, and **network**) from inbound packets are mapped to the corresponding 8 *dscp1* through *dscp8* values (0 to 63; defaults are 0, 8, 16, 24, 32, 40, 48, and 56). The resulting internal DSCP values are then used by QoS. The following table shows the default mapping.

Section 13-2

ToS	DSCP
0 (*routine*)	0 ("best effort")
1 (*priority*)	8 (AF class 1 "best effort")
2 (*immediate*)	16 (AF class 2 "best effort")
3 (*flash*)	24 (AF class 3 "best effort")
4 (*flash-override*)	32 (AF class 4 "best effort")
5 (*critical*)	40 (EF "best effort")
6 (*internet*)	48 (Internetwork control "best effort")
7 (*network*)	56 (Network control "best effort")

Note that no drop precedences are used by default. This gives DSCP values that differ slightly from those shown in Table 13-2 because the drop precedence bits are all 000. When you need to map CoS to DSCP values in a switch, alter the default mapping so that distinct drop precedences are used instead. To return to the default mapping, use the **clear qos ipprec-dscp-map** or **no mls qos map ip-prec-dscp** command.

— Enable IP precedence trust on one or more ports:

COS	`set port qos` *mod/port* `trust trust-ipprec`
IOS	`(interface) mls qos trust ip-precedence`

Trust only the inbound IP precedence value (ToS), from which the DSCP values will be derived.

g. *(Optional; Layer 3 only)* Trust the inbound DSCP value by default:

COS	`set port qos` *mod/port* `trust trust-dscp`
IOS	`(interface) mls qos trust dscp`

You can choose to trust only the inbound DSCP value, keeping the ToS and DSCP values intact. No other mapping derives the internal DSCP values.

h. *(Catalyst 3550 only)* Map DSCP values between QoS domains.

— Create a DSCP mutation map:

COS	N/A
IOS	`(global) mls qos map dscp-mutation` *dscp-mutation-name in-dscp* `to` *out-dscp*

When a switch port is at the boundary of a QoS domain, the inbound DSCP values can be mapped to a set of different DSCP values. The mutation map named *dscp-mutation-name* (text string) contains the inbound values *in-dscp* (up to 8 values 0 to 63 separated by spaces) that are mapped to corresponding new values *out-dscp* (up to 8 values 0 to 63 separated by spaces). The command can be repeated if more than eight DSCP values need to be mapped.

— Apply a mutation map to an interface:

COS	N/A
IOS	(interface) **mls qos dscp-mutation** *dscp-mutation-name*

By default, no DSCP mutation occurs on an interface. Otherwise, the mutation map named *dscp-mutation-name* (text string) is used. Each Gigabit Ethernet interface can have a different mutation map, whereas only one map can be used on each group of 12 10/100 Ethernet interfaces.

4 *(Optional)* Tune the ingress port queues.

TIP   By default, the ingress ports use the congestion avoidance and scheduling in Table 13-3.

Table 13-3   *Congestion Avoidance/Scheduling for Ingress Ports*

Queue Type	Threshold Number (Standard Queue) CoS: Percentage Tail-Drop or Low%/High% WRED							
	T1	T2	T3	T4	T5	T6	T7	T8
1q4t	0,1: 50%	2,3: 60%	4,5: 80%	6,7: 100%				
1p1q4t	0,1: 50%	2,3: 0%	4: 80%	6,7:100%				
1p1q8t	0: 40%/70%	1: 40%/70%	2: 50%/80%	3: 50%/80%	4: 60%/90%	6: 60%/90%	7: 70%/100%	

TIP   All port types assign frames with CoS 5 to their strict-priority queues (except 1q4t, which has none). The 1p1q0t ports have no thresholds; all frames with CoS values other than 5 are assigned to the standard queue and dropped when the queue is 100 percent full.

Section 13-2

a. *(Optional)* Tune the ingress queue ratio:

COS	`set qos rxq-ratio` *port-type queue1 queue2*
IOS	(interface) `rcv-queue queue-limit` *queue1 queue2*

CAUTION   When using this command, all ports cycle through a link-down and link-up process. In a production network, this causes a network outage while the ports are down and while they progress through the spanning-tree states again.

By default, the standard queue (queue 1) receives 80 percent of the available space, whereas the strict-priority queue (queue 2) receives 20 percent of the space. If QoS is disabled, the standard queue receives 100 percent of the space.

Estimate the ratio of normal and priority traffic coming into a switch port. Use the *queue1* and *queue2* values to set the percentage (1 to 99) for the two receive queues. These values must total 100 percent.

b. *(Optional)* Set the congestion-avoidance thresholds.

— *(Optional)* Use standard tail-drop receive queues:

COS	`set qos drop-threshold` *port-type* `rx queue` *queue-id threshold-percent-1 ... threshold-percent-n*
IOS	(interface) `rcv-queue threshold` *queue-id threshold-percent-1 ... threshold-percent-n* -OR- (interface) `wrr-queue threshold` *queue-id threshold-percent-1 ... threshold-percent-n*

For most switch port receive queues (1q4t, 1p1q4t, 2q2t, and 1p1q0t), standard tail-drop congestion-avoidance can be used. By default, frames with a CoS 5 are assigned to the strict-priority queue. All other frames are assigned to the standard queue.

The number of queue thresholds available is the number preceding the **t** in the queue type. For each threshold, you can assign the percentage of the buffer that is available to receive frames. The *threshold-percentage-n* values (1 to 100 percent) are given in sequential order. When the buffer rises above the threshold level, new inbound frames are dropped.

TIP On an IOS switch, the 1q4t queue is serviced by a *weighted round-robin* (WRR) algorithm. Therefore, the thresholds must be set with the **wrr-queue threshold** command.

— *(Optional)* Use *weighted random early detection* (WRED) receive queues:

COS	**set qos wred** *port-type* **queue** *queue-id* [*thr1-min:*] *thr1-max* [*thr2-min:*] *thr2-max*...
IOS	(interface) **rcv-queue random-detect min-threshold** *queue-id* *thr1-min* *thr2-min* ...
	(interface) **rcv-queue random-detect max-threshold** *queue-id* *thr1-max* *thr2-max* ...

For 1p1q8t port types, WRED is used. The *queue-id* is **1** (standard queue) or **2** (priority queue). Two limits are used for each of the eight queue thresholds: a minimum *thr1-min* (1 to 100 percent) and a maximum *thr1-max* (1 to 100 percent).

When the buffer is below the minimum level, no frames are dropped. As the buffer rises above the minimum but below the maximum, the chances that frames will be dropped increases. Above the maximum level, all frames are dropped.

TIP The IOS 1p1q8t receive queues also require the **wrr-queue random-detect** *queue-id* command to enable the WRED drop thresholds.

c. *(Optional)* Tune ingress scheduling and congestion avoidance:

COS	**set qos map** *port-type* **rx** *queue-id* *threshold-id* **cos** *cos-list*
IOS	(interface) **rcv-queue cos-map** *queue-id* *threshold-id* *cos-list* -OR-
	(interface) **wrr-queue cos-map** *queue-id* *threshold-id* *cos-list*

If the inbound CoS values are trusted from Step 3c or a QoS policy, frames with certain CoS values can be mapped and sent to specific ingress queues and thresholds. The *cos-list* can be a single value (0 to 7), multiple values separated by commas, or a hyphenated range of values. This mapping is set for all switch ports (COS switch) or per-interface (IOS switch).

The *port-type* is the type of queuing available, as seen by the **show port capabilities** (COS) or **show queueing interface** (IOS) command. The *queue-id* (**1** for standard or **2** for strict priority) and the *threshold-id* (1 to 4) identify the specific queue and threshold where inbound frames will be queued. The range of values is dependent upon the switch port hardware.

By default when QoS is enabled, CoS 0 through 7 are mapped to the standard ingress queue (queue 1). If a strict-priority queue (queue 2) is supported (queue type begins with **1p...**), CoS 5 is mapped there.

5 *(Optional; Layer 3 only)* Create a policer to control inbound packet flow.

a. *(Optional)* Use an aggregate policer:

COS	**set qos policer aggregate** *aggregate_name* **rate** *rate* **burst** *burst* {**drop** | **policed-dscp**} [**erate** *peak-rate* [**policed-dscp**]]
IOS	(global) **mls qos aggregate-policer** *aggregate-name rate burst* [*max-burst*] [**pir** *peak-rate*] [**conform-action** *action*] [**exceed-action** *action*] [**violate-action** *action*]

On a COS switch, the policer is defined by an average or CIR *rate* (0 or 32 to 8,000,000 in kbps), and is allowed to exceed this rate by a *burst* amount (1 to 32,000 in Kb). With a PFC2 module, you can also specify a PIR with the **erate** keyword and *peak-rate* (0 or 32 to 8,000,000 in kbps).

On an IOS switch, set the CIR *rate* (32,000 to 4,000,000,000 in bps) and the *burst* size (1000 to 512,000,000 bytes). With a PFC2 module, you can also specify a PIR with the **pir** keyword and a *peak-rate* (32,000 to 4,000,000,000 in bps) and a maximum burst size *max-burst* (1000 to 512,000,000 bytes).

TIP Notice that the COS and IOS switches have different concepts of *rate* and *burst* units. COS switches expect rates to be given as kilobits per second, and burst sizes in kilobits. IOS switches expect rates as bits per second, and burst sizes in bytes.

The policer can take the following actions, based on how it measures the traffic rate:

— **Conforming (in-profile, less than the CIR)**—Forwarded by default. An IOS switch allows a **conform-action** to be taken instead: **drop** (the frame is dropped and not forwarded), **policed-dscp-transmit** (the internal DSCP value is marked down by a mapping), or **transmit** (the frame is forwarded as is).

— **Exceeding (out-of-profile, exceeds the CIR)**—Dropped by
default. A COS switch allows **drop** (frame is not forwarded) or
police-dscp (the internal DSCP value is marked down by a
mapping). An IOS switch allows an **exceed-action** to be taken:
drop (the frame is dropped and not forwarded), **policed-dscp-transmit** (the internal DSCP value is marked down by a mapping),
or **transmit** (the frame is forwarded as is).

— **Violating (out-of-profile, exceeds the PIR)**—By default, the
action is the same as the Exceeding action. A COS switch can either
forward the frame or **police-dscp** (the internal DSCP value is
marked down by a mapping). An IOS switch allows a **violate-action** to be taken: **drop** (the frame is dropped and not forwarded),
policed-dscp-transmit (the internal DSCP value is marked down
by a mapping), or **transmit** (the frame is forwarded as is).

b. *(Optional)* Use a microflow policer:

COS	`set qos policer microflow` *microflow-name* `rate` *rate* `burst` *burst* `{drop	policed-dscp}`
IOS	See Step 8d, bullet two

On a COS switch, the policer is defined by an average or CIR *rate* (0 or 32 to 8000000
in kbps), and is allowed to exceed this rate by a *burst* amount (1 to 32000 in Kb).

TIP   On a Catalyst 6000 PFC2, you must enable microflow policing of bridged traffic to perform
any type of microflow policing. This is done with the command in Step 5c.

On an IOS switch, microflow policers are configured as a part of a policy map. See
Step 8d for more information.

The policer can take the following actions, based on how it measures the traffic rate:

— **Conforming (in-profile, less than the CIR)**—Forwarded by
default.

— **Exceeding (out-of-profile, exceeds the CIR)**—Dropped by
default. A COS switch allows **drop** (frame is not forwarded) or
police-dscp (the internal DSCP value is marked down by a
mapping).

| TIP | The *rate* value you specify for a CIR might be different from the value that is actually used. The QoS hardware uses values that are the specified *rate* rounded to the nearest multiple of the rate granularity as shown in Table 13-4. |

Table 13-4 *Granularity of CIR Rate Values*

CIR/PIR *rate* Range	Granularity of Actual Value
1–1,048,576 (1 mbps)	32,768 (32 kbps)
1,048,577–2,097,152 (2 mbps)	65,536 (64 kbps)
2,097,153–4,194,304 (4 mbps)	131,072 (128 kbps)
4,194,305–8,388,608 (8 mbps)	262,144 (256 kbps)
8,388,609–1,677,216 (16 mbps)	524,288 (512 kbps)
1,677,217–33,554,432 (32 mbps)	1,048,576 (1 mbps)
33,554,433–67,108,864 (64 mbps)	2,097,152 (2 mbps)
67,108,865–134,217,728 (128 mbps)	4,194,304 (4 mbps)
134,217,729–268,435,456 (256 mbps)	8,388,608 (8 mbps)
268,435,457–536,870,912 (512 mbps)	1,677,216 (16 mbps)
536,870,913–1,073,741,824 (1 gbps)	33,554,432 (32 mbps)
1,073,741,825–2,147,483,648 (2 gbps)	67,108,864 (64 mbps)
2,147,483,649–4,294,967,296 (4 gbps)	134,217,728 (128 mbps)
4,294,967,297–8,589,934,592 (8 gbps)	268,435,456 (256 mbps)

As a rule of thumb, the *burst* size should be set to 32 kilobits or greater. Because the *burst* size operates the token bucket, use caution when choosing a value. Packets that arrive and cause the token bucket to exceed the burst value can potentially be dropped.

Therefore, you should choose a *burst* value that is greater than the *rate* value divided by 4000 and also greater than the size of the largest frame you expect to receive. If you choose a *burst* that is too small, frames that are larger than the burst value will be out-of-profile, and can be dropped. Be aware that the QoS hardware uses values that are the specified *burst* rounded to the nearest multiple of the burst granularity as shown in Table 13-5.

Table 13-5 *Granularity of CIR Burst Values*

CIR/PIR *burst* Range	Granularity of Actual Value
1–32,768 (32 Kb)	1024 (1 Kb)
32,769–65,536 (64 Kb)	2048 (2 Kb)
65,537–131,072 (128 Kb)	4096 (4 Kb)

Table 13-5 *Granularity of CIR Burst Values (Continued)*

CIR/PIR *burst* Range	Granularity of Actual Value
131,073–262,144 (256 Kb)	8192 (8 Kb)
262,145–524,288 (512 Kb)	16,384 (16 Kb)
524,289–1,048,576 (1 Mb)	32,768 (32 Kb)
1,048,577–2,097,152 (2 Mb)	65,536 (64 Kb)
2,097,153–4,194,304 (4 Mb)	131,072 (128 Kb)
4,194,305–8,388,608 (8 Mb)	262,144 (256 Kb)
8,388,609–16,777,216 (16 Mb)	524,288 (512 Kb)
16,777,217–33,554,432 (32 Mb)	1,048,576 (1 Mb)
33,554,433–67,108,864 (64 Mb)	2,097,152 (2 Mb)
67,108,865–134,217,728 (128 Mb)	4,194,304 (4 Mb)
134,217,729–268,435,456 (256 Mb)	8,388,608 (8 Mb)
268,435,457–536,870,912 (512 Mb)	16,777,216 (16 Mb)

c. *(Optional; Layer 3 only)* Allow microflow policing of bridged traffic:

COS	`set qos bridged-microflow-policing {enable	disable}` *vlan-list*
IOS	(interface) `mls qos bridged`

Microflow policing is normally allowed only on Layer 3 switched traffic or on traffic that is switched between VLANs. However, you can use microflow policers for bridged (intra-VLAN) traffic on specific VLANs. Specify a *vlan-list* (COS) or use this command on the VLAN interfaces.

TIP   You must use this command on a PFC2 to perform any type of microflow policing.

d. *(Optional)* Define a DSCP markdown mapping:

COS	`set qos policed-dscp-map [normal	excess]` *internal-dscp:policed-dscp...*
IOS	(global) `mls qos map policed-dscp` *internal-dscp* `to` *policed-dscp*

The internal DSCP values *internal-dscp* are marked down to *policed-dscp* values. Internal DSCP values can be specified as single values, multiple values separated by commas, or as a hyphenated range. A COS switch requires a colon (:) between the internal and policed DSCP values, whereas an IOS switch requires the **to** keyword. More mappings can be given on a COS switch by separating them with spaces, and on an IOS switch by repeating this command.

A PFC2 module allows mappings for marking down DSCP values for **normal** (out-of-profile, above the CIR) or **excess** (in-violation, above the PIR) policed traffic.

6 *(Layer 3 only)* Define matching traffic for a QoS policy.

COS switches define the actual QoS policy by grouping **set qos acl** commands that have common ACL names. On IOS switches, the access lists are defined first, and QoS policies are defined separately.

In the following steps, source and destination addresses are given by *source-ip* and *destination-ip*, along with masks for wildcard matching (0-bit matches, 1-bit is wildcard). If any address is to be matched, you can replace the address and mask fields with the keyword **any**. If a specific host address is to be matched, you can replace the address and mask fields with the keyword **host** followed by its IP address.

On a COS switch, access lists are called *access control entries* (ACEs), and are held in an edit buffer as they are entered. Each ACE is numbered with an index. As you enter an ACE, you can control its relative location by using the **before** (insert the ACE before the one at *editbuffer-index*) or **modify** (replace the ACE at *editbuffer-index*) keywords.

COS switches also allow microflow or aggregate policers to be assigned to the ACE in this step. IOS switches assign policers to the QoS policies in Step 5.

For a COS switch, the QoS values of a frame or packet can also be set by the access list. One of the keywords **dscp** (set the DSCP value to **dscp**), **trust-cos** (derive DSCP from the frame's CoS value), **trust-ipprec** (derive DSCP from the packet's IP precedence value), or **trust-dscp** (use the existing DSCP value) can be used.

The **precedence** keyword can be used to match the IP precedence value, given as a number (0 to 7) or as a text string. Available values are **critical** (5), **flash** (3), **flash-override** (4), **immediate** (2), **internet** (6), **network** (7), **priority** (1), and **routine** (0).

The **dscp-field** (or IOS **dscp**) keyword can be used to match the DSCP bits contained in the DS byte of an IP packet. The *dscp* value can be given as a number (6 bits, 0 to 63) or as a text string name. Available names are **default** (000000), **ef** (101110), (Assured Forwarding, AF) **af11** (001010), **af12** (001100), **af13** (001110), **af21** (010010), **af22** (010100), **af23** (010110), **af31** (011010), **af32** (011100), **af33** (011110), **af41** (100010), **af42** (100100),

af43 (100110), (Class Selector, CS) **cs1** (precedence 1, 001000), **cs2** (precedence 2, 010000), **cs3** (precedence 3, 011000), **cs4** (precedence 4, 100000), **cs5** (precedence 5, 101000), **cs6** (precedence 6, 110000), and **cs7** (precedence 7, 111000).

An IOS switch also allows the **tos** keyword to match the ToS level (0 to 15). Available values are **max-reliability**, **max-throughput**, **min-delay**, **min-monetary-cost**, and **normal**.

a. *(Optional)* Match IP traffic by source address:

COS	`set qos acl ip` `acl-name` `{dscp` `dscp` `| trust-cos` `| trust-ipprec |` `trust-dscp}` `[microflow` `microflow-name]` `[aggregate` `aggregate-name]` `source-ip` `source-mask` `[precedence` `precedence` `| dscp-field` `dscp]` `[before` `editbuffer-index` `| modify` `editbuffer-index]`
IOS	(global) `access-list` `acc-list-number` `{permit` `| deny}` `ip` `source-ip` `source-mask` -OR- (global) `ip access-list standard` `acl-name` (access-list) `{permit` `| deny}` `source-ip` `[source-mask]`

The access list is referenced by its name *acl-name* (text string) or by its number *acc-list-number* (1 to 99 or 1300 to 1999).

b. *(Optional)* Match IP traffic by source, destination, and port number:

COS	`set qos acl ip` `acc-list` `{dscp` `dscp` `| trust-cos` `| trust-ipprec |` `trust-dscp}` `[microflow` `microflow-name]` `[aggregate` `aggregate-name]` `{tcp` `| udp}` `source-ip` `source-mask` `[operator` `[source-port]]` `destination-ip` `destination-mask` `[operator` `[dest-port]]` `[established]` `[precedence` `precedence` `| dscp-field` `dscp]` `[before` `editbuffer-index` `| modify` `editbuffer-index]`
IOS	(global) `access-list` `acc-list` `{permit` `| deny}` `protocol` `source-ip` `source-mask` `[operator` `[source-port]]` `destination-ip` `destination-mask` `[operator` `[dest-port]]` `[precedence` `precedence]` `[dscp` `dscp]` `[tos` `tos]` -OR- (global) `ip access-list extended` `acl-name` (access-list) `{permit` `| deny}` `protocol` `source-ip` `source-mask` `[operator` `[source-port]]` `destination-ip` `destination-mask` `[operator` `[dest-port]]` `[precedence` `precedence]` `[dscp` `dscp]` `[tos` `tos]`

The access list is referenced by its name *acl-name* (text string) or by its number *acc-list-number* (100 to 199 or 2000 to 2699).

An IP *protocol* can be specified. The protocol can be one of **ip** (any IP protocol), **tcp**, **udp**, **eigrp** (EIGRP routing protocol), **gre** (Generic Routing Encapsulation), **icmp** (Internet Control Message Protocol), **igmp** (Internet Group Management Protocol), **igrp** (IGRP routing protocol), **ipinip** (IP-in-IP tunnel), **nos**, **ospf** (OSPF routing protocol), or an IP protocol number (0 to 255).

An **operator** can be specified to determine how the source and destination port numbers are to be matched. You can use the operators **lt** (less than), **gt** (greater than), **eq** (equal to), **neq** (not equal to), or **range** (within a range given by two port number values). The source and destination ports are given as a number (0 to 65535) or as a text string port name.

Available TCP names are **bgp**, **chargen**, **daytime**, **discard**, **domain**, **echo**, **finger**, **ftp**, **ftp-data**, **gopher**, **hostname**, **irc**, **klogin**, **kshell**, **lpd**, **nntp**, **pop2**, **pop3**, **smtp**, **sunrpc**, **syslog**, **tacacs-ds**, **talk**, **telnet**, **time**, **uucp**, **whois**, and **www**. In addition, you can use the **established** keyword to match packets from established connections or packets that have either the RST or ACK bits set.

Available UDP names are **biff**, **bootpc**, **bootps**, **discard**, **dns**, **dnsix**, **echo**, **mobile-ip**, **nameserver**, **netbios-dgm**, **netbios-ns**, **ntp**, **rip**, **snmp**, **snmptrap**, **sunrpc**, **syslog**, **tacacs-ds**, **talk**, **tftp**, **time**, **who**, and **xdmcp**.

c. *(Optional)* Match ICMP traffic:

COS	**set qos acl ip** *acl-name* {**dscp** *dscp* | **trust-cos** | **trust-ipprec** | **trust-dscp**} [**microflow** *microflow-name*] [**aggregate** *aggregate-name*] **icmp** *source-ip source-mask destination-ip destination-mask* [*icmp-type* [*icmp-code*] | *icmp-message*] [**precedence** *precedence* | **dscp-field** *dscp*] [**before** *editbuffer-index* | **modify** *editbuffer-index*]
IOS	(global) **access-list** *acc-list* {**permit** | **deny**} **icmp** *source-ip source-mask destination-ip destination-mask* [*icmp-type* [*icmp-code*] | *icmp-message*] [**precedence** *precedence*] [**dscp** *dscp*] [**tos** *tos*]
	-OR-
	(global) **ip access-list extended** *acl-name*
	(access-list) {**permit** | **deny**} **icmp** *source-ip source-mask destination-ip destination-mask* [*icmp-type* [*icmp-code*] | *icmp-message*] [**precedence** *precedence*] [**dscp** *dscp*] [**tos** *tos*]

The access list is referenced by its name *acl-name* (text string) or by its number *acc-list-number* (100 to 199 or 2000 to 2699).

One or more of *icmp-type*, *icmp-type icmp-code*, or *icmp-message* can be added to the command line. The *icmp-type* field is the ICMP message type (0 to 15), and the *icmp-code* is an optional ICMP message code (0 to 255). The *icmp-message* field is a text string name, chosen from the following **administratively-prohibited**, **alternate-address**, **conversion-error**, **dod-host-prohibited**, **dod-net-prohibited**, **echo**, **echo-reply**, **general-parameter-problem**, **host-isolated**, **host-precedence-unreachable**, **host-redirect**, **host-tos-redirect**, **host-tos-unreachable**, **host-unknown**, **host-unreachable**, **information-reply**, **information-request**, **mask-reply**, **mask-request**,

mobile-redirect, **net-redirect**, **net-tos-redirect**, **net-tos-unreachable**, **net-unreachable**, **network-unknown**, **no-room-for-option**, **option-missing**, **packet-too-big**, **parameter-problem**, **port-unreachable**, **precedence-unreachable**, **protocol-unreachable**, **reassembly-timeout**, **redirect**, **router-advertisement**, **router-solicitation**, **source-quench**, **source-route-failed**, **time-exceeded**, **timestamp-reply**, **timestamp-request**, **traceroute**, **ttl-exceeded**, and **unreachable**.

d. *(Optional)* Match IGMP traffic:

COS	**set qos acl ip** *acl-name* {**dscp** *dscp* | **trust-cos** | **trust-ipprec** | **trust-dscp**} [**microflow** *microflow-name*] [**aggregate** *aggregate-name*] **igmp** *source-ip source-mask destination-ip destination-mask* [*igmp-type*] [**precedence** *precedence* | **dscp-field** *dscp*] [**before** *editbuffer-index* | **modify** *editbuffer-index*]
IOS	(global) **access-list** *acc-list* {**permit** | **deny**} **igmp** *source-ip source-mask destination-ip destination-mask* [*igmp-type*] [**precedence** *precedence*] [**dscp** *dscp*] [**tos** *tos*] -OR- (global) **ip access-list extended** *acl-name* (access-list) {**permit** | **deny**} **igmp** *source-ip source-mask destination-ip destination-mask* [*igmp-type*] [**precedence** *precedence*] [**dscp** *dscp*] [**tos** *tos*]

The access list is referenced by its name *acl-name* (text string) or by its number *acc-list-number* (100 to 199 or 2000 to 2699).

When the protocol is **igmp**, an additional IGMP message type field can be added for further filtering, chosen from the following: **dvmrp**, **host-query**, **host-report**, **pim**, and **trace**.

e. *(Optional)* Match IPX traffic:

COS	**set qos acl ipx** *acl-name* {**dscp** *dscp* | **trust-cos**} [**aggregate** *aggregate-name*] *protocol source-network* [*dest-net*.[*dest-node*] [[*dest-net-mask*.]*dest-node-mask*] [**before** *editbuffer-index* | **modify** *editbuffer_index*]
IOS	(global) **access-list** *access-list-number* {**deny** | **permit**} *source-network*[.*source-node*[*source-node-mask*]] [*destination-network*[.*destination-node* [*destination-node-mask*]]] -OR- (global) **ipx access-list standard** *acl-name* (access-list) {**permit** | **deny**} *source-network*[.*source-node* [*source-node-mask*]] [*destination-network*[.*destination-node* [*destination-node-mask*]]]

The access list is referenced by its name *acl-name* (text string) or by its number *acc-list-number* (800 to 899). Addresses are defined by *source-network* and *destination-network* (an 8-digit hex number, 1 to FFFFFFFE; -1 denotes all networks), *source-node* and *destination-node* (48-bit MAC address in dotted-triplet format), and *source-node-mask* and *destination-node-mask* (48-bit masks in dotted-triplet format; a 1 bit ignores or acts like a wildcard).

f. *(Optional)* Match MAC layer traffic:

COS	`set qos acl mac` *acl-name* `{dscp` *dscp* `| trust-cos}` `[aggregate` *aggregate-name*`]` `{`*source-mac source-mask* `| any}` `{`*dest-mac_dest-mask* `| any}` `[`*ether-type*`]` `[before` *editbuffer-index* `| modify` *editbuffer-index*`]`
IOS	(global) `mac access-list extended` *acl-name*
	(access-list) `{permit	deny}` `{`*source-mac source-mask* `| any}` `{`*dest-mac_dest-mask* `| any}` *ether-type*

The access list is referenced by its name *acl-name* (text string).

Both source and destination MAC addresses (*source* and *destination*) and masks (*source-mask* and *destination-mask*) are specified for matching. The addresses are 48-bit MAC addresses written as three groups of four hex digits separated by dots (that is, 0000.1111.2222). The mask fields specify masks to use for matching multiple addresses. A 1 bit in the mask causes that address bit to be ignored.

For COS switches, the *ether-type* field can be one of these values: **Ethertalk** (0x809b), **AARP** (0x8053), **dec-mop-dump** (0x6001), **dec-mop-remote-console** (0x6002), **dec-phase-iv** (0x6003), **dec-lat** (0x6004), **dec-diagnostic-protocol** (0x6005), **dec-lavc-sca** (0x6007), **dec-amber** (0x6008), **dec-mumps** (0x6009), **dec-lanbridge** (0x8038), **dec-dsm** (0x8039), **dec-netbios** (0x8040), **dec-msdos** (0x8041), **banyan-vines-echo** (0x0baf), **xerox-ns-idp** (0x0600), and **xerox-address-translation** (0x0601).

For IOS switches, the *ether-type* field can be one of these values: **aarp** (0x80f3), **amber** (0x6008), **appletalk** (0x809b), **diagnostic** (0x6005), **decnet-iv** (0x6003), **dec-spanning** (0x8038), **dsm** (0x8039), **etype-6000** (0x6000), **etype-8042** (0x8042), **lat** (0x6004), **lavc-acm** (0x6007), **mop-console** (0x6002), **mop-dump** (0X6001), **msdos** (0X8041), **mumps** (0x6009), **netbios** (0x8040), **vines-ip** (0x0bad), **vines-echo** (0x0baf), or **xns-idp** (0x0600).

g. *(COS only; optional)* Create default matching conditions.

TIP   When QoS is first enabled, the default action is to deliver traffic in a "best effort" fashion. This is done by setting the internal DSCP and CoS values to 0. No policing is configured or performed.

— *(Optional)* Set the IP default action:

COS	set qos acl default-action ip {dscp *dscp* | trust-cos | trust-ipprec | trust-dscp} [microflow *microflow-name*] [aggregate *aggregate-name*]
IOS	N/A

If no other IP ACE matches a frame, the internal DSCP value is derived as **dscp** (DSCP set to *dscp*), **trust-cos** (DSCP mapped from inbound CoS), **trust-ipprec** (DSCP mapped from inbound IP precedence), or **trust-dscp** (inbound DSCP is used). Default policers can be given with **microflow** and **aggregate**.

— *(Optional)* Set the IPX default action:

COS	set qos acl default-action ipx {dscp *dscp* | trust-cos} [microflow *microflow-name*] [aggregate *aggregate-name*]
IOS	N/A

If no other IPX ACE matches a frame, the internal DSCP value is derived as **dscp** (DSCP set to *dscp*) or **trust-cos** (DSCP mapped from inbound CoS). Default policers can be given with **microflow** and **aggregate**.

— *(Optional)* Set the MAC default action:

COS	set qos acl default-action mac {dscp *dscp* | trust-cos} [microflow *microflow-name*] [aggregate *aggregate-name*]
IOS	N/A

If no other MAC ACE matches a frame, the internal DSCP value is derived as **dscp** (DSCP set to *dscp*) or **trust-cos** (DSCP mapped from inbound CoS). Default policers can be given with **microflow** and **aggregate**.

7 *(IOS only)* Group matching traffic into a class map.

a. Create the class map:

COS	N/A
IOS	(global) **class-map** *class-name* [match-all | match-any]

For the class map *class-name* (text string), one or more matching conditions is specified. You can match against all of them (**match-all**, the default) or against any of them (**match-any**).

b. *(Optional)* Use an access list for matching candidate traffic:

COS	N/A
IOS	(cmap) **match access-group name** *acc-list*

The class map matches traffic that is permitted by the access list *acc-list* (named or numbered). This access list is configured in Step 6.

c. *(Optional)* Match against IP precedence values:

COS	N/A
IOS	(cmap) **match ip precedence** *ipprec1* [*...ipprecN*]

Up to eight IP precedence *ipprec* (0 to 7) values can be given to match against. Separate the values by spaces. Available values are **critical** (5), **flash** (3), **flash-override** (4), **immediate** (2), **internet** (6), **network** (7), **priority** (1), and **routine** (0).

d. *(Optional)* Match against DSCP values:

COS	N/A
IOS	(cmap) **match ip dscp** *dscp1* [*...dscpN*]

Up to eight DSCP values can be given to match against. These values should be separated by spaces.

The *dscp* values can be given as a number (6 bits, 0 to 63) or as a text string name. Available names are **default** (000000), **ef** (Express Forwarding, EF, 101110), (Assured Forwarding, AF) **af11** (001010), **af12** (001100), **af13** (001110), **af21** (010010), **af22** (010100), **af23** (010110), **af31** (011010), **af32** (011100), **af33** (011110), **af41** (100010), **af42** (100100), **af43** (100110), (Class Selector, CS) **cs1** (precedence 1, 001000), **cs2** (precedence 2, 010000), **cs3** (precedence 3, 011000), **cs4** (precedence 4, 100000), **cs5** (precedence 5, 101000), **cs6** (precedence 6, 110000), and **cs7** (precedence 7, 111000).

8 *(IOS only)* Define a QoS policy.

a. Create the policy:

COS	N/A
IOS	(global) **policy-map** *policy-name*

b. Use one or more class maps to find matching traffic.

— *(Optional)* Use an existing class map:

COS	N/A
IOS	(pmap) **class** *class-name*

If a class map is already defined, it can be referenced by its name *class-name* (text string).

— *(Optional)* Create a new class map:

COS	N/A
IOS	(pmap) **class** *class-name* {**access-group** *acc-list* | **dscp** *dscp1* [*…dscpN*] | **precedence** *ipprec1* [*…ipprecN*]}

A class map can also be created while the policy is being defined. This offers a more efficient way to define class maps.

c. *(Optional)* Set the QoS trust state:

COS	N/A
IOS	(pmap-class) **trust** {**cos** | **dscp** | **ip-precedence**}

IOS switches can selectively choose the source for the internal DSCP values from ingress traffic. For frames matching the class map, the DSCP value can be derived from **cos** (using the CoS-to-DSCP mapping), **dscp** (using the inbound DSCP as is), or **ip-precedence** (using the ToS-to-DSCP mapping).

d. Use a policer to control the bandwidth of matching traffic.

— *(Optional)* Use a named aggregate policer:

COS	N/A
IOS	(pmap-class) **police aggregate** *policer-name*

— The policer named *policer-name* (text string) controls the aggregate traffic from all the ingress ports to which it is assigned.

— *(Optional)* Define a per-interface policer for controlling one interface:

COS	N/A
IOS	(pmap-class) **police** [**aggregate** *policer-name*] [**flow**] *rate burst* [*max-burst*] [**pir** *peak-rate*] [**conform-action** *action*] [**exceed-action** *action*] [**violate-action** *action*]

When a policer is defined as a part of the policy, it operates only on the aggregate traffic from the ingress port where the policy is assigned. Use the **aggregate** keyword to define an aggregate policer or the **flow** keyword to define a microflow policer.

The Catalyst 3550 allows only an **exceed-action** to be specified.

TIP

To use microflow policers on an IOS switch, you must first enable the microflow functionality with the **mls qos flow-policing** command. In addition, microflow policing of bridged traffic must also be enabled on a PFC2 or to police multicast traffic. This is done with the **mls qos bridged** VLAN interface command.

Set the CIR *rate* (32,000 to 4,000,000,000 in bps) and the *burst* size (1000 to 512,000,000 bytes). With a PFC2 module, you can also specify a PIR with the **pir** keyword and a *peak-rate* (32,000 to 4,000,000,000 in bps) and a maximum burst size *max-burst* (1000 to 512,000,000 bytes).

TIP

The *rate* value you specify for a CIR or PIR might differ from the value that is actually used. See the *rate* and *burst* ranges and actual granularities shown in Step 5b.

As a rule of thumb, the *burst* size should be set to 32 kilobits (32 Kb for COS, 4096 bytes for IOS) or greater. Because the *burst* size operates the token bucket, use caution when choosing a value. Packets that arrive and cause the token bucket to exceed the burst value can potentially be dropped.

Therefore, choose a *burst* value that is greater than the *rate* value divided by 4000 and also greater than the size of the largest frame you expect to receive. If you choose a *burst* that is too small, frames that are larger than the burst value will be out-of-profile and can be dropped.

The policer can take the following actions, based on how it measures the traffic rate:

— **Conforming (in-profile, less than the CIR)**—Forwarded by default. An IOS switch allows a **conform-action** to be taken instead: **drop** (the frame is dropped and not forwarded), **set-dscp-transmit** *new-dscp* (the DSCP is set to *new-dscp*), **set-prec-transmit** *new-precedence* (the IP precedence is set to *new-precedence*) or **transmit** (the frame is forwarded as is).

— **Exceeding (out-of-profile, exceeds the CIR)**—Dropped by default. An IOS switch allows an **exceed-action** to be taken: **drop** (the frame is dropped and not forwarded), **policed-dscp-transmit** (the internal DSCP value is marked down by a mapping), or **transmit** (the frame is forwarded as is).

— **Violating (out-of-profile, exceeds the PIR)**—By default, the action is the same as the Exceeding action. An IOS switch allows a **violate-action** to be taken: **drop** (the frame is dropped and not forwarded), **policed-dscp-transmit** (the internal DSCP value is marked down by a mapping), or **transmit** (the frame is forwarded as is).

9 Apply a policy to a switch port or VLAN.

a. *(Layer 3 COS only)* Finalize the policy ACE:

COS	**commit qos acl** {*acl-name* | **all**}
IOS	N/A

ACE entries are stored in a temporary edit buffer as they are entered. After editing an ACE, you must commit either a specific ACE as *acl-name* (text string) or **all** (all ACEs) to NVRAM. As well, committed ACEs are compiled and written out to the switch hardware for use.

TIP   If an ACE was previously attached to a switch port, any changes to it go immediately into effect when it is committed again. To discard an uncommitted ACE from the edit buffer, use the **rollback qos acl** {*acl-name* \| **all**} command.

To amend a committed ACE, find the ACE index within the ACL by using the **show qos acl info** *acl-name* command. Then use the **clear qos acl** *acl-name index* command to remove the ACE at *index*. Add additional ACE entries if needed, and recompile the ACL with the **commit qos acl** command in this step.

b. Attach the policy to the port:

COS	**set qos acl map** *acl-name* {*mod/port* | *vlan*}
IOS	(interface) **service-policy input** *policy-name*

The policy (COS: *acl-name*; IOS: *policy-name*) is attached to the switch port for immediate use on ingress traffic. If the policy will be used for VLAN QoS, it is attached to the VLAN number *vlan* or the VLAN interface.

10 *(Optional)* Tune the egress port queues.

TIP

By default, the egress ports use the congestion avoidance and scheduling as listed in Table 13-6.

Table 13-6   *Queue Scheduling and Congestion-Avoidance Thresholds*

Queue Type	Threshold Number CoS: Percentage Tail-Drop or Low%/High% WRED					
	Standard Queue 1		Standard Queue 2		Standard Queue 3	
	T1	T2	T1	T2	T1	T2
2q2t	0,1: 80%	2,3: 100%	4,5: 80%	6,7: 100%		
1p2q2t	0,1: 50%	2,3: 60%	4: 80%	6,7: 100%		
1p3q1t	0,1: 100%		2,3,4: 100%		6,7: 100%	
1p2q1t	0,1,2,3: 70%/100%		4,6,7: 70%/100%			

All port types assign frames with CoS 5 to their strict-priority queues (except 2q2t, which has none).

a. *(Optional)* Tune the egress queue ratio:

COS	**set qos txq-ratio** *port-type queue1 queue2* [*queue3*] *queue-priority*
IOS	(interface) **wrr-queue queue-limit** *queue1 queue2* [*queue3*] *queue-priority*

CAUTION   When this command is used, all ports cycle through a link-down and link-up process.

Estimate the ratio of normal (low and high priority) and strict-priority traffic to the total amount of traffic going out of a switch port. Use the *queue1*, *queue2*, and optionally *queue3* values to set the percentages (1 to 100) for the standard transmit queues. Use the *queue-priority* value to set the percentage (1 to 100) of the strict-priority queue. These values must total 100 percent.

Table 13-7 lists how the switch port buffers are divided by default.

Table 13-7 *Switch Port Buffer Division Defaults*

Port Type	Low Priority	Medium Priority	High Priority	Strict Priority
2q2t	80% (queue1)	N/A	20% (queue2)	N/A
1p2q2t	70% (queue1)	N/A	15% (queue2)	15% (queue3)
1p3q1t	25% (queue1)	25% (queue2)	25% (queue3)	25% (queue4)
1p2q1t	50% (queue1)	N/A	30% (queue2)	20% (queue3)

b. *(Optional)* Adjust the weighting of transmit queue servicing:

COS	`set qos wrr` *port-type weight1 weight2* [*weight3*]
IOS	(interface) **wrr-queue bandwidth** *weight1 weight2* [*weight3*]

For *port-type* **2q2t**, **1p2q2t**, **1p3q1t**, and **1p2q1t**, the standard queues are serviced in a WRR fashion. The strict-priority queue is always serviced, regardless of any other queue. Then each standard queue is serviced in turn, according to its *weight* value; each queue's weight is relative to the others.

By default, ports with two queues have a ratio of 4:255, and ports with three queues have a ratio of 100:150:200. (When QoS is disabled, all queues are equally weighted at 255.)

TIP

The *weight* value for a queue specifies how many bytes are transmitted before moving to the next queue. A whole frame is always transmitted, even if you choose a *weight* value that is smaller. Therefore, make sure you choose a value for *weight1* (the lowest priority queue) that is at least as large as the MTU (the largest frame that can be sent). Then scale the other weight values proportionately.

The larger the weights for higher priority queues, the more time elapses before lower-priority queues are serviced. This increases the latency for lesser-priority queues.

After setting the weights for a port, confirm that the hardware is using an appropriate value. Use the **show qos info runtime** *mod/port* command and look at the transmit queue ratio information. The ratio and number of bytes are shown.

11 *(Optional; Layer 3 only)* Map internal DSCP values to egress CoS values:

COS	`set qos dscp-cos-map` *dscp-list:cos-value* ...
IOS	(global) **mls qos map dscp-cos** *dscp-list* **to** *cos-value*

The internal DSCP generates a final CoS value for each frame. The final CoS is written into the CoS fields of egress trunks and is also used to control egress scheduling and congestion avoidance.

DSCP values *dscp-list* can be a single value (0 to 63), a hyphenated range of values, or multiple values and ranges separated by commas. The CoS value is given by *cos-value* (0 to 7).

Table 13-8 shows the default DSCP-to-CoS map.

Table 13-8 *DSCP-to-CoS Map Default*

DSCP	0–7	8–15	16–23	24–31	32–39	40–47	48–55	56–63
CoS	0	1	2	3	4	5	6	7

The IOS command can be repeated several times, until all the CoS mappings are defined.

12 *(Optional)* Tune egress scheduling and congestion avoidance.

a. *(Optional)* Set the congestion-avoidance thresholds.

— *(Optional)* Use standard tail-drop receive queues:

COS	**set qos drop-threshold** *port-type* **tx queue** *queue-id threshold-percent-1 threshold-percent-2*
IOS	(interface) **wrr-queue threshold** *queue-id threshold-percent-1 threshold-percent-2*

For 2q2t switch ports, standard tail-drop congestion avoidance can be used. For each threshold, you can assign the percentage of the buffer that is available to transmit frames. The *threshold-percentage-n* values (1 to 100 percent) are given in sequential order. When the buffer rises above the threshold level, new outbound frames are dropped. By default, threshold 1 is set to 100 percent and threshold 2 is set to 60 percent.

— *(Optional)* Use WRED receive queues:

COS	**set qos wred** *port-type* **tx queue** *queue-id* [*thr1-min:*]*thr1-max* [*thr2-min:*]*thr2-max*...
IOS	(interface) **wrr-queue random-detect min-threshold** *queue-id thr1-min thr2-min ...* (interface) **wrr-queue random-detect max-threshold** *queue-id thr1-max thr2-max ...*

Section 13-2

For 1p2q2t, 1p3q1t, and 1p2q1t port types, WRED is used. The *queue-id* is **1** (standard low-priority queue) or **2** (standard high-priority queue)—except 1p3q1t ports, which add **3** (standard highest-priority queue). Two limits are used for each of the queue thresholds: a minimum *thr1-min* (1 to 100 percent) and a maximum *thr1-max* (1 to 100 percent).

When the buffer is below the minimum level, no frames are dropped. As the buffer rises above the minimum but below the maximum, the chances that frames will be dropped increases. Above the maximum level, all frames are dropped.

TIP

The IOS 1p3q1t and 1p2q1t transmit queues also require the **wrr-queue random-detect** *queue-id* command to enable the WRED drop thresholds.

---

b. *(Optional)* Tune egress scheduling:

COS	**set qos map** *port-type* **tx** *queue-id threshold-id* **cos** *cos-list*
IOS	(interface) **wrr-queue cos-map** *queue-id threshold-id cos-list*

Outbound frames with certain CoS values can be mapped and sent to specific egress queues and thresholds. The *cos-list* can be a single value (0 to 7), multiple values separated by commas, or a hyphenated range of values. This mapping is set for all switch ports (COS switch) or per-interface (IOS switch).

The *port-type* is the type of queuing available, as seen by the **show port capabilities** (COS) or **show queueing interface** (IOS) command. The *queue-id* (**1** for standard or **2** for strict priority) and the *threshold-id* (1 to 4) identify the specific queue and threshold where outbound frames are queued. The range of values depends on the switch port hardware.

The default mappings are shown in Table 13.6.

QoS Example

A Catalyst 6000 switch with a PFC2 module is used as the distribution or core layer switch. The access layer is broken down into several switch platform choices: a Catalyst 6000 with PFC2 (or a Catalyst 4000 with a Supervisor III), a Catalyst 4000, and a Catalyst 2900XL or 3500XL. Figure 13-5 shows a network diagram.

Figure 13-5 *Network Diagram for the QoS Example*

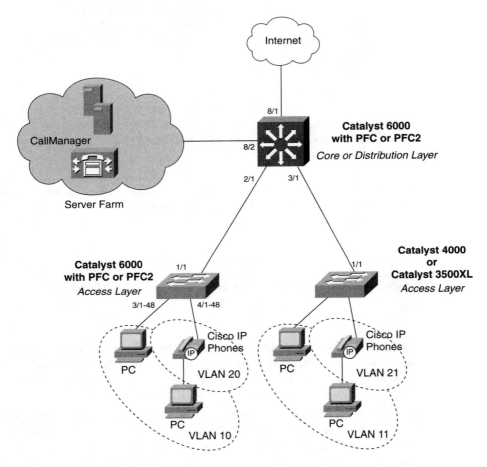

In this example, you want to use QoS to control two types of traffic:

- A peer-to-peer file-sharing protocol using TCP port 1214
- IP telephony traffic

Traffic on TCP port 1214 should be policed so that the cumulative rate is no more than 1 Mbps through the distribution switch. IP telephony, on the other hand, should be marked so that it receives the premium level of QoS.

Port 2/1 is a Gigabit Ethernet trunk connection to a Catalyst 6000 in the access layer. QoS is port-based, because the access layer switch can examine and mark all traffic on any VLAN within the trunk. Port 3/1 is a Gigabit Ethernet trunk connection to either a Catalyst 4000 or 3500XL in the access layer. These switches are not capable of examining and marking traffic at Layer 3, so the QoS is set to **vlan-based** (each VLAN is treated independently). The choice of access layer switch has been used to demonstrate the QoS configurations for the different switch platforms.

Because we are configuring QoS end-to-end in this network, we can safely assume that the access layer switches will classify and mark IP telephony control traffic (TCP ports 2000 to 2002) to DSCP 26 (AF31) and the *Real-Time Transfer Protocol* (RTP) or voice bearer packets to DSCP 46 (EF).

Port 8/1 is a Gigabit Ethernet connection toward the public Internet. As such, you will not trust any QoS information from that source. Port 8/2 is a Gigabit Ethernet connection into a server farm, where DSCP information can be trusted. The IP telephony server (a Cisco CallManager, for example) is located in the server farm.

For those ingress ports that are untrusted, a CoS-to-DSCP map and an IP precedence-to-DSCP map have been configured. These are slightly different from the default map, with adjustments to make CoS 3 map to DSCP 26 (AF31) and CoS 5 map to DSCP 46 (EF).

The aggregate policer named *Policer-1214* limits the throughput of matching traffic to 1000 kbps or 1 MBps. Traffic that exceeds this rate is dropped. The policer is applied to traffic that matches TCP port 1214 as a source or destination port. The traffic must be matched in both directions, because this is a peer-to-peer protocol, allowing file transfers in either direction. The policer and the matching ACL or class map is applied to ingress ports 2/1, 3/1, and 8/1—all the ports where file servers might be present.

IP telephony traffic is matched with an ACL on the COS switch and a class map on the IOS switch. TCP port ranges 2000 through 2002 represent IP telephony control traffic, between IP telephones and the CallManager. The DSCP value is set to 26 (AF31) for control traffic. This policy is applied only to VLAN 21, where IP Phones are located on the Catalyst 4000 or 3500XL access layer switches. The Catalyst 6000 access layer switch can do this marking for its IP Phones. The RTP or voice bearer traffic is always marked as CoS 5 by the IP Phones. This is mapped to DSCP 46 (EF) at the ingress ports.

Notice that the IOS switch uses a policer to mark the voice control traffic to DSCP 26. This is the only method that can be used for marking DSCP values. Fictitious CIR, burst, and PIR values are given (32000 bps). Because the traffic is transmitted for both conforming and nonconforming, the CIR and burst values don't matter.

Finally, the IP telephony traffic is scheduled at the egress port queues. By default, all traffic with CoS 5 (voice bearer traffic) is assigned to the strict-priority queue on all egress ports. A map is defined to assign frames with CoS 3 (IP telephony control traffic) to queue 2 threshold 1. This places the IP telephony control traffic ahead of normal traffic in queue 1, but behind the bearer traffic in the priority queue.

The distribution or core Catalyst 6000 switch configuration is shown first:

| COS | ```
set qos enable
set port qos 2/1 port-based
set port qos 2/1 trust trust-dscp
set port qos 3/1 vlan-based
set port qos 8/1 port-based
set port qos 8/1 trust untrusted
set port qos 8/1 cos 0
set port qos 8/2 port-based
set port qos 8/2 trust trust-dscp
set qos cos-dscp-map 0 8 16 26 32 46 48 56
set qos ipprec-dscp-map 0 8 16 26 32 46 48 56

set qos policer aggregate Policer-1214 rate 1000 burst 32 drop
set qos acl ip ACL-1214 dscp 0 aggregate Policer-1214 tcp any any
eq 1214
set qos acl ip ACL-1214 dscp 0 aggregate Policer-1214 tcp any eq
1214 any
commit qos acl ACL-1214
set qos acl map ACL-1214 2/1,3/1,8/1

set qos acl ip ACL-IPT-Control dscp 26 tcp any any range 2000 2002
commit qos acl ACL-IPT-Control
set qos acl map ACL-IPT-Control 21

set qos map 1p2q2t tx 2 1 cos 3
``` |
| IOS | ```
(global) mls qos
(global) interface gig 2/1
(interface) mls qos trust dscp
(global) interface gig 3/1
(interface) mls qos vlan-based
(global) interface gig 8/1
(interface) no mls qos trust
(interface) mls qos cos 0
(global) interface gig 8/2
(interface) mls qos trust dscp
(global) mls qos map cos-dscp 0 8 16 26 32 46 48 56
``` |

| IOS (*Cont.*) | ```
(global) mls qos aggregate-policer Policer-1214 1000000 32768
conform-action transmit exceed-action drop
(global) ip access-list extended ACL-1214
(acc-list) permit tcp any any eq 1214 dscp 0
(acc-list) permit tcp any eq 1214 any dscp 0
(acc-list) exit
(global) ip access-list extended ACL-IPT-Control
(acc-list) permit tcp any any range 2000 2002
(acc-list) exit
(global) class-map Class-1214 match-all
(cmap) match access-group name ACL-1214
(cmap) exit
(global) class-map Class-IPT-Control match-all
(cmap) match access-group 101

(global) policy-map Policy-1214-IPT
(pmap) class Class-1214
(pmap) police aggregate Policer-1214
(pmap) class Class-IPT-Control
(pmap) police 32000 32000 32000 conform-action set-dscp-transmit 26
exceed-action transmit
(pmap) exit

(global) interface gig 2/1
(interface) service-policy input Policy-1214-IPT
(interface) wrr-queue cos-map 2 1 3
(global) interface gig 3/1
(interface) service-policy input Policy-1214-IPT
(interface) wrr-queue cos-map 2 1 3
(global) interface gig 8/1
(interface) service-policy input Policy-1214-IPT
(interface) wrr-queue cos-map 2 1 3
``` |
|---|---|

The configuration for the access layer Catalyst 6000 switch is shown next. Port 1/1 is the uplink into the distribution or core layer, also within the QoS domain. Therefore, DSCP information is trusted. Ports 2/1 to 48 connect to end-user PCs, so the QoS information is untrusted and the inbound CoS values are marked to 0.

Ports 3/1 to 48 are connected to Cisco IP Phones. The inbound CoS values are trusted because they have been correctly handled by the IP Phones. The phones have been instructed to consider their access ports as untrusted and to mark their inbound CoS values to 0. These ports are also configured for VLAN-based QoS because all QoS policies will be applied to the voice VLAN as a whole.

One access list, *ACL-IPT-Control*, has been defined to classify IP telephony control traffic (TCP ports 2000 to 2002) and mark the internal DSCP values to 26 (AF31). This is done for all of VLAN 20 traffic.
```

The egress queue scheduling has been configured to assign frames with CoS 3 (IP telephony control traffic) to queue 2 threshold 1 on all 1p2q2t (Gigabit Ethernet) and 2q2t (10/100 phone) ports. By default, frames with CoS 5 (voice bearer traffic) are assigned to the strict priority queues:

COS	
| | ```
set qos enable
set port qos 1/1 trust trust-dscp
set port qos 2/1-48 trust untrusted
set port qos 2/1-48 cos 0
set port qos 3/1-48 trust trust-cos
set port qos 3/1-48 trust-ext untrusted
set port qos 3/1-48 vlan-based
set qos cos-dscp-map 0 8 16 26 32 46 48 56
set qos ipprec-dscp-map 0 8 16 26 32 46 48 56

set qos acl ip ACL-IPT-Control dscp 26 tcp any any range 2000 2002
commit qos acl ACL-IPT-Control
set qos acl map ACL-IPT-Control 20

set qos map 1p2q2t tx 2 1 cos 3
set qos map 2q2t tx 2 1 cos 3
``` |
| IOS | N/A |

Finally, the QoS configurations for the Catalyst 4000 (COS) and 3500XL (IOS) access layer switches are shown. Neither switch platform can classify inbound frames. Therefore, only the Catalyst 3500XL is configured to instruct directly connected Cisco IP Phones to rewrite the CoS value of their access ports to 0.

The Catalyst 4000 must trust any CoS value that the end device sends. However, some adjustment can be made to its queue scheduling. By default frames with CoS 3 (IP telephony control traffic, for example) are assigned to queue 1 threshold 2, along with CoS 2. Both CoS 3 and CoS 5 (voice bearer traffic) are assigned to queue 2 threshold 1 to improve the overall handling of voice traffic.

In this case, it is up to the next higher layer of switches to correctly handle the QoS policies:

COS	
| | ```
set qos enable
set qos map 2q1t 2 1 cos 3-5
``` |
| IOS | ```
(global) interface fast 0/1
(interface) switchport priority extend cos 0
(global) interface fast 0/2
(interface) switchport priority extend cos 0
(global) interface fast 0/3 …
``` |
```

Displaying Information About QoS

Table 13-9 documents some switch commands that you can use to display helpful information about QoS configuration and operation.

Table 13-9 *Commands to Display QoS Configuration and Operation Information*

Display Function	Switch OS	Command
QoS port information	COS	`show port qos` [*mod*[/*port*]]
	IOS	(exec) `show mls qos` {*type number* | **port-channel** *number* | **vlan** *vlan-id*]
Port queue scheduling and congestion avoidance	COS	`show port qos` [*mod*[/*port*]] -OR- `show qos info` {**runtime** | **config**} {*mod*/*port*} -OR- `show qos info config` *port_type* {**tx** | **rx**}
	IOS	(exec) `show queueing interface` {*type number* | **Null** *interface-number* | **vlan** *vlan-id*}
QoS mapping	COS	`show qos maps` {**config** | **runtime**} [{**cos-dscp-map** | **ipprec-dscp-map** | **dscp-cos-map** | **policed-dscp-map** {**normal-rate** | **excess-rate**}]
	IOS	(exec) `show mls qos maps`
Policers	COS	`show qos policer` {**config** | **runtime**} {**microflow** [*policer-name*] | **aggregate** [*policer-name*] | **all**}
	IOS	(exec) `show mls qos aggregate policer` [*aggregate-name*]
QoS policies	COS	`show qos acl editbuffer` -OR- `show qos acl info default-action` {**ip** | **ipx** | **mac** | **all**} `show qos acl info runtime` {*acl_name* | **all**} `show qos acl info config` {*acl_name* | **all**} [**editbuffer** [*editbuffer_index*]]
	IOS	(exec) `show class-map` [*class-name*] -OR- (exec) `show policy-map` *policy-map-name*
Policy activity on an interface	COS	`show qos acl map` {**config** | **runtime**} {*acl-name* | *mod*/*port* | *vlan* | **all**} -OR- `show qos statistics` {*mod*[/*port*] | **l3stats**}
	IOS	(exec) `show policy-map interface` [*type number* | **null** *interface-number* | **Vlan** *vlan-id*] [**input** | **output**]

13-3: QoS Data Export

- QoS statistics data can be gathered from sources within a switch and sent to a data collection device.

- QoS data export is limited to the Catalyst 6000 family.

- Statistics data is exported using a specific UDP port or a syslog facility.

- The sources of QoS data can be one of the following. The data fields shown are separated by a delimiter character when data is exported:

  - **Switch port**—Data export type 1, slot/port, number of ingress packets, ingress bytes, egress packets, egress bytes, and a time stamp.

  - **Aggregate policer**—Data export type 3, policer name, number of in-profile packets, out-of-profile packets exceeding the CIR, out-of-profile packets exceeding the PIR, and a time stamp.

  - **QoS policy class map**—Data export type 4, class map name, port, VLAN, or port-channel number, number of in-profile packets, out-of-profile packets exceeding the CIR, out-of-profile packets exceeding the PIR, and a time stamp.

Configuration

1 Specify how to send QoS statistics.

a. Select a destination for statistic collection:

COS	`set qos statistics export destination` *host* `[{`*port* `|` `syslog` `[`*facility-name severity*`]}]`
IOS	`(global)` `mls qos statistics-export destination {`*host-name* `|` *host-ip-address*`}` `[{`**port** *port-number* `|` **syslog** `[`**facility** *facility-name*`]` `[`**severity** *severity*`]}]`

By default, no statistics are sent to the destination. Statistics can be sent to the destination *host* (either IP address or host name) using a specific UDP *port* or through syslog (UDP port 514). If the **syslog** keyword is used, the syslog *facility-name* can be given as **kern, user, mail, daemon, auth, lpr, news, uucp, cron, local0, local1, local2, local3, local4, local5, local6** (the default), or **local7**. The syslog *severity* is one of **emerg, alert, crit, err, warning, notice, info,** or **debug** (the default). See section "12-1: Logging" for more information about syslog.

b. *(Optional)* Set the data export interval:

COS	`set qos statistics export interval` *interval*
IOS	`(global)` `mls qos statistics-export interval` *interval*

QoS statistics are sent to the destination every *interval* seconds (30 to 65,535 seconds; COS default 30 seconds, IOS default 300 seconds).

TIP Be careful when choosing an interval value. If the time is too long, the QoS statistics counters could reach their maximum values and wrap back to 0. If the time chosen is too short, the switch CPU load increases significantly. Begin with the default and make adjustments, taking notice of the effects on both CPU and counters.

---

c. *(Optional; IOS only)* Set the statistics delimiter:

COS	N/A
IOS	(global) **mls qos statistics-export delimiter** *character*

QoS statistics can be separated by a specific *character* (default pipe or |) if desired.

2 Enable data gathering on the switch:

COS	**set qos statistics export {enable	disable}**
IOS	(global) **mls qos statistics-export**

By default, no QoS statistics are gathered or exported.

3 Gather QoS statistics from one or more sources.

a. *(Optional)* Select a switch port:

COS	**set qos statistics export port** *mod/port* **{enable	disable}**
IOS	(interface) **mls qos statistics-export**

b. *(Optional)* Select an aggregate policer:

COS	**set qos statistics export aggregate** *policer-name* **{enable	disable}**
IOS	(global) **mls qos statistics-export aggregate-policer** *policer-name*

QoS statistics are gathered from the aggregate policer named *policer-name* (text string). The policer must be configured as described in section "13-2: QoS Configuration."

c. *(Optional; IOS only)* Select a QoS class map:

COS	N/A
IOS	(global) **mls qos statistics-export class-map** *classmap-name*

You can gather statistics about a specific portion of a more complex QoS policy if needed. Statistics are gathered from the QoS class map named *classmap-name* (text string). The class map must be configured as described in section "13-2: QoS Configuration."

QoS Data Export Example

QoS statistics are gathered on a switch and are sent to a collection host at 192.168.111.14 using the *local6* syslog facility and *debug* severity (the defaults). Data is collected and sent every 300 seconds. Statistics are gathered only for ports 3/1, 3/2, and the aggregate policer named *MyPolicer*:

COS	set qos statistics export destination 192.168.111.14 syslog
	set qos statistics export interval 300
	set qos statistics export enable
	set qos statistics export port 3/1-2 enable
	set qos statistics export aggregate MyPolicer enable
IOS	(global) **mls qos statistics-export destination** 192.168.111.14 **syslog**
	(global) **mls qos statistics-export interval 300**
	(global) **mls qos statistics-export**
	(global) **interface gig 3/1**
	(interface) **mls qos statistics-export**
	(global) **interface gig 3/2**
	(interface) **mls qos statistics-export**
	(global) **mls qos statistics-export aggregate-policer MyPolicer**

Displaying Information About QoS Data Export

You can use the following switch commands to display QoS statistic sources:

COS	show qos statistics export info
IOS	(exec) **show mls qos statistics-export info**

13-4: QoS Management

- *Common Open Policy Service* (**COPS**)—The protocol that communicates QoS policies and enforcement between devices on a network.

  COPS management is supported on the Catalyst 6000 COS switch family with a Layer 3 switching engine (PFC or PFC2).

- *Policy Decision Point* (**PDP**)—Maintains QoS policies and rules that will be enforced within the network. Traffic conditions can be polled and can affect how the policies are implemented. A typical PDP might be a host running Cisco *QoS Policy Manager* (QPM).

- *Policy Enforcement Point* (**PEP**)—A device consisting of physical interfaces, controlled by a PDP. QoS policies are sent down to a PEP, where they are enforced in a granular fashion. Typical PEPs are routers and switches.

  COPS configures QoS policies for PEP switch ports using role names rather than physical switch module and port numbers. This gives COPS a more abstract view of network QoS. All switch ports that will be controlled by COPS must be assigned arbitrary role names.

- *Resource Reservation Protocol* (**RSVP**)—Used to request and reserve bandwidth for a specific traffic flow. The reservation is set up end-to-end across a network.

  RSVP-for-COPS uses the COPS mechanism to gather and control RSVP requests.

- *Designated Subnet Bandwidth Manager* (**DSBM**)—One switch on a network segment is elected to coordinate all RSVP activity. All RSVP-for-COPS client devices forward RSVP messages to the DSBM.

QoS Management Configuration

1 Select the source for QoS policies.

a. Set the source for global policy information:

COS	`set qos policy-source {local	cops}`
IOS	N/A

By default, all QoS policy information is taken from the local switch configuration (**local**). Use the **cops** keyword to accept global QoS information from a COPS device instead.

Section 13-4

TIP Global QoS policies include all DSCP maps, both named and default ACLs, both microflow and aggregate policer definitions, port scheduling (CoS-to-queue mapping), congestion avoidance (queue thresholds), queue weighting, default port CoS, and mappings for ACLs to switch ports.

b. Set the source for specific switch ports:

COS	`set port qos policy-source` *mod/ports* {`local` | `cops`}
IOS	N/A

By default, QoS information for every switch port is taken from the local switch configuration (**local**). Use the **cops** keyword to accept QoS policy configuration for one or more switch ports (*mod/ports*) from a COPS device instead.

2 Communicate with COPS devices.

a. Identify one or more PDP servers:

COS	`set cops server` *ipaddress* [*port*] [`primary`] `diff-serv`
IOS	N/A

The PDP server is identified by its IP address *ipaddress*. An optional TCP *port* number can be given. You can specify one primary server with the **primary** keyword. The command can be repeated once without the **primary** keyword to specify a backup server.

b. Set the COPS domain name:

COS	`set cops domain-name` *domain*
IOS	N/A

The COPS domain name is set to *domain* (text string up to 31 characters; default is a null string). PDP devices can control PEP devices in the same domain.

c. *(Optional)* Set the COPS retry interval:

COS	`set cops retry-interval` *initial incr max*
IOS	N/A

Communication with the COPS server uses a retry interval. The switch waits for the *initial* interval (0 to 65,535 seconds, default 30 seconds) after the first failed exchange. After each subsequent failure, the retry interval is incremented by *incr* (0 to 65,535 seconds, default 30 seconds), up to the maximum timeout *max* (0 to 65,535 seconds, default 300 seconds).

3 Assign COPS roles to switch ports:

COS	**set port cops** *mod*/*port* **roles** *role1* [*role2*]...
IOS	N/A

By default, all switch ports have a null role. You can define one or more role names *role1*, *role2*, (text string up to 31 characters) and so on to a switch port. The total length of all role names assigned to a switch port cannot exceed 255 characters. You can define up to 64 roles on a switch.

4 *(Optional)* Use RSVP with COPS.

a. Enable RSVP support:

COS	**set qos rsvp** {**enable** | **disable**}
IOS	N/A

By default, RSVP support is disabled.

b. Identify the COPS PDP server:

COS	**set cops server** *ipaddress* [*port*] [**primary**] **rsvp**
IOS	N/A

The PDP server is identified by its IP address *ipaddress*. An optional TCP *port* number can be given. You can specify one primary server with the **primary** keyword. The command can be repeated once without the **primary** keyword to specify a backup server.

c. Allow the switch to participate in bandwidth management:

COS	**set port rsvp** *mod*/*port* **dsbm-election** {**enable** | **disable**} [*dsbm-priority*]
IOS	N/A

A switch can participate in an election to become a DSBM. Election is allowed on specific switch ports (*mod/port*). By default, DSBM participation is disabled. The switch priority *dsbm-priority* (128 to 255, default 128) determines the likelihood of winning the election, because the highest priority wins.

d. *(Optional)* Take action during the loss of a PDP server.

— *(Optional)* Set the DSBM timeout interval:

COS	`set qos rsvp policy-timeout `*`timeout`*
IOS	N/A

If the switch is the elected DSBM and it loses contact with the PDP server, it continues to function as the DSBM for *timeout* (1 to 65,535 minutes, default 30 minutes). During that time, only its cached RSVP policies are used. If the PDP server is not restored within that time, the switch reverts back to being an SBM client.

— *(Optional)* Handle RSVP requests during the timeout interval:

COS	`set qos rsvp local-policy {forward	reject}`
IOS	N/A

— By default, a switch continues to **forward** all RSVP path messages, even if the PDP server is not accessible. You can choose to **reject** all new or modified RSVP messages if desired.

Displaying Information About QoS Management

Table 13-10 lists some switch commands that you can use to display helpful information about QoS management.

Table 13-10 *Commands to Display QoS Management Information*

Display Function	Switch OS	Command
QoS policy source	COS	`show qos policy-source`
	IOS	N/A
COPS status	COS	`show cops info [diff-serv]`
	IOS	N/A
Switch port COPS roles	COS	`show cops roles`
	IOS	N/A

Table 13-10 *Commands to Display QoS Management Information (Continued)*

Display Function	Switch OS	Command
RSVP status	COS	`show qos rsvp info`
	IOS	N/A
Active RSVP flows	COS	`show qos rsvp flow-info`
	IOS	N/A

Further Reading

Refer to the following recommended sources for further information about the topics covered in this chapter.

IP Quality of Service by Srinivas Vegesna, Cisco Press, ISBN 1-57870-116-3

Differentiated Services (DiffServ) IETF Working Group at:
www.ietf.org/html.charters/diffserv-charter.html

The COPS Protocol, RFC 2748 at: www.faqs.org/rfcs/rfc2748.html

The RSVP Protocol at: www.isi.edu/div7/rsvp/rsvp.html

QoS Policing on the Catalyst 6000 at:
www.cisco.com/warp/customer/473/102.html

QoS on Catalyst 6000 Family Switches: Output Scheduling on the Catalyst 6000 with PFC Using Hybrid Mode at: www.cisco.com/warp/public/473/60.html

QoS on Catalyst 6000 Family Switches: Output Scheduling on the Catalyst 6000 with PFC Using IOS Native Mode at: www.cisco.com/warp/public/473/73.html

Understanding RACL/VACL/QoS ACL Hardware Resources in Catalyst 6000 Family Switches at: www.cisco.com/warp/public/473/79.html

Section 13-4

CHAPTER 14

Voice

See the following sections to configure and use these features:

- **14-1: Voice Ports**—Covers the commands necessary to configure switched Ethernet ports for IP telephony.
- **14-2: Voice QoS**—Presents guidelines and configuration suggestions that provide end-to-end *quality of service* (QoS) in a campus network.
- **14-3: Voice Modules**—Discusses the steps needed to configure voice gateway modules in Catalyst 4000 and 6000 switches.

14-1: Voice Ports

- Inline power is provided to a powered device as follows:
  - A phantom-powered device can be detected as a switch port becomes active.
  - A powered device loops the transmit and receive pairs back so that the switch detects its own 340 kHz test tone.
  - Power is applied to the port if the device is present; no power is applied if a normal Ethernet device is connected.
  - Inline power is provided over pairs 2 and 3 (RJ-45 pins 1,2 and 3,6) at 48V DC.
- Inline power is available on the following switch modules:
  - Catalyst 6000 Inline Power 48-port 10/100 Ethernet Switch Module (WS-X6348-RJ45V)
  - Catalyst 4000 Inline Power 48-port 10/100 Ethernet Switch Module (WS-X4148-RJ45V), with auxiliary DC power shelf and power entry module
  - Catalyst 3524XL

- Power can also be provided through an external 48-port power patch panel (WS-PWR-PANEL):
  - No detection of a phantom-powered device is performed.
  - Powered devices can be connected to a wall power adapter and the power patch panel. The devices use the patch panel as a backup power source.
  - Power is provided over pairs 1 and 4 (RJ-45 pins 4,5 and 7,8) at 48V DC.
- A Catalyst switch can send instructions to a Cisco IP Phone on how to present frames from its voice and data ports. This is done through *Cisco Discovery Protocol* (CDP) messages.
- The switch and phone can communicate over an 802.1Q trunk, with voice traffic in a separate *voice VLAN ID* (VVID). Voice *class of service* (CoS) information can be propagated across the trunk.
- A Cisco IP Phone performs the following steps during initialization:
1. Inline power is detected by the switch, if needed.
2. The phone triggers a CDP exchange. The actual amount of required power is sent to the switch, while the VVID number is sent to the phone. The phone can also receive instructions on how to extend the QoS trust boundary.
3. A special 802.1Q trunk is negotiated between the phone and the switch, if a VVID is to be supported. On Catalyst 4000 and 6000 switches, the trunk is negotiated through *Dynamic Trunk Protocol* (DTP) messages. On Catalyst 3500XL switches, DTP is not supported, so the trunk must be manually configured.
4. A DHCP request is made.
5. A DHCP reply is sent to the phone, containing the IP address and TFTP server address (DHCP option 150).
6. The TFTP server is contacted for a phone configuration file. A list of Cisco CallManager servers is also obtained.
7. Registration with a CallManager server is performed. A *directory number* (DN) is obtained so that calls can be placed and received.

Configuration

1. Use inline power for Cisco IP Phones.

   a. *(Optional)* Set the default power allocation:

COS	`set inlinepower defaultallocation` *value*
IOS	N/A

The amount of power allocated to a switch port is negotiated with the powered device. By default, 10.0 watts (0.24 amps at 42V DC) is supplied to each switch port. The default amount can be changed to *value* (2000 to 12500 mW, default 10000 mW).

TIP

The default power allocation is based on the total power available from the switch power supplies. If you change the default allocation, be sure that you don't exceed the available power when all powered devices are active. Use the **show environment power** COS command to see the total power available. You can also use the **show port inlinepower** COS command to find switch ports that exceed the available power.

Although the switch initially offers the default power allocation to the device, the amount of power can be changed to a value agreed upon by an exchange of CDP messages.

b. *(Optional)* Detect an inline-powered device:

COS	**set port inlinepower** *mod/port* {**off**	**auto**}
IOS	(interface) **power inline** {**auto**	**never**}

By default, the switch attempts to discover an inline-powered device on a switch port (**auto**). Use the **off** (COS) or **never** (IOS) keyword to disable inline power detection.

CAUTION

After a powered device has been detected and power has been applied to a switch port, the switch waits four seconds to see that the device has initialized and the link is established. If not, power is removed from the switch port.

If you unplug the powered device within the 4-second delay and plug a regular Ethernet device in its place, power will still be applied and the device could be damaged. Wait at least 10 seconds before swapping devices on a switch port.

2 Establish VLANs with the IP Phone.

TIP

A Cisco IP Phone can use an 802.1Q trunk to transport packets from two VLANs: the voice VLAN (voice packets) and the native VLAN (data packets, untagged). By default, a Cisco IP Phone transports both its voice packets and the data packets from a connected device over the native VLAN. All data is untagged.

After a switch has been configured to instruct an IP Phone to support a VVID number, the switch and phone must use an 802.1Q trunk between them. On Catalyst 3500XL switches, trunk negotiation is not supported and the 802.1Q trunk must be manually configured. The IP Phone will automatically use an 802.1Q trunk on its end of the connection.

For Catalyst 4000 and 6000 switches, a special-case 802.1Q trunk is negotiated with the IP Phone using CDP and the DTP. Once the phone is detected, the switch port becomes a *vlan2-access port*, supporting only the two voice and data VLANs. The port won't be shown in trunking mode from the **show trunk** command. In fact, it doesn't matter which trunking mode (*auto, desirable, on, or off*) is configured on the port—the special trunk will be negotiated through the DTP. Be sure that the trunk is not configured using the **nonegotiate** keyword, as DTP messages will not be sent or received and the trunk will not be automatically established.

The *Spanning Tree Protocol* (STP) is automatically supported over the IP Phone trunk as well. The **show spantree** command displays the STP state for both of the VLANs on the trunk.

---

a. *(Optional)* Use a VLAN for data.

— *(Optional)* Identify the switch-port access VLAN:

COS	`set vlan vlan-id mod/ports`
IOS	`(interface) switchport access vlan vlan-id`

— You can configure switch ports to support both PCs and IP Phones. For the case when a regular host (not an IP Phone) is connected to a switch port, the access VLAN should be set to *vlan-id* (1 to 1000 or 1025 to 4094). When a PC is connected, only the access VLAN is supported and no special trunking negotiations take place. See section "6-1: VLAN Configuration" for more information.

— Identify the switch-port native VLAN:

COS	`set vlan vlan-id mod/ports`
IOS	`(interface) switchport trunk native vlan vlan-id`

— Data from the access switch port on an IP Phone is carried over the native VLAN (untagged) of the special 802.1Q trunk. Therefore, you should identify the native VLAN number as *vlan-id* (1 to 1000 or 1025 to 4094). For a COS switch, the command is the same as setting the switch-port access VLAN.

b. *(Optional)* Instruct the phone to transport data and voice.

— *(Optional)* Use an 802.1Q trunk with a voice VLAN:

COS	`set port auxiliaryvlan` *mod*[*/port*] *vlan-id*
IOS	`(interface)` `switchport voice vlan` *vlan-id*

The IP Phone is instructed to use an 802.1Q trunk. Voice frames are tagged with VLAN *vlan-id* (1 to 4096 COS or 1 to 1001 IOS), whereas frames from the phone's data port are sent untagged (the native VLAN). The CoS value of the voice frames are carried in the 802.1p priority field.

— *(Optional)* Use an 802.1Q trunk with no voice VLAN:

COS	`set port auxiliaryvlan` *mod*[*/port*] `dot1p`
IOS	`(interface)` `switchport voice vlan dot1p`

The IP Phone is instructed to use an 802.1Q trunk and the 802.1p CoS priority field, but all voice frames are placed in the null VLAN (VLAN 0). Frames from the phone's data port are sent untagged (the native VLAN). This allows the voice priority information to be propagated, without requiring a separate voice VLAN.

— *(Optional)* Use an 802.1Q trunk with no VLAN information:

COS	`set port auxiliaryvlan` *mod*[*/port*] `untagged`
IOS	`(interface)` `switchport voice vlan untagged`

The IP Phone is instructed to send all voice frames untagged, over the native VLAN. As a result, no 802.1Q encapsulation is used, and no 802.1p CoS priority information can be propagated.

— *(Optional)* Don't instruct the phone at all:

COS	`set port auxiliaryvlan` *mod*[*/port*] `none`
IOS	`(interface)` `switchport voice vlan none`

The switch will not provide the IP Phone with a VVID to use. This is the default configuration. The phone will have no knowledge of a voice VLAN, and both voice and data frames are sent to the switch port over the same access VLAN.

c. *(Catalyst 3500XL only)* Manually configure the 802.1Q trunk.

— Select 802.1Q encapsulation:

COS	N/A
IOS	(interface) **switchport trunk encapsulation dot1q**

The 802.1Q trunk encapsulation is forced on the switch interface. The IP Phone automatically uses and expects an 802.1Q trunk.

— *(Optional)* Allow the voice and data VLANs on the trunk:

COS	N/A
IOS	(interface) **switchport trunk allowed vlan** *vvid,pvid*

— By default, all configured VLANs are allowed on the trunk. You can limit this to only the voice VLAN number (*vvid*) and the data VLAN number (*pvid*), to prevent any broadcast traffic on any other VLANs from using unnecessary bandwidth.

— Enable the trunk:

COS	N/A
IOS	(interface) **switchport mode trunk**

— The interface is in the static access mode by default. The trunk mode must be started manually with this command.

3 *(Optional)* Optimize the switch port for an IP Phone.

TIP

A COS switch can perform the actions of the following configuration steps with a single command: **set port host** *mod/port*.

Note that this command effectively disables trunking on the switch port; however, the switch port and the IP Phone still use a special form of 802.1Q trunking regardless.

a. Turn off EtherChannel support:

COS	**set port channel** *mod/port* **mode off**
IOS	(interface) **no channel-group**

Support for dynamic EtherChannel configuration using *Port Aggregation Protocol* (PAgP) is disabled, saving about 10 seconds of port startup time. See section "4-3: EtherChannel" for more information.

b. Enable Spanning Tree PortFast:

COS	`set spantree portfast` *mod/port* `enable`
IOS	`(interface)` `spanning-tree portfast`

The switch port is tuned for a faster STP startup time by bypassing the *listening* and *learning* STP states. The port can be moved into the *forwarding* state immediately. See section "7-3: STP Convergence Tuning" for more information.

Example

A Catalyst switch is configured to support an IP Phone on a port. The switch supports inline power, but the switch port might connect to a regular PC or to a Cisco IP Phone.

The port is set to automatically detect a device that supports inline power. The access or port VLAN ID (PVID) is set to VLAN number 55. If a PC is directly connected to the switch port, all data frames are transported over the access VLAN. If an IP Phone is connected, a two-VLAN 802.1Q trunk is negotiated. Data frames from a PC connected to the phone are carried untagged over the native VLAN 55 on the trunk. Voice frames to and from the phone are tagged and carried over the voice or auxiliary VLAN (VVID) 200 on the trunk.

The switch port is also configured to minimize the port-initialization delays due to PAgP and STP. This is optional, but can keep the IP Phones from waiting for switch-port delays before phone configuration data is downloaded:

COS	`set port inlinepower 4/1 auto`
	`set vlan 55 4/1`
	`set port auxiliaryvlan 4/1 200`
	`set port host 4/1`

IOS	`(global)` `interface fastethernet 0/1`
	`(interface)` `power inline auto`
	`(interface)` `switchport access vlan 55`
	`(interface)` `switchport trunk native vlan 55`
	`(interface)` `switchport voice vlan 200`
	`(interface)` `switchport trunk encapsulation dot1q`
	`(interface)` `switchport mode trunk`
	`(interface)` `no channel-group`
	`(interface)` `spanning-tree portfast`

Displaying Information About Voice Ports

Table 14-1 lists some switch commands that you can use to display helpful information about voice ports.

Table 14-1 *Switch Commands to Display Voice Port Information*

Display Function	Switch OS	Command
Inline power status	COS	`show port inlinepower` [*mod*[/*port*]]
	IOS	(exec) `show power inline` [*interface-id*] [**actual** | **configured**] -OR- (exec) `show cdp neighbor` [*interface-id*] **detail**
Access, native, and voice VLANs	COS	`show port` *mod/port* -OR- `show trunk` *mod/port* **detail**
	IOS	(exec) `show interface` [*interface-id*] **switchport**
Discovered device	COS	`show cdp neighbor` *mod/port* [**detail**]
	IOS	(exec) `show cdp neighbor` [*interface-id*] [**detail**]

14-2: Voice QoS

To support proper delivery of voice traffic in a hierarchical switched network, follow several QoS rules of thumb. See the basic network diagram in Figure 14-1.

- Access layer
  - A QoS trust boundary should be established as close to the end devices (at the access layer) as possible.
  - Let the IP Phone handle the trust boundary for attached PCs; the IP Phone should be trusted.
  - PCs running Cisco SoftPhone should be untrusted. Instead, the inbound voice traffic should be classified and the CoS and *differentiated services code point* (DSCP) values marked.
  - Normal PCs with no voice capability should be untrusted (CoS and *type of service* [ToS] set to 0).
  - On Catalyst 6000 switches, port trust can be VLAN-based and applied to the voice VLAN on all trusted ports.

- — Modify the CoS and ToS to DSCP maps so that 3 maps to DSCP 26 (AF31) and 5 maps to DSCP 46 (EF), where possible.
- — Uplinks into the distribution and core layers should trust DSCP values, if possible.
- — Schedule egress voice frames with CoS 3 to be assigned to the higher-priority queue. Frames with CoS 5 are automatically assigned to the strict-priority egress queue.

- Distribution and core layers

  - — If the DSCP values can be controlled by the access layer switches, trust them on those ports.
  - — If the access layer switches are Layer 2-only and can't classify or mark frames based on DSCP, set the DSCP values for voice frames in the higher-layer switches. This can be done on a voice VLAN for ports that are configured for VLAN-based trust.
  - — Modify the CoS and ToS to DSCP maps so that 3 maps to DSCP 26 (AF31) and 5 maps to DSCP 46 (EF), where possible.
  - — Schedule egress voice frames with CoS 3 to be assigned to the higher-priority queue. Frames with CoS 5 are automatically assigned to the strict-priority egress queue.

You can use several voice protocols within a network:

- **Voice control protocols**—Protocols that are used to register and set up calls:

  - — *Skinny Client Control Protocol* (SCCP), also known as *Simple Client Control Protocol*
  - — H.323
  - — *Session Initiation Protocol* (SIP)
  - — *Media Gateway Control Protocol* (MGCP)
  - — Megaco or H.248

- **Real-Time Transport Protocol (RTP)**—The UDP encapsulation of the actual voice-bearer packets. All voice protocols use RTP as the transport mechanism, after a call has been established.

Figure 14-1 *QoS Trust Considerations in a Switched Network*

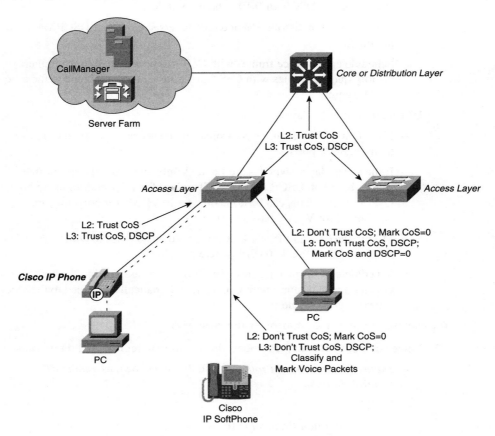

These voice protocols use the UDP or TCP port numbers shown in Table 14-2. These values can come in handy when you need to classify voice traffic for QoS in a Catalyst switch. Each of the voice-call control protocols should be marked as CoS 3 or DSCP 26 (AF31). The RTP voice-bearer packets should *always* be marked as CoS 5 or DSCP 46 (EF) to ensure timely delivery. RTP packet marking is usually done at the source, by definition.

Table 14-2 *Voice Protocol Port Numbers*

Voice Protocol	Port	Description
Skinny	TCP 2000	Skinny Client Control Protocol (SCCP)
	TCP 2001	Skinny Station Protocol (SSP)
	TCP 2002	Skinny Gateway Protocol (SGP)

Table 14-2   *Voice Protocol Port Numbers (Continued)*

Voice Protocol	Port	Description
H.323	TCP 1718	Gatekeeper messages
	TCP 1719	Gatekeeper RAS
	TCP 1720	H.225 call control
	TCP 11000 to 11999	H.245
SIP	UDP/TCP 5060	Default server ports; can also be arbitrarily chosen
MGCP	TCP 2427	Call agents to gateway
	TCP 2727	Gateway to call agents
Megaco	UDP/TCP 2944	Text call control messages
H.248	UDP/TCP 2945	Binary call control messages
RTP	UDP port negotiated by voice-call signaling protocol	Voice payload transport

Access Layer Configuration

TIP

The commands presented are broken out according to the switch platform that is used. The L3 switches have a Layer 3 switching engine, supported by the Catalyst 6000 with *Policy Feature Card* (PFC) or PFC2. The L2 switches have a Layer 2 switching engine, supported on the Catalyst 4000 and 5000 platforms. The Catalyst 2900XL and 3500XL models are labeled as 3500.

1 *(Optional)* Establish a trust boundary at the access layer.

a. *(Optional)* Trust QoS from a Cisco IP Phone:

COS L3	```set port qos mod/port vlan-based``` ```set port qos mod/port trust trust-cos```
IOS L3	```(interface) mls qos vlan-based``` ```(interface) mls qos trust cos```
COS L2	```set port qos mod/port trust trust-cos```
IOS L2	```(interface) mls qos trust cos```

IOS 3500	```(interface) switchport priority default 0```
	```(interface) no switchport priority override```
	```(interface) switchport priority extend cos 0```

A single QoS policy can be applied to all voice traffic from IP Phones on a common voice VLAN. This is only possible on Layer 3 switches. Otherwise, the inbound CoS values can be trusted when IP Phones classify and mark CoS from their own voice and data access ports. The IP Phone is instructed to control QoS trust with the configuration in Step 3.

TIP

A Cisco IP Phone marks its SCCP voice control packets with CoS 3, ToS 3, and DSCP 26 (AF31). The RTP voice bearer packets are marked with CoS 5, ToS 5, and DSCP 46 (EF). These are carried over the frames in the voice VLAN (VVID) of the 802.1Q trunk.

The IP Phone also marks traffic from its access switch port, if instructed to do so. By default, these frames are carried untagged over the native VLAN of the 802.1Q trunk, and have their ToS and DSCP values set to 0.

b. *(Optional)* Don't trust QoS from a PC running Cisco SoftPhone:

COS L3	`set port qos` *mod/ports* `cos 0`
	`set port qos` *mod/port* `trust untrusted`
IOS L3	`(interface)` `mls qos cos 0`
	`(interface)` `no mls qos trust`
COS L2	`set port qos` *mod/ports* `cos 0`
	`set port qos` *mod/port* `trust untrusted`
IOS L2	`(interface)` `mls qos cos 0`
	`(interface)` `no mls qos trust`
IOS 3500	`(interface)` `switchport priority default 0`
	`(interface)` `switchport priority override`

Although a SoftPhone PC produces voice control and bearer data packets, other applications running can attempt to mark the CoS in nonvoice packets. Because of this, you should not trust the QoS information coming from the PC. Set these switch ports to an untrusted state and configure Layer 3 switches in your QoS domain to classify and mark the voice control and bearer packets appropriately.

TIP

The Cisco SoftPhone application marks its SCCP voice control packets with CoS 0, ToS 0, and DSCP 0 (default). The RTP voice bearer packets are marked with CoS 5, ToS 5, and DSCP 46 (EF). These are carried over the access VLAN untagged because no inherent trunk is used.

c. *(Optional)* Don't trust QoS from a regular data-only host:

COS L3	`set port qos` *mod/ports* `cos 0` `set port qos` *mod/port* `trust untrusted`
IOS L3	`(interface)` `mls qos cos 0` `(interface)` `no mls qos trust`
COS L2	`set port qos` *mod/ports* `cos 0` `set port qos` *mod/port* `trust untrusted`
IOS L2	`(interface)` `mls qos cos 0` `(interface)` `no mls qos trust`
IOS 3500	`(interface)` `switchport priority default 0` `(interface)` `switchport priority override`

Frames that are untagged or that do not match any QoS-classifying *access control lists* (ACLs) will be marked with CoS value 0. This also causes the ingress DSCP values to be mapped to 0 by the CoS-to-DSCP mapping. (See the next step.)

2   *(Optional; Layer 3 only)* Adjust the ingress QoS-to-DSCP mappings:

| COS | `set qos cos-dscp-map 0 8 16 26 32 46 48 56`
`set qos ipprec-dscp-map 0 8 16 26 32 46 48 56` |
| IOS | `(global)` `mls qos map cos-dscp 0 8 16 26 32 46 48 56`
`(global)` `mls qos map ip-prec-dscp 0 8 16 26 32 46 48 56` |

You can make minor adjustments to the mappings so that CoS 3 maps to DSCP 26 (AF31) and CoS 5 maps to DSCP 46 (EF). The default values are slightly different and are not the standard values expected for voice traffic.

3   *(Optional)* Extend QoS trust into the IP Phone.

a. Set the phone access-port trust:

| COS | `set port qos` *mod/ports* `trust-ext {trusted | untrusted}` |
| IOS | `(interface)` `switchport priority  extend {trust | none}` |

A Cisco IP Phone has its own access layer switch port, where a PC can be connected. This port is **untrusted** (IOS **none**) by default, causing the CoS and IP Precedence values for inbound frames to be set to 0. To allow the PC to mark its own packets with IP Precedence values, set the mode to **trusted** (IOS **trust**).

b. Set the default phone access-port CoS value:

| COS | `set port qos` *mod/ports* `cos-ext` *cos-value* |
| IOS | `(interface)` `switchport priority  extend cos cos-value` |

— When the phone's access port is set to untrusted mode, the CoS value for all inbound data frames is set to *cos-value* (0 to 7, default 0) by the phone.

4 *(Layer 3 only)* Trust DSCP information on the uplink ports:

COS	`set port qos mod/ports trust trust-dscp`
IOS	`(interface) mls qos trust dscp`

Because the distribution and core layer switches are also within the QoS domain and are properly configured to follow the QoS requirements, you can safely assume that any QoS information coming from them has been examined and adjusted to conform to the QoS policies. As such, this information can be trusted over the uplink ports on an access layer switch.

5 *(Optional; Layer 3 only)* Apply a QoS policy to the voice traffic.

a. Define matching traffic with an ACL:

COS	`set qos acl ip acl-name dscp 26 tcp any any range 2000 2002` `set qos acl ip acl-name trust-cos ip any any`

IOS	`(global) ip access-list extended acl-name`
	`(access-list) permit tcp any any range 2000 2002 dscp 26`
	`(access-list) exit`

In this case, SCCP voice control TCP ports 2000, 2001, and 2002 are matched. These frames are given a DSCP value of 26 (AF31), even if this value was already set. This matching ACL is also necessary so that the CoS trust can be established on switch ports configured with the **set port qos trust trust-cos** command.

If other voice protocols are used, you can change the ACL to match against the appropriate port numbers.

b. *(Layer 3 IOS only)* Define the QoS policy:

COS	N/A

IOS	`(global) policy-map policy-name`
	`(pmap) class class-name access-group acl-name`
	`(pmap-class) trust cos`

The policy uses a class to match traffic from the ACL. CoS values are then trusted for matching traffic.

c. Apply the QoS policy to the voice VLAN:

COS	`commit qos acl` `acl-name` `set qos acl map` `acl-name` `voice-vlan`
IOS	`(global)` `interface vlan` `voice-vlan` `(interface)` `service-policy input` `policy-name`

You can apply the QoS policy to all ports carrying the voice VLAN. This is an efficient way to use a QoS policy on one specific VLAN within a trunk.

6 Configure voice scheduling on the egress ports.

Catalyst 2900XL and 3500XL switches have fixed scheduling on their egress ports. Voice control frames with CoS 3 are assigned to the lower-priority queue (queue 1), whereas CoS 5 frames go to the higher-priority queue (queue 2). There are no strict-priority queues.

COS L3	`set port qos` `mod/port` `port-based`
	`set qos map 1p2q2t tx 2 1 cos 3`
	`set qos map 2q2t tx 2 1 cos 3`

IOS L3	`(interface)` `no mls qos vlan-based` `(interface)` `wrr-queue cos-map 2 1 3`
COS L2	`set qos map 1p2q2t tx 2 1 cos 3` `set qos map 2q2t tx 2 1 cos 3`
IOS L2	`(interface)` `wrr-queue cos-map 2 1 3`
IOS 3500	N/A

By default, all frames with CoS 5 are sent to the strict-priority queue. Frames with CoS 3 are sent to the lowest-priority queue. The scheduling map makes sure that the voice control frames (CoS 3) are sent to a higher-priority queue, serviced ahead of other traffic.

Distribution and Core Layer Configuration

1 Establish a trust boundary.

a. *(Optional; Layer 3 only)* Trust VLAN-based QoS from an L2 access layer switch:

COS L3	`set port qos` `mod/port` `vlan-based` `set port qos` `mod/port` `trust trust-cos`
IOS L3	`(interface)` `mls qos vlan-based` `(interface)` `mls qos trust cos`
COS L2	N/A
IOS L2	N/A
IOS 3500	N/A

A Layer 2 access layer switch can classify and mark traffic based only on Layer 2 CoS values. As well, QoS is applied to the voice VLAN where IP Phone traffic is carried. A distribution or core layer switch can then apply QoS policies directly to the voice VLAN.

b. *(Optional)* Trust QoS from another distribution or core switch or a Layer 3 access layer switch:

COS L3	`set port qos` *mod/port* `port-based` `set port qos` *mod/port* `trust trust-dscp`
IOS L3	`(interface)` `no mls qos vlan-based` `(interface)` `mls qos trust dscp`
COS L2	`set port qos` *mod/port* `trust trust-cos`
IOS L2	`(interface)` `no mls qos trust cos`
IOS 3500	N/A

The QoS information from other switches in a QoS domain can be trusted. This assumes that *every* switch in the QoS domain has been configured to enforce QoS policies consistently.

QoS is port-based on these connections because every VLAN carried over the link will have its QoS values already examined and modified. A Layer 3 switch can trust the inbound DSCP information, but a Layer 2 switch can trust only the inbound CoS values.

c. *(Optional)* Don't trust QoS from sources outside the QoS domain:

COS L3	`set port qos` *mod/ports* `cos 0` `set port qos` *mod/port* `trust untrusted`
IOS L3	`(interface)` `mls qos cos 0` `(interface)` `no mls qos trust`
COS L2	`set port qos` *mod/ports* `cos 0` `set port qos` *mod/port* `trust untrusted`
IOS L2	`(interface)` `mls qos cos 0` `(interface)` `no mls qos trust`
IOS 3500	N/A

Frames that are untagged receive CoS value 0. This also causes the ingress DSCP values to be mapped to 0 by the CoS-to-DSCP mapping. (See the next step.)

2 *(Optional; Layer 3 only)* Adjust the ingress QoS-to-DSCP mappings:

COS	`set qos cos-dscp-map 0 8 16 26 32 46 48 56`
	`set qos ipprec-dscp-map 0 8 16 26 32 46 48 56`
IOS	`(global) mls qos map cos-dscp 0 8 16 26 32 46 48 56`
	`(global) mls qos map ip-prec-dscp 0 8 16 26 32 46 48 56`

You can make minor adjustments to the mappings so that CoS 3 maps to DSCP 26 (AF31) and CoS 5 maps to DSCP 46 (EF). The default values are slightly different and are not the standard values expected for voice traffic.

3 *(Optional; Layer 3 only)* Apply a QoS policy to the voice traffic.

a. Define matching traffic with an ACL:

COS	`set qos acl ip `*`acl-name`*` dscp 26 tcp any any range 2000 2002`
IOS	`(global) ip access-list extended `*`acl-name`*
	`(access-list) permit tcp any any range 2000 2002 dscp 26`
	`(access-list) exit`

In this case, the SCCP voice control TCP ports 2000, 2001, and 2002 are matched. These frames are given a DSCP value of 26 (AF31), even if this value was already set.

If other voice protocols are used, you can change the ACL to match against the appropriate port numbers.

b. *(Layer 3 IOS only)* Define the QoS policy:

COS	N/A
IOS	`(global) policy-map `*`policy-name`*
	`(pmap) class `*`class-name`*` access-group `*`acl-name`*

The policy uses a class to match traffic from the ACL.

c. Apply the QoS policy to the voice VLAN:

COS	`commit qos acl `*`acl-name`*
	`set qos acl map `*`acl-name`*` voice-vlan`
IOS	`(global) interface vlan `*`voice-vlan`*
	`(interface) service-policy input `*`policy-name`*

The QoS policy can be applied to all ports carrying the voice VLAN. This is an efficient way to use a QoS policy on one specific VLAN within a trunk.

4 Configure voice scheduling on the egress ports:

COS L3	`set port qos` *mod/port* `port-based`
	`set qos map 1p2q2t tx 2 1 cos 3`
	`set qos map 2q2t tx 2 1 cos 3`

IOS L3	`(interface)` `no mls qos vlan-based` `(interface)` `wrr-queue cos-map 2 1 3`
COS L2	`set qos map 1p2q2t tx 2 1 cos 3` `set qos map 2q2t tx 2 1 cos 3`
IOS L2	`(interface)` `wrr-queue cos-map 2 1 3`
IOS 3500	N/A

By default, all frames with CoS 5 are sent to the strict-priority queue. Frames with CoS 3 are sent to the lowest-priority queue. The scheduling map makes sure that the voice control frames (CoS 3) are sent to a higher-priority queue, serviced ahead of other traffic.

Voice QoS Example

See the QoS example in section "13-2: QoS Configuration," which presents a complete voice example, covering a variety of switch platforms in a layered network design.

14-3: Voice Modules

- **Catalyst 4000 access gateway**—Performs as a WAN router, H.323 voice over IP (VoIP) gateway, and an SCCP digital signal processor (DSP) farm for Cisco CallManager. The module also supports these interfaces:

    — One Gigabit Ethernet 802.1Q trunk into the switch backplane, supporting up to six VLANs

    — Two *voice/WAN interface cards* (VWIC)—One or two-port T1 or E1 trunks

    — One *voice interface card* (VIC)—Two-port *Foreign Exchange Station* (FXS), two-port *Foreign Exchange Office* (FXO), or two-port ISDN BRI/ST

    — One *WAN interface card* (WIC) slot—One-port 56/64 kbps DSU/CSU, two-port asynchronous/synchronous serial

- **Catalyst 4000 8-port RJ-21 FXS module**—VoIP gateway with 8 FXS interfaces for analog phone and fax devices.

- **Catalyst 4224 access gateway switch**—A combination device containing a 24-port 10/100 Ethernet switch, an 8-port FXS analog telephony module, and 3 slots for multiflex VWICs, VICs, and WICs.

- **Catalyst 6000 8-port voice T1 and services module**—VoIP gateway to 8 T1 (or E1) ISDN PRI or CAS trunks.

- **Catalyst 6000 24-port FXS module**—VoIP gateway for 24 analog stations.

Catalyst 4000 and 4224 Access Gateway Configuration

1 *(Catalyst 4000 only)* Open a *command-line interface* (CLI) session with the access gateway module:

COS	**session** *module*
IOS	N/A

From the switch supervisor CLI, a new Telnet session is opened to the access gateway module. This module uses a router IOS CLI for all configuration and display commands.

2 Configure the access gateway.

TIP

The Catalyst 4000 access gateway module and the Catalyst 4224 access gateway switch both use commands from the Cisco IOS software for routers. Refer to Chapter 12 "Voice and Telephony" in the *Cisco Field Manual: Router Configuration*, Cisco Press, ISBN 1-58705-024-2, or the *Cisco IOS Voice, Video, and Fax Configuration Guide* at www.cisco.com/univercd/cc/td/doc/product/software/ios122/122cgcr/fvvfax_c/index.htm for more complete configuration information.

In particular, you will configure the access gateway as a router and as an H.323 VoIP gateway. Chapter 12, "Switch Management," contains the necessary information to configure the voice ports, dial peers, H.323 gateways, and the QoS features needed for voice delivery. *Survivable Remote Site* (SRS) telephony is also covered there.

The Catalyst 4000 8-port FXS module must be configured from the access gateway module configuration session. It doesn't have a session interface of its own and can't be configured apart from the access gateway module.

Catalyst 6000 Voice Module Configuration

1 Identify the configuration servers.

a. *(Optional)* Use a DHCP server:

COS	`set port voice interface` *mod/port* `dhcp enable` [`vlan` *vlan*]
IOS	N/A

The module sends a DHCP request to obtain its own IP address. A DHCP server must also return the TFTP server address, DNS server address, and the default gateway address. For an 8-port T1/E1 module, each port must receive a unique IP address. The 24-port FXS module needs only one IP address for the module.

You can use the **vlan** keyword to assign the voice gateway port to a specific voice *vlan* number (1 to 1000 or 1025 to 4094).

TIP   To see the MAC address assigned to each voice gateway port or module, use the **show port voice** command.

b. *(Optional)* Don't use a DHCP server:

COS	`set port voice interface` *mod/port* `dhcp disable` *ipaddrspec* `tftp` *ipaddr* [`vlan` *vlan*] [`gateway` *ipaddr*] [`dns` [*ipaddr*] [*domain-name*]]
IOS	N/A

You can assign each voice gateway port static configuration values, if the use of a DHCP server is not practical or possible. The *ipaddrspec* field gives the IP address and mask in the form *ip-address/mask* (dotted-format mask), or *ip-address/bits* (number of mask bits 0 to 31), or *ip-address* (mask derived from the network class). For an 8-port T1/E1 module, each port must receive a unique IP address. The 24-port FXS module needs only one IP address for the module.

The **tftp** keyword identifies the TFTP server address as *ipaddr*. You can assign the voice gateway port to a specific voice VLAN by using the **vlan** keyword. The default gateway can be given with the **gateway** keyword. You can use the **dns** keyword to identify the DNS server at IP address *ipaddr*, using the domain *domain-name* (text string). If either DNS parameter is omitted, the DNS values from the switch supervisor are used. You define these with the **set ip dns server** and **set ip dns domain** commands.

2 Configure the voice gateway in Cisco CallManager.

After the module has its IP address and server information, it can download further configuration parameters. The addresses of Cisco CallManager servers are obtained from the TFTP server. The CallManager servers must be configured so that they can control all aspects of the module's operation.

Example

A Catalyst 6000 8-port T1 module is located in slot 2. It is configured to use a DHCP server for ports 2/7 and 2/8. Ports 1 through 6 are statically configured with their IP addresses, masks, TFTP server address 192.168.3.200, and default gateway address 192.168.217.1. All 8 ports are configured to use VLAN 21 as the voice VLAN. Notice that each T1 port requires a unique IP address.

Two Catalyst 6000 24-port FXS modules are located in slots 3 and 4. The module in slot 3 uses a DHCP server to obtain its configuration information. The module in slot 4 is statically configured. These modules require only a single IP address for all 24 ports:

COS	set port voice interface 2/1 dhcp disable 192.168.217.10 255.255.255.0 vlan 21 tftp 192.168.3.200 gateway 192.168.217.1
	set port voice interface 2/2 dhcp disable 192.168.217.11 255.255.255.0 vlan 21 tftp 192.168.3.200 gateway 192.168.217.1
	set port voice interface 2/3 dhcp disable 192.168.217.12 255.255.255.0 vlan 21 tftp 192.168.3.200 gateway 192.168.217.1
	set port voice interface 2/4 dhcp disable 192.168.217.13 255.255.255.0 vlan 21 tftp 192.168.3.200 gateway 192.168.217.1
	set port voice interface 2/5 dhcp disable 192.168.217.14 255.255.255.0 vlan 21 tftp 192.168.3.200 gateway 192.168.217.1
	set port voice interface 2/6 dhcp disable 192.168.217.15 255.255.255.0 vlan 21 tftp 192.168.3.200 gateway 192.168.217.1
	set port voice interface 2/7 dhcp enable vlan 21
	set port voice interface 2/8 dhcp enable vlan 21
	set port voice interface 3 dhcp enable vlan 21
	set port voice interface 4 dhcp disable 192.168.217.30/24 vlan 21 tftp 192.168.3.200 gateway 192.168.217.1
IOS	N/A

Displaying Information About Voice Modules

Table 14-3 lists some switch commands that you can use to display helpful information about Catalyst voice gateway modules.

Table 14-3   *Switch Commands to Display Catalyst Voice Gateway Module Information*

Display Function	Switch OS	Command
Voice port and server configuration	COS	`show port voice interface [mod[/port]]`
	IOS	N/A
T1/E1 CallManager and DSP status	COS	`show port [mod[/port]]`
	IOS	N/A
FXS port hook and line status	COS	`show port [mod[/port]]`
	IOS	N/A
Voice port *Facilities Data Link* (FDL) error statistics	COS	`show port voice fdl [mod[/port]]`
	IOS	N/A
T1/E1 port active-call information	COS	`show port voice active [mod[/port]] [all	call	conference	transcode] [ipaddr]`
	IOS	N/A
FXS port active-call information	COS	`show port voice active [mod[/port]] call`
	IOS	N/A

Further Reading

Refer to the following recommended sources for further information about the topics covered in this chapter.

Cisco IP Telephony Design Guides

Cisco IP Telephony Network Design Guide at: www.cisco.com/univercd/cc/td/doc/product/voice/ip_tele/network/index.htm

Cisco IP Telephony QoS Design Guide at: www.cisco.com/univercd/cc/td/doc/product/voice/ip_tele/avvidqos/

IP Telephony Solution Guide at: www.cisco.com/univercd/cc/td/doc/product/voice/ip_tele/solution/index.htm

Cisco IP Telephony Books

Cisco IP Telephony by David Lovell, Cisco Press, ISBN 1-58705-050-1

Deploying Cisco Voice over IP Solutions by Jonathan Davidson, Cisco Press, ISBN 1-58705-030-7

Integrating Voice and Data Networks by Scott Keagy, Cisco Press, ISBN 1-57870-196-1

Developing Cisco IP Phone Services by Deel, Nelson, and Smith; Cisco Press, ISBN 1-58705-060-9

Cisco CallManager Fundamentals by Smith, Alexander, Pearce, and Whetten; Cisco Press, ISBN 1-58705-008-0

Troubleshooting Cisco IP Telephony by Paul Giralt and Addis Hallmark, Cisco Press, ISBN 1-58705-075-7

Inline Power

IEEE P802.3af DTE Power via MDI at: http://grouper.ieee.org/groups/802/3/af/

Voice Protocols

Session Initiation Protocol (SIP), RFC 2543 at: ftp://ftp.isi.edu/in-notes/rfc2543.txt

H.323 ITU standards at http://www.itu.int/home/index.html

Multimedia Gateway Control Protocol (MGCP) v1.0, RFC 2705 at: ftp://ftp.isi.edu/in-notes/rfc2705.txt

Megaco at http://www.ietf.org/html.charters/megaco-charter.html and also www.ietf.org/rfc/rfc3015.txt

Real-Time Transport Protocol (RTP), RFC 1889 at: www.cs.columbia.edu/~hgs/rtp/

Voice QoS

CIM Voice Internetworking: VoIP Quality of Service, Cisco Systems, ISBN 1-58720-050-3

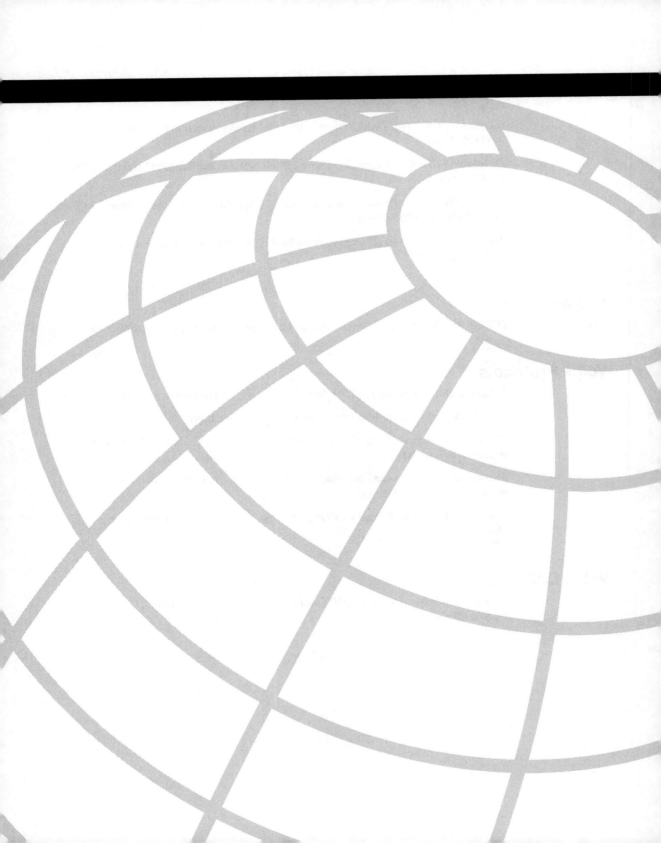

Cabling Quick Reference

Table A-1 lists the various types of *Gigabit Interface Converters* (GBICs) that you can use in Cisco Catalyst switches.

Table A-1   *Cisco Catalyst GBICs*

GBIC Type	Cisco Part Number	Media Connector	Media Type
1000BASE-T	WS-G5482	RJ-45	Category 5 UTP
Gigastack	WS-X3500-XL	Stack cable	Stack cable
	CAB-GS-50CM		50 cm stack cable
	CAB-GS-1M		1 m stack cable
1000BASE-SX	WS-G5484	SC	MMF[1]
1000BASE-LX/LH	WS-G5486	SC	MMF or SMF[2]
	CAB-GELX-625	SC	Mode conditioning patch cable
1000BASE-ZX	WS-G5487	SC	SMF

[1]   MMF = multimode fiber

[2]   SMF = single-mode fiber

Network cabling is always subject to distance limitations, which depend on the media used and the bandwidth supported. Table A-2 provides a quick reference by listing the maximum cabling distance of a variety of network media and cable types.

Table A-2   *Cabling Distances for Network Media and Cabling*

Media	Cable Type	Maximum Distance
10/100BASE-TX Ethernet	EIA/TIA Category 5 UTP[1]	100 m (328 ft)
100BASE-FX	MMF 62.5/125	400 m half-duplex
		2000 m full-duplex
	SMF	10 km
1000BASE-CX	STP[2]	25 m (82 ft)
1000BASE-T	EIA/TIA Category 5 UTP (4 pair)	100 m (328 ft)
1000BASE-SX	MMF 62.5 micron, 160 MHz/km	220 m (722 ft)
	MMF 62.5 micron, 200 MHz/km	275 m (902 ft)
	MMF 50.0 micron, 400 MHz/km	500 m (1640 ft)
	MMF 50.0 micron, 500 MHz/km	550 m (1804 ft)
1000BASE-LX/LH[3]	MMF 62.5 micron, 500 MHz/km	550 m (1804 ft)
	MMF 50.0 micron, 400 MHz/km	550 m (1804 ft)
	MMF 50.0 micron, 500 MHz/km	550 m (1804 ft)
	SMF 9/10	10 km (32,810 ft)
1000BASE-ZX	SMF	70 to 100 km
SONET	MMF (62.5 or 50.0 micron)	3 km (1.5 mi)
	SMI[4]	15 km (9 mi)
	Single-mode long reach	45 km (28 mi)
FDDI	MMF	2 km (1.2 mi)
	SMF	15 km (9.3 mi)
Token Ring (IEEE 802.5)	STP	500 m (1640 ft)
Token Ring (IEEE 802.5)	EIA/TIA Category 5 UTP	100 m (328 ft)
ISDN BRI	UTP, RJ-45	10 m (32.8 ft)

Table A-2   *Cabling Distances for Network Media and Cabling (Continued)*

Media	Cable Type	Maximum Distance
Async EIA/TIA-232	2400 baud	60 m (200 ft)
	4800 baud	30 m (100 ft)
	9600 baud	15 m (50 ft)
	19200 baud	15 m (50 ft)
	38400 baud	15 m (50 ft)
	57600 baud	7.6 m (25 ft)
	115200 baud	3.7 m (12 ft)
Sync EIA/TIA-449 with balanced drivers, including X.21 and V.35	2400 baud	1250 m (4100 ft)
	4800 baud	625 m (2050 ft)
	9600 baud	31 m (1025 ft)
	19200 baud	156 m (513 ft)
	38400 baud	78 m (256 ft)
	56000 baud	31 m (102 ft)
	T1 (1.544 mbps)	15 m (50 ft)

[1] UTP = unshielded twisted-pair

[2] STP = single twisted-pair

[3] When using 1000BASE-LX/LH GBICs with 62.5 micron multimode fiber, you must use a mode-conditioning patch cord for distances of more than 300 m (984 ft). See www.cisco.com/univercd/cc/td/doc/product/lan/cat5000/cnfg_nts/ethernet/5421_01.htm for installation and usage information.

[4] SMI = single-mode intermediate reach

In many cases, you might find that you need to know the pinout connections for various network cables. The RJ-45 connector is commonly used across many media, but with different pinouts for each. Table A-3 shows the pinout for an RJ-45 connector when used with specific media.

Table A-3 *RJ-45 Connector Pinouts Based on Media Type*

RJ-45 Pin	Router Console (DTE)	Ethernet UTP		Token Ring UTP	ISDN BRI S/T TE	ISDN BRI U	CT1/PRI CSU	CE1/ PRI	56/64kbps DSU/CSU[1]	T1/E1[1]
		10/100	1000							
1	RTS	TX+	TP0+	GND			Rcv Ring	TX Tip	TX Ring	RX
2	DTR	TX–	TP0–	GND			Rcv Tip	TX Ring	TX Tip	RX
3	TxD	RX+	TP1+	TX+	TX+			TX Shld		
4	GND		TP2+	RX+	RX+	Tip or Ring	Ring	RX Tip		TX
5	GND		TP2–	RX–	RX–	Tip or Ring	Tip	RX Ring		TX
6	RxD	RX–	TP1–	TX–	TX–			RX Shld		
7	DSR		TP3+	GND					RX Tip	
8	CTS		TP3–						RX Ring	

[1] An RJ-48 connector is actually used in these applications.

Back-to-Back Connections

In a lab setup or in certain circumstances, you might find that you need to connect two switches or two routers to each other in a back-to-back fashion. Normally, some other active device is used to connect router interfaces. For example, an Ethernet hub or switch, a Token Ring *media attachment unit* (MAU), and the *Public Switched Telephone Network* (PSTN) all perform an active role in interconnecting routers. If these are not available, as in a lab environment, a special cable is needed to make the back-to-back connection.

NOTE It is not possible to make a back-to-back cable to connect two Token Ring interfaces. Token Ring connections require an active device such as a MAU or a Token Ring switch to terminate the connection.

Ethernet Connections

Normally, a 10BASE-T or a 10/100BASE-TX host *network interface card* (NIC) connects to a switch through a *straight-through* Category 5 UTP cable. RJ-45 pins 1 and 2 form one pair, and pins 3 and 6 form another pair. To connect two Ethernet switch ports directly, however, you need a *crossover cable*.

A crossover cable connects the pair containing pins 1 and 2 on one end to the pair containing pins 3 and 6 on the other end. Likewise, pins 3 and 6 are connected to pins 1 and 2. Table A-4 lists the pinout connections for both RJ-45 ends of the crossover cable.

Table A-4   *RJ-45 Connector Pinouts for Crossover Cables*

RJ-45 Pin End A	Description End A	Description End B	RJ-45 Pin End B
1	TX+	RX+	3
2	TX–	RX–	6
3	RX+	TX+	1
4			4
5			5
6	RX–	TX–	2
7			7
8			8

Asynchronous Serial Connections

An asynchronous serial connection, such as the Aux port or a line on an access server, requires an RJ-45 connection. For a back-to-back link between two async ports on two different routers, you must use a *rollover cable*. Rollover cables are usually flat eight-conductor cables with RJ-45 connectors, fashioned so that pin 1 on one end goes to pin 8 on the other end, pin 2 goes to pin 7, and so forth. Cisco normally supplies a rollover cable with a console cable kit. Table A-5 shows the pinout connections for both ends of the rollover cable.

Table A-5   *RJ-45 Connector Pinouts for Rollover Cables*

RJ-45 Pin End A	Description End A	Description End B	RJ-45 Pin End B
1	RTS	CTS	8
2	DTR	DSR	7
3	TxD	RxD	6
4	GND	GND	5

continues

Table A-5 *RJ-45 Connector Pinouts for Rollover Cables (Continued)*

5	GND	GND	4
6	RxD	TxD	3
7	DSR	DTR	2
8	CTS	RTS	1

56/64-kbps CSU/DSU Connections

Normally, if a router has an integrated or external CSU/DSU for a 56/64-kbps serial interface, the CSU/DSU is connected to the service provider's termination box. The service provider or PSTN establishes the active circuit between two CSU/DSU units and routers.

Back-to-back serial connections can usually be made between the serial interfaces of two routers using one *data termination equipment* (DTE) serial cable and one *data communication equipment* (DCE) serial cable. One router becomes the DTE end, and the other becomes the DCE end and must provide the clock. If you have two routers with integrated CSU/DSUs, however, there is no way to access the physical serial interface. In this case, you can make a back-to-back 56/64 cable by crossing the transmit and receive pairs. Table A-6 shows the pinout connections of both RJ-48 (an RJ-45 will do) ends of the cable.

Table A-6 *RJ-48 Connector Pinouts for Back-to-Back 56/64 kbps CSU/DSU Connections*

RJ-48 Pin End A	Description End A	Description End B	RJ-48 Pin End B
1	TX Ring	RX Ring	7
2	TX Tip	RX Tip	8
3			3
4			4
5			5
6			6
7	RX Tip	TX Tip	1
8	RX Ring	TX Ring	2

T1/E1 CSU/DSU Connections

You can also make back-to-back connections between two routers with integrated T1/E1 CSU/DSUs using a specially made cable. Again, the transmit and receive pairs are crossed in the cable. Table A-7 lists the pinout connections of both RJ-48 (an RJ-45 will do) ends of the cable.

Table A-7   *RJ-48 Connector Pinouts for Back-to-Back T1/E1 CSU/DSU Connections*

RJ-48 Pin End A	Description End A	Description End B	RJ-48 Pin End B
1	RX (input)	TX (input)	4
2	RX (input)	TX (input)	5
3			3
4	TX (output)	RX (output)	1
5	TX (output)	RX (output)	2
6			6
7			7
8			8

Well-known Protocol, Port, and Other Numbers

Refer to the following sections for explanations and listings of well-known numbers:

- **B-1: IP Protocol Numbers**
- **B-2: ICMP Type and Code Numbers**
- **B-3: Well-known IP Port Numbers**
- **B-4: Well-Known IP Multicast Addresses**
- **B-5: Ethernet Type Codes**

B-1: IP Protocol Numbers

A higher-layer protocol is identified with an 8-bit field within an IPv4 packet called *Protocol*. The IPv4 header format is shown in Figure B-1 with the Protocol field shaded. Figure B-2 shows the IPv6 header format where the protocol number is stored in the shaded Next Header field.

Well-known or assigned IP protocols are registered with the *Internet Assigned Numbers Authority* (IANA). The information presented here is reproduced with permission from the IANA. For the most current IP protocol number assignment information, refer to www.iana.org/numbers.htm under the "Protocol Numbers" link.

Figure B-1 *IPv4 Header Format Showing the Protocol Field*

0		1	2	3
Version	Hdr len	Service type	Total length	
Identification			Flags	Fragment offset
Time to live		Protocol	Header checksum	
Source IP address				
Destination IP address				
IP options (if needed)				Padding
Data …				

Figure B-2 *IPv6 Base Header Format Showing the Next Header Field*

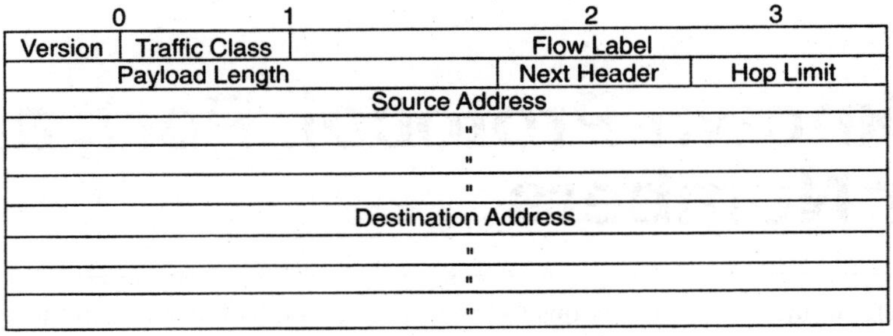

Table B-1 shows the registered IP protocol numbers, along with the protocol keyword (or acronym), the name of the protocol, and an RFC number (if applicable).

Table B-1 *Registered IP Protocol Numbers, Keywords, Names, and Associated RFCs*

Keyword Protocol References	Number
HOPOPT IPv6 Hop-by-Hop Option RFC 1883	0
ICMP Internet Control Message RFC 792	1
IGMP Internet Group Management RFC 1112	2
GGP Gateway-to-Gateway RFC 823	3
IP IP in IP (encapsulation) RFC 2003	4
ST Stream RFC 1190, RFC 1819	5

Table B-1 *Registered IP Protocol Numbers, Keywords, Names, and Associated RFCs (Continued)*

Keyword Protocol References	Number
TCP	6
Transmission Control	
RFC 793	
CBT	7
CBT	
EGP	8
Exterior Gateway Protocol	
RFC 888	
IGP	9
Any private interior gateway	
IANA (used by Cisco for IGRP)	
BBN-RCC-MON	10
BBN RCC Monitoring	
NVP-II	11
Network Voice Protocol	
RFC 741	
PUP	12
PUP	
ARGUS	13
ARGUS	
EMCON	14
EMCON	
XNET	15
Cross Net Debugger	
CHAOS	16
Chaos	
UDP	17
User Datagram	
RFC 768	

continues

Table B-1 *Registered IP Protocol Numbers, Keywords, Names, and Associated RFCs (Continued)*

Keyword Protocol References	Number
MUX	18
Multiplexing	
DCN-MEAS	19
DCN Measurement Subsystems	
HMP	20
Host Monitoring	
RFC 869	
PRM	21
Packet Radio Measurement	
XNS-IDP	22
XEROX NS IDP	
TRUNK-1	23
Trunk-1	
TRUNK-2	24
Trunk-2	
LEAF-1	25
Leaf-1	
LEAF-2	26
Leaf-2	
RDP	27
Reliable Data Protocol	
RFC 908	
IRTP	28
Internet Reliable Transaction	
RFC 938	
ISO-TP4	29
ISO Transport Protocol Class 4	
RFC 905	
NETBLT	30
Bulk Data Transfer Protocol	
RFC 969	

Table B-1   *Registered IP Protocol Numbers, Keywords, Names, and Associated RFCs (Continued)*

Keyword Protocol References	Number
MFE-NSP MFE Network Services Protocol	31
MERIT-INP MERIT Internodal Protocol	32
SEP Sequential Exchange Protocol	33
3PC Third Party Connect Protocol	34
IDPR Inter-Domain Policy Routing Protocol RFC 1479	35
XTP XTP	36
DDP Datagram Delivery Protocol	37
IDPR-CMTP IDPR Control Message Transport Protocol	38
TP++ TP++ Transport Protocol	39
IL IL Transport Protocol	40
IPv6 Ipv6	41
SDRP Source Demand Routing Protocol	42
IPv6-Route Routing Header for IPv6	43
IPv6-Frag Fragment Header for IPv6	44

continues

Table B-1 *Registered IP Protocol Numbers, Keywords, Names, and Associated RFCs (Continued)*

Keyword Protocol References	Number
IDRP	45
Inter-Domain Routing Protocol	
RSVP	46
Resource ReSerVation Protocol	
RFC 2205	
GRE	47
General Routing Encapsulation	
RFC 1701	
MHRP	48
Mobile Host Routing Protocol	
BNA	49
BNA	
ESP	50
Encap Security Payload	
RFC 2406	
AH	51
Authentication Header	
RFC 2402	
I-NLSP	52
Integrated Net Layer Security	
TUBA	
SWIPE	53
IP with Encryption	
NARP	54
NBMA Address Resolution Protocol	
RFC 1735	
MOBILE	55
IP Mobility	
RFC 2002	
TLSP	56
Transport Layer Security Protocol using Kryptonet key management	

Table B-1   *Registered IP Protocol Numbers, Keywords, Names, and Associated RFCs (Continued)*

Keyword Protocol References	Number
SKIP	57
SKIP	
IPv6-ICMP	58
ICMP for IPv6	
RFC 2463	
IPv6-NoNxt	59
No Next Header for IPv6	
RFC 2460	
IPv6-Opts	60
Destination Options for IPv6	
RFC 2460	
Any host internal protocol	61
IANA	
CFTP	62
CFTP	
Any local network	63
IANA	
SAT-EXPAK	64
SATNET and Backroom EXPAK	
KRYPTOLAN	65
Kryptolan	
RVD	66
MIT Remote Virtual Disk Protocol	
IPPC	67
Internet Pluribus Packet Core	
Any distributed file system	68
IANA	
SAT-MON	69
SATNET Monitoring	

continues

Table B-1 *Registered IP Protocol Numbers, Keywords, Names, and Associated RFCs (Continued)*

Keyword Protocol References	Number
VISA	70
VISA Protocol	
IPCV	71
Internet Packet Core Utility	
CPNX	72
Computer Protocol Network Executive	
CPHB	73
Computer Protocol Heart Beat	
WSN	74
Wang Span Network	
PVP	75
Packet Video Protocol	
BR-SAT-MON	76
Backroom SATNET Monitoring	
SUN-ND	77
SUN ND PROTOCOL-Temporary	
WB-MON	78
WIDEBAND Monitoring	
WB-EXPAK	79
WIDEBAND EXPAK	
ISO-IP	80
ISO Internet Protocol	
VMTP	81
VMTP	
RFC 1045	
SECURE-VMTP	82
SECURE-VMTP	
VINES	83
VINES	
TTP	84
TTP	

Table B-1   *Registered IP Protocol Numbers, Keywords, Names, and Associated RFCs (Continued)*

Keyword Protocol References	Number
NSFNET-IGP	85
NSFNET-IGP	
DGP	86
Dissimilar Gateway Protocol	
TCF	87
TCF	
EIGRP	88
EIGRP	
CISCO	
OSPFIGP	89
OSPFIGP	
RFC 2328	
Sprite-RPC	90
Sprite RPC Protocol	
LARP	91
Locus Address Resolution Protocol	
MTP	92
Multicast Transport Protocol	
AX.25	93
AX.25 Frames	
IPIP	94
IP-within-IP Encapsulation Protocol	
RFC 1853	
MICP	95
Mobile Internetworking Control Protocol	
SCC-SP	96
Semaphore Communications Sec. Pro.	
ETHERIP	97
Ethernet-within-IP Encapsulation	

continues

Table B-1 *Registered IP Protocol Numbers, Keywords, Names, and Associated RFCs (Continued)*

Keyword Protocol References	Number
ENCAP	98
Encapsulation Header	
RFC 1241	
Any private encryption scheme	99
IANA	
GMTP	100
GMTP	
IFMP	101
Ipsilon Flow Management Protocol	
PNNI	102
PNNI over IP	
PIM	103
Protocol Independent Multicast	
RFC 2362 (sparse mode)	
ARIS	104
ARIS	
SCPS	105
SCPS	
QNX	106
QNX	
A/N	107
Active Networks	
IPComp	108
IP Payload Compression Protocol	
RFC 2393	
SNP	109
Sitara Networks Protocol	
Compaq-Peer	110
Compaq Peer Protocol	

Table B-1 *Registered IP Protocol Numbers, Keywords, Names, and Associated RFCs (Continued)*

Keyword Protocol References	Number
IPX-in-IP	111
IPX in IP	
RFC 1234	
VRRP	112
Virtual Router Redundancy Protocol	
RFC 2328	
PGM	113
PGM Reliable Transport Protocol	
Any 0-hop protocol	114
IANA	
L2TP	115
Layer Two Tunneling Protocol	
RFC 2661	
DDX	116
D-II Data Exchange (DDX)	
IATP	117
Interactive Agent Transfer Protocol	
STP	118
Schedule Transfer Protocol	
SRP	119
SpectraLink Radio Protocol	
UTI	120
UTI	
SMP	121
Simple Message Protocol	
SM	122
SM	
PTP	123
Performance Transparency Protocol	
ISIS over IPv4	124

continues

Table B-1 *Registered IP Protocol Numbers, Keywords, Names, and Associated RFCs (Continued)*

Keyword Protocol References	Number
FIRE	125
CRTP Combat Radio Transport Protocol	126
CRUDP Combat Radio User Datagram	127
SSCOPMCE	128
IPLT	129
SPS Secure Packet Shield	130
PIPE Private IP Encapsulation within IP	131
SCTP Stream Control Transmission Protocol	132
FC Fibre Channel	133
Unassigned IANA	134 to 254
Reserved IANA	255

B-2: ICMP Type and Code Numbers

The *Internet Control Message Protocol* (ICMP) transports error or control messages between routers and other devices. An ICMP message is encapsulated as the payload in an IP packet. Figure B-3 shows the ICMP message format. Notice that in the case of an error condition, the first 8 bytes (64 bits) of the original datagram causing the error are included in the ICMP message. This provides the protocol and port numbers of the original message to be seen, making troubleshooting easier.

Figure B-3 *ICMP Message Format*

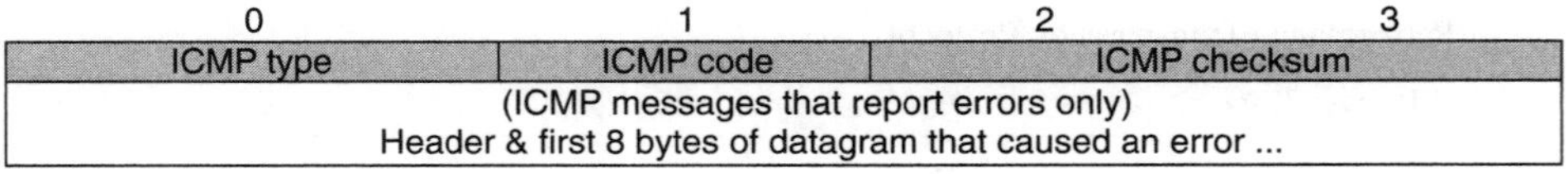

0	1	2	3
ICMP type	ICMP code	ICMP checksum	
(ICMP messages that report errors only) Header & first 8 bytes of datagram that caused an error ...			

ICMP type codes are registered with the IANA. The information presented here is reproduced with permission from the IANA. For the most current ICMP type code number assignment information, refer to www.iana.org/numbers.htm under the "ICMP Type" link.

Table B-2 shows the assigned ICMP type numbers, ICMP codes (where applicable), a brief description, and a reference to an RFC.

Table B-2   *Assigned ICMP Type Numbers, Codes, Descriptions, and Associated RFCs*

Type	Code	Name	Reference
0		Echo Reply	RFC 792
1		Unassigned	
2		Unassigned	
3		Destination Unreachable	RFC 792
	0	Net Unreachable	
	1	Host Unreachable	
	2	Protocol Unreachable	
	3	Port Unreachable	
	4	Fragmentation Needed and Don't Fragment Was Set	
	5	Source Route Failed	
	6	Destination Network Unknown	
	7	Destination Host Unknown	
	8	Source Host Isolated	
	9	Destination Network Is Administratively Prohibited	
	10	Destination Host Is Administratively Prohibited	
	11	Destination Network Unreachable for Type of Service	
	12	Destination Host Unreachable for Type of Service	
	13	Communication Administratively Prohibited	RFC 1812
	14	Host Precedence Violation	RFC 1812
	15	Precedence Cutoff in Effect	RFC 1812
4		Source Quench	RFC 792
5		Redirect	RFC 792
	0	Redirect Datagram for the Network (or Subnet)	
	1	Redirect Datagram for the Host	

continues

Table B-2   *Assigned ICMP Type Numbers, Codes, Descriptions, and Associated RFCs (Continued)*

Type	Code	Name	Reference
	2	Redirect Datagram for the Type of Service and Network	
	3	Redirect Datagram for the Type of Service and Host	
6		Alternate Host Address	
	0	Alternate Address for Host	
7		Unassigned	
8		Echo	RFC 792
9		Router Advertisement	RFC 1256
10		Router Solicitation	RFC 1256
11		Time Exceeded	RFC 792
	0	Time to Live Exceeded in Transit	
	1	Fragment Reassembly Time Exceeded	
12		Parameter Problem	RFC 792
	0	Pointer Indicates the Error	
	1	Missing a Required Option	RFC 1108
	2	Bad Length	
13		Timestamp	RFC 792
14		Timestamp Reply	RFC 792
15		Information Request	RFC 792
16		Information Reply	RFC 792
17		Address Mask Request	RFC 950
18		Address Mask Reply	RFC 950
19		Reserved (for Security)	
20 to 29		Reserved (for Robustness Experiment)	
30		Traceroute	RFC 1393
31		Datagram Conversion Error	RFC 1475
32		Mobile Host Redirect	
33		IPv6 Where-Are-You	
34		IPv6 I-Am-Here	
35		Mobile Registration Request	
36		Mobile Registration Reply	

Table B-2   *Assigned ICMP Type Numbers, Codes, Descriptions, and Associated RFCs (Continued)*

Type	Code	Name	Reference
37		Domain Name Request	
38		Domain Name Reply	
39		SKIP	
40		Photuris	
	0	Reserved	
	1	Unknown Security Parameters Index	
	2	Valid Security Parameters, but Authentication Failed	
	3	Valid Security Parameters, but Decryption Failed	
41 to 255		Reserved	

B-3: Well-known IP Port Numbers

Transport layer protocols identify higher-layer traffic with 16-bit fields called *port numbers.* A connection between two devices uses a source and a destination port, both contained within the protocol data unit. The *User Datagram Protocol* (UDP) header format is shown in Figure B-4 with the source and destination port fields shaded. The UDP checksum is optional for IPv4. Figure B-5 shows *Transmission Control Protocol* (TCP) header format with the source and destination port fields shaded.

Figure B-4   *UDP Datagram Format Showing Port Fields*

0	1	2	3
UDP source port		UDP destination port	
UDP message length		UDP checksum	
Data ...			

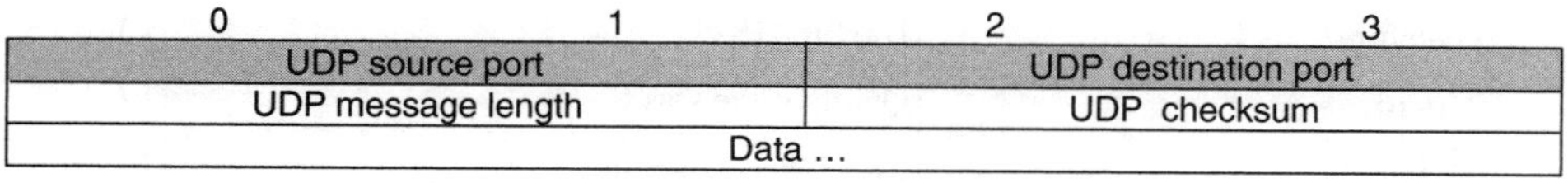

Figure B-5   *TCP Segment Format Showing Port Fields*

0	1	2	3
TCP source port		TCP destination port	
Sequence number			
Acknowledgment number			
Hdr len	Reserved	Code bits	Window
Checksum		Urgent pointer	
Options (if necessary)			Padding
Data			
Data ...			

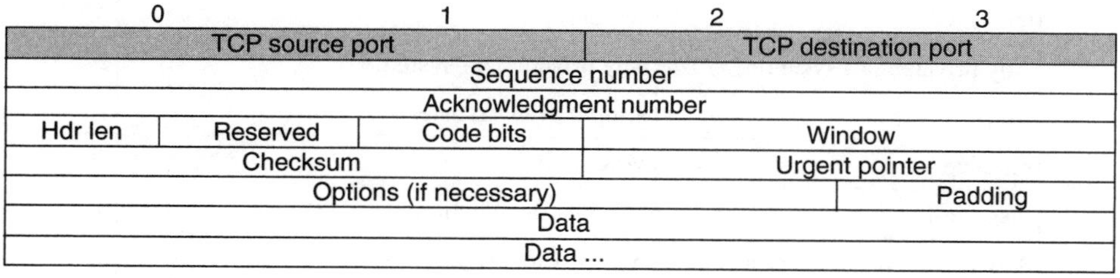

Both UDP and TCP port numbers are divided into the following ranges:

- Well-known port numbers (0 through 1023)
- Registered port numbers (1024 through 49151)
- Dynamic or private port numbers (49152 through 65535)

Usually, a port assignment uses a common port number for both UDP and TCP. A connection from a client to a server uses the well-known port on the server as a *service contact port*, whereas the client is free to dynamically assign its own port number. For TCP, the connection is identified by the source and destination IP addresses, as well as the source and destination TCP port numbers.

Well-known or assigned IP protocols are registered with the IANA. The information presented here is reproduced with permission from the IANA. For the most current IP protocol number assignment information, refer to www.iana.org/numbers.htm under the "Port Numbers" link.

Table B-3 shows some commonly used protocols, their port numbers, and a brief description. The IANA has recorded around 3350 unique port numbers. Because of space limitations, only a small subset of these port numbers are presented here.

Table B-3 *Commonly Used Protocols and Associated Port Numbers*

Keyword	Description	UDP/TCP Port
echo	Echo	7
discard	Discard	9
systat	Active Users	11
daytime	Daytime (RFC 867)	13
qotd	Quote of the Day	17
chargen	Character Generator	19
ftp-data	File Transfer [Default Data]	20
ftp	File Transfer [Control]	21
ssh	SSH Remote Login Protocol	22
telnet	Telnet	23
Any private mail system	Any private mail system	24
smtp	Simple Mail Transfer	25
msg-icp	MSG ICP	29
msg-auth	MSG Authentication	31
Any private printer server	Any private printer server	35

Table B-3 *Commonly Used Protocols and Associated Port Numbers (Continued)*

Keyword	Description	UDP/TCP Port
time	Time	37
name	Host Name Server	42
nameserver	Host Name Server	42
nicname	Who Is	43
tacacs	Login Host Protocol (TACACS)	49
re-mail-ck	Remote Mail Checking Protocol	50
domain	Domain Name Server	53
Any private terminal address	Any private terminal address	57
Any private file service	Any private file service	59
whois++	whois++	63
tacacs-ds	TACACS-Database Service	65
sql*net	Oracle SQL*NET	66
bootps	Bootstrap Protocol Server	67
bootpc	Bootstrap Protocol Client	68
tftp	Trivial File Transfer	69
gopher	Gopher	70
Any private dial out service	Any private dial out service	75
Any private RJE service	Any private RJE service	77
finger	Finger	79
http	World Wide Web HTTP	80
www	World Wide Web HTTP	80
www-http	World Wide Web HTTP	80
hosts2-ns	HOSTS2 Name Server	81
xfer	XFER Utility	82
Any private terminal link	Any private terminal link	87
kerberos	Kerberos	88
dnsix	DNSIX Securit Attribute Token Map	90
npp	Network Printing Protocol	92

continues

Table B-3 *Commonly Used Protocols and Associated Port Numbers (Continued)*

Keyword	Description	UDP/TCP Port
dcp	Device Control Protocol	93
objcall	Tivoli Object Dispatcher	94
acr-nema	ACR-NEMA Digital Imag. & Comm. 300	104
rtelnet	Remote Telnet Service	107
snagas	SNA Gateway Access Server	108
pop2	Post Office Protocol (version 2)	109
pop3	Post Office Protocol (version 3)	110
sunrpc	SUN Remote Procedure Call	111
Mcidas	McIDAS Data Transmission Protocol	112
ident/auth	Authentication Service	113
audionews	Audio News Multicast	114
sftp	Simple File Transfer Protocol	115
uucp-path	UUCP Path Service	117
sqlserv	SQL Services	118
nntp	Network News Transfer Protocol	119
ntp	Network Time Protocol	123
pwdgen	Password Generator Protocol	129
cisco-fna	Cisco FNATIVE	130
cisco-tna	Cisco TNATIVE	131
cisco-sys	Cisco SYSMAINT	132
ingres-net	INGRES-NET Service	134
profile	PROFILE Naming System	136
netbios-ns	NetBIOS Name Service	137
netbios-dgm	NetBIOS Datagram Service	138
netbios-ssn	NetBIOS Session Service	139
imap	Internet Message Access Protocol	143
sql-net	SQL-NET	150
sgmp	SGMP	153
sqlsrv	SQL Service	156
pcmail-srv	PCMail Server	158

Table B-3   *Commonly Used Protocols and Associated Port Numbers (Continued)*

Keyword	Description	UDP/TCP Port
sgmp-traps	SGMP-TRAPS	160
snmp	SNMP	161
snmptrap	SNMPTRAP	162
cmip-man	CMIP/TCP Manager	163
send	SEND	169
print-srv	Network PostScript	170
xyplex-mux	Xyplex	173
mailq	MAILQ	174
vmnet	VMNET	175
xdmcp	X Display Manager Control Protocol	177
bgp	Border Gateway Protocol	179
mumps	Plus Five's MUMPS	188
irc	Internet Relay Chat Protocol	194
dn6-nlm-aud	DNSIX Network Level Module Audit	195
dn6-smm-red	DNSIX Session Managementt Module Audit Redirect	196
dls	Directory Location Service	197
dls-mon	Directory Location Service Monitor	198
src	IBM System Resource Controller	200
at-rtmp	AppleTalk Routing Maintenance	201
at-nbp	AppleTalk Name Binding	202
at-3	AppleTalk Unused	203
at-echo	AppleTalk Echo	204
at-5	AppleTalk Unused	205
at-zis	AppleTalk Zone Information	206
at-7	AppleTalk Unused	207
at-8	AppleTalk Unused	208
qmtp	The Quick Mail Transfer Protocol	209
ipx	IPX	213

continues

Table B-3   *Commonly Used Protocols and Associated Port Numbers (Continued)*

Keyword	Description	UDP/TCP Port
vmpwscs	VM PWSCS	214
softpc	Insignia Solutions	215
dbase	dBASE UNIX	217
imap3	Interactive Mail Access Protocol (version 3)	220
http-mgmt	http-mgmt	280
asip-webadmin	AppleShare IP WebAdmin	311
ptp-event	PTP Event	319
ptp-general	PTP General	320
pdap	Prospero Data Access Protocol	344
rsvp_tunnel	RSVP Tunnel	363
rpc2portmap	rpc2portmap	369
aurp	AppleTalk Update-Based Routing Protocol	387
ldap	Lightweight Directory Access Protocol	389
netcp	NETscout Control Protocol	395
netware-ip	Novell NetWare over IP	396
ups	Uninterruptible power supply	401
smsp	Storage Management Services Protocol	413
mobileip-agent	MobileIP-Agent	434
mobilip-mn	MobilIP-MN	435
https	HTTP protocol over TLS/SSL	443
snpp	Simple Network Paging Protocol	444
microsoft-ds	Microsoft-DS	445
appleqtc	Apple QuickTime	458
ss7ns	ss7ns	477
ph	Ph service	481
isakmp	isakmp	500
exec	Remote process execution	512
login	remote login by Telnet	513
shell	cmd	514
printer	spooler	515

Table B-3   *Commonly Used Protocols and Associated Port Numbers (Continued)*

Keyword	Description	UDP/TCP Port
ntalk	ntalk	518
utime	unixtime	519
ncp	NCP	524
timed	timedserver	525
irc-serv	IRC-SERV	529
courier	rpc	530
conference	chat	531
netnews	readnews	532
netwall	For emergency broadcasts	533
iiop	iiop	535
nmsp	Networked Media Streaming Protocol	537
uucp	uucpd	540
uucp-rlogin	uucp-rlogin	541
klogin	klogin	543
kshell	krcmd	544
appleqtcsrvr	appleqtcsrvr	545
dhcpv6-client	DHCPv6 Client	546
dhcpv6-server	DHCPv6 Server	547
afpovertcp	AFC over TCP	548
rtsp	Real Time Stream Control Protocol	554
remotefs	rfs server	556
rmonitor	rmonitord	560
monitor	monitor	561
nntps	nntp protocol over TLS/SSL (was snntp)	563
whoami	whoami	565
sntp-heartbeat	SNTP HEARTBEAT	580
imap4-ssl	IMAP4 + SSl (use 993 instead)	585
password-chg	Password Change	586
eudora-set	Eudora Set	592

continues

Table B-3 *Commonly Used Protocols and Associated Port Numbers (Continued)*

Keyword	Description	UDP/TCP Port
http-rpc-epmap	HTTP RPC Ep Map	593
sco-websrvrmg3	SCO Web Server Manager 3	598
ipcserver	SUN IPC server	600
sshell	SSLshell	614
sco-inetmgr	Internet Configuration Manager	615
sco-sysmgr	SCO System Administration Server	616
sco-dtmgr	SCO Desktop Administration Server	617
sco-websrvmgr	SCO WebServer Manager	620
ldaps	LDAP protocol over TLS/SSL (was sldap)	636
dhcp-failover	DHCP Failover	647
mac-srvr-admin	MacOS Server Admin	660
doom	doom Id Software	666
corba-iiop	CORBA IIOP	683
corba-iiop-ssl	CORBA IIOP SSL	684
nmap	NMAP	689
msexch-routing	MS Exchange Routing	691
ieee-mms-ssl	IEEE-MMS-SSL	695
cisco-tdp	Cisco TDP	711
flexlm	Flexible License Manager	744
kerberos-adm	Kerberos administration	749
phonebook	Phone	767
dhcp-failover2	dhcp-failover2	847
ftps-data	FTP protocol, data, over TLS/SSL	989
ftps	FTP protocol, control, over TLS/SSL	990
nas	Netnews Administration System	991
telnets	Telnet protocol over TLS/SSL	992
imaps	imap4 protocol over TLS/SSL	993
ircs	irc protocol over TLS/SSL	994
pop3s	POP3 protocol over TLS/SSL (was spop3)	995
sunclustermgr	SUN Cluster Manager	1097

Table B-3   *Commonly Used Protocols and Associated Port Numbers (Continued)*

Keyword	Description	UDP/TCP Port
tripwire	TRIPWIRE	1169
shockwave2	Shockwave 2	1257
h323hostcallsc	H323 Host Call Secure	1300
lotusnote	Lotus Notes	1352
novell-lu6.2	Novell LU6.2	1416
ms-sql-s	Microsoft SQL Server	1433
ms-sql-m	Microsoft SQL Monitor	1434
ibm-cics	IBM CICS	1435
sybase-sqlany	Sybase SQL Any	1498
shivadiscovery	Shiva	1502
wins	Microsoft Windows Internet Name Service	1512
ingreslock	ingres	1524
orasrv	Oracle	1525
tlisrv	Oracle	1527
coauthor	Oracle	1529
rdb-dbs-disp	Oracle Remote Data Base	1571
oraclenames	oraclenames	1575
ontime	ontime	1622
shockwave	Shockwave	1626
oraclenet8cman	Oracle Net8 Cman	1630
cert-initiator	cert-initiator	1639
cert-responder	cert-responder	1640
kermit	kermit	1649
groupwise	groupwise	1677
rsvp-encap-1	RSVP-ENCAPSULATION-1	1698
rsvp-encap-2	RSVP-ENCAPSULATION-2	1699
h323gatedisc	h323gatedisc	1718
h323gatestat	h323gatestat	1719
h323hostcall	h323hostcall	1720

continues

Table B-3   *Commonly Used Protocols and Associated Port Numbers (Continued)*

Keyword	Description	UDP/TCP Port
cisco-net-mgmt	cisco-net-mgmt	1741
oracle-em1	oracle-em1	1748
oracle-em2	oracle-em2	1754
tftp-mcast	tftp-mcast	1758
www-ldap-gw	www-ldap-gw	1760
bmc-net-admin	bmc-net-admin	1769
bmc-net-svc	bmc-net-svc	1770
oracle-vp2	Oracle-VP2	1808
oracle-vp1	Oracle-VP1	1809
radius	RADIUS	1812
radius-acct	RADIUS Accounting	1813
hsrp	Hot Standby Router Protocol	1985
licensedaemon	Cisco license management	1986
tr-rsrb-p1	Cisco RSRP Priority 1 port	1987
tr-rsrb-p2	Cisco RSRP Priority 2 port	1988
tr-rsrb-p3	Cisco RSRP Priority 3 port	1989
stun-p1	Cisco STUN Priority 1 port	1990
stun-p2	Cisco STUN Priority 2 port	1991
stun-p3	Cisco STUN Priority 3 port	1992
snmp-tcp-port	Cisco SNMP TCP port	1993
stun-port	Cisco serial tunnel port	1994
perf-port	Cisco perf port	1995
tr-rsrb-port	Cisco Remote SRB port	1996
gdp-port	Cicso Gateway Discovery Protocol	1997
x25-svc-port	Cisco X.25 service (XOT)	1998
tcp-id-port	Cisco identification port	1999
dlsrpn	Data Link Switch Read Port Number	2065
dlswpn	Data Link Switch Write Port Number	2067
ah-esp-encap	AH and ESP Encapsulated in UDP packet	2070
h2250-annex-g	H.225.0 Annex G	2099

Table B-3   *Commonly Used Protocols and Associated Port Numbers (Continued)*

Keyword	Description	UDP/TCP Port
ms-olap3	Microsoft OLAP	2382
ovsessionmgr	OpenView Session Manager	2389
ms-olap1	MS OLAP 1	2393
ms-olap2	MS OLAP 2	2394
mgcp-gateway	Media Gateway Control Protocol Gateway	2427
ovwdb	OpenView NNM daemon	2447
giop	Oracle GIOP	2481
giop-ssl	Oracle GIOP SSL	2482
ttc	Oracle TTC	2483
ttc-ssl	Oracle TTC SSL	2484
citrixima	Citrix IMA	2512
citrixadmin	Citrix ADMIN	2513
call-sig-trans	H.323 Annex E call signaling transport	2517
windb	WinDb	2522
novell-zen	Novell ZEN	2544
clp	Cisco Line Protocol	2567
hl7	HL7	2575
citrixmaclient	Citrix MA Client	2598
sybaseanywhere	Sybase Anywhere	2638
novell-ipx-cmd	Novell IPX CMD	2645
sms-rcinfo	SMS RCINFO	2701
sms-xfer	SMS XFER	2702
sms-chat	SMS CHAT	2703
sms-remctrl	SMS REMCTRL	2704
mgcp-callagent	Media Gateway Control Protocol Call Agent	2727
dicom-iscl	DICOM ISCL	2761
dicom-tls	DICOM TLS	2762
citrix-rtmp	Citrix RTMP	2897
wap-push	WAP Push	2948

continues

Table B-3 *Commonly Used Protocols and Associated Port Numbers (Continued)*

Keyword	Description	UDP/TCP Port
wap-pushsecure	WAP Push Secure	2949
h263-video	H.263 Video Streaming	2979
lotusmtap	Lotus Mail Tracking Agent Protocol	3007
njfss	NetWare sync services	3092
bmcpatrolagent	BMC Patrol Agent	3181
bmcpatrolrnvu	BMC Patrol Rendezvous	3182
ccmail	cc:mail/lotus	3264
msft-gc	Microsoft Global Catalog	3268
msft-gc-ssl	Microsoft Global Catalog with LDAP/SSL	3269
Unauthorized Use by SAP R/3	Unauthorized Use by SAP R/3	3300 to 3301
mysql	MySQL	3306
ms-cluster-net	MS Cluster Net	3343
ssql	SSQL	3352
ms-wbt-server	MS WBT Server	3389
mira	Apple Remote Access Protocol	3454
prsvp	RSVP Port	3455
patrolview	Patrol View	4097
vrml-multi-use	VRML Multiuser Systems	4200 to 4299
rwhois	Remote Who Is	4321
bmc-reporting	BMC Reporting	4568
sip	SIP	5060
sip-tls	SIP-TLS	5061
pcanywheredata	PcANYWHEREdata	5631
pcaywherestat	pcANYWHEREstat	5632
x11	X Window System	6000 to 6063
bmc-grx	BMC GRX	6300
bmc-perf-agent	BMC PERFORM AGENT	6767
bmc-perf-mgrd	BMC PERFORM MGRD	6768
sun-lm	SUN License Manager	7588
http-alt	HTTP Alternate (see port 80)	8080

Table B-3   *Commonly Used Protocols and Associated Port Numbers (Continued)*

Keyword	Description	UDP/TCP Port
cp-cluster	Check Point Clustering	8116
patrol	Patrol	8160
patrol-snmp	Patrol SNMP	8161
wap-wsp	WAP connectionless session service	9200
wap-wsp-wtp	WAP session service	9201
wap-wsp-s	WAP secure connectionless session service	9202
wap-wsp-wtp-s	WAP secure session service	9203
wap-vcard	WAP vCard	9204
wap-vcal	WAP vCal	9205
wap-vcard-s	WAP vCard Secure	9206
wap-vcal-s	WAP vCal Secure	9207
bmc-perf-sd	BMC-PERFORM-SERVICE DAEMON	10128
h323callsigalt	h323 Call Signal Alternate	11720
vofr-gateway	VoFR Gateway	21590
quake	quake	26000
flex-lm	FLEX LM (1–10)	27000 to 27009
traceroute	traceroute use	33434
reachout	REACHOUT	43188

B-4: Well-Known IP Multicast Addresses

Some client server applications use a multicast packet to send large streams of data to many hosts with a single transmission. The multicast packet uses special addressing at Layer 3 and Layer 2 to communicate with clients that have been configured to receive these packets. The multicast packet contains a Class D IP address to specify the group of devices that are to receive the packet. This group is known as the *multicast group*, and the IP address translates directly to a multicast Ethernet address. The Ethernet multicast address has the first 24 bits set to 01-00-5E, the next bit is set to 0, and the last 23 bits are set to match the low 23 bits of the IP multicast address. Figure B-6 shows how Layer 3 multicast addresses translate to Layer 2 Ethernet addresses.

Figure B-6   *Layer 3-to-Layer 2 Multicast Translation*

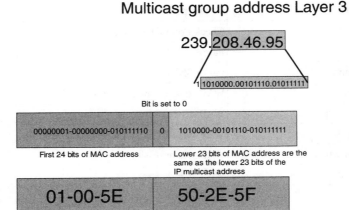

Multicast group address Layer 3

239.208.46.95

Translates into Layer 2 MAC address

Well-known or assigned IP protocols are registered with the IANA. The information presented here is reproduced with permission from the IANA. For the most current IP protocol number assignment information, refer to www.iana.org/numbers.htm under the "Multicast Addresses" link.

Host extensions for IP multicasting (RFC 1112) specifies the extensions required of a host implementation of the Internet Protocol to support multicasting. The multicast addresses are in the range 224.0.0.0 through 239.255.255.255. Current addresses are listed in the table that follows.

The range of addresses between 224.0.0.0 and 224.0.0.255, inclusive, is reserved for the use of routing protocols and other low-level topology discovery or maintenance protocols, such as gateway discovery and group membership reporting. Multicast routers should not forward any multicast datagram with destination addresses within this range, regardless of its TTL.

Table B-4 shows the registered multicast addresses, along with the application, and the RFC number (if applicable) or other reference.

Table B-4   *Registered Multicast Addresses and Associated Applications, RFCs, and References*

Group, Application, and References	Address
Base address (reserved) RFC 1112	224.0.0.0
All systems on this subnet RFC 1112	224.0.0.1

Table B-4   *Registered Multicast Addresses and Associated Applications, RFCs, and References (Continued)*

Group, Application, and References	Address
All routers on this subnet	224.0.0.2
Unassigned	224.0.0.3
DVMRP Routers RFC 1075	224.0.0.4
OSPFIGP OSPFIGP all routers RFC 2328	224.0.0.5
OSPFIGP OSPFIGP designated routers RFC 2328	224.0.0.6
ST Routers RFC 1190	224.0.0.7
ST Hosts RFC 1190	224.0.0.8
RIP2 Routers RFC 1723	224.0.0.9
EIGRP Routers	224.0.0.10
Mobile agents	224.0.0.11
DHCP Server/Relay agent RFC 1884	224.0.0.12
All PIM routers	224.0.0.13
RSVP-ENCAPSULATION	224.0.0.14
all-cbt-routers	224.0.0.15
designated-sbm	224.0.0.16
all-sbms	224.0.0.17

continues

Table B-4   *Registered Multicast Addresses and Associated Applications, RFCs, and References (Continued)*

Group, Application, and References	Address
VRRP	224.0.0.18
IPAllL1Iss	224.0.0.19
IPAllL2Iss	224.0.0.20
IPAllIntermediate Systems	224.0.0.21
IGMP	224.0.0.22
GLOBECAST-ID	224.0.0.23
Unassigned	224.0.0.24
router-to-switch	224.0.0.25
Unassigned	224.0.0.26
Al MPP Hello	224.0.0.27
ETC Control	224.0.0.28
GE-FANUC	224.0.0.29
indigo-vhdp	224.0.0.30
shinbroadband	224.0.0.31
digistar	224.0.0.32
ff-system-management	224.0.0.33
pt2-discover	224.0.0.34
DXCLUSTER	224.0.0.35
DTCP Announcement	224.0.0.36
Zeroconfaddr	224.0.0.37 to 224.0.0.68
Reserved	224.0.0.69 to 224.0.0.100
cisco-nhap	224.0.0.101
HSRP	224.0.0.102
MDAP	224.0.0.103
Unassigned	224.0.0.104 to 224.0.0.250
mDNS	224.0.0.251
Unassigned	224.0.0.25 to 224.0.0.255
VMTP Managers Group RFC 1045	224.0.1.0

Table B-4   *Registered Multicast Addresses and Associated Applications, RFCs, and References (Continued)*

Group, Application, and References	Address
NTP (Network Time Protocol)	224.0.1.1
RFC 1119	
SGI-Dogfight	224.0.1.2
Rwhod	224.0.1.3
VNP	224.0.1.4
Artificial Horizons – Aviator	224.0.1.5
NSS (Name Service Server)	224.0.1.6
AUDIONEWS (Audio News Multicast)	224.0.1.7
SUN NIS+ Information Service	224.0.1.8
MTP (Multicast Transport Protocol)	224.0.1.9
IETF-1-LOW-AUDIO	224.0.1.10
IETF-1-AUDIO	224.0.1.11
IETF-1-VIDEO	224.0.1.12
IETF-2-LOW-AUDIO	224.0.1.13
IETF-2-AUDIO	224.0.1.14
IETF-2-VIDEO	224.0.1.15
MUSIC-SERVICE	224.0.1.16
SEANET-TELEMETRY	224.0.1.17
SEANET-IMAGE	224.0.1.18
MLOADD	224.0.1.19
Any private experiment	224.0.1.20
DVMRP on MOSPF	224.0.1.21
SVRLOC	224.0.1.22
XINGTV	224.0.1.23
microsoft-ds	224.0.1.24
nbc-pro	224.0.1.25
nbc-pfn	224.0.1.26
lmsc-calren-1	224.0.1.27
lmsc-calren-2	224.0.1.28

continues

Table B-4   *Registered Multicast Addresses and Associated Applications, RFCs, and References (Continued)*

Group, Application, and References	Address
lmsc-calren-3	224.0.1.29
lmsc-calren-4	224.0.1.30
ampr-info	224.0.1.31
Mtrace	224.0.1.32
RSVP-encap-1	224.0.1.33
RSVP-encap-2	224.0.1.34
SVRLOC-DA	224.0.1.35
rln-server	224.0.1.36
proshare-mc	224.0.1.37
Dantz	224.0.1.38
cisco-rp-announce	224.0.1.39
cisco-rp-discovery	224.0.1.40
gatekeeper	224.0.1.41
iberiagames	224.0.1.42
nwn-discovery	224.0.1.43
nwn-adaptor	224.0.1.44
isma-1	224.0.1.45
isma-2	224.0.1.46
telerate	224.0.1.47
Ciena	224.0.1.48
dcap-servers RFC 2114	224.0.1.49
dcap-clients RFC 2114	224.0.1.50
mcntp-directory	224.0.1.51
mbone-vcr-directory	224.0.1.52
Heartbeat	224.0.1.53
sun-mc-grp	224.0.1.54
extended-sys	224.0.1.55
pdrncs	224.0.1.56

Table B-4   *Registered Multicast Addresses and Associated Applications, RFCs, and References (Continued)*

Group, Application, and References	Address
tns-adv-multi	224.0.1.57
vcals-dmu	224.0.1.58
Zuba	224.0.1.59
hp-device-disc	224.0.1.60
tms-production	224.0.1.61
Sunscalar	224.0.1.62
mmtp-poll	224.0.1.63
compaq-peer	224.0.1.64
iapp	224.0.1.65
multihasc-com	224.0.1.66
serv-discovery	224.0.1.67
Mdhcpdisover RFC 2730	224.0.1.68
MMP-bundle-discovery1	224.0.1.69
MMP-bundle-discovery2	224.0.1.70
XYPOINT DGPS Data Feed	224.0.1.71
GilatSkySurfer	224.0.1.72
SharesLive	224.0.1.73
NorthernData	224.0.1.74
SIP	224.0.1.75
IAPP	224.0.1.76
AGENTVIEW	224.0.1.77
Tibco Multicast1	224.0.1.78
Tibco Multicast2	224.0.1.79
MSP	224.0.1.80
OTT (One-way Trip Time)	224.0.1.81
TRACKTICKER	224.0.1.82
dtn-mc	224.0.1.83
jini-announcement	224.0.1.84

continues

Table B-4   *Registered Multicast Addresses and Associated Applications, RFCs, and References (Continued)*

Group, Application, and References	Address
jini-request	224.0.1.85
sde-discovery	224.0.1.86
DirecPC-SI	224.0.1.87
B1Rmonitor	224.0.1.88
3Com-AMP3 dRMON	224.0.1.89
ImFtmSvc	224.0.1.90
NQDS4	224.0.1.91
NQDS5	224.0.1.92
NQDS6	224.0.1.93
NLVL12	224.0.1.94
NTDS1	224.0.1.95
NTDS2	224.0.1.96
NODSA	224.0.1.97
NODSB	224.0.1.98
NODSC	224.0.1.99
NODSD	224.0.1.100
NQDS4R	224.0.1.101
NQDS5R	224.0.1.102
NQDS6R	224.0.1.103
NLVL12R	224.0.1.104
NODS1R	224.0.1.105
NODS2R	224.0.1.106
NODSAR	224.0.1.107
NODSBR	224.0.1.108
NODSCR	224.0.1.109
NODSDR	224.0.1.110
MRM	224.0.1.111
TVE-FILE	224.0.1.112
TVE-ANNOUNCE	224.0.1.113
Mac Srv Loc	224.0.1.114

Table B-4 *Registered Multicast Addresses and Associated Applications, RFCs, and References (Continued)*

Group, Application, and References	Address
Simple Multicast	224.0.1.115
SpectraLinkGW	224.0.1.116
Dieboldmcast	224.0.1.117
Tivoli Systems	224.0.1.118
pq-lic-mcast	224.0.1.119
HYPERFEED	224.0.1.120
Pipesplatform	224.0.1.121
LiebDevMgmg-DM	224.0.1.122
TRIBALVOICE	224.0.1.123
Unassigned (Retracted 1/29/01)	224.0.1.124
PolyCom Relay1	224.0.1.125
Infront Multi1	224.0.1.126
XRX DEVICE DISC	224.0.1.127
CNN	224.0.1.128
PTP-primary	224.0.1.129
PTP-alternate1	224.0.1.130
PTP-alternate2	224.0.1.131
PTP-alternate3	224.0.1.132
ProCast	224.0.1.133
3Com Discp	224.0.1.134
CS-Multicasting	224.0.1.135
TS-MC-1	224.0.1.136
Make Source	224.0.1.137
Teleborsa	224.0.1.138
SUMAConfig	224.0.1.139
Unassigned	224.0.1.140
DHCP-SERVERS	224.0.1.141
CN Router-LL	224.0.1.142
EMWIN	224.0.1.143

continues

Table B-4 *Registered Multicast Addresses and Associated Applications, RFCs, and References (Continued)*

Group, Application, and References	Address
Alchemy Cluster	224.0.1.144
Satcast One	224.0.1.145
Satcast Two	224.0.1.146
Satcast Three	224.0.1.147
Intline	224.0.1.148
8x8 Multicast	224.0.1.149
Unassigned	224.0.1.150
Intline-1	224.0.1.151
Intline-2	224.0.1.152
Intline-3	224.0.1.153
Intline-4	224.0.1.154
Intline-5	224.0.1.155
Intline-6	224.0.1.156
Intline-7	224.0.1.157
Intline-8	224.0.1.158
Intline-9	224.0.1.159
Intline-10	224.0.1.160
Intline-11	224.0.1.161
Intline-12	224.0.1.162
Intline-13	224.0.1.163
Intline-14	224.0.1.164
Intline-15	224.0.1.165
marratech-cc	224.0.1.166
EMS-InterDev	224.0.1.167
itb301	224.0.1.168
rtv-audio	224.0.1.169
rtv-video	224.0.1.170
HAVI-Sim	224.0.1.171
Nokia Cluster	224.0.1.172
host-request	224.0.1.173

Table B-4   *Registered Multicast Addresses and Associated Applications, RFCs, and References (Continued)*

Group, Application, and References	Address
host-announce	224.0.1.174
ptk-cluster	224.0.1.175
Proxim Protocol	224.0.1.176
Unassigned	224.0.1.177 to 224.0.0.255
"rwho" Group (BSD) (unofficial)	224.0.2.1
SUN RPC PMAPPROC_CALLIT	224.0.2.2
SIAC MDD Service	224.0.2.64 to 224.0.2.95
CoolCast	224.0.2.96 to 224.0.2.127
WOZ-Garage	224.0.2.128 to 224.0.2.191
SIAC MDD Market Service	224.0.2.192 to 224.0.2.255
RFE Generic Service	224.0.3.0 to 224.0.3.255
RFE Individual Conferences	224.0.4.0 to 224.0.4.255
CDPD Groups	224.0.5.0 to 224.0.5.127
SIAC Market Service	224.0.5.128 to 224.0.5.191
Unassigned IANA	224.0.5.192 to 224.0.5.255
Cornell ISIS Project	224.0.6.0 to 224.0.6.127
Unassigned IANA	224.0.6.128 to 224.0.6.255
Where-Are-You	224.0.7.0 to 224.0.7.255
INTV	224.0.8.0 to 224.0.8.255
Invisible Worlds	224.0.9.0 to 224.0.9.255
DLSw Groups	224.0.10.0 to 224.0.10.255
NCC.NET Audio	224.0.11.0 to 224.0.11.255
Microsoft and MSNBC	224.0.12.0 to 224.0.12.63
UUNET PIPEX Net News	224.0.13.0 to 223.0.13.255
NLANR	224.0.14.0 to 224.0.14.255
Hewlett Packard	224.0.15.0 to 224.0.15.255
XingNet	224.0.16.0 to 224.0.16.255

continues

Table B-4   *Registered Multicast Addresses and Associated Applications, RFCs, and References (Continued)*

Group, Application, and References	Address
Mercantile & Commodity Exchange	224.0.17.0 to 224.0.17.31
NDQMD1	224.0.17.32 to 224.0.17.63
ODN-DTV	224.0.17.64 to 224.0.17.127
Dow Jones	224.0.18.0 to 224.0.18.255
Walt Disney Company	224.0.19.0 to 224.0.19.63
Cal Multicast	224.0.19.64 to 224.0.19.95
SIAC Market Service	224.0.19.96 to 224.0.19.127
IIG Multicast	224.0.19.128 to 224.0.19.191
Metropol	224.0.18.192 to 224.0.19.207
Xenoscience, Inc.	224.0.19.208 to 224.0.19.239
HYPERFEED	224.0.19.240 to 224.0.19.255
MS-IP/TV	224.0.20.0 to 224.0.20.63
Reliable Network Solutions	224.0.20.64 to 224.0.20.127
TRACKTICKER Group	224.0.20.128 to 224.0.20.143
CNR Rebroadcast MCA	224.0.20.144 to 224.0.20.207
Talarian MCAST	224.0.21.0 to 224.0.21.127
WORLD MCAST	224.0.22.0 to 224.0.22.255
Domain Scoped Group	224.0.252.0 to 224.0.252.255
Report Group	224.0.253.0 to 224.0.253.255
Query Group	224.0.254.0 to 224.0.254.255
Border Routers	224.0.255.0 to 224.0.255.255
ST Multicast Groups RFC 1190	224.1.0.0 to 224.1.255.255
Multimedia Conference Calls	224.2.0.0 to 224.2.127.253
SAPv1 Announcements	224.2.127.254
SAPv0 Announcements (deprecated)	224.2.127.255
SAP Dynamic Assignments	224.2.128.0 to 224.2.255.255
DIS transient groups	224.252.0.0 to 224.255.255.255
MALLOC (temp - renew 1/01)	225.0.0.0 to 225.255.255.255
VMTP transient groups	232.0.0.0 to 232.255.255.255
Static Allocations (temp - renew 03/02)	233.0.0.0 to 233.255.255.255

Table B-4   *Registered Multicast Addresses and Associated Applications, RFCs, and References (Continued)*

Group, Application, and References	Address
Administratively Scoped	239.0.0.0 to 239.255.255.255
IANA	
RFC 2365	
Reserved	239.0.0.0 to 239.63.255.255
IANA	
Reserved	239.64.0.0 to 239.127.255.255
IANA	
Reserved	239.128.0.0 to 239.191.255.255
IANA	
Organization-Local Scope	239.192.0.0 to 239.251.255.255
RFC 2365	
Site-Local Scope (reserved)	239.252.0.0 to 239.252.255.255
RFC 2365	
Site-Local Scope (reserved)	239.253.0.0 to 239.253.255.255
RFC 2365	
Site-Local Scope (reserved)	239.254.0.0 to 239.254.255.255
RFC 2365	
Site-Local Scope	239.255.0.0 to 239.255.255.255
RFC 2365	
rasadv	239.255.2.2

B-5: Ethernet Type Codes

A listing of commonly used Ethernet type codes is maintained by the IANA. The information presented here is reproduced with permission from the IANA. For the most current Ethernet type code number assignment information, refer to www.iana.org/numbers.htm under the "Ethernet Numbers" link. Table B-5 shows the Ethernet type code numbers in hexadecimal format, along with a description.

Table B-5   *Ethernet Type Codes*

Hex Value	Description
0000 to 05DC	IEEE 802.3 Length Field
0101 to 01FF	Experimental
200	XEROX PUP (see 0A00)
201	PUP Addr Trans (see 0A01)
400	Nixdorf
600	XEROX NS IDP
660	DLOG
661	DLOG
800	Internet IP (IPv4)
801	X.75 Internet
802	NBS Internet
803	ECMA Internet
804	Chaosnet
805	X.25 Level 3
806	ARP
807	XNS Compatibility
808	Frame Relay ARP (RFC 1701)
081C	Symbolics Private
0888 to 088A	Xyplex
900	Ungermann-Bass net debug
0A00	Xerox IEEE802.3 PUP
0A01	PUP Address Translation
0BAD	Banyan VINES
0BAE	VINES Loopback (RFC 1701)
0BAF	VINES Echo (RFC 1701)
1000	Berkeley Trailer negotiation
1001 to 100F	Berkeley Trailer encapsulation/IP
1600	Valid Systems
4242	PCS Basic Block Protocol
5208	BBN Simnet

Table B-5 *Ethernet Type Codes (Continued)*

Hex Value	Description
6000	DEC Unassigned (experimental)
6001	DEC MOP Dump/Load
6002	DEC MOP Remote Console
6003	DEC DECNET Phase IV Route
6004	DEC LAT
6005	DEC Diagnostic Protocol
6006	DEC Customer Protocol
6007	DEC LAVC, SCA
6008 to 6009	DEC Unassigned
6010 to 6014	3Com Corporation
6558	Trans Ether Bridging (RFC 1701)
6559	Raw Frame Relay (RFC 1701)
7000	Ungermann-Bass download
7002	Ungermann-Bass dia/loop
7020 to 7029	LRT
7030	Proteon
7034	Cabletron
8003	Cronus VLN
8004	Cronus Direct
8005	HP Probe
8006	Nestar
8008	AT&T
8010	Excelan
8013	SGI diagnostics
8014	SGI network games
8015	SGI reserved
8016	SGI bounce server
8019	Apollo Domain
802E	Tymshare

continues

Table B-5   *Ethernet Type Codes (Continued)*

Hex Value	Description
802F	Tigan, Inc.
8035	Reverse ARP
8036	Aeonic Systems
8038	DEC LANBridge
8039 to 803C	DEC Unassigned
803D	DEC Ethernet Encryption
803E	DEC Unassigned
803F	DEC LAN Traffic Monitor
8040 to 8042	DEC Unassigned
8044	Planning Research Corp.
8046	AT&T
8047	AT&T
8049	ExperData
805B	Stanford V Kernel exp.
805C	Stanford V Kernel prod.
805D	Evans & Sutherland
8060	Little Machines
8062	Counterpoint Computers
8065	Univ. of Mass. @ Amherst
8066	Univ. of Mass. @ Amherst
8067	Veeco Integrated Auto.
8068	General Dynamics
8069	AT&T
806A	Autophon
806C	ComDesign
806D	Computgraphic Corp.
806E to 8077	Landmark Graphics Corp.
807A	Matra
807B	Dansk Data Elektronik
807C	Merit Internodal

Table B-5   *Ethernet Type Codes (Continued)*

Hex Value	Description
807D to 807F	Vitalink Communications
8080	Vitalink TransLAN III
8081 to 8083	Counterpoint Computers
809B	Appletalk
809C to 809E	Datability
809F	Spider Systems Ltd.
80A3	Nixdorf Computers
80A4 to 80B3	Siemens Gammasonics Inc.
80C0 to 80C3	DCA Data Exchange Cluster
80C4	Banyan Systems
80C5	Banyan Systems
80C6	Pacer Software
80C7	Applitek Corporation
80C8 to 80CC	Intergraph Corporation
80CD to 80CE	Harris Corporation
80CF to 80D2	Taylor Instrument
80D3 to 80D4	Rosemount Corporation
80D5	IBM SNA Service on Ether
80DD	Varian Associates
80DE to 80DF	Integrated Solutions TRFS
80E0 to 80E3	Allen-Bradley
80E4 to 80F0	Datability
80F2	Retix
80F3	AppleTalk AARP (Kinetics)
80F4 to 80F5	Kinetics
80F7	Apollo Computer
80FF to 8103	Wellfleet Communications
8107 to 8109	Symbolics Private
8130	Hayes Microcomputers

continues

Table B-5 *Ethernet Type Codes (Continued)*

Hex Value	Description
8131	VG Laboratory Systems
8132 to 8136	Bridge Communications
8137 to 8138	Novell, Inc.
8139 to 813D	KTI
8148	Logicraft
8149	Network Computing Devices
814A	Alpha Micro
814C	SNMP
814D	BIIN
814E	BIIN
814F	Technically Elite Concept
8150	Rational Corp
8151 to 8153	Qualcomm
815C to 815E	Computer Protocol Pty Ltd
8164 to 8166	Charles River Data System
817D	XTP
817E	SGI/Time Warner prop.
8180	HIPPI-FP encapsulation
8181	STP, HIPPI-ST
8182	Reserved for HIPPI-6400
8183	Reserved for HIPPI-6400
8184 to 818C	Silicon Graphics prop.
818D	Motorola Computer
819A to 81A3	Qualcomm
81A4	ARAI Bunkichi
81A5 to 81AE	RAD Network Devices
81B7 to 81B9	Xyplex
81CC to 81D5	Apricot Computers
81D6 to 81DD	Artisoft
81E6 to 81EF	Polygon

Table B-5   *Ethernet Type Codes (Continued)*

Hex Value	Description
81F0 to 81F2	Comsat Labs
81F3 to 81F5	SAIC
81F6 to 81F8	VG Analytical
8203 to 8205	Quantum Software
8221 to 8222	Ascom Banking Systems
823E to 8240	Advanced Encryption System
827F to 8282	Athena Programming
8263 to 826A	Charles River Data System
829A to 829B	Inst Ind Info Tech
829C to 82AB	Taurus Controls
82AC to 8693	Walker Richer & Quinn
8694 to 869D	Idea Courier
869E to 86A1	Computer Network Tech
86A3 to 86AC	Gateway Communications
86DB	SECTRA
86DE	Delta Controls
86DD	IPv6
86DF	ATOMIC
86E0 to 86EF	Landis & Gyr Powers
8700 to 8710	Motorola
876B	TCP/IP Compression (RFC 1144)
876C	IP Autonomous Systems (RFC 1701)
876D	Secure Data (RFC 1701)
880B	PPP
8847	MPLS Unicast
8848	MPLS Multicast
8A96 to 8A97	Invisible Software
9000	Loopback
9001	3Com(Bridge) XNS Sys Mgmt

continues

Table B-5 *Ethernet Type Codes (Continued)*

Hex Value	Description
9002	3Com(Bridge) TCP-IP Sys
9003	3Com(Bridge) loop detect
FF00	BBN VITAL-LanBridge cache
FF00 to FF0F	ISC Bunker Ramo
FFFF	Reserved (RFC 1701)

Additional Catalyst Modules

Refer to the following sections to configure and use these features:

- **C-1: Catalyst 6000 Intrusion Detection System Module**—Presents the steps needed to configure and maintain the *Intrusion Detection System Module* (IDSM) as part of a security plan.

- **C-2: Catalyst 6000 Network Analysis Module**—Describes the configuration steps to use a *Network Analysis Module* (NAM) to monitor data from various sources in the switch.

- **C-3: Catalyst 6000 Switch Fabric Module**—Explains the *Switch Fabric Module* (SFM) and how to monitor it.

- **C-4: Catalyst 6000 FlexWAN Module**—Describes the FlexWAN module and how to configure its interfaces. These other Catalyst switch modules are covered in other sections of this book:

  - **Catalyst 4000 Access Gateway**—Section "14-3: Voice Modules"
  - **Catalyst 4000 8-port RJ-21 FXS Module**—Section "14-3: Voice Modules"
  - **Catalyst 6000 8-port Voice T1 and Services Module**— Section "14-3: Voice Modules"
  - **Catalyst 6000 24-port FXS Module**—Section "14-3: Voice Modules"
  - **Catalyst 6000 Content Switching Module**—Chapter 10, "Server Load Balancing (SLB)"

C-1: Intrusion Detection System Module

- The IDSM can analyze a data stream and recognize intrusions or malicious activity based on a set of attack signatures.

- The IDSM can monitor up to 100 Mbps of data. If the data rate rises above that maximum, some packets will be lost and attacks could go unrecognized.

- You can subscribe to receive IDS bulletins describing new signature updates, service packs, or product news. Enter your email address and a password at www.cisco.com/warp/public/779/largeent/it/ids_news/subscribe.html.

- The IDSM has two logical switch ports: a capture or "sniffing" port (port 1), and a control port (port 2).

- Monitored traffic must be sent to the capture port. Only the VLANs of which that capture port is a member can be monitored. The capture port can be a trunk, allowing all VLANs on the trunk to be monitored.

- The IDSM is controlled by an external application. If an attack is detected, the IDSM sends an alarm to the management application. This can be Cisco Secure Director, Cisco Secure Policy Manager, or HP OpenView.

- Multiple IDSMs can be installed in a single Catalyst 6000 chassis. Each IDSM can be configured to monitor a different data stream, each up to 100 Mbps.

Configuration

1 Access the IDSM.

   a. Open a *command-line interface* (CLI) session with the IDSM:

COS	**session** *module*
IOS	**session slot** *module* **processor 1**

   A CLI session is initiated with the IDSM module in chassis slot *module*. To close the session, type the escape sequence **^-]**, **control-]**, or the **exit** command.

   b. Log in as the administrator:

IDSM	login: *username*
	Password: *password*

   Use the administrator *username* (text string; default "ciscoids") and *password* (text string; default "attack").

   c. *(Optional)* Change the administrator password:

IDSM	(exec) **configure terminal**
	(global) **password**

   You should change the password to something different from the default. The password is a text string of up to 15 characters.

   d. *(Optional)* Initially configure the IDSM:

IDSM	(exec) **setup**

After the setup mode begins, the IDSM prompts for all the necessary parameters. These values are needed for both the local IDS sensor and the remote IDS director:

— IP address, subnet mask, and default gateway.

— Host name (up to 256 characters), host ID (1 to 65,535), and Post Office Protocol UDP port (256 to 65,535; default 45,000). The host ID is a number that uniquely identifies the IDSM among other IDS sensors in an organization.

— Organization name (up to 256 characters) and ID (1 to 65,535). Within an IDS domain, the sensors and their managing directors must have a common organization ID and name.

e. *(Optional)* Test network connectivity to the IDSM.

— Ping a remote host:

| IDSM | (exec) **diagnostics** |
| | (diag) **ping** *ip-address* |

— Trace the route to a remote host:

| IDSM | (exec) **diagnostics** |
| | (diag) **traceroute** *ip-address* |

2   *(Optional)* Shut down the IDSM.

CAUTION   Before you can remove the IDSM from the switch chassis, you must properly shut it down. Use one of the shutdown methods in this step to bring about an orderly shutdown, and wait for the shutdown process to be completed. A completed shutdown process is indicated when the status LED goes from green to either amber or is off. Then you can safely remove the module.

a. Module shutdown from the IDSM CLI:

| IDSM | (exec) **shutdown** |

b. *(Optional)* Module shutdown or reset from the switch CLI:

COS	`set module shutdown` *module*
	-or-
	`reset` *module*
IOS	(exec) `hw-module module shutdown` *module*
	-or-
	(exec) `hw-module module` *module* `reset`

You can shut down the IDSM in slot *module* with the **shutdown** keyword. If the switch is then rebooted or power cycled, the IDSM will reboot also. To restore the IDSM to service, use the **reset** keyword.

c. *(Optional)* Remove or restore power to the IDSM:

COS	`set module power down` *module*
	-or-
	`set module power up` *module*
IOS	(global) `no power enable module` *module*
	-or-
	(global) `power enable module` *module*

d. *(Optional)* Use the IDSM shutdown button as a last resort.

You can use a small pointed object such as the end of a paper clip to push the Shutdown button on the IDSM module front panel. The button is located to the right of the status LED.

3 Instruct the IDSM to begin intrusion detection.

From an external management application, such as Cisco Secure Director, you can select the set of attack signatures that the IDSM uses. Refer to that application's documentation for more information.

4 Specify the traffic source to monitor.

a. *(Optional)* Monitor specific traffic.

— Select interesting traffic with a *VLAN access control list* (VACL):

COS	`set security acl ip` *acl-name* {**permit** | **deny** | **redirect** {*adj-name* | *mod/port*}} *protocol src-ip-spec dest-ip-spec* [**precedence** *precedence*] [**tos** *tos*] [**fragment**] **capture** [**before** *editbuffer_index* | **modify** *editbuffer_index*] [**log**]
IOS	(global) `access-template` {*acl-number* | *acl-name*} {*temporary-list-name*} *src-ip-spec dest-ip-spec* [**timeout** *minutes*]
	(global) `vlan access-map` *name* [*seq#*]
	(vlan-acc-map) `match` {**ip address** {*acl-number* | *acl-name*}}

The traffic to be captured or monitored by the IDSM should have both the **permit** and **capture** keywords added. Other traffic to be forwarded but not captured should have the **permit** keyword only. Mark any traffic that is not to be forwarded with the **deny** keyword. Be sure to add a **permit ip any any** line at the end of the VACL so that all other traffic not specified is forwarded.

The simplest case is to capture all traffic on a VLAN with the **permit ip any any capture** command.

Refer to section "11-5: VLAN ACLs" for complete information about configuring VACLs.

— Apply the VACL to hardware:

COS	`commit security acl {`*acl-name*`	`**all**`}`
IOS	N/A

A COS switch must first compile the VACL and download it into the switching hardware. You can compile and commit a single VACL as *acl-name*, or **all** configured VACLs.

— Copy the interesting traffic to the IDSM:

COS	`set security acl capture-ports `*mod*`/1`
IOS	`(vlan-acc-map) `**action forward capture** `{`*interface slot*`/1}`

Traffic that is matched by the VACL is copied to the capture port, which is the IDSM slot number and port number 1.

— Apply the VACL to one or more VLANs:

COS	`set security acl map `*acl-name vlan*
IOS	`(global) `**vlan filter** *map-name* **vlan-list** *vlan-list*

The VLAN access list named *acl-name* (text string of up to 32 characters) is applied to examine traffic on VLAN number *vlan* (1 to 1005 or 1025 to 4094).

— Gauge the amount of monitored traffic.

Make sure the bandwidth of captured or monitored traffic doesn't rise above 100 Mbps. This ensures that the IDSM is able to examine all the packets involved in every traffic flow.

You can configure an additional VACL capture to an unused Gigabit Ethernet interface. The data that is copied to the IDSM capture port is also copied to the unused switch port. Then you can use the **show mac** *mod/port* or **show interface** command to measure the amount of data that is being captured.

COS	**set security acl capture-ports** *mod/port*
IOS	(vlan-acc-map) **action forward capture** {*interface slot/number*}

b. *(Optional)* Monitor a SPAN source.

TIP

See section "12-3: SPAN" for complete configuration information about *Switched Port Analyzer* (SPAN) or port monitoring.

— *(Optional)* Monitor a switch port:

COS	**set span** *src-mod/src-ports dest-mod/***1** [**rx** | **tx** | **both**] [**inpkts** {**enable** | **disable**}] [**learning** {**enable** | **disable**}] [**multicast** {**enable** | **disable**}] [**filter** *vlans...*] [**create**]
IOS	(global) **monitor session** *session* **source interface** *type number* [**rx** | **tx** | **both**]
	(global) **monitor session** *session* **destination interface** *type* **1**
	(global) **monitor session** *session* **filter vlan** *vlans*

The traffic source is identified as a specific switch port. The destination is the IDSM port 1. Specific VLANs can be filtered for monitoring by using the **filter** keyword.

— *(Optional)* Monitor a VLAN:

COS	**set span** *src-vlans dest-mod/***1** [**rx** | **tx** | **both**] [**inpkts** {**enable** | **disable**}] [**learning** {**enable** | **disable**}] [**multicast** {**enable** | **disable**}] [**create**]
IOS	(global) **monitor session** *session* **source vlan** *vlans* [**rx** | **tx** | **both**]
	(global) **monitor session** *session* **destination interface** *type* **1**

One or more VLANs can be given as sources of traffic to be monitored. The destination is the IDSM port 1.

— Gauge the amount of monitored traffic.

Make sure the bandwidth of captured or monitored traffic specified in Steps 4b and 4c don't rise above 100 Mbps. This ensures that the IDSM is able to examine all the packets involved in every traffic flow.

The easiest way to control the traffic rate to the IDSM is to choose a source switch port that has 100 Mbps bandwidth.

Otherwise, you can use the **show top** *n* command to display the highest utilized switch ports.

5 *(Optional)* Upgrade the IDSM software.

a. Select the active hard drive partition:

COS	`set boot device hdd:`*partition mod*
IOS	N/A

The IDSM in slot number *mod* runs the software image in *partition*: **1** (application partition, the default) or **2** (maintenance partition). After the IDSM is running the image in the active partition, the other partition can be upgraded.

b. *(Optional)* Install a cached image from the inactive partition.

— Enter the diagnostics mode:

IDSM	`(exec)` **diag**

— Verify that the correct image is cached:

IDSM	`(diag)` **ids-installer system /cache /show**

— Install the cached image:

IDSM	`(diag)` **ids-installer system /cache /install**

— Reload the IDSM:

COS	**reset** *module* **hdd:1**
IOS	`(global)` **hw-module module** *module* **reset hdd:1**

The IDSM reloads, running the image on the application partition (partition 1).

c. *(Optional)* Install an image from an FTP server.

— Enter the diagnostics mode:

IDSM	(exec) **diag**

— *(Optional)* Identify IP addresses for the upgrade process:

IDSM	(diag) **ids-installer netconfig /configure /ip=**ip-addr **/subnet=**mask **/gw=**gw-ip-addr

The IDSM uses the specified IP address *ip-addr*, subnet mask, and gateway address *gw-ip-addr* when upgrading the application partition from an FTP server.

— Download the image from an FTP server:

IDSM	(diag) **ids-installer system /nw /install /server=**ip-addr **/user=**account **/save={yes	no} /dir=**ftp-path **/prefix=**file-prefix

The IDSM contacts the FTP server at *ip-addr*, using the user account name *account* (text string). After the image has been downloaded from the server and installed, it can also be cached on the IDSM by using the **yes** keyword. The image is found in the FTP directory *ftp-path*, as the filename *file-prefix* (text string) but not including the *.dat* extension.

— Reload the IDSM:

COS	**reset** module **hdd:1**

The IDSM reloads, running the image on the application partition (partition 1).

6 *(Optional)* Upgrade IDSM with service packs.

a. *(Optional)* Check the active version:

IDSM	(exec) **show config**

b. Download the service pack to an FTP server.

TIP   You can find the IDSM service packs at the Software Center on Cisco.com: www.cisco.com/
kobayashi/sw-center/sw-ciscosecure.shtml. Look under "Cisco Intrusion Detection System
(IDS)." The Catalyst 6000 IDS Module software is collected under the "Latest Software"
link. (You need to have a registered user account on CCO, and a current maintenance
contract, to access the Software Center link.)

c. Apply the service pack:

IDSM	(exec) **configure terminal**
	(config-term) **apply servicepack site** *ftp-ip-addr* **user** *account* **dir** *path* **file** *filename*

The IDSM contacts the FTP server at IP address *ftp-ip-addr* using the username
account (text string). The service pack is found stored in the *path* directory under the
name *filename* (text string, including the *.exe* extension).

You can remove the last applied service pack with the **remove servicepack** command.

7 *(Optional)* Upgrade the IDS signature database.

a. *(Optional)* Check the active version:

IDSM	(exec) **show config**

b. Download the signature database to an FTP server.

TIP   You can find the IDSM signature databases or updates at the Software Center on
Cisco.com: www.cisco.com/kobayashi/sw-center/sw-ciscosecure.shtml. Look under
"Cisco Intrusion Detection System (IDS)." The Catalyst 6000 IDS Module software is
collected under the "Latest Software" link. (You need to have a registered user account on
CCO, and a current maintenance contract, to access the Software Center link.)

c. Apply the signature update:

IDSM	(exec) **configure terminal**
	(config-term) **apply signatureupdate site** *ftp-ip-addr* **user** *account* **dir** *path* **file** *filename*

The IDSM contacts the FTP server at IP address *ftp-ip-addr* using the username *account* (text string). The signature update is found stored in the *path* directory under the name *filename* (text string, including the *.exe* extension).

You can remove the last applied signature update with the **remove signatureupdate** command.

Displaying Information About the IDSM

Table C-1 lists the switch commands that you can use to display helpful information about the IDSM.

Table C-1 *Commands to Display IDSM Information*

Display Function	Switch OS	Command
IDSM versions	IDSM	`show version`
IDSM configuration	IDSM	`show configuration`
VACLs for capturing	COS	`show security acl info all`
	IOS	(exec) `show vlan filter [{`**access-map** *map-name*`}	{`**vlan** *vlan-id*`}]`
VACLs mapped to VLANs	COS	`show security acl map {`*acl-name*	*vlan*	**all**`}`
	IOS	(exec) `show vlan access-map [`*map-name*`]`
Active SPAN sessions	COS	`show span`
	IOS	(exec) `show port monitor`

C-2: 6000 Network Analysis Module

- The NAM monitors traffic on a switch and offers analysis using Remote Monitoring (RMON), RMON2, and Simple Network Management Protocol (SNMP) MIBs.

- Traffic sourced by a VLAN or a SPAN switch port can be monitored.

- *Netflow data export* (NDE) information can be collected and analyzed by the NAM.

- The NAM can be managed by these applications:

  — NAM Traffic Analyzer—An internal web-based application

  — CiscoWorks TrafficDirector

  — NetScout nGenius *Real-Time Monitor* (RTM)

  — CiscoWorks2000 (via SNMP)

Configuration

1 Access the NAM.

a. Assign the NAM management port to a VLAN:

COS	N/A
IOS	(global) **interface gigabitethernet** *mod*/**1**
	(interface) **switchport access vlan** *vlan-number*

On an IOS switch, the NAM management port (port 1) must be assigned to a *vlan-number* so that the NAM traffic can be switched to and from the management application.

A COS switch doesn't require this step. Instead, the NAM management port is automatically assigned to the VLAN associated with the sc0 switch interface.

b. Open a CLI session with the NAM:

COS	**session** *module*
IOS	**session slot** *module* **processor 1**

A command-line session is initiated with the NAM module in chassis slot *module*. To close the session, type the escape sequence **^-]** or **control-]**.

c. Log in as the administrator:

NAM	login: **root**
	Password: *password*

Use the administrator username **root** and *password* (text string; default "root").

d. *(Optional)* Change the administrator password:

NAM	(exec) **password root**

You should change the root password to something different from the default. The password is a text string of up to 15 characters.

e. *(Optional)* Initially configure the IP parameters.

— Set the IP address:

NAM	(exec) **ip address** *ip-address subnet-mask*

The NAM is managed by using its IP address. Make sure the IP address is appropriately chosen to match the management port VLAN.

— Set the broadcast address:

NAM	(exec) **ip broadcast** *broadcast-address*

The broadcast address should be set according to the IP network and subnet mask of the NAM management port.

— Set the host name and domain name:

NAM	(exec) **ip host** *name*
	(exec) **ip domain** *domain-name*

The NAM identifies itself by its host name and domain name (text strings).

— Set the default gateway:

NAM	(exec) **ip gateway** *default-gateway*

Specify the IP address of the default gateway on the NAM management port's local network.

— Identify one or more name servers:

NAM	(exec) **ip nameserver** *ip-address* [*ip-address* …]

f. Initially configure the SNMP parameters.

— Identify the system location:

NAM	(exec) **snmp location** *location*

The system *location* (text string) is used to describe where the NAM is physically located.

— Identify the system contact:

NAM	(exec) **snmp contact** *contact*

Give the name of the person or group to be contacted for NAM maintenance as *contact* (text string).

— Identify the system name:

NAM	(exec) **snmp name** *name*

The NAM is identified as *name* (text string) in SNMP queries.

— *(Optional)* Identify the read-write community string:

NAM	(exec) **snmp community** *community-string* **rw**

The SNMP management application can read or write MIB variables only if it uses the *community-string* (text string) that is configured on the NAM.

— Identify the read-only community string:

NAM	(exec) **snmp community** *community-string* **ro**

The SNMP management application can only read MIB variables if it uses the *community-string* (text string) that is configured on the NAM.

g. *(Optional)* Test network connectivity to the NAM.

— Ping a remote host:

NAM	(exec) **ping** [**-nv**] [**-c** *count*] [**-i** *wait*] [**-p** *pattern*] [**-s** *packetsize*] {*hostname* | *ip-address*}

ICMP echo packets are sent to the remote host at *hostname* (text string) or *ip-address*. To display addresses as numbers rather than host names, use the **–n** flag. For more detail, use the verbose **–v** flag. The number of packets can be given as **–c** *count*. With the **–i** option, the NAM will pause *wait* seconds between echo packets. The echo packets can be filled with a *pattern* (up to 16 bytes in hexadecimal) by using **–p**. The size of the echo packet can be set with **–s** to *packetsize* bytes.

— Trace the route to a remote host:

NAM	(exec) **traceroute** [**-Inv**] [**-f** *first-ttl*] [**-m** *max-ttl*] [**-p** *port*] [**-s** *source-addr*] [**-t** *tos*] [**-w** *wait-time*] {*hostname* | *ip-address*}

Traceroute probe packets are sent to the remote host at *hostname* (text string) or *ip-address*. UDP probes are used, unless the **–I** flag forces ICMP echo packets. To display addresses as numbers rather than host names, use the **–n** flag. For more detail, use the verbose **–v** flag. The initial and maximum time-to-live (number of hops) are given by **–f** and **–m**, respectively.

The UDP port number used is given by the **–p** option. A source address other than the NAM management port can be given by **–s**. The *type of service* (ToS) value can be given by **–t**. With the **–w** option, the NAM will allow *wait* seconds for the probe response to return.

2 *(Optional)* Shut down the NAM.

CAUTION Before you can remove the NAM from the switch chassis, you must shut it down properly. Use one of the shutdown methods in this step to bring about an orderly shutdown and wait for the shutdown process to be completed. This is indicated when the status LED changes from green to amber or is off. Then you can safely remove the module.

---

a. Module shutdown from the NAM CLI:

NAM	(exec) **shutdown**

b. *(Optional)* Module shutdown or reset from the switch CLI:

COS	**set module shutdown** *module*
	-or-
	reset *module*
IOS	(exec) **hw-module module shutdown** *module*
	-or-
	(exec) **hw-module module** *module* **reset**

You can shut down the NAM in slot *module* with the **shutdown** keyword. If the switch is then rebooted or power cycled, the NAM will reboot also. To restore the NAM to service, use the **reset** keyword.

c. *(Optional)* Remove or restore power to the NAM:

COS	set module power down *module*
	-or-
	set module power up *module*
IOS	(global) no power enable module *module*
	-or-
	(global) power enable module *module*

d. *(Optional)* Use the NAM Shutdown button as a last resort.

You can use a small pointed object such as the end of a paper clip to push the Shutdown button on the NAM module front panel. The button is located to the right of the status LED.

3 Select the traffic source to monitor.

a. *(Optional)* Monitor NDE information.

TIP   The NAM can be configured to collect NDE information from one or more sources. To enable the local switch containing the NAM to be an NDE source, follow the configuration steps presented here. If the local switch is a COS-only switch, you must also configure the Multilayer Switch Feature Card (MSFC)/MSFC2 to generate NDE information. Refer to section "8-6: Network Data Export" for complete configuration information.

— Enable NDE on a Policy Feature Card (PFC):

COS	set snmp extendedrmon netflow {enable	disable} *mod*
	set mls nde {enable	disable}
	set mls nde version {1	7	8}
IOS	(global) mls nde sender [version *version*]

For a PFC/PFC2, Layer 3-switched traffic can be reported as NDE version 7. On a COS switch, the PFC can be enabled to send NDE data to the NAM in slot *mod*.

— *(Optional)* Enable NDE on Layer 3 interfaces:

COS	N/A
IOS	(interface) ip route-cache flow

For an MSFC/MSFC2, routed traffic can be reported as NDE version 1, 5, or 6. NDE must then be enabled on any Layer 3 interfaces where the MSFC routes traffic.

— Identify the NDE source:

COS	N/A
IOS	(global) **ip flow-export source** [{*interface interface-number*} | {**null** *interface-number*} | {**port-channel** *number*} | {**vlan** *vlan-id*}]

NDE packets will be sent using the source address specified. Either an interface (Ethernet, null, or EtherChannel) or a VLAN can be used as the source.

— Identify the NDE collector:

COS	**set mls nde** *ip-address* **3000**
IOS	(global) **mls rp nde-address** *ip-address* (global) **ip flow-export destination** *ip-address* **3000**

The NAM at *ip-address* will receive the NDE information over UDP port 3000, which is required by the NAM.

— *(Optional)* Define the flow mask used to generate netflow data:

COS	N/A
IOS	**mls flow** {**ip** {**destination** | **destination-source** | **full**} | {**ipx** {**destination** | **destination-source**}}

The NDE sends flow information based on the destination address (**destination**, the default), both destination and source (**destination-source**), or both destination and source addresses and ports (**full**).

— *(Optional)* Use flow filters to report only specific traffic flows:

COS	**set mls nde flow** [**exclude** | **include**] [**destination** *ip-address mask*] [**source** *ip-address mask*] [**protocol** *protocol*] [**src-port** *number*] [**dst-port** *number*]
IOS	(global) **mls nde flow** {**exclude** | **include**} {**destination** *ip-address mask* | **source** *ip-address mask* {**dest-port** number | **src-port** number}}

NDE will export flows that match (**include**) or don't match (**exclude**) the remaining filter parameters. Filtering can be performed based on destination IP address (**destination**), destination port number (**dest-port**), source IP address (**source**), and source port number (**src-port**).

b. *(Optional)* Monitor a SPAN session.

— *(Optional)* Monitor a switch port:

COS	**set span** *src-mod/src-ports dest-mod*/1 [**rx** | **tx** | **both**] [**inpkts** {**enable** | **disable**}] [**learning** {**enable** | **disable**}] [**multicast** {**enable**| **disable**}] [**filter** *vlans...*] [**create**]
IOS	(global) **monitor session** *session* **source interface** *type number* [**rx** | **tx** | **both**]
	(global) **monitor session** *session* **destination interface gigabitethernet** *mod*/1
	(global) **monitor session** *session* **filter vlan** *vlans*

The traffic source is identified as a specific switch port. The destination is the NAM port 1. Specific VLANs can be filtered for monitoring by using the **filter** keyword.

— *(Optional)* Monitor a VLAN.

COS	**set span** *src-vlans dest-mod*/1 [**rx** | **tx** | **both**] [**inpkts** {**enable** | **disable**}] [**learning** {**enable** | **disable**}] [**multicast** {**enable** | **disable**}] [**create**]
IOS	(global) **monitor session** *session* **source vlan** *vlans* [**rx** | **tx** | **both**]
	(global) **monitor session** *session* **destination interface gigabitethernet** *mod*/1

One or more VLANs can be given as sources of traffic to be monitored. The destination is the NAM port 1.

4 *(Optional)* Upgrade the NAM software.

a. Make the upgraded partition inactive:

COS	**reset** *module* **hdd:***partition*
IOS	(global) **hw-mod module** *module* **reset hdd:***partition*

To upgrade the application partition (1), reload the NAM and run from the maintenance *partition* (2). Alternatively, if the maintenance partition software must be upgraded, run from the application *partition* (1).

b. Install an image from an FTP server:

NAM	(exec) **upgrade** *ftp-url*

The NAM can download a software image from any FTP server (including CCO at ftp.cisco.com), provided that it can reach the server over the network. First, make sure you can ping the server.

The software image is located by its URL, *ftp-url*. Use the format *ftp://host/absolute-path/filename* for a server that supports anonymous FTP. Otherwise, you can specify a username and password by using the format *ftp://user@hostname/absolute-path/filename*.

c. Reload the NAM into the application partition:

COS	**reset** *module* **hdd:1**
IOS	(global) **hw-mod module** *module* **reset hdd:1**

5 *(Optional)* Apply a software patch to the NAM.

a. Make sure the NAM is running the application image.

b. Download and apply the patch.

NAM	(exec) **patch** *ftp-url*

The NAM can download a patch file from any FTP server (including CCO at ftp.cisco.com), provided that it can reach the server over the network. First, make sure you can ping the server.

The patch is located by its URL, *ftp-url*. Use the format *ftp://host/absolute-path/filename* for a server that supports anonymous FTP. Otherwise, you can specify a username and password by using the format *ftp://user@hostname/absolute-path/filename*.

6 *(Optional)* Access the NAM's HTTP server.

a. Install a strong crypto (3DES) patch:

NAM	(exec) **patch** *ftp-url*

The NAM must first have a patch applied that will enable 3DES cryptographic features. You can find the strong crypto patch on the Cisco FTP site in a location such as ftp://ftp.cisco.com/cisco/crypto/3DES/lan/catalyst/6000/nam/cisco-nam-strong-crypto-patchK9-1.0-1.i386.rpm.

b. Select the secure HTTP port:

NAM	(exec) `ip http secure port port`

The TCP port used for secure HTTP access is given as   *port* (1 to 65535). This is typically 8080.

c. Enable the NAM HTTP server:

NAM	(exec) `ip http server enable`

d. *(Optional)* Use self-signed certificates for secure server connections:

NAM	(exec) `ip http secure generate self-signed-certificate`

The self-signed certificate is generated by the NAM itself and is delivered to the HTTP clients for secure HTTP sessions.

e. *(Optional)* Use a *certificate authority* (CA) for secure server connections.

    — Request a certificate from the CA:

NAM	(exec) `ip http secure generate certificate-request`

This command prompts you for the necessary information about your organization and server. A certificate request is then displayed as several lines of printed characters. To actually request the certificate, you have to copy and paste the request information into a request message that is manually sent to the CA. The CA should send a reply with the certificate data.

Install the certificate:

NAM	(exec) `ip http secure install certificate`

This command will prompt you for the certificate information. Copy and paste the lines of certificate characters, including the lines that mark the beginning and end of the certificate. End the certificate data by typing a period and then pressing the Enter key.

Displaying Information About the NAM

Table C-2 lists the switch commands that you can use to display various helpful information about the NAM.

Table C-2 *Commands to Display NAM Information*

Display Function	Switch OS	Command
SNMP configuration	NAM	`show snmp`
IP configuration	NAM	`show ip`
CPU usage	NAM	`show cpu`
Memory usage	NAM	`show memory`
Version and serial number	NAM	`show bios`
HTTP certificates	NAM	`show certificate` `show certificate-request`
Installed features	NAM	`show patches` `show options`

C-3: Catalyst 6000 Switch Fabric Module

- The SFM provides a 256 Gbps crossbar switching fabric. It dedicates two 8 Gbps ports to each module in a Catalyst 6500 chassis. (Each port operates at 16 Gbps full-duplex.)

- Fabric-enabled modules can connect to only one of the two dedicated SFM ports. Fabric-only modules can connect to both SFM ports.

- The SFM provides several modes of connectivity between modules:

  - **Flow-through mode**—Used when nonfabric-enabled modules are installed; data passes through the normal backplane buses.

  - **Truncated mode**—Used when fabric-enabled modules are communicating, but some nonfabric-enabled modules are installed. Data passes through a fabric channel unless a nonfabric-enabled module is involved.

  - **Compact mode**—Used when only fabric-enabled modules are installed in the switch. Data passes through a fabric channel as a compact version, yielding the best switching performance.

- Two SFMs can be installed in a switch for redundancy. The SFM in the upper slot functions as the primary, and the SFM in the lower slot as the secondary.

- Refer to Chapter 2, "Switch Functionality" for more information about the Catalyst 6000 family architecture.

Configuration

1 *(Optional)* Choose a switching mode:

COS	`set system switchmode allow {truncated	bus-only}`
IOS	N/A

The switch can allow the **truncated** mode (the default) to be used, if a low number of nonfabric-enabled modules are installed. If all the modules are fabric-enabled, the SFM is allowed to enter compact mode. If the **bus-only** keyword is used, the SFM is forced into flow-through mode.

2 *(Optional)* Choose a fallback mode:

COS	`set system crossbar-fallback {bus-mode	none}`
IOS	N/A

If the SFM fails, the switch can begin using the normal system bus (**bus-mode**, the default). If the **none** keyword is used instead, no traffic will be switched during the SFM failure.

3 *(Optional)* Change the LCD display banner:

COS	`set banner lcd` *d message d*
IOS	(global) `fabric lcd-banner` *d message d*

Normally, the LCD display on SFM modules shows the Cisco Systems logo and name. You can specify a *message* (text string, up to 800 characters) that begins and ends between the delimiter character *d*. The delimiter character cannot appear in the message. The message can be entered as one or more lines of text.

You can enter tokens within the message, causing the current token values to display. The switch host name can be substituted for the token *$(hostname)*, and the domain name for the token *$(domain)*.

Displaying Information About the SFM

Table C-3 lists the switch commands that you can use to display helpful information about the SFM.

Table C-3   *Commands to Display SFM Information*

Display Function	Switch OS	Command
Switch mode and channel status	COS	`show fabric channel switchmode [`*`mod`*`]`
	IOS	`show fabric status [module {`*`mod`* `| all}]` `show fabric switching-mode [module {`*`mod`* `| all}]`
Allowed switch mode	COS	`show system switchmode`
	IOS	N/A
Fabric counters	COS	`show fabric channel counters [`*`mod`*`]`
	IOS	`show fabric errors [module {`*`mod`* `| all}]`
Fabric utilization	COS	`show fabric channel utilization`
	IOS	`show fabric utilization [module {`*`mod`* `| all}]`

C-4: Catalyst 6000 FlexWAN Module

- The FlexWAN module supports up to two Cisco 7200/7500 series router WAN port adapters in any combination.

- Up to eight FlexWAN modules can be installed in a Catalyst 6000 switch chassis.

- Any port adapter can be used except Ethernet, Fast Ethernet, Token Ring, FDDI, channel port adapters, encryption service modules, compression service modules, and double-wide port adapters.

Configuration

Interfaces on FlexWAN port adapters are configured according to the Cisco IOS Software command syntax. The configuration commands are entered on either an MSFC/MSFC2 module or on the Catalyst 6000 Supervisor running native Cisco IOS Software. The Supervisor must have both MSFC and PFC modules installed before the FlexWAN module can be configured and used.

When configuring the FlexWAN interfaces, you need to use this interface numbering format:

COS	N/A
IOS	`(global)` **`interface`** *`mod`*`/`*`bay`*`/`*`port`*

The *mod* field is the module or slot number of the FlexWAN module. The *bay* field specifies the port adapter number within the FlexWAN module. The *port* field is the port or interface number within the port adapter.

For complete coverage of the Cisco IOS Software interface configuration commands, refer to *Cisco Field Manual: Router Configuration* by David Hucaby and Steve McQuerry, Cisco Press, ISBN: 1-58705-024-2.

Extending VLANs Within Layer 3 Switches

Some Layer 3 switches will perform Layer 3 processing only at the interface level in hardware and have no concepts of VLANs and VLAN databases. Routers also fall into this category. This appendix explains how to set up a broadcast domain between ports on a device with only Layer 3 interfaces. This appendix also explains how to map these broadcast domains to ISL or 802.1Q trunks to extend a switch VLAN into a Layer 3 device.

- A Layer 3-only device, such as a router or a 2948G-L3 switch, is specialized to process packets based on Layer 3 header information.

- Within a Layer 3 device, bridging software can be enabled and ports can be assigned to bridge groups.

- All ports in a common bridge group are in the same broadcast domain.

- By default a Layer 3 device will still attempt to route an IP, IPX, or AppleTalk packet unless otherwise directed.

- Layer 3 devices have no knowledge of VLANs that exist in switches but can understand 802.1Q or ISL tags coming from a switch.

- By mapping a bridge group to an ISL or 802.1Q VLAN, the broadcast domain of a VLAN can be extended into a Layer 3 switch.

Using Integrated Routing and Bridging (IRB) to Extend a VLAN

The following steps describe the process for creating a broadcast domain within the Layer 3 device and then mapping that to the VLAN through a trunk link:

1 Create a bride group.

IOS	(global) **bridge** *number* **protocol ieee**

In global configuration mode, the **bridge** command creates a bridge group. The *number* option specifies the group; numbers can range from 1 to 255. If your VLAN on the switch is within this range, it is recommended to create a bridge group with the same number as the VLAN. The **protocol** option should always be **ieee** when working with switches because the switch does not understand the Digital Equipment Corporation *Spanning-Tree Protocol* (STP), and bridge loops may occur.

2 Enable routing and bridging for the protocol.

IOS	(global) **bridge irb**

In global configuration mode, the **bridge irb** command allows both routing and bridging for configured protocols. By default a Layer 3 switch or router will not bridge any routable protocol, such as IP, even if an interface is configured for bridging. To make the interface bridge the traffic, you could disable IP routing completely (not a likely option) or enable the IRB function.

NOTE   Depending on the operating system (OS), you might have to add another command when IRB is enabled. The command **no bridge** *number* **route ip** might display in the configuration after you enable IRB. This command disables IP routing on any interface that is in the bridge group specified by the *number* option. If the command is not automatically entered, you will have to manually enter the command if you want to bridge between the interfaces.

---

3 Assign interfaces to the bridge group.

IOS	(interface) **bridge-group** *number*

In interface configuration mode, the **bridge-group** command adds a port to the bridge group. When a port is a member of the bridge group, all the interfaces in that group can communicate at Layer 2. Essentially the interfaces are in the same Broadcast domain, just like interfaces in the same VLAN on a Layer 2 switch. The *number* option specifies to which group an interface belongs. When an interface becomes a member of the group, it begins running the STP on that interface as well.

4 Create a subinterface on a trunk link.

IOS	(global) **interface** type number.subintnumber

To extended the VLAN from a switched network into the router or Layer 3 device, you must get traffic from the Layer 2 switch with some indication of the VLAN associated with the traffic. You can do so through a trunk link. On the interface attached to the switch trunk link, you are going to create a subinterface. The **interface** command followed by the *type* (FastEthernet or GigabitEthernet) and the *number.subintnumber* option creates the subinterface. Each VLAN that will be mapped to the Layer 3 device will have its own subinterface. It is recommended that the subinterface number (the one after the dot) be the same as the VLAN that will map to that subinterface. For example, VLAN 3 connected to interface FA 0/1 would have a subinterface FA 0/1.3.

5 Specify the encapsulation type and VLAN number.

IOS	(subinterface) **encapsulation** {**dot1q**	**isl**} *vlannumber* [**native**]

On the subinterface that was created in Step 4, you must specify the trunking encapsulation and the VLAN number that will be associated with this subinterface. The **encapsulation** command specifies this information. The **dot1q** or **isl** command specifies the trunk type, and the *vlannumber* specifies the VLAN.

NOTE   802.1Q trunk links do not tag for the native VLAN. On the Layer 3 switch, you must specify the native option for the subinterface attached to the native 802.1Q VLAN to prevent that VLAN from being tagged (typically VLAN 1).

6 Add the VLAN to the bridge group.

IOS	(subinterfac) **bridge-group** *number*

By adding the bridge group to the subinterface, you have added the VLAN from the switch to the bridge group on the router or Layer 3 device. This means all the interfaces on the Layer 3 device in the bridge group, and all the ports on the switch in the VLAN are in the same broadcast domain and effectively the same VLAN.

7 Routing for the broadcast domain.

a. Enable routing for the bridge group.

IOS	(global) **bridge** *groupnumber* **route ip**

In Step 2, either you or the router disabled the routing function on the Layer 3 device for interfaces in the bridge group for the IP protocol. If you want the Layer 3 device to route for all the devices in this broadcast domain (including those in the switch VLAN), you must first enable routing for this bridge group with the **bridge** *groupnumber* **route ip** command.

b. Create the virtual Layer 3 interface.

IOS	(global) **interface bvi** *groupnumber*

When you enable routing for these interfaces, bridging will cease to function until you create a virtual Layer 3 interface to be used by the group. The **interface bvi** command creates that virtual interface for all the members of the bridge group.

c. Assign an IP address to the Layer 3 interface.

IOS	(bvi-interface) **ip address** *address mask*

After you create the interface, you must assign it a Layer 3 address. This address becomes the gateway for all the devices in the bridge group and the VLAN.

Feature Example

The following example shows VLAN 20, VLAN 55, and VLAN 103 mapped to bridge groups within a Layer 3 switch (such as a 2948G-L3). Interfaces 1 through 4 on the Layer 3 device are to be mapped to VLAN 20, interfaces 11 and 12 are to be mapped to VLAN 55, and interfaces 25 and 26 are to be mapped to VLAN 103. Interface G 49 will provide the 802.1Q trunk connection to the Layer 2 switch. The switch will also be providing Layer 3 functions for VLAN 55 and VLAN 103. Figure D-1 shows the connections for this example. The configuration that follows would be entered on the Layer 3 switch.

Figure D-1   *VLAN Extensions*

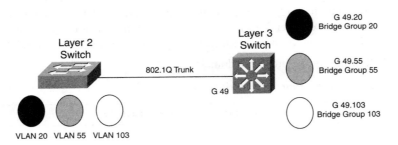

```
L3Switch(config)#bridge 20 protocol ieee
L3Switch(config)#bridge 55 protocol ieee
L3Switch(config)#bridge 103 protocol ieee
L3Switch(config)#bridge irb
L3Switch(config)#interface Fastethernet 1
L3Switch(interface)#bridge-group 20
L3Switch(interface)#interface Fastethernet 2
L3Switch(interface)#bridge-group 20
L3Switch(interface)#interface Fastethernet 3
L3Switch(interface)#bridge-group 20
L3Switch(interface)#interface Fastethernet 4
```

```
L3Switch(interface)#bridge-group 20
L3Switch(interface)#interface Fastethernet 11
L3Switch(interface)#bridge-group 55
L3Switch(interface)#interface Fastethernet 12
L3Switch(interface)#bridge-group 55
L3Switch(interface)#interface Fastethernet 25
L3Switch(interface)#bridge-group 103
L3Switch(interface)#interface Fastethernet 26
L3Switch(interface)#bridge-group 103
L3Switch(interface)#interface Gigabitethernet 49.20
L3Switch(interface-subif)#encapsulation dot1q 20
L3Switch(interface-subif)#bridge-group 20
L3Switch(interface-subif)#interface Gigabitethernet 49.55
L3Switch(interface-subif)#encapsulation dot1q 55
L3Switch(interface-subif)#bridge-group 55
L3Switch(interface-subif)#interface Gigabitethernet 49.103
L3Switch(interface-subif)#encapsulation dot1q 103
L3Switch(interface-subif)#bridge-group 103
L3Switch(interface-subif)#bridge 55 route ip
L3Switch(config)#bridge 103 route ip
L3Switch(config)#interface BVI 55
L3Switch(interface)#ip address 192.168.55.1 255.255.255.0
L3Switch(config)#interface BVI 103
L3Switch(interface)#ip address 192.168.103.1 255.255.255.0
```

INDEX

Symbols

(*, G) common shared tree structure, 232
(S, G) shortest path tree structure, 232

Numerics

56/64-kbps CSU/DSU back-to-back
  connections, 444
802.1Q
  GVRP
    configuring, 164
    dynamic VLAN creation, 165
    example configuration, 165–166
  trunking
    native VLAN switching, 154
    voice traffic transport, 418
802.1X port authentication, configuring, 322–324

A

abbreviated commands, typing, 7
access layer, applying QoS to voice traffic, 425–429
Access layer functionality, 27
access ports, 145
accessing
  modules, 49
  switch devices
    authentication, 316–318
    permit lists, 319–320
    SSH, 321–322
ACEs (access control entries), 372, 386
ACLs, VLAN ACLs, 309
  COS configuration, 310–311
  IOS configuration, 311–314
activating MISTP instances, 185
active commands, disabling, 10
adding entries to switching table, 73
addresses, well-known IP multicast, 473–485
adjacency table (CEF), 212–215
AF (Assured Forwarding) service levels, 369
aggressive mode (UDLD), 179
aging time (switching table), setting, 74
alias commands, 58
applying QoS policies, 395–397

assigned ICMP type codes, 458–461
assigned IP protocol numbers, 447–458
assigning
  IP management address, 39
  static switching table entries, 73
  traffic to QoS policies, 386–392
  VLAN ports
    dynamic, 145–148
    static, 145
    verifying, 148
asynchronous back-to-back connections, 443
ATM LANE (Asynchronous Transfer Mode LAN
  Emulation), 99
  configuring, 100–105
  displaying information, 107
  example configuration, 105–106
authentication, 322–324
  configuring, 316–317
  example configuration, 318–319
  RADIUS, 317–318
  TACACS, 317
authorization
  passwords, recovering, 44
  privileged passwords, 43
  user-level passwords, 42
auto trunking mode (COS), 153
autoconfig, 39
automatic IP management address assignment, 38

B

back-to-back connections
  56/64-kbps CSU/DSU, 444
  asynchronous, 443
  Ethernet, 443
  T1/E1 CSU/DSU, 445
backward compatibility, alias commands, 58
banners
  character limitations, 37
  configuring, 36–37
  example configuration, 37
BID (bridge ID), 176
blocking state (STP), 178
boot parameters, synchronizing, 61–62
booting
  from ROM Monitor, 18
  images from Flash, 57

T

W

X